MW01286135

Eyewitness Textures

Eyewitness Textures

*User-Generated Content and Journalism
in the Twenty-First Century*

EDITED BY

Michael Lithgow and Michèle Martin

McGill-Queen's University Press
Montreal & Kingston • London • Chicago

© McGill-Queen's University Press 2024
Chapter 5 is © CBC 2024

ISBN 978-0-2280-1922-0 (cloth)
ISBN 978-0-2280-1923-7 (paper)
ISBN 978-0-2280-1975-6 (ePDF)

Legal deposit first quarter 2024
Bibliothèque nationale du Québec

Printed in Canada on acid-free paper that is 100% ancient forest free (100% post-consumer recycled), processed chlorine free

Some of the research supporting this publication was funded by the Social Sciences and Humanities Research Council.

Funded by the Government of Canada   Financé par le gouvernement du Canada

Canada Council for the Arts   Conseil des arts du Canada

We acknowledge the support of the Canada Council for the Arts.

Nous remercions le Conseil des arts du Canada de son soutien.

McGill-Queen's University Press in Montreal is on land which long served as a site of meeting and exchange amongst Indigenous Peoples, including the Haudenosaunee and Anishinabeg nations. In Kingston it is situated on the territory of the Haudenosaunee and Anishinaabek. We acknowledge and thank the diverse Indigenous Peoples whose footsteps have marked these territories on which peoples of the world now gather.

Library and Archives Canada Cataloguing in Publication

Title: Eyewitness textures : user-generated content and journalism in the twenty-first century / edited by Michael Lithgow and Michèle Martin.

Names: Lithgow, Michael, 1965- editor. | Martin, Michèle, 1944– editor.

Description: Includes bibliographical references and index.

Identifiers: Canadiana (print) 20230473636 | Canadiana (ebook) 20230473709 | ISBN 9780228019220 (cloth) | ISBN 9780228019237 (paper) | ISBN 9780228019756 (ePDF)

Subjects: LCSH: Journalism – Technological innovations. | LCSH: User-generated content.

Classification: LCC PN4784.T34 E94 2024 | DDC 070.4 – dc23

This book was designed and typeset by Peggy & Co. Design in 11/14 Minion Pro.

Contents

Figures and Tables

Figures

Tables

Prologue

Truth and Technology in the Age of Digital Witnessing

LILIE CHOULIARAKI

User-generated content (UGC), especially mobile phone footage from conflict zones, has challenged journalists' monopoly on the storytelling of war, raising questions about disinformation and fake news. It is, in particular, the truth status of UGC that monopolizes public and scholarly debates on conflict reporting: Is the image real? Who is it attributed to? What was the context in which it was taken? What interests may it be serving? These are important and urgent concerns; however, this discussion challenges this dominant agenda by asking what the cost is of an exclusive focus on truth. I argue that it is important for us to take a step back from this dominant "paradigm of veridiction," which centres on truth as the only journalistic requirement for UGC reporting, and to turn our attention to the geopolitical ramifications of how that content is produced and mediated – to what, after Yuval Harari, I call the "paradigm of flesh witnessing." This move from the institutional to the geopolitical opens up a new space for us to think about UGC not simply as a genre of conflict reporting but also as a form of embodied communication that is conducted under conditions of risk to life. Within the paradigm of "flesh witnessing," mobile phone users, from civilians to militants to humanitarian workers to refugees, are simultaneously conflict participants, who may die or kill as they film, and it is precisely this embodied fragility of reporting that turns their stories into important moral and emotional appeals for global news publics. Flesh witnessing, I argue, signals a new practice of listening to the voices of conflict that, by drawing attention to how these actors speak and what they say, has the potential to restore conflict reporting as a testimony to bodily vulnerability.

My discussion focuses on social media images from UGC recorded in crisis and conflict zones. I reflect on the ways in which such images and news stories are contextualized and used in Western journalism. I am concerned about the kinds of rationalities that drive this work of contextualization. What are the dominant frameworks within which it is possible to conceptualize, speak about, and manage such content, in academic but also professional and public discourse?

I am also concerned about the implications of such rationalities for crisis and war reporting – that is, the way they shape our understanding of migration flows and conflict zones. Put another way, does UGC really change how we engage with conflicts and crises? The questions I am asking are these: How is the use of UGC discussed in the academic world, professional practices, and the public sphere? Can UGC really make a difference in the ways we engage with conflicts and crises?

The first rationality of UGC, the techno-institutional rationality of convergence, is a rationality that celebrates sharing and connectivity through digital platforms. It celebrates the fact that we can sit at home and watch on our phone the footage of an illegal crossing filmed on another phone's camera by a refugee sailing in the Mediterranean – UGC as a techno-institutional process of convergence; UGC as an ethico-political process of witnessing.

The second rationality is that of UGC as ethico-political process of witnessing. Instead of focusing on UGC as citizens' acts of content sharing, this rationality approaches UGC as citizens' acts of bearing witness in times of life and death. Unlike convergence, which foregrounds technological capacity, witnessing highlights human precarity, the threat of violence, and death in times of crisis and conflict.

This is not a dominant rationality. Even though it does sometimes surface in public debate – an example being the photograph of Alan Kurdi, the Syrian toddler who was found dead on a Turkish beach, which turned viral after it was disseminated on 2 September 2015. So my point here is that we must take seriously the nature of UGC as witnessing, for that is an argument in its favour. For before these became images for us to consume, people often risked their lives to film them so as to make their precarity visible to the world. Ignoring this historical trajectory empties UGC of its moral urgency. And this, as we shall see, has costs. Before we get to the costs, let me briefly elaborate on the debates that define each of these two rationalities.

Convergence

Convergence relies on the technological compatibility between Web 2.0 and various platforms that make it possible for content to be remediated instantaneously from one to the next: from the mobile phone, to Twitter, to the BBC website, and back to social media. It is precisely this remediation that has been hailed as the single most important digital development in news journalism, for it blurs the boundaries of professional reporting and integrates non-professionals with the practices of institutional news-making.

From a convergence perspective, then, a video of migrants taken by amateurs and included in a news story is what Melissa Wall and Sahar El Zahed call the "collaborative news clip" – a piece of video that finds its way into news coverage through intermediary social media platforms. Today, as the authors say, "much of the reporting of the conflict that appears in the international news media has fallen to amateurs, often activists within the conflict itself."[1]

Early accounts of convergence were positive. This integration of UGC into institutionalized news was seen as a positive development that was helping democratize journalism. It gave voice to people and changed the authority relations between professionals and users. Axel Bruns was one of the first (back in 2007) to hail the emergence of "produsers"; he regarded "citizen media" as a new form of participatory content creation within a new "networked commons."[2] Adrienne Russell similarly talked about audiences moving from the periphery to the centre of news production. The former head of BBC World, Richard Sambruk, described journalism today as a "collaborative project" in which citizens contributed to the making of the news just as journalists do.

In my work, I have described this paradigm as a shift from a journalism of reporting (where professionals offer an "impartial" overview of crisis or conflict) to a journalism of digital witnessing (where citizens, immersed in the events as they happen, offer their own partial and often deeply emotional perspective). Mette Mortensen refers to eyewitness news images as "ushering a new era of conflict reporting,"[3] and she has more recently talked about "connective witnessing" to capture this new productive synergy between professionals and protest activists on the ground.

In the past two or three years, however, things have changed. The turning point was the revelation in 2016 that malevolent actors (individual or state) were contaminating platforms with "ordinary voices" that were, in fact, manipulating online traffic to achieve specific political ends. This has resulted in a change of perspective.

Today, research on convergence focuses on disinformation – a buzzword of our times. Criticism of disinformation is directed both at news organizations themselves for compromising truth for profit and at social media platforms whose business models privilege virality over credibility. Alice Marwick and Rebecca Lewis in their recent report on disinformation note that the news media's "dependence on social media analytics and metrics ... makes them vulnerable to ... media manipulation."[4]

Making a bolder point, Pablo Bozckowsi and Eugenia Michelstein in their book *The News Gap* state that convergent journalism has little to do with democracy. It is basically a market choice for major news networks. Journalists want to maximize their viewerships and revenues, and that is why they are constantly, the authors say, "monitoring, reproducing and imitating citizen content."[5] The dominance of the profit-driven model – clickbaiting – and the proliferation of non-institutional sources online (from trolls to terrorists) have together created the perfect storm for journalism by nurturing a milieu of content remediation in which the spread of rumour and fake news blurs the boundary between fact and fiction, thereby undermining citizens' trust, public debate, and the democratic process.

Convergence is now under intense scrutiny. That scrutiny inevitably goes beyond news in Western democracies, encompassing debates on crisis and conflict reporting beyond the West. Three specific critical arguments about convergence in crisis and conflict zones deserve our attention:

1 Regarding the political economy of platforms and in the context of conflict reporting, it is worth considering Tarleton Gillespie's critique of how social media logics of profit participate in propaganda cascades – for instance, how YouTube's algorithms

and recommendation systems helped ISIS circulate its beheading videos among the site's 1.8 billion users, greatly boosting ISIS's propaganda campaign.[6]

2   Regarding anxieties about technological progress – for example, how new technologies always outpace old verification skills – Robert Chesney and Danielle Citron warn about the growing presence of deepfakes in this age of "post-truth geopolitics."[7] They contend that hard-to-detect AI-generated images of real people and circumstances (deepfakes) are injecting new risks into conflict zones, spreading fake news and thereby inciting further violence.

3   The techno-solutionist argument seeks to remedy the risks of fake news by resorting to the same AI or algorithmically driven programs that create disinformation in the first place. Recent work in this context analyzes a Ukrainian fact-checking app, "StopFake," which monitors Russian-driven propaganda in Ukraine and flags trolls and fake news.

This triple debate about disinformation constitutes a vital agenda for liberal democracies, which rely on truthful journalism and informed deliberation. I now want to ask a different set of questions, which together will draw us toward the ethico-political paradigm of UGC. Returning to the migrants' videos mentioned earlier, there are several legitimate questions to ask that we do not usually ask. What about *those* people? Isn't it *their* "content" our media are using? Where are *they* within the rationality of convergence? Should *they* not figure in our discussions about the news they generate?

These are equally important questions for our liberal democracies to ask. As Luc Boltanski argues, the political communities of today's West are founded on more than simply the (inward-looking/nation-based) principle of a well-informed citizenry; they also embrace the (outward-looking) principle of cosmopolitan citizenship and care for the other: the poor, the vulnerable, the suffering.[8] Put another way, humanitarianism and human rights are integral to liberal democracy just as much as the deliberative public sphere. So why do we not ask these questions? Perhaps the terminology we are using has something to do with this. Perhaps the problem – at least in part – lies with the very acronym UGC.

UGC offers a new conception of the audience of news as user – the produser – but it also hides something significant, something that, in the context of conflict and crisis reporting, is important, indeed existential. The term UGC hides the bodies of those who make the recordings under conditions of risk to life. A video is not just UGC. It is the use of the mobile phone as a testimonial technology, a technology that bears witness to the precariousness of bodies in moments of crisis.

Flesh Witnessing

In "Beyond Verification: Flesh Witnessing and the Significance of Embodiment in Conflict News" (2022), Omar al-Ghazzi and I introduce the term "flesh witnessing" for discussing mobile phone videography. For us, flesh witnessing refers to embodied and mobile testimonies of distant suffering that reach Western news publics as potential generators of emotion, reflection, and action. The term flesh witnessing was first used by Yuval Harari to refer to the special status that stories of returning combatants, who had felt war "on their skin," acquired in early twentieth century.[9]

My use of the term here expands flesh witnessing to encompass all forms of digital testimony recorded by those who risk their bodies in conflict zones today. In its sensitivity to embodied precarity, it draws on work done by diverse scholars such as Judith Butler, Elaine Scarry, and Karin Fierke, as well as previous work of my own on distant suffering and humanitarian communication. In the past, soldiers and war correspondents were the only flesh witnesses at the battlefront; since then, the landscape of testimony has changed – today, civilians, NGOs, militants, terrorists, refugees, and others also claim the news scene, increasingly defining the content of news from conflict zones.

At the heart of this transformation is, as David Patrikarakos reminds us, "the extraordinary ability of social media to endow ordinary individuals ... with the power to change both the physical battlefield and the discourse around it."[10] I would like now to focus on the challenges this rationality of flesh witnessing raises for journalism today. Flesh witnessing both respects and interrupts the rationality of convergence in times of crisis and conflict. It does not suggest that we *a priori* treat such content as testimony of genuine suffering; it suggests, rather, that we open up a space for understanding flesh witnessing in terms just

Figure 0.1   Yemen crisis

as rich and complex as those for the rationality of convergence. What power relations and struggles shape the testimonial potential of UGC in our media environment? How do these relations of convergent news regulate the remediations of flesh witnessing?

I would like to present a possible critical agenda for flesh witnessing. Three themes will help us understand how the power relations of news media shape the rationality of embodied precarity: invisibility, skepticism, and introversion.

Invisibility. On 14 May the *Guardian* reported that 85,000 children had died of starvation in Yemen since 2016. Although there exists UGC from Yemen, it rarely becomes front-page news or goes viral. It simply does not meet the criteria of Western newsworthiness.

UGC invisibility is less a technological problem and more a geopolitical one insofar as the remediation of the conflict depends on the strategic interests and security priorities that journalism serves. In other words, UGC may offer the potential for testimonials of atrocity, yet it rarely challenges the power relations of Western journalism and its norms for remediating atrocity. Here, I insist that *rarely* does not mean *never* – recall the international scandal the US military faced after the leak of the Abu Ghraib amateur images back in 2004, during the second Iraq war. So rarely does not mean never – critique is possible.

Figure 0.2   The Bana Al Abed tweet

But as long as historical hierarchies of location and human life remain in place such scandals will be fleeting and fragmented rather than capable of challenging the global order.

Skepticism. UGC is viewed with profound suspicion. For instance, Bana Al Abed, a seven-year-old girl who, with the help of her mother, tweeted from Aleppo during the deadly siege of the 2016, dominated the news not only because of her dramatic messages but importantly also because of the controversy over her authenticity. Who was she? What interests did she represent? Even when her account was verified, armies of trolls and individual users kept undermining its credibility and authenticity. Such cases of uncertainty, as Koen Leurs argues, render flesh witnessing unstable and in need of constant reiteration and verification.[11] UGC news becomes here more about proving that one is real than about reporting on atrocity and suffering.

Introversion. Introversion is about appropriating UGC in news stories and discussions that reflect our own concerns instead of addressing the testimonial claims of vulnerable others.

In our LSE study on the 2015 migration "crisis," we focused on how refugee selfies were remediated in institutional news in nine Eastern and Central European nations. Our key finding was that not a single refugee selfie appeared in our news spaces. Instead, news images represented the

A group of Syrian men pose for snap using selfie stick

Figure 0.3   *Sunday Express,*
10 September 2015

Figure 0.4   *The Independent,* 19 August 2015. "It is surreal:
The 'tragic' plight of migrants arriving on the beach."

act of selfying (figures 0.3 and 0.4). The focus was on looking at them doing it and on the politicians posing with them (figure 0.5) (focus on internal politics).

There was no attempt to "meet" the other's face; to listen to their voices or stories or to attend to their perspective, except for the BBC story (figure 0.6), the only one that included a face-to-face encounter with refugees. The story exposed refugee selfies as fake. They had been taken by an actor who was posing as a migrant to document his dangerous journey to Europe; in fact, they were part of a branding campaign for an SP advertising firm.

What does all this tell us about the power relationships of flesh witnessing from conflict and crisis zones? Or, as I was asking earlier, can UGC really change how the news invites us to engage with conflicts and crises? Invisibility, skepticism, and introversion, I argue, are manifestations of a particular practice of power that governs the circulation of UGC content in Western news. In journalism studies the term for this kind of selective exclusion is gate-watching. But it makes more sense to call it a practice of bordering.

The term "bordering" has long referred to the geopolitical and military practices of power that keep migrant flows outside Western zones of safety and prosperity for the purpose of keeping us "safe." It refers to a territorial border. I use the term bordering to talk about how the news excludes or restricts remediations of UGC in order to highlight the geopolitical logic of security that regulates not only territories but also institutions.[12] Such practices of bordering, diverse and nuanced as they are, leave little space for testimonials of the flesh, for the voices of precarious bodies to be heard and attended to in the news spaces of our liberal communities. Even though these communities are historically informed by the principles of humanitarianism and human rights – by what philosopher Richard Rorty called a "culture of sympathy" – these principles are employed selectively. Invisibility, skepticism, and introversion consistently eclipse, resist, or appropriate vulnerable others and their UGC testimonials in news.

Conclusion

In this discussion, I have presented two rationalities that inform debates about UGC: convergence and flesh witnessing. Unlike the rationality of convergence, initially celebrated but later critiqued, where technology

Figure 0.5   *The Independent*, 1 April 2015. Selfies with Western leaders.
"Germany's refugee crisis has left it as bitterly divided as Donald Trump's America."

Figure 0.6   "Migrant hoax," BBC, 3 August 2015.

presents a problem but also offers a solution (i.e., disinformation detection apps – the rationality of), flesh witnessing is implicit, but never acknowledged in our academic and public discourse. Instead, it is constantly rendered irrelevant, invisible, or suspicious.

While convergence dominates, raising urgent questions about the nature of our liberal democracies, flesh witnessing is marginal. It is rarely acknowledged and, when it is, only rarely does it succeed in informing public debate. The two, of course, are not separate. Rather, convergence and flesh witnessing go hand in hand. Specifically, the rationality of the former – the need to verify and monetize information – marginalizes the latter. How? Skepticism, for example, has to do with the pluralization of witnesses. (UGC comes from the killers as much as from their victims and is entangled in the disinformation wars between rival geopolitical interests – how do we know that White Helmets are "humanitarians"?) Conflict content is notoriously hard to verify. But what about verification that respects lives? And stands up for people's rights?

Introversion has much to do with the business model of social-media-driven news, where clicks are monetized. In this economy of attention, platforms algorithmically promote what sells. Promoting familiar faces, such as celebrities or politicians, is more profitable than promoting refugees at a camp in Jordan, Lesbos, or Lampedusa. The geopolitics of bordering can amount to a market politics of profit.

My aim here is not to moralize news practitioners or to propose a revolution in news production. Both would be out of place. My aim has been rather to slightly shift the perspective away from the rationality of convergence and make visible another set of moral and political concerns in the news use of UGC. Flesh witnessing alerts us to UGC no longer just as content, but as bodies reaching out, communicating their predicament. This raises the following set of questions:

- Should the produsers of war testimonials be treated as content or as journalists who risk their lives to provide major Western news outlets with stories and images of the battlefield?
- Should remediation sustain its current practices of bordering? If so, how can it balance verification as security with the ethical and political concern of listening?
- Should news organizations go beyond the economy of attention and offer space and time for more contextual, historicized, and personalized pieces on conflicts and their journalists?

If these questions/proposals appear too idealistic or even irrelevant in the convergence paradigm of fake news and disinformation, perhaps we need to remember that it is the dearth of a sustained culture of empathy, humanity, and inclusion that breeds the worst kind of anti-democratic populist rhetoric and its "othering" of distant sufferers in our political communities (particularly in Europe and the United States). It is precisely the power of bordering – territorial and narrative – that authoritarian populists want to nurture and reproduce today. The wall with Mexico in the United States and the Brexit vote in the United Kingdom are only two, but perhaps the most prominent, consequences of an exclusive persistence on a techno-social rationality of verification that, important as it may be, nonetheless marginalizes – when it does not throw into suspicion – the significance of testimony and its potentially humanizing impact on citizen witnesses from conflict zones. At a moment in time when so much is at stake, opening up new ways of thinking about Western war reporting and reconsidering the place that such reporting reserves for the voices of those who suffer most in those wars, serves, I believe, a crucial intellectual purpose for scholars of communication and journalism – it reclaims what it means to be a cosmopolitan citizen in Western democracies today.

Notes

1 Wall and El Zahed, "Embedding," 3.
2 Bruns, "Towards."
3 Mortensen, "Conflictual."
4 Marwick and Lewis, *Media*, 1.
5 Boczkowski and Mitchelstein, *News Gap*.
6 Gillespie, "Politics."
7 Chesney and Citron, "Deepfakes."
8 Boltanski, *Distant*.
9 Harari, *Ultimate*.
10 Patrikarakos, *War*, 5.
11 Leurs, "Practicing."
12 See Chouliaraki and Georgiou, *The Digital Border*, for the idea of bordering.

Bibliography

Boczkowski, Pablo J., and Eugenia Mitchelstein. *The News Gap: When the Information Preferences of the Media and the Public Diverge*. Cambridge, MA: MIT Press, 2013.

Boltanski, Luc. *Distant Suffering: Morality, Media, and Politics*. Cambridge, MA: Cambridge University Press, 1999.

Bruns, Alex. "Towards Produsage: Futures for User-Led Content Production." In *Proceedings of Cultural Attitudes towards Communication and Technology*, Tartu, Estonia, 2007, 275–84.

Chesney, Robert, and Danielle Citron. "Deepfakes and the New Disinformation War." *Foreign Affairs* 11 (2018).

Chouliaraki, Lilie, and Omar al-Ghazzi. "Beyond Verification: Flesh Witnessing and the Significance of Embodiment in Conflict News." *Journalism* 23, no. 3 (2022): 649–67.

Chouliaraki, Lilie, and Myria Georgiou. *The Digital Border: Mobility, Technology, Power*. New York: NYU Press, 2022.

Chouliaraki, Lilie, and Rafal Zaborowski. "Voice and Community in the 2015 Refugee Crisis: A Content Analysis of News Coverage in Eight European Countries." *International Communication Gazette* 79, nos 6–7 (2017): 613–35.

Gillespie, Tarleton. "The Politics of 'Platforms.'" *New Media and Society* 12, no. 3 (2010): 347–64.

Harari, Yuval. *The Ultimate Experience: Battlefield Revelations and the Making of Modern War Culture, 1450–2000*. Springer, 2008.

Leurs, Koen. "Practicing Critical Media Literacy Education with 4 Young Migrants: Lessons Learned from Participatory Active Action Research Project." *International Communication Gazette*, November 2019.

Marwick, Alice, and Rebecca Lewis. *Media Manipulation and Disinformation Online*. New York: Data and Society Research Institute, 2017.

Mortensen, Mette. "Conflictual Media Events, Eyewitness Images, and the Boston Marathon Bombing (2013)." *Journalism Practice* 9, no. 4 (2015): 536–51.

Patrikarakos, David. *War in 140 Characters: How Social Media Is Reshaping Conflict in the Twenty-First Century*. New York: Basic Books, 2017.

Wall, Melissa, and Sahar El Zahed. "Embedding Content from Syrian Citizen Journalists: The Rise of the Collaborative News Clip." *Journalism* 16, no. 2 (2015): 163–80.

Eyewitness Textures

New Voices, New Practices, New Discourses

The Transformation of Journalism through the Eyewitness Experiences of User-Generated Content

MICHAEL LITHGOW AND MICHÈLE MARTIN

This book uniquely brings together the voices and experiences of both professional journalists and academic researchers from Asia, South America, North America, and Europe, to address the important and far-reaching changes taking place in response to the growing importance of user-generated content (UGC) in news coverage. UGC encompasses all forms of primarily non-professional media content production incorporated by journalists into news stories. UGC provides journalists with immediate on-the-scene content for breaking news events around the world.

The discursive implications of UGC encompass not only the growing complexities of gathering, verifying, and integrating UGC materials into professional news practices, but also the growing significance of UGC in shaping news outcomes, audience expectations for immediate and visually compelling records of newsworthy events, audience expectations about their role in news discourse, and public commentary about news stories. UGC amounts to *de facto* collaboration between professionally trained journalists and witnesses to news events, and the public has come to expect that the latter point of view (recorded through the lenses of smart phones and other digital apparatus) will help define news narratives. Traditional journalists encounter untrained witnesses and must contend with them for influence over the framing and meaning of news events. A transformed newsscape is emerging in which the shifting complexities of journalism practices are producing new kinds of news narratives that not only respond to changing audience expectations for proximal and immediate news coverage but also usurp in a sense the journalist's once unique role as observer by situating the public's experience centre stage in their role as eyewitnesses to the events that affect their lives.

UGC refers to text, audio, photographs, video, and metadata produced outside of the routines of traditional journalism; these are then incorporated into professional news production processes.[1] As Santos points out, there are many dimensions to UGC – a user is publishing data in a non-professional capacity, on a platform that is more or less free from curatorial criteria, where the data published were generated by the user and intended for circulation and use by others.[2] Naab and Sehl similarly identify three qualities of UGC: original contribution, created outside of professional routines, made accessible to the public.[3] UGC presents a resource for journalists, who still, though, must do the boundary work of determining what can be admitted into their workflows and news outcomes as legitimate elements of journalism.[4]

The epistemic foundations of the legitimacy of journalism as a discourse are grounded in the conventions of journalism training that produce professional actors who have learned a method for representing reality to audiences. The conventions of journalism practice such as objectivity, fairness, newsworthiness, verification, and so on have been historically the foundation of trust between news organizations and their audiences, and this foundation is tied to the expectation and understanding that news materials are gathered and assembled by journalists trained in these professional conventions.[5] Even professionally trained journalists performing outside of these conventions – for example, columnists – are understood to be producing something other than news. UGC challenges these categorical distinctions and presents materials that emerge from radically different contexts, that is, untrained citizens playing eyewitness to historical events. These differences are the foundation of UGC's fascinating complexity and suggest why it presents such an interesting field of study. These epistemic complexities are explored in the chapters that make up the academic sections of this collection. It is our contention that UGC presents an epistemically unique addition to news discourses, one that destabilizes and challenges news conventions tied to the central role of the trained journalist in establishing the relations of trust between news media organizations and the public, and that in doing so asserts in historically unpreced-ented ways voices and perspectives of people whose experiences might otherwise have been obscured, neglected, or simply excluded through the routines of journalistic professionalism.

The production and circulation of UGC has become commonplace as social media platforms have grown in their ability to embrace mass participation and video technologies via phones, which have become ubiquitous tools in most places in the world.[6] UGC evidences an act of "witnessing" that blurs the traditional boundaries between producers and consumers of news content[7] and transforms media viewers and consumers into what Axel Bruns describes as "produsers,"[8] a term that recognizes the hybrid quality of amateur production as blurring traditional boundaries between those who make the news and those who are its audiences. For Mette Mortensen, "eyewitness" in a media context "involves an individual sharing his or her experience of watch-ing or attending a certain event by making a statement, performance or representation."[9] Mortensen states that "eyewitness images" are auto-recorded, subjective, and ambiguous in terms of media institutions, as they emerge from a participatory stance of some kind (happened to be there, intended to be there, etc.) and are often decontextualized, as they eliminate the distance between seeing and saying.[10] However, based on the results of some of the chapters in this collection, the degree to which this is the case often depends on the discourses in which the images eventually end up and the choices made by journalists who incorporate the fragmentary elements of UGC into the narratives through which news stories derive their sensibilities.

It is important here to specify the distinction we make between the expression "user-generated content" and "citizen journalism," a form of news production by untrained and self-taught members of the public that includes current affairs–based blogging, photo and video sharing, and posting eyewitness commentary on current events.[11] As Goode has argued, citizen journalism can be used quite broadly to include activities like "re-posting, linking, 'tagging' (labeling with keywords), rating, modifying or commenting upon news materials posted by other users or by professional news outlets, whereby citizens participate in the news process without necessarily acting as 'content creators.'"[12] Radsch argues that citizen journalists generally have an activist orientation in the sense that the intention is to produce an alternative to traditional news, using similar journalistic practices but with different goals.[13] According to Noor, citizen journalism describes the "journalistic activities of ordinary people" who are reporting "on the issues confronting them."[14] In chapter 12 in this volume, Kang similarly argues for recognition of the important distinctions to be made between the journalistic intentionalities that organize citizen journalism outcomes and UGC. We take the position that the qualitative difference between posting a video clip of an event and reporting on that event is not only worth exploring but also of critical importance in contemporary newsrooms. The newsroom accounts in Part I demonstrate that seeking out the reporting outcomes of amateur journalists is the exception, not the rule. In fact, curating and incorporating UGC into news narratives produced by professional journalists has emerged as a raison d'être of contemporary newsrooms struggling to keep up with the tsunami of UGC flooding the global circuits of digital media circulation. Professional journalists continue to report the news in news media organizations, but with a new resource. Our focus is on UGC created by amateurs who are recording and documenting events to which they are witnesses or in which they are participants, which is then incorporated into the news by professional journalists.

Nevertheless, as alluded to, there are exceptions that challenge any sense of absolute categorical distinction. In chapter 6 the authors describe France 24's *Observers* program, in which professional journalists collaborate with UGC creators to produce a unique hybrid form of professional/amateur reportage. France 24 journalists are also engaged in receiving, sourcing, and verifying video and photographic recordings of news events provided by the general public, materials that after verification are shared with the whole of the France 24 news organization for use in reportage. But France 24 sometimes provides production support for "observers" – trusted members of the public reporting on local events, and they produce news reports by introducing and contextualizing UGC contributions either for their website or for one of their television programs. The boundaries between categories in this sense are unstable, but the outcomes in all categories are groundbreaking.

A second and even more unusual exception is described in chapter 8 by Kenzie Burchell and Jennifer Fielding. Here the focus is on a blog created by photojournalists to discuss aspects of their professional lives *that exceed the limitations for legitimate discourse in their professional journalism routines.* These photojournalists use the blog to express feelings and to describe the many complexities and tensions in photojournalism practices that bring together professionals from international news agencies with amateurs in settings where news events are taking place. The blog becomes a platform for UGC because the feelings and experiences expressed by the journalists fall outside the conventions of journalism discourse and rest precisely on the epistemic fault line that has emerged between UGC and traditional news, pointing to the depth and significance of transformation taking place in response to the growing worldwide availability and significance of UGC for journalists and audiences.

The use of UGC is now widespread among traditional news media seeking to take advantage of visual content to which they would not otherwise have access and that their own workers have not (yet) produced.[15] The range of periods covered by this collection provides the opportunity to witness how UGC has grown into an integral resource for what some scholars describe as "networked journalism," a term being used to describe changing practices associated with the ways digital technologies and networks have gradually transformed possibilities for information sharing.[16] Networked journalism is a newer concept reflecting the growing central role of content derived online from social media, blogs, independent websites, and so on, and reflects a shift in traditional practices toward understanding journalists as functioning nodes within a vast network of information flows that are constantly being updated from many sources, including traditional and emerging sources.[17] UGC is an increasingly important element in these journalism networks in part because it responds to consumer and market demands for "immediate" information and can enhance perceptions of "authenticity"[18] and proximity to events.[19, 20] But proximity and authenticity does not always equate with evidence. As some works in this collection show, questionable quality of images and lack of verification not only have *not* been absolute barriers to their use in professional reportage, but would appear to have been used to justify their inclusion in news reports, perhaps with attribution to another media source[21] or, as some of the chapters below and others have observed, by labelling the unverified amateur footage as "unverified."[22] The evidentiary value of the UGC in these cases is unclear, raising questions about why they would be included in coverage at all. And while these are largely historical anomalies, or if not necessarily historical, part of the growing pains of a profession in transition, such observations draw attention to important epistemic tensions between UGC and how it is put to use. As the chapters from journalists in this collection describe, today's newsrooms are demonstrating a growing proficiency and efficiency with verification procedures, and these kinds of anomalies are far more rare. Indeed, there have been recent efforts to develop standards of verification, an indication of the institutional value and acceptance of amateur content within professional news routines.[23] But the underlying tensions between origins and use remain a central territory in need of further investigation.

Lilie Chouliaraki, who authored the prologue to this collection, has argued that UGC contributions to Western journalism challenge "existing hierarchies of place and human life ... towards recognizing the voice of distant others."[24] And while distance can be significantly conceived in cultural terms, the observation is especially resonant in contexts in which non-Western members of publics are recording images that are then circulated in Western news discourses. Chouliaraki is arguing for a new understanding of journalism in a converged, twenty-first century networked and digital environment, one whose practices more and more emphasize deliberation and witnessing over the traditional emphasis on the provision of information. In this context, UGC represents a remediation of ordinary voices into news network discourses.[25] It is an epistemic shift that underscores the profound and far-reaching changes brought about by new technologies and new practices in the twenty-first century.

Part I: UGC and Changing Newsroom Practices

We turn now to the chapters in this book. The place we begin is with the practitioners – the journalists – whose practices are the methods and means by which UGC circulates in and through the discourses aimed at audiences for conventional, professional news. The emerging newsroom practices described in the chapters in Part I provide an essential experiential foundation with which to begin our examination of the phenomenon of UGC. The journalists' accounts make clear the distinction we uphold in this book between UGC and citizen journalism; the former give rise to the many emerging practices described in Part I in a way that the latter does not.[26] In chapter 2, Derek Bowler, head of

Social Newsgathering for the European Broadcasting Union (EBU), describes the ways in which a vast global news organization with a collective reach to more than 1 billion audience members in fifty-six countries[27] has transformed its practices by incorporating UGC from all over the world. Bowler describes the meteoric rise of UGC activities at the EBU and the challenges that organization has faced as those activities have entered its global practice. At the heart of the EBU's interest in UGC has been a desire to bring the public "closer" to the events that make up the news by allowing the public to participate through eyewitness content. In chapter 3, Natalie Miller, former editor at the BBC UGC Hub, describes similarly rapid changes in practice at the BBC in response to the growing significance of UGC. Early interest in and use of UGC by journalists was met with significant skepticism from others in the newsroom. Miller describes specific examples from her experiences at the BBC, illllustrating the uphill battle that UGC once faced in being accepted as a legitimate source, as well the changing labour practices that emerged as it gradually came to be accepted as a core news-gathering activity.

In chapter 4, journalist Shauna Rempel describes how one private sector news organization, Global News, adjusted to UGC in terms of both benefits and complications. Rempel discusses the complexities involved in searching for relevant UGC and establishing consent, as well as the emerging issue of the trauma that newsroom journalists experience when they must view the often traumatic events depicted in UGC.

In chapter 5, Andree Lau and colleagues describe how journalists at the Canadian Broadcasting Corporation (CBC) handled UGC footage depicting violence against BIPOC communities. Through case examples of urgent contemporary relevance such as ongoing violence against Black and Indigenous communities in North America, the authors explore new conditions for BIPOC journalists in the newsroom in connection with the proximity of UGC to events of violence against BIPOC citizens. This empirical chapter is of particular importance in understanding new and emerging conditions of practice for journalists.

Chapter 6 considers two unique appropriations of UGC for news outcomes. The first, France 24, has established a unique collaborative relationship with UGC producers, not just training them but sometimes also collaborating with them to make programming. This practice, which they call the Observer Program, is a hybrid of amateur and professional news coverage, accompanied by the gathering and verifying of UGC that is more common in other newsrooms. The chapter describes the development of this program, relations with UGC producers, and what makes this kind of news production unique. The second account is about Storyful, which has commercialized UGC by offering a gathering and verification service that at times includes contextualizing narratives for news organizations. Storyful's clients can acquire verified UGC for journalists to use in news production, or UGC that has been context-ualized into news narratives ready for public consumption.

These first-person accounts of newsroom practices demonstrate through the experiences of professionals the far-reaching and profound changes to news conventions that have been occurring in response to the rise of UGC as a significant element of news coverage. These chapters serve as the cornerstone for the analysis that follows in Parts II and III, in that they offer concrete depictions of how UGC has been taken up in the crucible of the newsroom, a workplace that never sleeps and that must transform itself "on the fly," improvising new practices to accommodate and put to use new technical affordances as they emerge.

Part II: User-Generated Content and the Changing Landscape of News Outcomes

UGC, with its unique origins outside the traditional conventions of news production, has given rise to discursive content with surprisingly complex epistemic implications. In Part II, some of the many textures, dimensions, and territories of meaning of UGC are explored, including the role that UGC plays in the destabilization of news organization mon-opolies over production cycles. UGC presents a far more complicated array of meaning potentials than the common notions of "cell phone footage" or "eyewitness account" might suggest.

In chapter 7, Michael Lithgow and Michèle Martin revisit the Arab Spring as a useful historic snapshot of a changing profession. At the time, newsrooms were only just starting to explore UGC as a staple of coverage and routines for handling UGC in newsrooms were either rare or still being formed. In addition to the now less common practice of using unverified UGC in news stories, the seemingly obvious evidentiary value of UGC was not its only discursive use. As the authors explore, UGC appeared to have many discursive functions, not least among which was creating a sense of urgency and proximity to events. At times it implicitly supported ideological metanarratives unrelated (or only indirectly related) to the specific events being reported.

In chapter 8, Kenzie Burchell and Jennifer Fielding explore how emerging genres of witnessing intersect with shifting journalistic practices influenced by, and adjusting to, the wider landscape of UGC practices of witnessing and bearing witness. Their discussion emerges from a multilingual comparison of international agency coverage of the ongoing Syrian war and its associated military campaign and humanitarian crises. The case study focuses on *AFP Correspondents*, a blog for photojournalists and their editors that stands in contrast to the traditional output of the international news agency Agence France Presse (AFP). The blog posts of the amateur photojournalists turned AFP freelance "stringers," who reported from within the Syrian conflict when others could not, reveal an analytical gap in understanding diverging genres for war reporting in a landscape increasingly influenced by amateur journalism and other UGC practices.

The unique epistemic possibilities of UGC are further explored in chapter 9 by Michael Lithgow, who analyzes amateur video decontextualized from the news stories in which it appears. In a close examination of UGC that appeared in CBC coverage of the first hundred days of the Arab Spring uprising, he argues that the trauma evidenced in the amateur video recorded the state violence undergirding a repressive version of civic identity, and that through this witnessing of the abject by citizens whose fabric of civic identity was being both torn asunder and woven anew, new audience subjectivities were made possible. UGC that presents an insider's perspective raises questions for audiences about accountability. In this case, Lithgow argues, amateur video of the Arab Spring uprising interpellated an engaged and interconnected subjectivity rooted in the unique aesthetic sensibilities of eyewitness video.

Part III: User-Generated Content
Journalism around the World

In the third and final section of the book, the chapters explore journalism around the world in response to the growing significance of UGC. Despite UGC's seemingly obvious role as "eyewitness evidence" to news events, news discourse from around the world suggests a more

complex array of discursive possibilities. In Part III, each chapter analyzes a unique role that UGC has played somewhere in the global news
stream, including in Latin America, Africa, and Europe. UGC has shaped
news discourse by narrativizing news events in ways aligned with,
and sometimes opposed to, the narrativizing practices of conventional
journalists. UGC can set news agendas. It can both extend and limit
the discursive violence and trauma of terrorist spectacles. And it has
been observed playing a central role in asserting cultural identities
and exposing discrimination. The epistemic complexities described in
Part II, it would seem, give rise to discursive complexity.

Marcelos Santos in chapter 10 considers UGC as a source for narrating
extraordinary events – here, a street protest against the impeachment of
Brazilian ex-president Dilma Rousseff. By focusing on the patterns
of UGC creation and diffusion through Twitter that emerged during
a large and particularly important demonstration during the crisis,
Santos was able to map the extent to which this particular UGC not only
challenged the meanings being developed for the crisis by professionally
created media but also helped define public understanding at a time of
great political turmoil.

The unique epistemic status of UGC comes under scrutiny in
chapter 11, written by Inkyu Kang, who considers the popular citizen
journalism project OhmyNews in South Korea. Kang argues that despite
a widely inconsistent use of the terms "UGC" and "citizen journalism,"
so as to often conflate everything amateurs do into one encompassing
category, UGC should be recognized as distinct from citizen journalism.
The latter often reflects the various proclivities of conventional journalism, Kang argues, including an urge toward balance, verification,
objectivity, and so on – proclivities generally absent from the eyewitness
recording of events by bystanders or participants. UGC as a unique type
of news resource represents a key conceptual shift in journalism in the
twenty-first century.

UGC as its own channel of discourse is explored in chapter 12, where
Carolina Escudero examines coverage of terrorist attacks perpetuated
by the Islamic State in Barcelona and Cambrils, in the Spanish region of
Catalonia, on 17 and 18 August 2017. The chapter utilizes the recommen-
dations of the Audiovisual Council of Catalonia (CAC) and the Catalan
Journalists' College (CPC) for the analysis of the UGC published by two
Spanish mainstream media: the newspapers *La Vanguardia* and *El País*.

The study specifically examines a four-stage process of remediation, corrective actions, creativity, and humour used in the production and/ or dissemination of UGC images of the terrorist attacks. In these events and subsequent coverage, the potential for unintentionally widening the political violence perpetrated by the terrorist groups through the sharing of UGC recordings of the attacks was modulated – again through UGC – by images of kittens posted by members of the public in response to calls from state authorities to limit the circulation of images of the attacks. Escudero argues that in this instance, UGC functioned as a form of counterterrorism through collective gestures aimed at limiting the spread of images intended to destabilize the social order.

In chapter 13, Eugene Brown Nyarko Agyei and Sara Akrofi-Qwarcoo argue that the increased presence and recirculation of UGC coupled with the rise of online news platforms has produced an intermedia agenda-setting relationship between online news websites and social media in Ghana.

Finally, chapter 14 by Babatunde Ojebuyi and Abiodun Salawu is a unique examination of UGC use in news coverage in Nigeria, a country that has one of the highest rates of Internet use in Africa. In this setting, UGC not only presents important news events but also plays a role in identity formation through assertions of group identity, assertions that reflect an emerging form of discourse that is adding to ongoing threats to Nigerian social stability.

The growing importance of UGC in news production is a phenomenon of interest to scholars and journalists worldwide, yet the depth and breadth of this transformation of journalism is perhaps under-appreciated. Newsrooms are being restructured. New positions and editorial teams are being created. The skills required of professional journalists have expanded to include verification and curation skills in an increasingly complex digital mediascape. New relationships are being forged between members of the general public and professional journalists whose symbiotic interest in public information and welfare is destabilizing the epistemic foundation of a discourse grounded in assumptions about the journalist's non-involvement in the affairs being reported on. UGC presents eyewitness evidence from people in close proximity to events and often, as well, from participants who, sensing something of significance occurring, record images with their smart phones or perhaps share descriptions in social media. Journalists are being decentred as the only source of "truth" in news discourse, a discourse undergoing epistemic upheaval as journalists come to increasingly play a curatorial role in the gathering, verifying, and integrating of UGC into news outcomes. The necessarily collaborative dimensions of these practices point to perhaps the most important transformation in newsroom routines from our perspective. New relations afforded by UGC are embodied, on the one hand, in the recordings by individuals of events that affect their lives and the lives of others in their communities, and on the other hand, in emerging relationships between journalists, editors, and newsrooms and UGC producers, a range of relationship types unprecedented in their complexity and necessity. UGC is here to stay and is transforming how we understand news coverage, journalists' professional roles, and the role of the general public as witnesses to the events in their own lives. Our hope is that this book will offer a valuable contribution to this growing and important field of study.

Notes

1 See Harkin et al., *Deciphering*; Kaplan and Haenlein, "Users"; Popple and Thornham, *Content*; Singer and Ashman, "User-generated"; van Dijck, "Users"; and Wahl-Jorgensen, "Resisting."

2 Santos, "So-called."

3 Naab and Sehl, "Studies."

4 Johnson and Dade, "Local."

5 It is worth noting that news values such as objectivity, fairness, and newsworthiness have their own range of interpretations, for example, those of the *New York Times* as to compared Fox News. Consequently the use of UGC will also reflect different methods of news production and perceptions of what is and isn't legitimate news discourse.

6 Commentary re digital divide

7 See Wahl-Jorgenson, "Resisting." For more on witnessing, see the Prologue, as well as chapters 8 (Burchell and Fielding) and 9 (Lithgow) in this book.

8 Bruns, "Towards."

9 Mortensen, *Journalism*, 19.

10 Mortensen, "Witnessing" and *Journalism*.

11 See Allan and Thorsen *Citizen Journalism*, vols 1 and 2; and Goode, "Social." See also chapter 11 (Kang) in this book for more on the difference between citizen journalism and user-generated content.

12 Goode, "Social," 1288.
13 Radsch, *Cyberactivism*.
14 Noor, "Citizen," 55.
15 See Allan and Peters, "Visual"; Anden-Papadopoulos, "Media"; Anden-Papadopoulos and Pantti, "Reimagining"; Mortensen, "Witnessing" and *Journalism*; and Mortensen and Kristensen, "Amateur."
16 See Van der Haak et al., "Future."
17 See Beckett, *Value*; and Duffy and Dhabi, "Networked."
18 See Ahva and Hellman, "Citizen"; and Wahl-Jorgensen et al., "Audience."
19 See Pantti, "Getting Closer?"
20 For more on the perception of authenticity and proximity, see chapters 7 (Lithgow and Martin) and 10 (Santos).
21 See Mortensen and Kristensen, "Amateur."
22 See MacFarquhar, "Syrian"; and Cockburn, "Is it the End."
23 See Silverman, *Verification Handbook* and *Verification Handbook for Disinformation*.
24 Chouliaraki, "I Have a Voice," 51; also mentioned in her symposium paper.
25 Choiliaraki, "I Have a Voice" and "Witnessing."
26 The exception being, as noted, the work of Observers working with France 24.
27 https://www.ebu.ch/publications/research/open/infographic/the-ebu-community-in-numbers.

Bibliography

Ahva L., and M. Hellman. "Citizen Eyewitness Images and Audience Engagement in Crisis Coverage." *International Communication Gazette* 77, no. 7 (2015): 668–81.

Allan, S., and C. Peters. "Visual Truths of Citizen Reportage: Four Research Problems." *Information, Communication and Society* 18, no. 11 (2015): 1348–61.

Allan, S., and E. Thorsen, eds. *Citizen Journalism: A Global Perspective*, vol. 1. New York: Peter Lang, 2009.

– *Citizen Journalism: A Global Perspective*, vol. 2. New York: Peter Lang, 2014.

Anden-Papadopoulos, K. "Media Witnessing and the 'Crowd-Sourced Video Revolution.'" *Visual Communication* 12, no. 3 (2013): 341–57.

Anden-Papadopoulos, K., and M. Pantti. "Reimagining Crisis Reporting: Professional Ideology of Journalists and Citizen Eyewitness Images." *Journalism* 14, no. 7 (2013): 960–77.

Beckett, C. *The Value of Networked Journalism*. London: POLIS, London School of Economics, 2010.

Bruns, A. "Towards Produsage: Futures for User-Led Content Production." In *Proceedings of Cultural Attitudes towards Communication and Technology*, Tartu, Estonia, 2006, 275–84. http://eprints.qut.edu.au.

Chouliaraki, L. "I Have a Voice: The Cosmopolitanism and Ambivalence of Convergent Journalism." In *Citizen Journalism: Global Perspectives*, edited by S. Allan and E. Thorsen, vol. 2, 51–66. New York: Peter Lang, 2014.

– "Witnessing without Responsibility." Keynote talk at Eyewitness Textures Symposium, 23–4 May 2019, MacEwan University, Edmonton, Canada.

Cockburn, P. "Is It the End of Sykes-Picot? Patrick Cockburn on the War in Syria and the Threat to the Middle East." *London Review of Books* 6 (June 2013): 3, 5.

Duffy, M.J., and A. Dhabi. "Networked Journalism and Al-Jazeera English: How the Middle East Network Engages the Audience to Help Produce News." *Journal of Middle East Media* 7, no. 1 (2011): 1–23.

Goode, L. "Social News, Citizen Journalism, and Democracy." *New Media and Society* 11, no. 8 (2009): 1287–305.

Harkin, J., K. Anderson, L. Morgan, and B. Smith, eds. *Deciphering User-Generated Content in Transitional Societies: A Syrian Coverage Case Study*. Centre for Global Communication Studies, Annenberg School for Communication, University of Pennsylvania, 2012.

Johnson, Brett G., and Caroline Dade. "Local Broadcast Journalism, User-Generated Content, and Boundary Work." *Media Practice and Education* 20, no. 3 (2019): 260–76. https://doi.org/10.1080/25741136.2018.1464742.

Kaplan, A., and M. Haenlein. "Users of the World, Unite! The Challenges and Opportunities of Social Media." *Business Horizons* 53 (2010): 59–68. https://doi.org/10.1016/j.bushor.2009.09.003.

MacFarquhar, N. "Syrian Newspapers Emerge to Fill Out War Reporting. Challenging Sources That Are Seen as Skewed." *New York Times*, 2 April 2013, International section, 4, 7.

Mortensen, Mette. *Journalism and Eyewitness Images: Digital Media, Participation, and Conflict*. New York: Routledge, 2015.

– "Witnessing War: Proximity and Distance." Keynote talk at Eyewitness Textures Symposium, 23–4 May 2019, MacEwan University, Edmonton, Canada.

Mortensen M., and N. Kristensen. "Amateur Sources of Breaking the News, Meta Sources Authorizing the News of Gaddafi's Death." *Digital Journalism* 1, no. 3 (2013): 352–67.

Naab, Teresa K., and Annika Sehl. "Studies of User-Generated Content: A Systematic Review." *Journalism* 18, no. 10 (2017): 1256–73.

Noor, Rabia. "Citizen Journalism vs. Mainstream Journalism: A Study on Challenges Posed by Amateurs." *Athens Journal of Mass Media and Communications* 3, no. 1 (2017): 55–76.

Pantti, M. "Getting Closer?" *Journalism Studies* 14, no. 2 (2013): 201–18.

Popple, S., and H. Thornham. *Content Cultures: Transformations of User-Generated Content in Public Service Broadcasting.* New York: I.B. Tauris, 2014.

Radsch, Courtney. *Cyberactivism and Citizen Journalism in Egypt.* New York: Palgrave Macmillan US, 2016.

Santos, M.L.B.D. "The 'So-Called' UGC: An Updated Definition of User-Generated Content in the Age of Social Media." *Online Information Review* 46, no. 1: 95–113. https://doi.org/10.1108/OIR-06-2020-0258.

Silverman, C. *Verification Handbook: An Ultimate Guide for Digital Age Sourcing for Emergency Coverage.* Maastricht: European Journalism Centre, 2014.

Silverman, C., ed. *Verification Handbook for Disinformation and Media Manipulation: A Definitive Guide for Investigating Platforms and Online Accounts to Reveal Inauthentic Activity and Manipulated Content.* Maastricht: European Journalism Centre, 2019.

Singer, J.B., and I. Ashman. "User-Generated Content and Journalistic Values." In *Citizen Journalism: Global Perspectives*, edited by S. Allen and E. Thorsen, 233–54. New York: Peter Lang, 2009.

Van der Haak, Bregtje, Michael Parks, and Manuel Castells. "The Future of Journalism: Networked Journalism." *International Journal of Communication* 6 (2012): 16.

van Dijck, J. "Users Like You? Theorizing Agency in User-Generated Content." *Media, Culture, and Society* 31, no. 1 (2009) 41–58.

Wahl-Jorgensen, Karin. "Resisting Epistemologies of User-Generated Content." In *Boundaries of Journalism*, edited by Matt Carlson and Seth C. Lewis, 167–83. New York: Routledge, 2015.

Wahl-Jorgensen, K., A. Williams, and C. Wardle. "Audience Views on User-Generated Content: Exploring the Value of News from the Bottom Up." *Northern Lights* 8, no. 1 (2010): 177–94.

PART ONE

User-Generated Content and Changing Newsroom Practices

2

Ethical Use of Eyewitness Content

How Public Service Media Are Rebuilding Trust in News

DEREK BOWLER

The European Broadcasting Union (EBU) is the world's leading alliance of public service media. With 115 member organizations in fifty-six countries and an additional thirty-four associates in Asia, Africa, Australasia, and the Americas, its members operate nearly 2,000 television, radio, and online channels and services in addition to a wealth of content across other platforms. Together they reach an audience of more than 1 billion worldwide, broadcasting in more than 160 languages. One of the core services at the Geneva-headquartered union, the Eurovision News Exchange, facilitates exchanges of news material among member organizations while also providing original coverage through its News Events team and international partners.[1]

In 2017, the EBU and its members embarked on a new era of news-gathering by forming the Eurovision Social Newswire (ESN), a collaborative community that helped members harness the power of reliable eyewitness media for their platforms by discovering, verifying, and clearing content obtained from social media, sometimes referred to as user-generated content (UGC). Since its inception, the ESN has provided organizations with upwards of forty verified and cleared-for-use items per day, complementing members' own material and allowing them to tell audiences about stories they may not have been able to explore otherwise. The daily collaboration at the ESN gave rise to EBU *Eyewitness News Principles and Guidelines*, a member-adopted document introducing guidelines and best practices for ethical and transparent social news-gathering; it also served as a guide for applying these principles to the editorial policies and practices of individual members. In this chapter, we will look at the origins of the ESN, how it became a core service of the EBU, and what is entailed in using eyewitness media in ways that are both ethical and transparent.

Origins

On the day the forty-fifth president of the United States began what would turn out to be his only term in office, the EBU was embarking on a journey into the unknown. As Donald J. Trump took the oath of office, millions of people around the world tuned in to watch an inauguration day marred by violence. More than 200 people were arrested in Washington, D.C., that day after activists clashed with police, leaving destroyed businesses and burned-out vehicles in their wake.

While lenses focused on the US Capitol, some 4,000 miles away, two journalists in Geneva, Switzerland, were navigating their way through the noise of social media platforms to discover, verify, and clear content pertaining to the unrest.

The User-Generated Content Verification Network (UGCVN), a WhatsApp group of EBU members with an interest in UGC verification, had been in existence for more than eighteen months, allowing members to communicate and share intelligence about pieces of eyewitness media on the news agenda. Now, for the first time in the group's existence, the EBU was working to self-source content and make it available for members to broadcast. Some sixty-two videos showing unrest were cleared for use for EBU members in a little over thirteen hours. The sudden and vast influx of real-time content and intelligence gave rise to questions about how the EBU could harness the new form of output while remaining true to the union's cooperation and collaboration ethos.

By March 2017, after consultations with members, the EBU had decided to rebrand and expand the UGCVN, which now became the ESN, a collaborative community of journalists, researchers, fact-checkers, and editors working together to discover, verify, and clear eyewitness media from the real-time Web.

For the ESN to work as a core service on par with any social news-gathering newsroom globally, it had to offer a consistently valuable service to member organizations. It had to provide a collaborative space for members to interact, gather real-time intelligence, access verification support and content emerging on social media, and provide skills training for members through collaboration with other members.

Slack, the popular communication platform that several organizations were already using, was chosen as the community's workspace. Its chat rooms, known on the platform as "channels," allowed members to separate out the conversation into areas of interest or specific geographic regions. For instance, members gathered in the "#Newsroom" for general chat and queries, while information on debunked claims and misrepresented content was found in "#debunks." For content, given the sheer volume being cleared for use daily, members were directed to channels based on geographic region or topic; this enabled users to navigate organized feeds of content.

In early 2017, the ESN began to build Twitter lists to aid the news team and members' news-gathering efforts. Carefully curated Twitter lists now play a pivotal role in news-gathering, allowing users to get closer to the story from anywhere in the world by listening to known, official, and trusted sources much closer to an event.

Twitter lists and real-time intelligence gave rise to priority alerts for members. Taking verified information from Twitter and providing it to members in an easily digestible format allowed members to prepare for certain stories rather than wait for the traditional wire services to inform them of stories they needed to chase.

The ESN was a community-based service; even so, the EBU needed to be the driving force behind verification support and content-clearing. Discovering, verifying, and clearing the content before contextualizing it and presenting it to the membership for use was done by a two-person team in Geneva. That team also provided training materials and regular blog posts and tutorials for members regarding how to verify content on a large scale from anywhere in the world. These activities were, and remain, the cornerstone for ESN operations today.

Integration with the Existing Exchange

When a new service emerges in a news organization, the attention and focus it receives can seem to push everything else into the shadows. Innovation brings enthusiasm and hunger for success, but it can also bring a sense of trepidation to the broader newsroom and raise questions about the future. The ESN's purpose was and remains the same: to add value to the Eurovision News Exchange and its members. Although collaborative communication tools such as Slack, Google Hangouts, and Trello introduced added complications to the Geneva newsroom – more tabs, more logins, more notifications – they were designed to support the newswire's workflow and bring a sense of agility and flexibility to a real-time desk.

The year 2017 offered no shortage of moments for testing the ESN, its workflows, and its overall value to members. The massacres in Las Vegas and Texas, the attacks in Westminster and on London Bridge, and the Barcelona and Cambrils attacks[2] all played out heavily on social media. For the first time, the News Exchange and its members were not just waiting for live content from collaborating members and other agencies; they were also anticipating what might come from the ESN. While the service's value is not measured by its successes in tragedy, in each of these events, the ESN provided members with verified and cleared content in a timely manner, allowing members to tell stories quickly and effectively through the eyes of witnesses.

The Verification Process

Since the advent of social media, the verification of eyewitness media has become a much-hyped activity in newsrooms.[3] Social media intelligence agencies, media hubs, and visual investigation teams have all added to the mystique and allure of what essentially is just good investigative journalism. The Five Ws – who, what, where, when, and why – underpin any journalistic investigation, never more so than in social newsgathering. With verification, there is no magic – you are simply applying the five Ws to a new medium.

The three indicators used by the ESN team to verify content are the source, location, and date.

THE SOURCE

Who is the uploader?
What are they filming?
Where are they filming?
When did they get there?
Why are they sharing this content?

THE LOCATION

Are there any identifying landmarks in the footage/image?
Is there signage or licence plates that offer clues to a location?
What type of terrain/environment is in the shot?

THE DATE

Is there an indicator of the day (event, newspaper, TV, speech)?
What are the weather conditions in the content, and how do they
    compare with official weather reports?
Does the footage tally with other footage shared from that location
    on that day?
Does the day tally with official sources?

The verification process is nearly always straightforward. Only rarely, when an in-depth analysis of content is required, can mistakes happen. Instances like this arise when you may not have the necessary language skills in your newsroom to accurately examine all indicators and factors in a piece of content, or when the content is in a remote area and is not easily accessible by open-source mapping services such as Google Maps, or – the worst-case scenario – when there is a rush to use the content in a news story.

One of the biggest news stories of 2018 was the rescue of a junior football team and their coach after heavy rains flooded the Tham Luang Lang Non cave in Chiang Rai province, Thailand. For almost three weeks, the world was captivated as emergency officials and volunteers tried to free the boys from their perilous situation. As rescue efforts continued, news organizations were left scrambling to get content from inside the cave. For days, official reports described the conditions the boys found themselves in: a dark, tight cave that only one diver at a time could reach. Yet no video from inside the cave emerged, however much viewers wanted to see it.

Two weeks after the event began, a video emerged on social media described as showing a diver taking part in the rescue – squeezing through an underwater section of the Tham Luang Lang Non cave with an oxygen tank. The low-resolution video spread across social media like wildfire, quickly garnering views, likes, and shares wherever it was posted. It seemed that with every posting the video came with new intelligence, no matter where you saw it. "Extremely complicated & long operation #ThaiCaveRescue," one Twitter user wrote. A Facebook user, whose version of the video had been watched more than two million times, wrote: "These are the conditions that the Derbyshire Rescuers have to contend with during their rescue operation of the 12 Thais in the Chiang Rai Caverns." One Australian news outlet broadcast the material, describing it as showing "how tight the conditions are through the Thai cave system for divers to rescue the 12 boys and their soccer coach."

When everyone is sharing a video like this, and each version tells its tale, it is even more important to go through a detailed verification process. Undertaking the video's verification at the request of EBU members, the ESN team found a high-resolution version of the video dating back to 2012. A YouTube user had filmed the footage while cave diving in Fennimore, Wisconsin, six years prior to the incident in Thailand.

While there are many tools, applications, and third parties to aid in the verification process, there is no replacement for critical thinking and the journalistic approach. If you can establish the three indicators with a high degree of certainty, you can consider the content verified. However, that is not the end of the process.

The final step in the verification process is engaging with the source to attain clearance to use the material. Of course, speaking directly to the source is crucial in obtaining permission. Knowing their perspective and motivation for sharing content is critical for verifying whether a piece of content is legitimate.

The ESN does not use content without the permission and informed consent of the originator and copyright holder. This is the basis of the ethical and transparent social news-gathering practice on which the ESN was founded. Only after written permission has been given by the originator is the content contextualized and presented to EBU members.

The Agile Newsroom

The coronavirus pandemic has played a key role in redefining how news organizations view their newsrooms. For many, the newsroom was a haven where only certain job functions and roles could be performed. With governments introducing tight restrictions and social distancing measures in a bid to curb the spread of the virus, newsrooms were forced to adapt their workflows to allow colleagues to work from outside the brick-and-mortar office.

When the ESN began, one of its priorities was to design a social newsroom and show how existing proprietary technology at the EBU combined with third-party tools would allow for a flexible, or agile, newsroom. The resulting flexibility in workflow allowed the team to react to breaking news at a moment's notice, no matter the time or location. With the news industry and many organizations in a trans-formative state, it is not always possible for newsrooms to carefully monitor social media for emerging content. Based on how well its agile newsroom functioned, the ESN's members were keen to learn how to incorporate these workflows and verification processes into their own newsrooms.

The ESN organized the Agile Newsroom, a three-day interactive event during which members worked together to discover, verify, and clear content for use. The workshop aimed to allow newsroom journalists to enhance their verification skills and find new workflows by working in teams and learning from one another. The inaugural event was held at the headquarters of the Austrian public service broadcaster Österreichischer Rundfunk (ORF) in October 2017, with fifty-five journalists from twenty-three EBU members working together to identify, verify, and clear eyewitness media from around the world. The success of the inaugural event led to a second Agile Newsroom in Sarajevo in 2018, where sixty journalists gathered to hone their social newsgathering skills.

In a 2018 report published by the EBU, external observers found the Agile Newsroom's immersive experience to be "challenging and rewarding." Also, attendees returned to their news organizations con-fident in the new skills they had acquired.[4]

EBU Eyewitness News Principles and Guidelines

Social media today constitute the Wild West of journalism, a competi-tive space in which news organizations race against one another in the battle for content. News outlets employ an array of tools and techniques to entice content producers to part with their much sought after bounty, thus blurring the lines between journalism and content-for-clicks. The thirst for content has spawned a new industry within journalism: third-party licensing. In major breaking news stories, hundreds of journalists might ask one uploader, who happened to be in the right place at the right time to capture the picture of the day, for the use of their content. Increased competition for exclusivity on third-party content has seen the window of opportunity for news organizations to acquire non-exclusive rights to material shrink, especially for bigger international news events.

In the race to publish, journalists, under pressure to secure the best content emerging on social media, can lose track of their journalistic principles and ethics. So can news organizations that consider everything online to be fair use, using content no matter what the copyright holder says.

Recognizing the importance and value that UGC retains, while at the same time recognizing that the social mediascape has become a battleground for content, the EBU decided that it was important to provide a principled and ethical structure regarding the use of UGC. This would enhance public service media as a trusted source of information for the public. Since its adoption by members in 2018, the EBU *Eyewitness News Principles and Guidelines* has provided a set of guidelines and principles, adherence to which is determined by each member voluntarily (see Addendum 1 for a summary of key principles). The principles and guidelines offer a code of practice and conduct under which the ESN team operates, encouraging greater transparency in news-gathering for the originator and the viewing audience.

The members of the EBU recognize the importance of establishing social news-gathering principles and guidelines for them to build upon as the use of eyewitness media grows in their newsrooms. The financial pressures that news organizations find themselves facing in the current climate mean that the use of third-party material is increasing. In such a climate, having a standard to adhere to allows for confident use of this material by organizations. It also brings to light the pitfalls of using content under a "fair use" policy without the expressed permission of the copyright holder, which could have severe financial repercussions for organizations.

Members of the EBU have embraced these principles and guidelines, with some importing sections into their own news-gathering structures. The document has reinforced the importance of the ethical use of UGC;

it has also provided members with the building blocks to become more confident in social news-gathering. This has led to a new stream of content for public service media, opening a new fount of stories for audiences across the world.

In Closing

Over the past decade, trust in the media has been tested like never before. News organizations had once been lauded for their factual and unbiased reporting; today they find themselves ridiculed by alternative news sources and right-leaning government actors.

Public service media are the bedrock of any democratic society. They enable the public to access information (which is a fundamental right) and express diverse opinions. They also foster pluralism. To those ends, they must maintain their independence, both financial and editorial, while adapting to meet audience demands in the digital age.

The ever-increasing role that UGC plays in output has brought an acute awareness of the pitfalls that come with it. In this era of "alternative facts," never before have the five Ws been so important in all facets of the newsroom, especially in the relatively young field of social news-gathering.

When UGC is handled with the highest ethical standards, news organizations need not fear it. Adapting journalistic skills to discover, forensically examine, and acquire permission for the use of UGC allows for its ease of use, ensuring the building of confidence within an organization as well as trust among its audience.

While all news organizations want to be first, they also have a duty to the audience to be right. Adherence to a set of ideals such as the EBU *Eyewitness Principles and Guidelines* offers organizations something reliable with which to navigate and decipher the news amidst all the noise emerging on social media.

We are quickly approaching a turning point in the industry in the use of UGC. The varying standards that organizations adopt in handling UGC are shedding a spotlight on the unethical use of third-party content by news media. Payment or no payment? Courtesy or no courtesy? Even issues of copyright and permission are bringing considerable scrutiny to organizations and practitioners operating in this space. Organizations need to hold themselves to a higher standard: Go through a strict verification process. Ask for permission. Be transparent about who will use or have access to the content. Accept no as an answer. Show courtesy to the copyright holder and recognize their contribution to your output.

While regulation may not be the answer, industry-wide adoption of ethical principles and guidelines is on the horizon for those working for traditional media organizations and agencies.

Although just one pillar of the trusted EBU alliance, the ESN operation has shown that commitment to journalistic principles and ethical news-gathering standards plays an ever-important role in navigating real-time news, while ethical and transparent consistency raises trust in the organization's operations.

However, bringing the ESN from concept to core service has not been without its challenges. The idea of digital transformation and adoption of new work processes and content has raised several questions, most notably, Why do we need this? Why now? Why can't things stay the same?

At the EBU, the Eurovision News Exchange has been delivering high-quality and respected broadcast material for more than sixty years to homes worldwide. The key to the ESN's successful integration into the service was to understand the existing services, identify what members wanted, and find a way to serve specific markets in ways that complimented the existing service.

Essential to that integration has been buy-in from the newsroom. To achieve that, you have to bring people into the process. At the News Exchange, outlining the research and analysis, mapping, and clearly communicating the potential journey and vision for the service has brought a greater understanding of the possibilities that such a service can offer while also identifying those who are ready to begin working on the service. But it is crucial to understand when undergoing a digital transformation that it is normal for people within an organization to resist change. Integrating new systems and processes into an organization takes time, and not everyone immediately wants that change.

What we learned from creating the ESN and incorporating it into the organization was that precision beats power, and timing beats speed. Know your audience, make precise and deliberate decisions, and communicate with your people.

Addendum I

EBU Eyewitness News Principles and Guidelines at a Glance

TRANSPARENCY
- We will be transparent about the source of the Eyewitness News Content.
- We will require the explicit crediting of content when it is editorially necessary to indicate the source of the content.

SOURCE
- In general, we do not solicit eyewitnesses to produce free material.
- We protect our sources.
- Journalists and producers should consider the physical and emotional welfare of originators. They will be sensitive to the situation an originator might be in when contacting them to receive permission for the use of their content.
- We will guard against using eyewitness media [UGC] in situations that might be dangerous to the person who created it or to others in the images.
- We will stress to possible providers of eyewitness media that they must not take risks to gather information or imagery.

PAYMENT, COPYRIGHT, AND LICENSING
- We will not distribute eyewitness media content unless we're certain we have the rights to do so.
- We will seek informed consent for the use of eyewitness media through direct communication with the individual who created it.
- We respect the rights of the copyright holder.
- We ensure that copyright holders are able to give informed consent to our use of their material.
- We will not pay for Eyewitness News Content nor commission such content from suppliers.
- We respect the request of the copyright holder to withdraw material from future use.
- We do not use "fair use" concepts in dealing with eyewitness media, and if news public interest exceptions are used, we apply the principles of the supplier's jurisdiction. This would be based upon the work's copyright status in its country of origin and the copyright law within said country.

COURTESY

- We give a courtesy crediting the owners of the eyewitness material to acknowledge their contribution and collaboration in our news production. Wherever the content appears, whether it be in broadcast or online, the originator's name will appear on screen recognizing them as the owner.
- We respect the right of the copyright holder to seek payment or reimbursement should their required courtesy not be adhered to.

GRAPHIC MATERIAL

- We respect the privacy of victims of violence and do not seek out shocking, disturbing, and extreme content gratuitously.
- We will be sensitive to the impact that exposure to graphic content may have on eyewitnesses and editorial staff.
- We will obscure or pixelate images only when the intent is to protect the identity of someone in the image or to protect viewers from gory or graphic material.
- We avoid material that exploits children or infringes on their rights unless there are important public interest reasons [at stake].
- We avoid identifying – by name or photo – children who are connected with a crime as perpetrators, victims, or witnesses.
- We obtain a parent's permission before clearing content from a child under the age of 16.

PRIVACY

- We will not gather content that infringes on the privacy of individuals or is secretly recorded unless clearly in the public interest to do so.
- We consider the standard for publishing material about private individuals who are thrust into the public eye as higher than that for public individuals.

ACCURATE AND RELEVANT

- We will verify and check all eyewitness content. We will correct and notify [about] all mistakes.
- We consider eyewitness media an extension of our own journalism.
- We don't run such material unless we're sure it's authentic.
- We partner with other organizations and the public to verify the accuracy of eyewitness media.
- We will provide accurate context for our reporting.
- We will ensure sources are reliable.

CONNECTED AND ACCOUNTABLE

- We encourage reciprocity in exchanges with non-journalists. In the spirit of collaboration, we acknowledge copyright holders' contributions to our news production and follow up on requests to share news items featuring their material.
- We will engage with our audiences about our use of eyewitness content and the principles we adopt when using it.

THE WELL-BEING OF STAFF AND CONTRIBUTORS

- We will support staff and contributors who may be confronted with graphic or otherwise disturbing content, ensuring awareness and openness in dealing with these issues in our newsrooms.[5]

Notes

1 Ezez, "About the EBU."
2 For more on the Barcelona terrorist attacks, see chapter 12 (Escudero).
3 For more on the verification process, see chapters 3 (Miller) and 11 (Kang).
4 Ezez, "50 Ways."
5 Ezez, EBU Eyewitness News.

Bibliography

Ezez. "About the EBU." Geneva: European Broadcasting Union, 2021. https://www.ebu.ch/about.

– EBU Eyewitness News Principles and Guidelines. Geneva: European Broadcasting Union, 2018. https://www.ebu.ch/files/live/sites/ebu/files/Services/News%20Exchange/EBU_Eyewitness_News_Principles_and_Guidelines-2020_19112020.pdf.

– EBU News Report 2018. "50 Ways to Make it Better." Geneva: European Broadcasting Union, 2018. https://www.ebu.ch/files/live/sites/ebu/files/Publications/Reports/login_only/EBU_News_Report_2018_EN.pdf.

3

The Origins, Development, and Future of the User-Generated Content Team at the BBC

NATALIE MILLER

It is not easy to be ahead of the game and predict the next move in media trends or indeed in audience trends, but that is what the BBC did back in 2005 when it began a trial involving six journalists using the BBC News website to source user-generated content. Fifteen years later, that un-catchy term still exists but the team has gone through some significant changes: no longer six, we are now eleven, and we no longer just use the BBC News website – with the development of social media our sources of material as well as our staff have expanded. I have been fortunate enough to witness some, if not all, of those changes. This is a brief introduction to the BBC's User-Generated Content team, or UGC team, its development, and a few key changes that have been made to it, along with, perhaps, a glimpse into its future.

How It All Began

On Boxing Day in 2004 a tsunami hit multiple countries in Southeast Asia, causing mass devastation across the region.[1] The effects of this tsunami were felt not just in the region itself but around the globe. It was a world-spanning event over the course of which millions of people took pictures, made phone calls, and sent emails to friends, family, and the media. They described and pictured what happened.

The BBC received hundreds of messages in the days and weeks after the event, and because there was no central place at the time for people to reach out to us, they instead emailed and sent pictures to the programmes they watched or listened to. Individual programmes across the BBC all received content, and all of them used that content but none of them shared it; at the time it was not even considered.

But what if there was one team assigned to dealing with this content, checking it, processing it, and then making sure all programmes could use it? The idea was simple: to develop a User-Generated Content Hub. The UGC Hub, as it became known, was set up in January 2005 following the tsunami for a six-month trial to see if it was worthwhile. The trial was to end at the end of July 2005.

Although the UGC Hub was useful in those first five months, not many programs saw it as an important part of journalism, and it took many years for the hub to become a critical part of all BBC News output. In the early days, producers on the team were assigned to work with certain programs: we worked with TV, radio, and online programs. But while every program editor had access to the team and its work, and indeed each producer was in daily contact with programs offering stories and content, only a few editors saw the value and used the material we provided. Even so, with the help of these enthusiasts of UGC, we were able to establish a reputation for providing accurate and newsworthy material from the public.

But the majority of editors in the newsroom at this time thought news should be the sole preserve of journalists. It was they who should be finding the news, sourcing it, verifying it, ensuring it was balanced, adding context, and then reporting it. Journalists were also the ones who decided what stories the public would be interested in; for them, the only purpose of the public was to *consume* the news.

Many editors found it difficult to imagine the change that was about to take place. The term "citizen journalist" was already well used, but the view was that even if the public did become more involved in the news-making process, they did not have the skill, the knowledge, or the training to present a balanced viewpoint and tell the story. There was also a concern about accuracy: could we trust these members of the public to tell us the truth? It took a while for these news editors to grasp that members of the public did not need to be involved in the entire process; they could simply be a part of it, with trained journalists verifying the content they were sharing, putting that material into context, and providing a balanced viewpoint.

A turning point came in July 2005 toward the end of the BBC's UGC trial. In July 2005 London was attacked; bombs went off in four locations, killing fifty-two people. It was only after our work on that day that the real value of the UGC team began to be acknowledged.[2]

I was on my way to work that morning, as a producer on Radio 5 Live fixing guests to come and talk on the radio. I was on a train, like many others, when the bombs went off. My first thought as I got off the train and was told all tube lines had closed was to phone work, from a payphone, to tell them I was going to be late, and then to phone home and tell them I was okay. I had no idea what was going on, just that there were no trains and no cell phone signals and a lot of confusion.

My team was not aware of what had happened. They were reporting signal failures and electrical faults, but even at that time the UGC team was starting to receive word that it was not a mass signal failure, as was being reported, but a bomb – in fact, multiple bombs had gone off on the London Underground and on a London bus. They not only had people emailing to say this, they also had photos, images from inside the tunnels as people were evacuating and photos of a bus in Tavistock Square. As former UGC assistant editor Matthew Eltringham wrote in his blog of July 2010:

> We had credible intelligence of every single one of the four bombs by 9:58am – including one that told us of the Tavistock Square bomb by 9:55am; just ten minutes after it had happened. At that time the BBC, and the rest of the media, were still reporting that there had been some kind of signaling or electrical fault. These erroneous reports moved one eyewitness, Lou Stern, to send in his pictures of the bus bomb because, as he put it, it clearly wasn't a signalling fault.[3]

The team that had been set up to source images of breaking news wasn't just getting images and eyewitnesses, *it was breaking the news itself*. It was clear from that moment that the small team provided a vital resource. One of the team's producers, Victoria Park,[4] summed up the unique nature of the team and its development:

> When I started not many people had heard of UGC, let alone knew what it meant. But I joined the team knowing that UGC was

going to be very important to news story telling. And this was due to one event that had stuck in my mind 12 months previously. In January of 2009, a US airliner on a domestic flight with 155 people onboard crashed into the Hudson River in New York City but with no loss of life. One of the very first pictures to be posted was taken by Janis Krums from Florida. Mr Krums, who was on a ferry, took a picture on his phone and immediately posted it on Twitpic. In the first few minutes after the crash, his picture of the plane was being shared around the world. This was the beginning of an important shift in the way news stories were to be sourced. And, in 2010, I was excited to be a part of it.

How Social Media Changed Our Work

I was excited to be part of this team, as for me talking to people at the heart of a story was key to being a journalist. I joined the team in 2007 just as things were really about to change. Up until that point the team had used forms and email addresses trailed on the BBC News Channel and the BBC News website to get content. It was, and to this day still is, a successful way to source content from our audiences. But things can change very quickly.

Back in 2007 very few BBC journalists were actively using social media for personal use, let alone work. However, in the hub we were always looking for new ways to reach our audiences – audiences in places we as journalists couldn't get to, or couldn't get to in time. When we heard about a microblogging site – a place where you could blog in 140 characters – we thought it had potential. At the time, this site – Twitter – seemed like a fantastic way to get more content. In 2007, 60,000 tweets were being sent each day; even if Twitter users sent just two or three tweets a day, that still meant a potential 20,000 people around the world who could be in the right place at the right time to take, and post, video or photos. The potential for news-gathering was huge. The BBC has more than 6,500 journalists working in 181 cities in 117 countries around the world,[5] but even the BBC does not have people everywhere.

The UGC team had the first officially branded BBC account on Twitter, an account we still use today, among other accounts on other social media platforms. But while the introduction of social media into newsrooms had many advantages, especially in reaching and connecting with audiences, it wasn't long before we realized that the platforms also posed a number of problems.

Finding content was not always easy. At first it was not too hard to search through posts, but with more and more people using the platforms to share material, sifting through content became more challenging. Users had begun resharing content, sometimes hundreds or thousands of times, which made it difficult to locate the original content.

There was also the growing issue of credibility. Who were the people sharing this material? What were their motives? Had the content been altered in any way? Was it real? And did we have the right, legally and ethically, to use it? These were all questions that needed to be answered before any UGC could be published. While these issues were not insurmountable, they did mean changing how we worked. We had tools to help us, but we added verification processes, which – problematic for a journalist working on a breaking story – added time.

All the while, the UGC team's reputation at the BBC was growing, and newsrooms were now depending on our ability to use social media to find people at the heart of the story to comment on major breaking news events.

Using WhatsApp for Social News-Gathering

There were some stories that had always left us frustrated, and earthquakes were one of them. Earthquakes take out power lines, phone lines, and electrical supplies, and in those situations it's almost impossible to get hold of people. But in 2015 that changed. In March of that year an earthquake struck Nepal, and within minutes, pictures and videos were being sent to us. Even more important, in addition to having the content we had a way to get in touch with people and interview them and verify the material. We did all this via WhatsApp.

Since then, WhatsApp has become one of the primary ways we gather content. When we ask our users to get in touch, we make sure to include our WhatsApp number. It is an easy, convenient, and cheap way for people to keep in touch with us. It is also an easy way for them to share content with us.

WhatsApp has enabled us to reach audiences quickly and efficiently, but it has also opened the door to a range of new problems, not only because a lot of the conversations on WhatsApp are private, but also because it is very easy to share content that may be misleading or inaccurate, or simply not yours to share. Content is often shared and forwarded between people and groups many times before it reaches us, so finding the original source is often tricky if not impossible. It is crucial for journalists to find the original source and speak to them, not only to establish copyright and permission to use the material but also to gather facts and verify the content.

Twitter and WhatsApp are not the only sources of UGC. Today we search platforms like Facebook, Instagram, Snapchat, YouTube, and TikTok. This list will change and grow as more platforms are developed and users move between them.

Where the Audience Goes, We Follow

We monitor all these platforms because our audiences have embraced them. When I started with the team I had a mobile phone. I used it to make phone calls and send text messages. It could take photos, but it was not connected to the Internet, so I could only tweet via text. However, the availability of smart phones, cheaper data packages, faster connection speeds, and better-quality phone cameras has meant more content can be shared.

The journalists who spend their time searching for UGC on social media need to follow the audience. It is not just journalists who rely on the platforms; so do the people who use them. For example, while we still use Twitter to find content on breaking stories, we also use Snapchat. Snapchat's map feature enables us to locate clips easily and adds a level of verification, besides providing a valuable source of content. In fact, for every story we use a variety of social media as well as our forms and other sources of direct messaging to gather content.

There will perhaps come a point when there are simply too many platforms for us to follow, too many accounts to keep up to date, and we will have to decide which ones are worthwhile. Perhaps they will be the ones with the greatest numbers of users, the widest geographic reach, or the greatest range of content, or perhaps we will have to dip in and out of various themed or location-based sites depending on the stories we are covering. With an ever-increasing demand for content and more organisations chasing the same material, it is more important than ever to build a trusting relationship with our audience. We want them to come to us first, we want them to tell us what is going on. We can only build that relationship by speaking their language on the platforms they use. TV news is either dead or dying. Younger audiences simply do not sit down at the same time each day to watch a news broadcast prepared by one organization. They watch on the go, when they want to, they pick and choose between news organizations, and they watch different types of content in different places. If we can build a brand and a reputation, if we are on the same platforms as they are, if we can tailor our content and talk to them in their language, then maybe they will choose us as a trusted news source, and maybe when something happens or when they chance upon a BBC story they will get in touch with us. If we don't follow our audience, this simply will not happen.

We were early adopters of this content, but we are no longer the only ones looking for it. Today, all broadcasters and news agencies look for, and use, UGC. Already we have started to change the way we look for material. Increasingly we are using third-party sites to help us source content from various social networks; their use of artificial intelligence helps us pick through the content to find material we want. Some news agencies today focus solely on finding and verifying UGC.

I think there will always be room for agencies working in this field. Traditional news agencies were trusted sources that were in places we couldn't get to quickly; they had stringers around the world providing content. The new social agencies will operate in much the same way. For broadcasters that can afford to sign up they will be an additional source of content. We will still need to work with them to ensure the content has been verified and is authentic. As they diversify and follow audiences across various platforms, we will likely use them more and more. Audiences too are seeing the value of these agencies, and indeed are seeing the value of the content they are capturing. Many now sell their own pictures and videos to the highest bidder.

But while there is competition, there is also collaboration. We have been working with other organizations to share our verification work and to share content. Sharing is important, for we need to keep in mind the pressure a lot of media attention can place on someone who is not expecting it or is not used to it. If one team finds, verifies, and clears material, why can't others benefit too?

The BBC has many relationships with broadcasters around the world, and when we clear content we always ask the users if they will let us share their content with our international broadcasting partners. The BBC does not acquire the rights to the content; the rights are always retained by the users. So it is important that we make it clear to them that when they give us permission to use their content, they may also see it on international broadcasters.

The Importance of Verification

The UGC hub now uses a variety of sources to track, trace, and clear content. We have had to change how we verify that content. When I started at the hub in 2007 we did not talk about verification quite as much as we do now, but even then we did journalistic checks on the people we were speaking to and the content we were being sent. However, verification soon became our mantra, and we have developed new ways to verify the content we find.

At first, every picture that was sent to us had exif (exchangeable image file) data, which told us the time, date, and location a photo was taken. Nowadays, as material is shared, then reshared and scraped from the Internet, then shared via social media or private channels such as WhatsApp, the overall picture of where an image originated is no longer clear.

Verification has become our most valuable skill: the importance of knowing whether a picture or video is genuine cannot be understated, especially in this era of disinformation and fake news.[6] And while the development of tech has made it easier for images and videos to be manipulated, it has also made it easier for us to detect that manipulation.

We use many tools – mapping tools to find information about location, tools that tell us about the weather, tools that analyze the position of shadows, and street view and satellite imagery to find locations and cross-check those with the images we have.[7] We use video location searches and tools developed by aid agencies to map disasters. And tools to detect image manipulation. Some of the tools we use, such as maps and street views, have been around for a long time and were not developed with verification in mind. Meanwhile, new tools are being developed, some of them for the express purpose of helping journalists verify content. But while tools like these are useful in the verification process, it is also crucial to ask a lot of questions, use common sense, and apply journalistic instincts.

It is easy to share a photo and say it is something it is not. That is the most common type of fakery the UGC team has to deal with. Quite often, people share things they genuinely believe are true. For those whose intent is to mislead, AI-generated images known as "fakes" and "deep fakes" are getting easier to create. As Tom Gerken,[8] who joined the team in 2017, said:

> I think in the future, journalists will have no choice but to be skilled up in most everything that we do in UGC. I'm unconvinced that you'll be able to be a journalist in 2040 unless you know how to verify a video online, as by then "fake news" will surely have proliferated to a point where it's next to impossible for normal people to distinguish it.
>
> Look at the advancement of "deep fakes," and pair it with Adobe's frightening "Photoshop for voice" which is in development. Very soon people with a malicious intent will be able to make it look and sound as if someone said something they didn't.
>
> Our role and that of other news organizations will be to distinguish what is real and what is not. We can't expect social media companies to do it.

People Are Our Best Resource

We also rely on the expertise of the people we work with to aid in the verification process. BBC journalists around the world are an incredible resource because of their knowledge, local knowledge, and language skills. Local knowledge in particular is key to verifying content, so when something happens in another country, these people become invaluable.

Consider this example. Our team was trying to verify a video claiming to have been filmed in the days following an earthquake in Iran. The video showed a heartwarming scene – a little boy collecting aid for his family with his young sister. It was a scene of hope in a story about utter devastation. Verification can take a long time, and every editor wanted to use this video straight away, so the pressure was on to find the origins and establish the facts. That day we were fortunate to have an Iranian journalist as part of the team. He looked at this clip and said no, it didn't sound right – simply that. We needed more time to investigate.

To him, the accents in the video were wrong. The earthquake had happened in the mountainous border region of the country, more than 400 miles from Tehran, yet the people in the video were speaking with Tehrani accents.

We looked closer at the background. This earthquake had wiped out entire villages, but in the background there was no rubble. We also tried to find the person who had filmed the video. It was being shared widely on Telegram, privately and securely, making it nearly impossible to find out where it had come from. However, eventually we found someone who helped lead us to the owners, who confirmed our suspicions that the video had not been filmed in the aftermath of the earthquake but was actually a little boy collecting food for a festival in Tehran.

We were then able to tell the rest of the BBC not to use this video in this context, for had not been filmed in the aftermath of the earthquake. We often get criticized for not being quick when it comes to giving an answer on a video, but accuracy is more important than speed, and in this case we were right to take our time.

In this instance we were also fortunate enough to have a journalist from Iran on hand. That is not always the case, but we always do have the ability to tap into the knowledge of other BBC journalists around the world. Whenever we are involved with a global story, whether it is an explosion in Beirut, an attack in Syria, or unrest in Sudan, we always approach teams on the ground for their help and expertise.

The first step in verification is to speak to the person who owns the footage or image. In some cases that simply is not possible – we cannot find that person, or we might be putting them and their family in danger simply by talking to them. In these cases, we seek out local BBC journalists.

When it is not possible to speak to the owner or a BBC contact, we ascertain as much as we can about the content from what we can see and hear ourselves. In these circumstances we can rarely be 100 percent confident about a source, but we can usually make some assumptions as to the accuracy of the material provided, and that, along with other sources and information, can help form a more complete picture of an event or incident.

Working Together Makes Us Stronger

At the BBC all news teams across the organization can ask the UGC team to help with verification. In addition to that, the BBC Academy, an internal training unit, now offers a dedicated verification training course to all new journalists joining the organization, not just those joining the UGC hub. And it's not just journalists at the hub who can help with verification. More and more journalists are working together to stop the spread of inaccurate information.

For example, in 2017 the UGC hub along with other European broadcasters joined a project launched by First Draft News called CrossCheck. The aim was to find and verify claims being made during the French election. Each broadcaster had its own remit, but we worked together to separate fact from fiction, report accurately, and expose misleading and confusing claims that were circulating online. The CrossCheck team has gone on to work on other elections.

The Impact of Vicarious Trauma

We are acutely aware of the impact traumatic events have on people who witness them. Merely watching this type of content, or hearing people describe it, can do our journalists harm. That is why vicarious trauma, like verification, has become a key word in our vocabulary.[9] In addition to developing workflows around social news-gathering and verification, we have developed systems and workflows to help us as journalists deal with graphic material.

We have guidelines in place that we follow while working on a story. For example, we no longer watch and listen to videos in their entirety; instead, we watch in sections and listen to the audio separately. We also take turns working on stories that we know will deliver graphic content so that no one person is overwhelmed, and on the day of a major event we rotate people wherever possible. We now ask anyone sending us content to mark it clearly to let us know whether it is graphic; that way, we know what to expect when we open that email. We have meetings outside of the work environment specifically to discuss any story that has had an impact on our mental health. Chatting with other colleagues about our experiences can help, but sometimes it is also necessary to chat with a professional, and to that end we have a system of support available to us twenty-four hours a day and managers are trained to spot signs of trauma in colleagues and refer them to our dedicated team of mental health professionals. These professionals are on hand for everyone in the UGC team and throughout the BBC.

The Future of UGC

Technology has forced journalists to adapt. In many ways it has made our lives easier, allowing us to find and verify more content. It has also allowed us to open doors to new audiences and new stories. But with these advantages have come new and distinct challenge.. Smart phones and social media accounts have had a significant impact on our work, but so – even more – has our understanding of UGC's potential. UGC now plays a key part in our work every single day.

Many journalists needed time to adapt to UGC. Having a team dedicated to this type of work did help. We were at the forefront of using social media tools to find, source, and verify this content. We were in touch with our audience every day and could see the types of questions and stories they were talking about and were interested in. Not only did we become the team that sourced this content, we also led the way in helping others understand and see its value. We encountered many problems as we grew and developed in this work, not least the impact of vicarious trauma on journalists and producers, but we were able to develop systems to help us cope with those situations. We used our knowledge to develop courses and showed others how to use the tools we used every day to source and verify material and how to avoid the pitfalls. In short, we have helped all journalists at the BBC become UGC journalists.

But what does the future hold for the UGC team? I fear we will become the victims of our own success. More and more journalists are becoming proficient in sourcing and verifying content, and that is a good thing, but with more skills will the BBC newsroom still need a dedicated UGC team to do this work? I don't think it will.

It makes sense to have every journalist know how to use social media to find content quickly, how to verify the authenticity of that content, and how to speak to those in traumatic situations who are sharing material. The tools and skills developed by journalists working in social news-gathering are critical for all journalists, regardless of their day-to-day role. Perhaps the next stage for this small but dedicated team will be more deep-dive investigations and collaborations with other teams on specific projects, programs, and documentaries. And while the UGC team is busy working in the dark corners of the Web trying to debunk deep fakes and find the truth about content, the rest of the newsroom will be gathering news and content through social media.

In the future I would like to see journalists have tools that will help with this process, tools that not only search for the content but also help to verify it. I'd like to see more work done by social platforms too, to help mitigate vicarious trauma, not just for journalists who are sourcing material but for everyone on their platforms. Content should be filtered and warnings added so that everyone knows what they are about to see and can make informed decisions about whether to view it.

Every journalist working in a dangerous environment, whether a protest or a war zone, has dedicated training before being allowed to go to those areas and cover those stories, and likewise every journalist searching through social media should have dedicated training as preparation for the type of content they might see. The impact of vicarious trauma cannot be underestimated, and newsrooms of the future will need to account for it and prepare their journalists just like they would when sending them to report directly on traumatic stories.

However the future newsroom develops, the need for UGC and verification work will not vanish; in fact it will become more crucial than ever. I believe that demand for it will continue to grow. But however the UGC team at the BBC changes and adapts, for us our audience will always be at the heart of everything we do.

Notes

1 For more discussion on the Boxing Day tsunami, see chapters 9 (Lithgow) and 12 (Escudero).
2 See also the discussion on the London bombings in chapter 12 (Escudero).
3 Eltringham, "UGC."
4 Victoria Park, private correspondence, 2019. Published with permission.
5 BBC News Press team, May 2019.
6 For more on fake news, see the Prologue and chapters 4 (Remple) and 6 (Lithgow and Martin).
7 For more on such "digital forensics techniques," see chapter 10 (Santos).
8 Tom Gerken, private correspondence, 2019. Published with permission.
9 For more on vicarious trauma, or secondary trauma, and its effect on the mental health of journalists, see chapters 4 (Rempel) and 5 (Lau et al.).

Bibliography

Eltringham, Matthew. "UGC Five Years On." BBC (blog), 6 July 2010. https://www.bbc.co.uk/blogs/collegeofjournalism/entries/1cc3d19f-5cb7-3f14-b598-76833d680c61.

4

The Global News Audience

User-Generated Content at a
Canadian National Broadcast News Network

SHAUNA REMPEL

Multiplatform entities like Global News rely on user-generated content (UGC) to develop an audience and power their channels. UGC brings myriad benefits and opportunities to enrich and diversify news coverage, but also potential pitfalls that require strong news judgment, ongoing training, and careful consultation. At Global, UGC allows us to capture moments that traditional news teams might otherwise miss, thanks to citizen journalists armed with smart phones and Twitter accounts. But those same amateur photos or videos can generate a host of complications when it comes to verifying their truthfulness and sorting out usage rights. Adding to that, the sometimes disturbing nature of the content raises questions about what both journalists and the news audience can handle. This chapter explores those benefits and pitfalls, as well as the tools we can use to source, verify, and clear UGC for use on broadcast, digital, and social media platforms. This chapter will also examine how Global News uses UGC on a daily basis, providing several recent case studies.

About the Organization

Global News, under its parent company Corus Entertainment, is a national network of local newsrooms and bureaux across Canada. It is a multimedia organization with four thriving platforms: the legacy businesses of television and radio broadcasting and the new media businesses of digital and social. Its website, globalnews.ca, is run largely by a Toronto-based national online team.

Within that framework is a small social media–focused team that administers dozens of accounts across Twitter, Facebook, Instagram, YouTube, Pinterest, TikTok, and more. That team is commonly referred to as the "social desk." The social media specialists collaborate daily with video producers, graphic designers, and developers, as well as local newsrooms across the country, as they interact with their social media audience of more than 9 million followers, fans, and subscribers.

A motto at Global News is that "social media is part of everyone's job." UGC has now been baked into everyone's role, whether they work behind the scenes or on camera, and whether they specialize in radio, digital, TV, or social media. This is necessary because although the social team is operational seven days a week, it is not an around-the-clock operation. So having social media–minded staff in newsrooms coast to coast, in four different time zones, helps ensure that we never miss a key piece of UGC.

Explanation of Terms

When discussing UGC, this chapter includes both solicited and unsolicited submissions from the audience. Various parts of this multi-platform business use terms such as "viewer," "listener," "reader," and "user"; on the social media desk we feel that "audience member" is the most inclusive appellation.

Solicited submissions are prompted by *callouts* or *calls to action*, in which a Global News account or a representative specifically asks for an audience member to respond in a certain way. For example, a staff reporter may ask on Facebook for a potential source to contact them for an interview, or the @globalnews Twitter account may solicit photos and testimonials for a #MothersDay campaign.

Unsolicited submissions take the form of news tips, photos, video, and other content sent to newsrooms electronically, via email, direct messages (DMs) on Facebook, Twitter, or Instagram, or the comments on those social media accounts.

Globalnews.ca ✓
@globalnews   • • •

Whether you're a new mom or a grandmother,
#MothersDay is always special. Show how you'll
celebrate - and who you'll celebrate with - for the
#MotherOfAllDays18 photo challenge trib.al/ukqRlnM

Figure 4.1   @globalnews Twitter, Mother's Day.

Consent

For both solicited and unsolicited submissions, we operate on the assumption that consent to use the content is implied. That is, in sharing the content with us, the audience member is giving us consent to use it on our platforms. Even with implied consent, we endeavour to get the audience member's permission in writing for use on all platforms. This practice is in keeping with that of many news outlets, which use a version of the following: "Do you consent to [news outlet] using this video/photo/image, with credit, on all our platforms?"

It is important in a multiplatform news organization to stipulate that consent is granted for *all* platforms, to ensure that we have the option of using that content anywhere. It may not actually be used on all platforms, but we ask anyway to give ourselves some editorial flexibility. Generally, the Global News journalist who is corresponding with the audience member will obtain this blanket consent and then communicate to colleagues working across the chain that this step has been taken. As part of this correspondence, the journalist also confirms that the audience member owns the content and is the copyright holder. It is crucial that we confirm who has original ownership of the content so that there are no unexpected copyright claims after we have published or broadcast it.

How UGC Is Sourced

Journalists on the centralized social media desk and in local markets across Canada monitor several communication channels for UGC to make sure we are staying on top of the latest newsworthy content. On a daily basis, sometimes many times each day, journalists check email, DMs, hashtags, and mentions for content the audience is sharing with us. They also one or more of the services we use to help track newsworthy UGC.

For several years, we have paid the Storyful social media wire service to provide verified UGC from around the world, including videos and photos that are trending or going viral on social media platforms.[1] Storyful bills itself as the world's first social newswire and as a premium service for not only media but also for business leaders and investors who want to keep a finger on the pulse of social media activity.[2] It was founded in 2010 in Dublin, Ireland, and acquired in 2013 by Rupert Murdoch's News Corporation.[3] Other wire services such as Reuters News Agency offer a "Media Solution"; these services gather UGC for a fee or on a subscription basis.[4] Again, Reuters does the bulk of the verification on behalf of Global News and other clients.

Another paid service, Dataminr,[5] uses artificial intelligence (AI) to provide breaking news and "pre-viral" tweets so that journalists can get a jump on stories as they develop. Dataminr is a Twitter partner and is subscribed to by 650 newsrooms around the world. Clients receive alerts based on their chosen interests, which might be politics, entertainment, sports, or breaking news situations such as natural disasters. Like Storyful, Dataminr has diversified over the years; in addition to news organizations, it has corporate and public sector clients such as police services, which use the AI Pulse tool for surveillance. Once a journalist clicks on an alert, she is taken directly to a tweet and can decide from there if it is worth further exploration.

CrowdTangle, a free service purchased by Facebook in 2016, can be programmed to help journalists monitor "overperforming" public posts on Reddit subreddits, Facebook pages, and Instagram accounts.[6] YouTube has been discontinued as a platform monitored by CrowdTangle, and Twitter access has been curtailed over the years. The service is especially useful for tracking photos, videos, and information from public figures such as politicians or celebrities who have unrestricted public accounts on Facebook and Instagram.

How UGC Is Obtained

Twitter is the easiest platform for obtaining photos because journalists can simply download directly from the tweet, while Facebook is easiest for obtaining video because the settings generally allow for straightforward downloading. On other platforms it is simply a matter of taking a screenshot or using a third-party app to record a video or asking the audience member to send it directly.

For its paying customers, Storyful makes social media content available for downloading or embedding on a case-by-case basis. Some people who partner with Storyful only allow their photo or video to be embedded as it originally appeared on their own social media account. News organizations have less control over embedded content, which cannot be edited and cannot be used if deleted by the original user.

Different Uses of UGC

To augment breaking news coverage. This is especially useful when we can't have Global News journalists on the ground immediately. Let's use an example of a huge fire in a rural area. A Global crew is on its way to the scene, and until it gets there, a UGC video of the burning trees and smoke-filled skies is used to tide us over until they arrive. Other times, the most dramatic moment – for example, a barn collapsing in flames – has already passed but was captured by citizens with cell phones.

To power our Instagram accounts. UGC videos and photos can help us update the main Global News Instagram account multiple times a day, and local accounts at least daily. Trending videos are a good fit for the main @globalnews account, while many local accounts use more "beautiful" content such as photos of nature sent in by users.

Globalnews.ca ✔ @globalnews

September 24, 2019

Justin Trudeau sits down in first interview since brownface scandal

Liberal leader Justin Trudeau sits down with Global National's Dawna Friesen while making a campaign stop in Burnaby, B.C. This is Trudeau's first sit-down interview since images emerged of him in brown and blackface last week. #cdnpoli #elxn43 Photo via @GlobalNational

Figure 4.2   @globalnews Twitter, 24 September 2019

In some markets, audience members regularly use hashtags such as #YourManitoba or #GlobalBCWeatherWindow as a way of submitting images for consideration by Global News editors.

To highlight our own reporters' work. When our audience is reacting favourably on Twitter to a story we have covered, we curate and publish those favourable tweets using the Twitter Moments curation tool. This is an easy way to reflect audience opinion while continuing to draw attention to our coverage. This is also quite effective for exclusives, such as a 2019 interview with Canadian Prime Minister Justin Trudeau in the wake of a scandal involving racist make-up.[7]

To create made-for-social videos. These videos may be lightly edited "raw" footage, along with the Global News logo and a bit of text making it clear where the video was shot and by whom. Other times we do a heavier edit with a short script that appears as text on the screen; this is known as text-on-video or TOV format.

To earn revenue via monetization opportunities. Facebook and Twitter offer publishers the opportunity to make money from ads that appear before or during videos that appear on their platforms. These pre-roll and mid-roll monetization programs can be lucrative for both the social media platform and the publisher, which split the advertising revenue. UGC provides a regular source of footage that can be turned into monetized made-for-social videos.

To create brand awareness. When a new editorial product is launched, such as a weather-focused mobile app, or there are changes to broadcast show formats or on-air hosts, a UGC callout can help spread the word. Sometimes a small prize is involved. For example, audience members may be encouraged to post something about the weather app for a chance to win a Global News–branded umbrella.

To build audience engagement. By reflecting the life of a community, we hope to attract an engaged audience whose members feel that they have some agency in aspects of our editorial programming. An engaged audience that interacts with us on social media is more likely to be a loyal audience, across our platforms.

Benefits

UGC acts as a backup set of eyes and ears when we do not have staffers on the ground. UGC is of course used to create new content for social media, digital, and broadcast platforms. But it also helps us locate sources so that we can piece together the story – the audience members posting the UGC can confirm dates, times, locations, and other crucial details during interviews. It helps us with both discovery and coverage. If we see a crucial piece of information or something captured on camera, we can use it to convey the story to our audience. UGC allows us to keep up with our competition when a situation is developing. To use the earlier example of a fire in a rural area, let's imagine that one news outlet is on the scene and has dramatic images of a barn burning down. If we can't match the coverage with our own staff-shot images, UGC is the next best thing – or even better, perhaps a citizen has already captured the best moment.

Callouts for UGC are an effective way to engage with our audience on our various platforms and to make *them* feel engaged and connected. Audience members like to see their own voices or photos reflected in our content. Many of our callouts are done via Instagram's vertical stories, which have the added advantage of a quick turnaround, as people respond directly to the post and all the responses are aggregated and easily shareable. UGC creates for us a virtuous circle of social media practitioners both consuming and creating content, which Global News can then share with a larger audience – all while earning revenue.

Drawbacks

"Brand-safe" content. One challenge that Global News and other news outlets face when participating in monetization programs run by Facebook and Twitter is the stipulation that videos must be "brand-safe" for advertisers. Generally this means no crime news or any of the three Ds: death, disaster, or danger. There are a host of other restrictions that make it difficult for a news outlet to create the necessary volume of advertiser-friendly videos to make programs profitable.

Misinformation, disinformation, hoaxes, and other fakery. As with anything involving social media, the twin spectres of misinformation and disinformation are always looming for news outlets. If a publisher is taken in by "fake news," the fallout can be detrimental to the publisher's reputation. Staff are trained to be suspicious of anything that seems too amazing – it very possibly is not true. We track down the original poster of the content to ask them to confirm information and provide more details to prove the veracity of the UGC. The interview usually starts with asking them to attest that they indeed shot the video and therefore own the rights to it, because trending content can be misappropriated by other users looking to gain from the attention. This is a time-consuming process and can result in less-conscientious competitors beating us to publication. Before publication, journalists and their managers discuss the steps they have taken to verify the UGC and whether we as a news organization feel comfortable using it.

Many news organizations use Storyful to help verify viral videos and other UGC. But relying on a for-profit service such as this has both benefits and drawbacks. Once the videos are verified and added to the newswire's premium content library, they may only be available for a fee. Essentially, news outlets must make a choice: either try to source and verify the UGC themselves, or spend limited resources on a service that does the verification for them.

Secondary trauma. The content that journalists must immerse them-selves in can be graphic and disturbing.[8] Often they must watch and rewatch violent footage or parse the horrific details of testimonials from audience members. In pursuit of the story, journalists wade into the darkest corners of the Web, including the undermoderated comment sections of social media sites and blogs. Journalists themselves are subject to abuse online, often in the form of social media messages from trolls. To counteract this, many news organizations such as Global News limit the amount of time that journalists spend dealing with potentially disturbing UGC. It is recommended that journalists work on UGC-related tasks in short bursts, interspersed with their other duties. While social media is a part of everyone's job, we have chosen not to make UGC verification a full-time job, out of concern for the well-being of employees. Global News also has an employee assistance program that offers trauma counselling and other support services.

Fair dealing. This is the limited exception to copyright for the purposes of news reporting, review, or criticism, and is an issue that social media teams must take seriously. Using a copyright-protected work without obtaining consent or paying copyright royalties can be a minefield for news outlets. Fair dealing is allowed as a legal defence for copyright infringement, but only if certain criteria are met and certain conditions are fulfilled. If it turns out that a news outlet does not have a strong case for fair dealing, it can open the organization up to costly legal action. Also, it is in the best interests of a reputable news organization to make fair dealing claims in a responsible manner. After all, the news organization is also a copyright holder, and if the situation was reversed, it would not want to see its content used by others without permission any more than is necessary.

Making a claim often comes down to whether that content is inte-gral to the story that is being told. Can the story be told *without* this particular content? If so, then it likely won't meet the criteria for a fair dealing claim. However, every claim of fair dealing has its own set of circumstances, so training and consultation are needed to make sure the right decision is made.

Training

Training is necessary to ensure that all staff are armed with basic knowledge around verification and fair dealing, as well as best practices around giving credit and obtaining consent.[9] While training sessions are offered to all staff members on a rolling basis, there is a core group of senior journalists who tend to make the calls for the more complex cases.

Storyful does a good job of differentiating *misinformation*, which is inaccurate information shared by people who may themselves have been misled, from *disinformation*, which was cooked up specifically to deceive.[10] However, misinformation and disinformation can have the same detrimental effect. Storyful subscribers can access training and other support when separating misinformation and disinformation from legitimate content.

Another resource that Global News and other news organizations find useful when training is the *Verification Handbook*, authored by Craig Silverman and other verification experts.[11] This free downloadable PDF has been updated several times. The original document focused on emergency reporting. A second version focused on how to accurately incorporate open data and open-source information into investigative reporting.[12] The latest version delves into disinformation and media manipulation on social media.[13]

Case Studies

The following are just a few examples of how UGC is used at Global News.

TRENDING HASHTAGS

Social media is full of pseudo-"hashtag holidays," some of which are celebrated almost solely in the digital space. These trending hashtags are often light-hearted and include "national" or "world" to make them sound more official: #NationalPieDay or #WorldEmojiDay. Trending hashtags can be great audience engagement opportunities and help strengthen loyalty to the news brand. Audience members find it easy to interact with these hashtags.

The trending nature of the topics means that little to no prompting is needed; audience members are already creating content. Often we are simply inserting ourselves into the ongoing conversation. We may follow up with users by arranging an interview, but generally, whatever the public has shared on social media is enough to go on.

Let's say a hashtag is trending on Twitter early in the morning. A TV morning show will record a segment – that originally aired live in one of the local markets – about the trending hashtag and post the video directly to Twitter, Facebook, and Instagram. The tweets and replies to it form the backbone of a curated Twitter Moment, which includes other Twitter users employing the hashtag.[14] Twitter Moments have been made for light-hearted topics, an example being #TakeOurKids ToWorkDay, which featured staff tweets.[15] An example of a more serious news use of UGC in a Twitter Moment would be #HongKongProtest, which entailed rounding up photos of that 2019 movement.[16] If there are enough responses, a producer will gather them and use a social media video creation service such as Wochit[17] to make a made-for-social video of public tweets, Instagram posts, and Facebook posts.

Trending hashtags also inspire daily social media polling, which we discuss next.

DAILY POLLING

Global News is in the habit of posting one-day polls on Twitter, Facebook, Instagram Stories, and LinkedIn. Trending hashtags are reliable fodder for questions, while other polls may play off the top news stories of the day. That may include queries on the economy, government policies, or (especially for several months in 2020) the coronavirus pandemic. Because they are so easy to interact with, and because people often want to add their own "write-in candidate" for an option that has not been listed, these are low-hanging fruit when it comes to engagement. Social media polling regularly garners tens of thousands of responses. The polls originate on our owned and operated accounts, so we have control over the content. There is implied consent with all the responses.

Many of the polls stand alone as social-only content. But occasionally the polling will be used to create content for other platforms. For example, to mark the end of a decade, the Global News social media desk ran a series of polls in December 2019 asking audience members about the top moments of the previous ten years.[18]

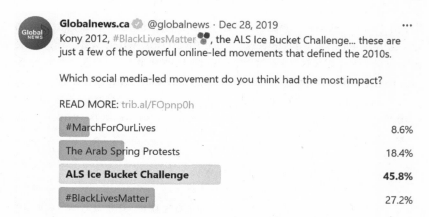

Globalnews.ca ✔ @globalnews · Dec 28, 2019   •••

Kony 2012, #BlackLivesMatter ✊🏿, the ALS Ice Bucket Challenge... these are just a few of the powerful online-led movements that defined the 2010s.

Which social media-led movement do you think had the most impact?

READ MORE: trib.al/FOpnp0h

#MarchForOurLives	8.6%
The Arab Spring Protests	18.4%
ALS Ice Bucket Challenge	**45.8%**
#BlackLivesMatter	27.2%

Figure 4.3   @globalnews Twitter, 28 December 2019

NEWS TIP ON LETHBRIDGE DEER DEATH

In January 2019, Lethbridge, Alberta, resident Erica Pritchard captured a disturbing incident on her cell phone of a police officer running over a deer multiple times with his patrol vehicle as the animal lay dying on a street in the city's north end.[19] Pritchard said she was driving when she witnessed a car slam into the rear end of a young deer, apparently breaking its back legs. Pritchard said that when the Lethbridge officer arrived on the scene, he ran back and forth over the injured animal twice with his truck.

Given Global News's focus on audience engagement within local markets, getting a video in this manner is not that unusual. But this particular video, with its shocking violence and disturbing details, was UGC that made headlines across the country and beyond.

Pritchard sent this unsolicited piece of UGC exclusively to the local Global Lethbridge newsroom. We conducted an interview to verify aspects of her story and sought comment from the Lethbridge police. We also examined the video itself closely for clues that it was shot where and when Pritchard alleged the incident took place. Assessing and editing videos like this one can be hard on the staff members involved, and journalists were offered support, including counselling through the employee assistance program.

Global News had this story exclusively, and then we kept covering it, from the initial scoop to the public protest against the police officer involved,[20] to the outcome of the Alberta Serious Incident Response

Team (ASIRT) investigation.[21] The video was edited and came with multiple warnings for viewers to use discretion when watching. One of the warnings was a black slate with text that appeared on screen before the video started. That warning is especially important on social media because videos often autoplay, and a black warning slate allows audience members to make an informed choice to pause and watch, or keep scrolling.

FIRST TIME I WAS CALLED

This UGC-powered series stems from a story that Global News anchor Farah Nasser recalled from her childhood: her earliest memory of experiencing discrimination.[22] From that negative experience, we set out on a challenging project called "First Time I Was Called." The objective was threefold: (1) to give closure to those who have been labelled, (2) to create an opportunity for empathy, and (3) to counteract the "bystander effect."[23]

When #FirstTimeIwasCalled hit Facebook, Twitter, and Instagram, the conversation exploded. The Global News social media team moderated conversations on our social media accounts so that the dialogue stayed constructive and candid. It was at times raw, at other times nuanced, but always lively as Canadians discussed the thorny issues of prejudice and discrimination. Thousands of people bravely shared their stories. Canadian public figures weighed in. The social media execution for the project won a major industry award.[24]

The emphasis was on public conversation, primarily on our owned and operated social media accounts. As the project unfolded, we followed up by conducting interviews with some participating audience members.

While this was a social media–focused project, it also drove coverage on television and radio as well as in-person and online. On the globalnews.ca website, we published several round-ups of curated social media conversations, and each sparked even more social media conversation. Project members worked with teachers to create a syllabus about the impact of hurtful words. Nasser hosted a discussion for an international journalism event about the series.[25]

Figure 4.4   #FirstTimeIWasCalled graphic, Global News.

YOUR CORONAVIRUS QUESTIONS

In January 2020, as the world grappled with the growing threat of the novel coronavirus, a Global News community manager noticed that social media users were turning to us with questions about the virus. We realized that our audience needed reliable information to make sense of the unprecedented and uncertain times.

We started small in late January, by answering questions we had gathered from comments and messages on our Facebook, Instagram, and Twitter posts. Then a simple callout revealed a thirst for factual, jargon-free answers. So we stepped it up by employing our regional newsrooms and our flagship broadcast TV program, Global National, as well as our dozens of social media accounts, to gather the questions that were top of mind for Canadians. We set up email addresses and created a coronavirus microsite with "Your Questions" on prominent display, then made promotional ads telling people where to find it.[26] We took a multiplatform approach to engage with people in the method of their choice.

Whenever possible, we conducted and recorded interviews with those asking the questions. We then sought out experts who could answer the questions in a factual way. Because the official response varied across the provinces and territories, we sought out experts who could tailor their answers to the appropriate region.

The strong response we received from our audience showed we were meeting a need. We received thousands of questions sent to specially created email addresses, plus more sent directly to reporters. Our social media posts on the topic routinely received hundreds of responses. People have thanked us for "reassuring and informative" coverage, praised us for "outstanding journalism," and thanked us for the service we provided.[27]

The questions have inspired dozens of articles and videos for globalnews.ca, including several pieces aimed at answering questions from children. We dedicated two episodes of the daily *Wait, There's More* podcast to answering audience questions. One podcast episode focused entirely on questions from children.[28] In our British Columbia market, Global BC produced four town halls that posed audience questions directly to medical and political officials.[29] Lead broadcast reporter Jeff Semple made dozens of guest appearances on network radio and TV programs, spanning four time zones, to help ensure that Canadians received answers to their questions. When possible, we replied directly to audience members via social media and pointed them to the answers.

Conclusion

Global News enjoys a strong relationship with the community it serves, and UGC is a way to keep it vibrant and engaged. Interacting with audience members on social media can build loyalty among users, who see themselves reflected in our coverage. UGC can lead to exclusives and award-winning, agenda-setting journalism. It can even power a growing revenue stream based on pre-roll and mid-roll ads for videos that play on Twitter, Facebook, and YouTube. Clearly, a strong supply of UGC has its benefits, especially in an ever-competitive news media market.

But there are costs and risks. Some are financial – staff members must be given time, training, and resources to properly source and verify social media. Alternatively, outsourcing the work to social media sourcing and verification services requires a budget. Getting it wrong, especially when it comes to copyright claims, could mean the news organization incurs costly licensing and legal fees.

Some costs and risks are harder to quantify but are no less important. The reputational hit when we get it wrong is more fodder for those critics who say the media is "fake news," and this can be incredibly demoralizing for staff members who fall for misinformation or disinformation and allow it to go out under the Global News banner.

Secondary trauma resulting from repeated immersion in graphic, disturbing imagery can lead to employee job dissatisfaction and turnover, not to mention negative effects on a journalist's mental health and overall well-being. Social media have replaced the street corner – instead of polling the "man on the street," as in the past, we do our polling on Twitter or Facebook. But the digital street corner can be a dark and even dangerous place. Journalists doing their jobs on social media are subject to harassment and exposed to graphic imagery.

Allocating more resources to social media verification services would help offset the workloads and emotional burdens experienced by journalists in our newsrooms, even as it potentially adds to the workloads and burdens of staffers in newsrooms at Reuters, Storyful, and the like. Adding more mental health and wellness supports for social media journalists could help address the fallout from secondary trauma and prevent burnout. Some of this support can be incorporated into UGC-related training for staff. Training has to be offered regularly to account for turnover and shiftwork. A holistic approach to social media training for journalists is best: the curriculum needs to cover nuts-and-bolts learning about matters such as how to spot disinformation, when to make a fair dealing claim, and how to obtain consent. Newsroom trainers must also instruct journalists on how to handle harassment and empower them to practise self-care – to know when to disengage from social media monitoring, step away from the keyboard, and go for a walk. I am hopeful that advances in AI, which is already incorporated into social media algorithms and services for sourcing and verifying, will help journalists filter raw UGC as they search for newsworthy content. AI can already be used to identify nudity, symbols, logos, hate speech, and more, and I predict this will become a vital part of the journalist's toolbox. While sometimes it is necessary to view swastikas as part of the news-gathering process, it would be reassuring to have the option to choose to avoid such exposure by letting AI-powered software filter it out.

While there are pitfalls, UGC is an integral part of Global News's nationwide network. The media climate, with its growing competitiveness and shrinking profit margins, has cemented UGC's role in the news cycle. The pervasiveness of social media ensures that it will always have a role. With the right process in place, news publishers like Global News can create a virtuous circle of audience-powered engagement and content that crosses platforms from social media to broadcast and digital.

Notes

This chapter is based on a 2019 presentation by the author, who left Global News in 2020. This chapter serves as a snapshot of newsroom workflows, approaches, and available tools and processes from that era.

1 For an in-depth discussion of Storyful, see chapter 6 (Lithgow and Martin).
2 Storyful, "Our Story."
3 Deans, "News Corp."
4 Reuters, Media Solutions: User Generated Content.
5 Dataminr, https://www.dataminr.com.
6 Newton, "Facebook."
7 "Archived Coverage," *Global News.*
8 For more on secondary trauma, or vicarious trauma, and its effect on the mental health of journalists, see chapters 3 (Miller) and 5 (Lau et al.).
9 For more on the verification process, see chapters 2 (Bowler) and 11 (Kang).
10 "Misinformation and Disinformation," *Storyful.*
11 Silverman et al., *Verification,* 2014.
12 Silverman et al., *Verification,* 2015.
13 Silverman et al., *Verification,* 2020.
14 "About Moments," Twitter.
15 Global News (@GlobalNews), 6 November 2019.
16 Global News (@GlobalNews), 22 August 2019.
17 Wochit, https://www.wochit.com.
18 Omar et al., "Top Moments."
19 Russell and Battochio, "Made Me Feel."
20 Small, "Dozens."
21 Bourne, "No Charges.
22 Nasser, "Farah Nasser."
23 Rempel, "Sparking."
24 "RTDNA Canada Announces Network Award Winners" (2019)
25 Nasser, "Farah Nasser."
26 Global News Coronavirus Hub (n.d.)
27 Emails sent to staff members (2020).
28 Crosby, "Kids."
29 "Global BC Town Hall."

Bibliography

"About Moments." Twitter. Accessed June 2020. https://help.twitter.com/en/using-twitter/twitter-moments.

"Archived Coverage: Trudeau Sits Down with Global News in 1st Interview Since Brownface Scandal." *Global News*, 25 September 2019. https://globalnews.ca/news/5943732/justin-trudeau-interview-canada-election.

Bourne, Kirby. "No Charges after Lethbridge Officer Repeatedly Ran Over Deer in January." *Global News*, 26 June 2019. https://globalnews.ca/news/5434425/lethbridge-police-officer-deer-no-charges.

Crosby, Jennifer. "Kids Put Their COVID-19 Questions to the Experts." *Global News*, 3 April 2020. https://globalnews.ca/news/6754047/kids-put-their-covid-19-questions-to-the-experts.

Deans, Jason. "News Corp Buys Storyful for £15M." *Guardian*, 20 December 2013. https://www.theguardian.com/media/2013/dec/20/news-corp-buys-storyful-social-news.

"Global BC Town Hall: Dr. Bonnie Henry and Adrian Dix Take Your COVID-19 Questions." *Global News*, 9 April 2020. https://globalnews.ca/news/6792103/global-bc-town-hall-coronavirus.

Global News Coronavirus Hub. "Coronavirus." *Global News*, n.d. https://globalnews.ca/tag/coronavirus.

Global News (@globalnews). "#HongKongProtest: IN PHOTOS." Twitter, 22 August 2019. https://twitter.com/i/events/1164571088849948672.

Global News (@globalnews). "It's #takeourkidstoworkday!" Twitter, 6 November 2019. https://twitter.com/i/events/1192100269749886976.

"Misinformation and Disinformation." *Storyful* (blog). 24 September 2018. https://storyful.com/thought-leadership/misinformation-and-disinformation.

Nasser, Farah. "Farah Nasser: My First Experience with Racism." *Global News*, 6 April 2018. https://globalnews.ca/news/4063582/farah-nasser-my-first-experience-with-racism.

Newton, Casey. "Facebook Buys CrowdTangle, the Tool Publishers Use to Win the Internet: Understanding How News Goes Viral." *Verge*, 11 November 2016. https://www.theverge.com/2016/11/11/13594338/facebook-acquires-crowdtangle.

Omar, Nida, Sara Hussein, and Jessica Maxwell. "Top Moments of the Decade, as Told by Global News Readers." *Global News*, 31 December 2019. https://globalnews.ca/news/6351891/top-moments-of-the-decade-2019-readers.

Rempel, Shauna. "Sparking a Conversation: Social Media Users React to #FirstTimeIWasCalled." *Global News*, 24 November 2018. https://globalnews.ca/news/4123461/social-media-firsttimeiwascalled.

Reuters News Agency. "Media Solutions: User Generated Content." https://www.reutersagency.com/en/media-solutions/user-generated-content.

"RTDNA Canada Announces Network Award Winners." *Radio Television Digital News Association*, 12 May 2019. http://rtdnacanada.com/rtdna-canada-announces-network-award-winners-2.

Russell, Andrew, and Matthew Battochio. "'Made Me Feel Really Sick': Lethbridge Woman Captures Video of Officer Repeatedly Running Over Injured Deer." *Global News*, 9 January 2019. https://globalnews.ca/news/4827328/lethbridge-police-video-officer-repeatedly-running-over-deer.

Small, Kaylen. "Dozens Protest Lethbridge Police Officer Who Ran Over Injured Deer Multiple Times." *Global News*, 14 January 2019. https://globalnews.ca/news/4843366/protest-lethbridge-police-officer-deer-death.

Silverman, Craig, Steve Buttry, Claire Wardle, Trushar Barot, Malachy Browne, Mathew Ingram, Patrick Meier, et al. *Verification Handbook: A Definitive Guide to Verifying Digital Content For Emergency Coverage*. Brussels: European Journalism Centre, 2014. https://datajournalism.com/read/handbook/verification-1.

Silverman, Craig, Rina Tsubaki, Hank Van Ess, Paul Myers, Khadija Sharife, Giannina Segnini, Eliot Higgins, et al. *Verification Handbook For Investigative Reporting: A Guide To Online Search And Research Techniques For Using UGC And Open Source Information In Investigations*. Brussels: European Journalism Centre, 2015. https://datajournalism.com/read/handbook/verification-2.

Silverman, Craig, Claire Wardle, Joan Donovon, Brandy Zadrozny, Vernise Tantuco, Gemma Bagayaua-Mendoza, Ben Collins, et al. *Verification Handbook for Disinformation and Media Manipulation*. Brussels: European Journalism Centre, 2020. https://datajournalism.com/read/handbook/verification-3.

Storyful. "Our Story." https://storyful.com/about.

Managing the Impact of Eyewitness Videos of Violence against Racialized Communities on the Public and on Journalists

ANDREE LAU, ASHA TOMLINSON, TASHAUNA REID,
TAMIKA FORRESTER, JILLIAN TAYLOR, AND JORGE BARRERA

A moose swimming in a suburban backyard pool. A white police officer kneeling on a handcuffed Black man's neck. A house fire. A car crash. An Indigenous woman dying on a hospital bed. A celebrity playing with a puppy.

The visuals whip by, as you scroll your phone, your laptop, your TV. As media consumers, we are now used to the whiplash scene changes that the democratization of video recording and distribution have brought, but the process that media outlets must use in deciding whether or not to amplify certain user-generated content (UGC) – generally defined as any text, image, video, or audio created by the public – still requires careful consideration.

Amid this contemporary wave of unfiltered, unchecked, and unceasing UGC, mainstream news broadcasters, including the Canadian Broadcasting Corporation (CBC), must continue to adhere to the journalistic principles of accuracy, fairness, balance, and responsibility. At the same time, we must evolve our editorial decision-making processes to acknowledge and reflect the harms, as well as the value, that such videos create for certain communities – for both the audience and for our journalists.

In this chapter, we share how CBC News manages user-generated videos, especially of actions by those in positions of authority against people from Black and Indigenous communities. The decision-making process involves considering verification, sensitivity, and editorial standards, as well as the impact on Black and Indigenous journalists who cover such content. In particular, this chapter presents the views of five CBC News staff, who candidly discuss how they process UGC both as journalists and as viewers, and how newsrooms must evolve to better support them as they engage with such footage.[1]

A Year of Deepening Awareness

The year 2020 saw growing public awareness in North America about anti-Black and anti-Indigenous racism, largely driven by harrowing videos of violence against members of those communities by police officers – videos often recorded by bystanders and more often than not streamed live on platforms like Facebook.

In May in Minneapolis, a teen heading to the store for snacks recorded a police arrest and shared it on social media.[2] The world watched – over and over again – while (former) officer Derek Chauvin, who is white, knelt on George Floyd's neck for more than nine minutes.[3] The Black man's death sparked protests across the United States and around the world as well as a resurgence of the Black Lives Matter movement.

Decades ago, few people would have seen such footage unless it was presented by a newscast. Today, there is little time for this sort of "gatekeeping." By the time videos like these reach journalists, the public has likely already seen them multiple times, with dubious information or little or no context.[4]

Against this backdrop, senior editors at the CBC must screen the footage and then convene to discuss how – or whether at all – to broadcast the footage on television, radio, Web pages, and/or social media accounts. First, there are the absolute questions:

- How did we verify that this UGC is real? Who recorded it and under what circumstances? Can we confirm the time and place that it occurred?
- How much context do we have? How much do we still need to gather?
- What happened before and after the UGC that is *not* shown?
- Who else can we contact to verify its provenance and the circumstances?
- Is there public service benefit of broadcasting and distributing this UGC?

Regarding depictions of violence in UGC, the CBC's Journalistic Standards and Practices (JSP) are clear: "We reflect the reality of the situations we report. We also respect the sensibilities of our viewers, listeners, and readers."[5] This means that senior journalists discuss the impact of such visuals in relation to the time of day and the context in which such material is appearing. Graphic video or audio during a morning show, for example, is ill-advised when we know that the audience may include children getting ready to go to school, whereas an excerpt as part of a packaged report during a late-night newscast may be more acceptable. All explicit or disconcerting materials come with a warning, whether it is from an announcer or reporter on TV or radio, a line in an online story, or a graphic board in a digital video.

The JSP also states: "Violence, nudity and sexuality are never presented without good reason. They may be justified when they are important to an understanding of the world we live in. Where they are necessary, we present them without undue exploitation, voyeurism or sensationalism and without trivializing, encouraging or glorifying. We treat painful scenes with discretion and restraint and without prolonging them unduly."[6]

The Trauma of Watching Graphic News Footage

In recent years, more consideration has been given to the kind of impact and even trauma that results from viewing these visuals. Research by the University of Bradford's Pam Ramsden found that 18 per cent of study participants who watched disturbing news footage on social media "are experiencing lasting effects such as negative stress reactions, anxiety and in some cases post-traumatic stress disorders or vicarious PTSD."[7] The ramifications run deeper for people of colour. A 2018 study published in *The Lancet* found that the mental health of Black individuals living in US communities where police killed unarmed Black Americans declined markedly in the two months after they were exposed to video and news reports of these deaths.[8] They also showed signs of trauma, said the report.

In October 2020, Ottawa police constable Daniel Montsion was acquitted in the death of Abdirahman Abdi.[9] There had been surveillance footage of the 2016 confrontation between the Black man and the white officer, who had punched Abdi several times in the head while wearing reinforced or "plated" gloves. In the online coverage of the verdict, CBC News digital editors decided not to embed that video footage. The need to avoid creating more trauma was greater than the value of presenting the recorded violence to our audiences again.

But what about the racialized journalists who must screen, analyze, edit, and report this footage as part of their job? There is no escaping the personal intersection of their lived experiences with the professional requirements of objectivity and balance. We reached out to several CBC journalists for their reflections regarding the toll such UGC took on them, the considerations they had to weigh that staff who are not racialized may not have to think about, and what newsroom leaders must understand to properly support them.

A Dying Mother's Video

In September 2020, Joyce Echaquan, a mother of seven, went to a Quebec hospital with stomach pains.[10] *Having had prior negative experiences with staff, and French not being her primary language, Echaquan streamed and recorded her hospital interactions on Facebook Live. That day, she broadcast her own UGC that showed her being insulted and sworn at by hospital staff as she lay dying on a bed. The Quebec coroner's office and local health authority are investigating, and a nurse and an orderly have been dismissed in relation to the case. Here are the reflections of Jillian Taylor, a CBC journalist based in Manitoba and a member of the Fisher River Cree Nation.*

I watched the video through an article, so partly as a journalist, partly as a viewer/reader. I couldn't get through the whole thing. Her screams were so gut-wrenching. I didn't watch the whole thing with sound on, because it's something I've covered and dealt with my whole career and it just gets to be too much. So I actually made the choice not to listen with the sound on.

In publicizing such stories, there are the channels you need to go through: you need to talk to the family, you need to get consideration because you need to know that you're not causing further harm to them – because for Indigenous people, it's always important to get a family's permission, to get a community's permission before you publish the name of someone who's died, or share a video [recorded by a bystander] like that, because it's so traumatizing based on all of the wrongs and harms that have been done to First Nations, Indigenous people in Canada.

Figure 5.1.   CBC journalist Jillian Taylor covers the national inquiry into missing and murdered Indigenous women and girls in Thompson, Manitoba, in March 2018. Photo: Lyzaville Sale/CBC

But also, there is value in showing Canadians, because Canadians maybe don't have a full picture of the discrimination, the systemic racism that Indigenous people go through. A lot of people think it's surface racism, like being followed in the grocery store or a department store. They think it's that type of racial profiling, just based on the way you look. And they think higher of teachers, law enforcement, lawyers, medical people, because they're professionals, they're educated, so you would assume that they're going to treat all of their patients or clients with the same level of respect. But that is not the reality. So when you see a UGC video like this, of Joyce crying out in pain, being berated by negative comments as she's dying, that is systemic racism and there's no denying it there.

Being First Nations myself, you can always see your own family and friends in these stories. You can always relate it to a personal experience. The pain and the impacts of colonization, residential schools, systemic racism – it affects us all, regardless of where we come from.

For me, in Manitoba, I covered the Brian Sinclair story extensively when it happened in 2008. Sinclair was an Indigenous man who died of a treatable bladder infection after sitting in his wheelchair for thirty-four hours in the ER waiting room of the Health Sciences Centre in Winnipeg. An inquest heard he was never asked if he was waiting for medical care and [he] received no medical attention, even as he vomited several times.[11] Later, it emerged [that] staff assumed he was homeless, intoxicated, or had already been seen and was waiting for a ride. I could see my uncles in him, I could see my uncles in Brian Sinclair. And to think, what if one of my relatives was ignored to death? You can separate it because it's not your family it's happening to, but you always think of your family when you're in one of these situations.

All journalists feel empathy and they would feel sympathy for the person and for the relatives, but they don't feel it on a personal level. They don't feel it deep inside. I'm assuming most – especially non-Indigenous or non-POC journalists – wouldn't have the experience of oppression or discrimination against them. So it's a different level. It's oftentimes that non-Indigenous, non-POC journalists just cannot understand and won't. And it's not a slight against them. It's just the reality of growing up as a BIPOC[12] person in Canada.

I have spent a lot of hours crying over missing and murdered Indigenous women – that's been the primary focus of my career. It's hard because you feel this duty to do the community justice by telling these stories and by telling them in a way that you know you can be respectful to the family and honour the family while still informing Canadians. But then at the end of the day, you're feeling so impacted when you go home, and you're drained. So a lot of my career, I pushed through that, and then as I got a little bit more experienced or as more senior in my newsroom, I would just say I can't do this one. I need a break. I need to be on something else, and I would have those conversations with my managers. And now I'm an assignment producer because it was time for me not to be talking to those families directly anymore. I couldn't take these girls and these women's stories home any longer, so I've moved behind the scenes.

So as a manager or newsroom leader, if you have a BIPOC journalist, it's really good to check if they're comfortable covering something, and if they are and they want to cover it, it's good to be checking in to see how they're doing along the way. Because like I said, we see our family and our friends in these stories of injustices, so it can hit us on a different level. That doesn't mean we're biased, it just means that we have a deeper understanding, and we might take it home a little bit harder than other journalists will. Even if it's an uncomfortable conversation for a producer to have, that's OK: "Hey, I know you're a member of the BIPOC community and this is a story about harm to BIPOC people. Are you OK covering this?" It's OK to ask. And it's a good thing to ask.

An Encounter That Ended Their Lives

Tashauna Reid is a senior reporter with CBC News who has worked in newsrooms across the country in Toronto, Edmonton, and Fredericton.

Philando Castile's last breaths were broadcast live on a Facebook video stream, captured by his girlfriend who sat in the car next to him as he died. His four-year-old daughter would bear witness to his tragic killing: shot at close range by a police officer during a traffic stop. The day before, on 5 July 2016, another African American, Alton Sterling, was killed outside of a store. The men lived in different states, had different circumstances, but the story in essence was the same: an encounter with police that ended their lives.

As a reporter in the newsroom, I remember seeing the repeated headlines of these two Black men's violent deaths and then stepping into a studio to discuss the ensuing global outrage. There were protests and demonstrations, celebrities speaking out, and news conferences from both police and politicians.

Most people can choose not to watch a video (recorded by the public) or to not share it with others, but as a journalist, our job on any given day is to do just that. We are tasked with reporting the facts. We have to watch each frame of a video or listen to audio recordings of a 911 call to ensure we are correctly reporting the events as we learn them. As a Black journalist, this cycle of watching and listening to violence enacted against Black people over and over (through UGC) carries its own trauma and weight. Every single time it happens, it's just as painful as the last. You remember the names, the sound of gunshots, the screams, the laboured breathing, and the cries for "Mama." You try to focus on the job you have to do, but you are constantly managing your own grief and pain.

The lack of diversity in Canadian media means you may be the only Black person, or one of the few, in the newsroom and there may not be much understanding or support from your peers.

There are also sensitivities that everyone who has a hand in shaping editorial coverage – from managers to producers to editors – needs to consider, especially an awareness of their own unconscious biases at play. There can be an assumption of guilt when it comes to Black victims, with questions coming up like: Why didn't they just listen to the police? Does the victim have a criminal record? Or suggestions that the victim must have done something wrong for police to react in a violent way.

These stories can also be triggering for our audience, who are bombarded with these videos on social media and television. Newsrooms must be cautious and respectful about how and when we use these videos and consider the impact, particularly for Black audiences. Building inclusive newsrooms will help create balance in our reporting and strengthen our storytelling. The way anti-Black racism plays a role in these news events needs to be part of editorial discussions and considerations.

The Story Can Get Very Personal Very Quickly

Tamika Forrester is senior producer for the CBC's Being Black in Canada website and was a member of the CBC News network social team.

A newsroom is a place where people become accustomed to all sorts of news, and where for many journalists, seeing an unarmed Black man being assaulted or killed by police becomes another tragic story. However, journalists who are BIPOC often do not have that privilege. For us, the story can get very personal very quickly. Suddenly as a Black mother, I find myself thinking, "Oh my gosh, this could happen to my Black son." Then it goes deeper with thoughts of why things like this keep happening. It's often difficult to suppress, and you look around knowing that your white colleagues don't really have these fears.

The morning after George Floyd was killed in the United States, I knew it was *the* lead story of the day for our Snapchat team. Yet I deliberately didn't pitch it, as I prayed someone else would write the horrific story. No such luck. An hour later, the assignment landed in my lap and I stared at my computer screen in tears. I had many words to say, but couldn't write a single one. I then took a deep breath and proceeded to ask if I could be excused from the story. Fortunately, my producer was very understanding, but is this the case for all BIPOC journalists? I struggled with the fact that this was my job and I simply couldn't do it.

Maybe editors can go beyond simply assigning a story, and ask if a journalist is in fact OK to cover such a story. The simple question humanizes the newsroom and sends the message that even if you don't understand how your BIPOC colleague is feeling, at least it signals that you care.

Following Floyd's death, several of my Black colleagues shared their thoughts on social media, including myself. Due to the CBC's Journalistic Standards and Practices, we often shy away from personal posts because of the need to remain objective, but in that instance, we weren't just journalists, we were Black Canadians reacting to a horror against our own community. This was suddenly our lived experience and not commenting would have been difficult to swallow. These very comments alerted our bosses to the fact that we were struggling and that we felt overwhelmed. As a result, various managers reached out and offered support.

The question is, does that happen in every newsroom? Managers and executives should be looking to make self-care and psychological support a mandatory part of the journalistic process, especially after a heavy or difficult news cycle.

A Different Lens

Asha Tomlinson, an award-winning investigative journalist with CBC News, is also the co-creator, co-producer, and host of the series Being Black in Canada.

I was not assigned to the George Floyd story but I still sought out the details, researched every angle, and inadvertently internalized it all. While I've covered numerous stories about anti-Black brutality throughout my career, this was the first time I was looking at it through a different lens. You see, I now have a toddler son – a Black boy. And while people smile at him, talk to him, and comment on his cuteness, I suspect that ten years from now, he'll be regarded by some as a menace. It dawned on me that I will have to have the "talk" with him eventually. I will have to explain these very complicated and sad dichotomies of life.

I started to write about my feelings. I wanted to share my pain and show solidarity with all the other Black parents out there carrying the same burdens. Critical conversations were happening. And people from all backgrounds were listening. Becoming allies. Standing up for what's right.

Figure 5.2.   CBC journalist Asha Tomlinson, seen in this undated photo, is an award-winning investigative journalist with CBC News. Photo: CBC

A number of journalists were finally lifting the veil on racism in their lives and doing so unapologetically. We could no longer stay silent or try to be objective because, at the end of the day, there's nothing objective about racism and discrimination. There should be no partisanship when it comes to this issue. There's no grey area. And that motivated me even more to share my story. I wrote about how these UGC videos and countless tragedies have affected me, especially as a new mother.

Here are excerpts from my personal essay published in CBC News:

> It took me a long time to watch that [UGC George Floyd] video. It was incredibly heartbreaking and infuriating to see Floyd begging for his life while a white police officer kept his knee on his neck until he died. His calls for "mama" haunt me.
>
> I wept for Floyd's family. For Black men like my husband, brother, and father. For Black children. And especially for Black boys like my nephew and my two-year-old son ...
>
> He can't comprehend what's happening around him. How do I explain this underbelly? The ugly side of society where a Black man can be seen as a threat, his life dehumanized and disposable.[13]

That was just a portion of the essay. But it provides insight into the thoughts running through my mind at the time. Of course, I had to make a case for why it should be published. I had to explain that part of our job as journalists is to open minds and provide a window into the lived experiences of others, including our own. I will always stay true to my journalistic principles but I cannot erase my Blackness and I cannot ignore the realities of what being Black in Canada means to me, my family, friends, and the wider population.

That's why seeing these UGC videos play out over and over again is triggering and traumatizing. But we find ways to cope and to continue to tell these stories with the hope that one day we won't have to see the hashtag Black Lives Matter trending because another Black life was cut short.

Uncompromising Visceral Truth

Jorge Barrera, who was born in Caracas, has spent almost his whole career reporting on Indigenous issues, from Yellowknife to northern Saskatchewan to northwestern Ontario. He is based in Ottawa for the CBC *News Indigenous unit.*

While eyewitness videos of trauma and injustice against Indigenous people can be disturbing and impactful, a reporter's obligation and experience of bringing the context behind such trauma leaves much more of a personal mark than the visceral footage itself.

I covered the death of a young man who was found hanging from a tree in a park across from the courthouse in Thunder Bay. And sitting with his mother describing what she's been through and all the unanswered questions about how he died, and then showing me photographs of her son – that left a pretty deep mark because you're next to such intense pain and loss and violent death.[14] When you delve into these stories, they become very, very real.

Reporting on youth suicides and talking to family members or a mother of a child who committed suicide and seeing that child's photo – for me, that has marked me more than social media depictions of violence against Indigenous people. Reporters in my unit cover trauma a lot and so we're always processing that. People share some of their darkest, most painful moments with us and because trauma is so prevalent in many Indigenous experiences, it's part of what we cover.

The UGC created by Joyce Echaquan was especially harrowing because it encapsulates a lot of stories I have already been told, and to see it capture her final moments, that's probably the hardest social media video that I've seen in terms of the realm that I cover. But it's like sitting next to someone and having them describe that. This story came out because it spread on Facebook, so maybe five years ago, that wave wouldn't have happened. There's a general population engaged on social media who are hyperaware of where the debate is, and so that also helps force the story out. Because Canadian media decision-makers are generally a conservative lot, they may not have reported on it at all. One thing that has changed is that the voices of those who say they are marginalized are taken a lot more seriously now than they used to be.

I do believe that those types of UGC videos allow people to understand the realities more, because it's reaching them at a place they are already consuming information. It helps them form their ideas and grow. There is an uncompromising visceral truth to a video catching a moment of violent exercise of power on the defenceless body, like the video of Ahmaud Arbery, an unarmed twenty-five-year-old Black man who was fatally shot while jogging, or the George Floyd video. Those are jarring. And for the people whose daily lives are separate and basically on another plane than the existence of many Black Americans and Black Canadians who see the same types of events happen in their communities, in their neighbourhoods, to family members, those videos sometimes break that plane and force some people to realize there is this other reality that they didn't know about. Because the injustice, the imbalance of power, and the violence that they're seeing through a medium that they rely on more and more for truth is so obvious. While it does retraumatize people who are already connected to that community, if reported on selectively and not to the point of desensitizing, then it can be a way for a mind to change, or for a small shift in a debate.

Conclusion

UGC has become a powerful means to document injustice. Some argue that the proliferation of such UGC negates the need for journalists and media outlets. But it is clear that public broadcasters such as CBC News continue to have an important role in verifying publicly created visuals or audio, and bringing as full context as possible to the surface using those foundational questions mentioned earlier in the introduction. Such material has been created by the public and not by our staff, but it is still our duty to carefully consider both the harms and the value of disseminating that UGC through the lens of our JSP so as to "reflect the reality of the situations we report" and to "respect the sensibilities of our viewers, listeners and readers."[15]

Just as UGC has evolved over the years, so must the way CBC News assigns, selects, edits, and presents eyewitness material, for both our audience and our staff. It must do so in a transparent and productive manner. Most contemplation in newsrooms of the past focused on the effect of UGC on audiences. Today, the impact that UGC of Black and Indigenous people being harmed has on Black and Indigenous journalists who work in those newsrooms must be just as carefully considered. The support provided for the well-being of racialized staff acknowledges that societal systems including policing, health care, and, yes, journalism are fraught with inequities. It also creates a trust and respect for their lived experiences, thus augmenting the CBC's connection to the range of communities we serve.

A significant survey of more than 1,200 Canadian media workers released in May 2022 found a startling amount of stress, anxiety, depression, and substance use in the industry; more than half of respondents said they had sought medical help to deal with work-related stress and trauma. This kind of dedicated tracking and evidence helps keep the spotlight on the toll the work takes and on the ongoing resources that are required to support journalists.

In 2022, CBC News appointed a veteran journalist in a new role: "journalist and well-being champion." His work includes delivering a new training program for staff and managers that addresses the unique workplace challenges and psychological harms faced by journalists, including those whose work intersects with UGC. The public broadcaster also offers training programs for staff to help with resiliency, stress, and exposure to graphic content.

We have also made clear to staff that they are under no obligation to engage on social media platforms using their personal accounts as part of their work for CBC, and that they can step away from social media whenever they need to for their mental health, especially since we know so much UGC comes through those tools.

Speaking openly and systemically about such harms and trauma, and having newsroom leaders with shared lived experiences who can support racialized staff, is helping shape nuanced approaches to how we use UGC in our newsrooms.

UGC can be powerful. Combined with our journalists' research, analysis, and expertise, it can be transformative.

Notes

1 For more on the effect of UGC on the mental health of journalists, see chapters 3 (Miller) and 4 (Rempel).
2 See Kaur, "Teen."
3 Bogel-Burroughs, "Prosecutors."
4 For more on gatekeeping, see chapter 8 (Burchell and Fielding).
5 CBC Journalistic Standards and Practices, CBC.
6 Ibid.
7 Ramsden, "Vicarious."
8 See Bor et al., "Police."
9 "Const. Daniel Montsion," CBC.
10 See Shingler, "Investigations."
11 See "Brian," CBC.
12 Black, Indigenous, and people of colour.
13 Tomlinson, "Raising."
14 Barrera, "Timothy."
15 "CBC Journalistic Standards and Practices," CBC News.

Bibliography

Barrera, Jorge. "Timothy Atlookan's Mom May Never Know What Led to Son's Death but Police Aay it's Not Suspicious." CBC News, 2020. https://www.cbc.ca/news/indigenous/thunder-bay-timothy-atlookan-death-1.5389796.

Bogel-Burroughs, Nicholas. "Prosecutors Say Derek Chauvin Knelt on George Floyd for 9 Minutes 29 Seconds, Longer Than Initially Reported." New York Times, 30 March 2021. https://www.nytimes.com/2021/03/30/us/derek-chauvin-george-floyd-kneel-9-minutes-29-seconds.html.

Bor, Jacob, Atheendar Venkataramani, David R. Williams, and Alexander C. Tsai. "Police Killings and their Spillover Effects on the Mental Health of Black Americans: A Population-Based, Quasi-Experimental Study." *Lancet*, 2018. https://www.thelancet.com/journals/lancet/article/PIIS0140-6736(18)31130-9/fulltext#seccestitle80.

"Brian Sinclair's Death 'Preventable' But Not Homicide, Says Inquest Report." CBC *News*, 2014. https://www.cbc.ca/news/canada/manitoba/brian-sinclair-s-death-preventable-but-not-homicide-says-inquest-report-1.2871025.

British Psychological Society. "Viewing Violent News on Social Media Can Cause Trauma." *EurekAlert!*, 2015. https://www.eurekalert.org/pub_releases/2015-05/bps-vvn050615.php.

CBC Journalistic Standards and Practices. CBC *News*, 1993, revised 2021. https://cbc.radio-canada.ca/en/vision/governance/journalistic-standards-and-practices.

"Const. Daniel Montsion Not Guilty in Death of Abdirahman Abdi." CBC *News*, 2021. https://www.cbc.ca/news/canada/ottawa/daniel-montsion-abdirahman-abdi-judgment-1.5765173.

Kaur, Harmeet. "The Teen Who Sparked a Global Movement With Her Video of George Floyd's Final Moments Receives an Award for Her Bravery." CNN, December 12, 2020. https://www.cnn.com/2020/12/09/us/teen-recorded-george-floyd-award-trnd/index.html.

Pearson, Matthew and Seglins, Dave. "Taking Care Report." *Canadian Journalism Forum on Violence and Trauma*, 2022. https://www.journalismforum.ca/taking-care-report.

Ramsden, Pam. "Vicarious Trauma, PTSD and Social Media: Does Watching Graphic Videos Cause Trauma?" *Journal of Depression and Anxiety* 6, no. 3 (2017). https://www.longdom.org/proceedings/vicarious-trauma-ptsd-and-social-media-does-watching-graphic-videos-cause-trauma-37421.html.

Shingler, Benjamin. "Investigations Launched after Atikamekw Woman Records Quebec Hospital Staff Uttering Slurs Before Her Death." CBC *News*, 2020. https://www.cbc.ca/news/canada/montreal/quebec-atikamekw-joliette-1.5743449.

Tomlinson, Asha. "Raising a Young Black Man in North America Today Means Fear, Faith and Hope that Change Will Come." CBC *News*, 2020. https://www.cbc.ca/news/canada/raising-young-black-man-1.5594179.

6

France 24 and Storyful

Two Unique Approaches to User-Generated Content in the Newsroom

MICHÈLE MARTIN AND MICHAEL LITHGOW

The preceding chapters have provided an overview of the ways the BBC (UK), Global News (Canada), the CBC (Canada), and the EBU (Europe) developed specific systems for handling UGC in their newsrooms that correspond not only to their needs but also to their ideology and politics. In all cases, the UGC producers remain at arm's length from the news organizations that use UGC content produced independently and outside of the conventional guidelines of professional journalism.

This chapter examines two very different approaches to UGC. The first is France 24's *The Observers* program, whose professional journalists work with UGC creators around the world to create a unique, hybrid form of news coverage. The second is Storyful, often cited as the first commercial social media newswire, whose employees identify, verify, curate, and license UGC for redistribution to news publishers. In each case, albeit in different ways, UGC has usurped the traditional journalist's role as primary content producer, by either replacing the traditional journalist altogether or creating a new partnership of sorts in which traditional journalists collaborate with UGC creators to generate an original form of news coverage.

France 24 and the System of *The Observers*[1]

The Observers program on France 24 (F24) presents a very different approach from the other channels covered in this collection. Founded in 2006, *The Observers* creates opportunities for F24 journalists to collaborate directly with UGC producers to create unique hybrid forms of news coverage.[2]

F24 is part of the France Medias Monde group, funded by the French government. The project provides a platform on which members of the public can share photos and videos on relevant news events. *The Observers* has four different websites operating in four languages (French, English, Arabic, and Persian) and presents a short TV show on F24 in weekly and monthly editions. The news produced by the website covers international current affairs, using eyewitness accounts from "observers," namely people who are "at the heart of an event." Anyone who witnesses an interesting event can contribute to *The Observers* by sending videos or photos indicating the location and date of its occurrence. A team of professional journalists in Paris verify and contextualize any observer's content received, after which the UGC is either put on the website or integrated into F24 TV news. Although *The Observers* news team has its own system for verifying and authenticating UGC, it also collaborates with a host of verification agencies, including the International Fact-Checking Network, Crosscheck, Storyful, and Facebook's Third-Party Fact-Checking Program. Today, *The Observers* news team verifies all UGC content used by the F24 news organization. In annual surveys with French audiences, *The Observers* television program is ranked as the second most popular show on F24.[3]

The Observers was launched by journalists Julien Pain and Derek Thomson. At the time, Pain had been working for some years for Reporters Without Borders (RWB), where he had developed an important network of informants. Thomson was head of new media at F24. After meeting at a conference and realizing they shared many of the same ideas, together they built a service based on informants living in different parts of the world who could share content on the Internet. As Thomson describes it: "He had a network of human rights activists around the world. I had a television network. So we got together and started *The Observers*."[4]

The idea was to create a platform on which F24 journalists and UGC creators around the world could work together to bring stories to public attention. At the beginning, Pain organized a system of "observers" based on his international contacts, who would provide videos of events taking place in diverse places around the world[5]; he also began to use what was available on social media. *The Observers* began producing in French and English but soon added Arab and Persian to its mix.[6] The success was such that F24 began to build a group of journalists to help with the various tasks attached to the use of UGC in news production. By 2015, the group had grown to seven regular journalists; as of 2020, nine were mentioned on the website.

As the journalists at F24 attached to the observers system grew in number, so did the number of users who contributed UGC. In 2015, Pain reported that F24 had about 4,000 observers and around 100 regular contributors. More recent estimates put the number of observers at closer to 5,000, with between 100 and 200 of them being highly trusted regular contributors.[7] These are not traditional "correspondents," Pain insisted, but individuals providing news content to the F24 *Observer* site, sometimes in collaboration with F24 journalists and sometimes independently.[8] "It is very much a collaboration," explained Thomson. "This is not citizen journalism. This is collaborative journalism. That's something that's very important."[9]

HOW THE SYSTEM WORKS

UGC comes to F24 in different ways. Much of it is submitted directly to *The Observer* website; some is gathered from social media; and some is sought out by F24 – for example, if there is a breaking news story in a region, F24 may contact a trusted observer there to ask if footage is available.[10] After verification, this kind of UGC material makes its way into F24 news coverage after being contextualized by F24 journalists into a news story, either on *The Observers* website or in other F24 news programming. Less frequently, with highly trusted observers, F24 will send a news team to where the observer is located to collaborate on a news piece, with F24 providing camera operators and journalists to assist the observer in the news gathering.[11]

When the journalists at F24 find amateur images on social networks, they attempt to contact the creators of these images, and if that is not possible, then someone with first-hand knowledge of the events depicted. When they are able to verify and authenticate the contributors' accounts, those accounts can be integrated in the network if the contributors wish it.[12] Some individuals may send France 24 information about events they have witnessed and documented via photo or video. In such cases, when the journalists are satisfied with the information provided, they offer to integrate these individuals into the network.

When F24 journalists have checked the authenticity of the information and supporting documentation, they publish it as an online article, introduced by one of their journalists, who, according to the F24 website, "give[s] the context and explain who our observers are and why their account is pertinent. That is followed by a first-person account from our observer, taken from a telephone interview or an exchange via social media."[13]

Pain suggests that the motives of observers who offer F24 UGC on a regular basis are diverse.[14] For some it is an opportunity to have UGC video integrated into news coverage, a way to have contact with traditional reporters, or a way to access training on how to write and present an issue; others are motivated by the local celebrity that can come once their video is recirculated through F24's website, even if their names are not mentioned (Pain has asserted that observers choose to have their names mentioned or not, but many refuse because they are afraid of retribution from authorities[15]). On rare occasions, some amateur producers have been compensated with a small amount of money or equipment (such as a video camera), although this practice has stopped.[16]

VERIFYING UGC

Integration of UGC into a news clip depends on different criteria: it may be that the topic cannot be covered by professional reporters at the time the UGC is received, or that the subject does not compete with what traditional reporters are covering.[17] Otherwise, when the topic is already being covered by traditional reporters, the news editors keep only what is complementary. Questioned about the rivalry between UGC producers and professional reporters, Pain asserted that he did not care about offending traditional journalists since it is the role of their union to defend them. His main concern when working with the Observer program was to use UGC to produce a more pertinent and efficient journalism.

Before UGC video can be part of an F24 news clip, it has to go through a thorough process of verification, not unlike that used by Storyful (see below); this includes examining the circumstances surrounding the event.[18] According to Pain, F24 prefers not to have a scoop than to risk being wrong: "We don't publish fake news!" he says, adding that unverified UGC is a "rumour" or fake news.[19] "In any case, people could go on the Internet to see the unverified videos. Furthermore, an observer could send his/her video to other stations as well. So it is better to personalize the news around the UGC."

"The journalist's job is to be a journalist and to treat any first-time observer exactly the way you treat any first time source, any person you don't know," explained Thomson, who became the director of *The Observers* in 2017. "So you confirm their identity. You confirm everything they tell you, crosscheck it against published information. You call the authorities where necessary, call the NGOs and various structures. And then once they've spoken to you and they've been truthful one time ... the second time it goes faster. The observers, when we recruit them, we put into a database their contact information, their interests, their location, and they become a resource if we keep using them."[20]

On first contact with the *Observers* team, amateur producers are submitted to the same treatment as any other news source: they are asked to provide photo and video documentation, some information on their access to the event they have covered, and their motivation for contacting F24. Journalists at F24 crosscheck the given information against additional sources: written reports, local news, experts, and even "pertinent governmental or nongovernmental agencies or other concerned parties."[21] Once observers have passed these checks and have contributed to the website, "they become a trusted source we can turn to for future reports."[22]

As for the UGC itself, F24 journalists verify photos and videos sent in by observers (whether or not they are the source of the images) using the following methodology[23]:

- Contact the author of the image (if not an observer).
- Check to see whether the image has been previously posted elsewhere (Google Image search, InVID, Amnesty's YouTube Dataviewer, etc.).
- Examine the image for signs of manipulation, tampering, or photomontage.
- Show the image to other observers with first-hand knowledge of the issue or location.
- Show the image to expert sources with knowledge of the issue or location.
- Compare the image with published accounts of the same event.

The *Observers* website also offers a Verification Guide, a series of "how-to" articles aimed at non-journalists (i.e., potential contributors to the *Observers* website) describing practices for verifying images: how to detect a photo or video that has been manipulated, how to verify a photo or video found online, using your phone to verify images, and basic tricks to avoid Internet hoaxes.[24]

REMUNERATION

Remuneration is perhaps the issue that has varied the most over the years, particularly due to the development of technologies such as smart phones and platforms such as the Internet, Instagram, Facebook, and so on. At one time *The Observers* rewarded reliable observers by providing them with a high-quality camera, but this practice was stopped because "now everyone has a smartphone."[25]

Remuneration follows a pattern. When the amateurs are on the spot and take the initiative to send their production, there is no remuneration. But when F24 initiates contact to request that an observer send a video, compensation is provided.

THE STATUS OF OBSERVERS

The status of the observers within the F24 news system is unclear and unstable. They could be viewed as more than amateurs, since they are sometimes paid, as well as trained, by traditional journalists, but, as Pain clearly stated, they are in no way correspondents or traditional reporters, even those who are already recognized as such in their own part of the world.[26] And new projects at F24 continue to complexify these relations. At the time of our interviews with the *Observer* news team, they described something they were exploring called "oriented UGC."[27] In a program called *Pas 2 Quartier*, F24 had asked youth in Paris suburbs (*les banlieues*) to film themselves and issues in the communities where they lived. F24 journalists then used the footage to build news stories for the *Observers* website and television show.

How to describe the relationship that exists between traditional journalists at F24 and producers of amateur videos? According to Pain, there is no competition between traditional and amateur reporters, although in a very few cases, amateurs have been hired into regular positions. But relationship-building is a core responsibility for journalists working with observers, and moreover, F24 journalists are deeply committed to the well-being and safety of observers who are sharing UGC. The boundaries between amateur and traditional reporters seem to have blurred over the years, even as each group retains a well-defined function in the news production process.

Storyful

Storyful[28] was started in 2010 by journalist Mark Little, at a time when most newsrooms were only beginning to realize the significance of UGC in daily news routines. Storyful focuses on curating visual UGC: identifying, locating, and verifying video information relevant to breaking news stories and then making verified UGC available to news publishers. In December 2013, Storyful was purchased by Rupert Murdoch's News Corp. At the time of the interviews for this chapter in 2018, Storyful was distributing more than 500 videos per week to more than 90 publishing partners, including the *New York Times*, the Sun Newspaper Group in the UK, the *Washington Post*, ABC News, the *Telegraph*, and CNN. UGC video that has been verified for use by clients is distributed to subscribers through a daily newsfeed called the Newswire.

Storyful was an early adopter: it recognized the importance of verified UGC as a resource at a time when other news organizations were scrambling to make sense of both the volume of material available and its significance, especially during the Arab Spring uprising, which started in 2010. At the time, there were few if any standardized verification procedures for UGC, and newsrooms found themselves all too often incorporating unverified UGC into their news coverage.[29] Alan O'Riordan, standards editor at Storyful, recalls working at a different news agency while covering the Arab Spring and the early months of the Syrian war.[30] "That was the phrase you saw: unverified video. What we do now is verified video … It's gone from being the Wild West to being something that is verifiable." Today, Storyful is one of the leaders in a trend toward standardizing and routinizing the use of UGC in newsrooms.

The Storyful news team focuses on three levels of verification: (1) verifying the original source – that is, who made the actual recording; (2) verifying the location; and (3) verifying the date. "When something happens," explains O'Riordan, "you don't have to wait until the reporter gets there [to the site of breaking news] to report back. But what is coming back, obviously, is from someone you've never met, someone you've never spoke[n] to, you don't know who they are, you don't know what their motives are, and what we do is try to build that picture before we can stand over something and say, 'We think this what it says it is, and here's why.'"[31]

There are two kinds of content in the Storyful newsroom. After picking up a signal that something is happening somewhere in the world, Storyful journalists find and verify relevant UGC for clients. This is the first kind. Once key visual content has been sourced and verified, and permission to use it has been secured, the Storyful team writes up background and context for the clip. This is the second kind of content. Together, the verified video materials, a transparent record of the level of verification completed, and contextualizing text are distributed to clients through the Newswire, a paid subscription service in which fees are based on the size of the organization and/or the amount of content being accessed. Storyful does its best to verify with 100 per cent certainty, but that is not always possible. Verification transparency allows the client to decide for itself what has been adequately verified for its purposes. A subscriber gets a login account and can download content as needed. The contextualizing text is written like a traditional news story; clients can then republish it in whole or in part, or simply use it as a guide when assessing the clip's significance.

But even verification does not address all of the journalistic concerns raised about video materials created by strangers. A verified video may still show only part of a story – for example, UGC created by a partisan in a conflict. The video clip may be what it purports to be, but the clip alone may not reflect the complexity of a situation. This is addressed by the contextualizing narratives produced by Storyful journalists for the UGC materials that go in the Newswire. "So we navigate that space and use that stuff [UGC] as an objective record as much as we can," says Joe Galvin, director of news at Storyful. "And to apply a standard of: is this a fair reflection of what actually happened, visually speaking? And then can we elaborate on the complexities in the copy we will provide and the context we provide."[32] Also, if Storyful journalists learn that one of their sources of UGC is partisan, they will share that information in the verification transparency report for clients: "The goal is always to provide both sides of the stories – you know, to make sure our clients have the full context of what's going on."[33]

Storyful journalists look for content on any and all social media platforms – vк in Russia, Instagram, Facebook, Twitter, Snapchat, and so on. They use algorithms that help search for content by keyword as well as other metadata indexes, including third-party tools such Datas-Minr, CrowdTangle, NewsWhip, Spike, Brandwatch, and Netalytic. They also have their own in-house team of digital tools developers building proprietary tech for internal and client use.

Client needs also drive decisions. "We do have to be aware of our clients and our clients' needs, and each of those clients have very different news values," explains O'Riordin. "So we're trying to cater our content provision to suit all of those clients in these values." Time is the greatest source of pressure affecting the value of uGc to news discourse. Fifteen to twenty minutes to get proper rights clearance verification is not uncommon, but sometimes clients require it much faster.

Storyful does not commission content and does not provide training for content creators. The general practice, once content is located, is to secure rights in exchange for attribution, or sometimes – such as when a particularly unique video clip *is* the story – for payment. Storyful will enter into licensing agreements based on a revenue-sharing model that pays content creators based on the number of clients and customers who upload the video. "It all comes down to respecting the needs or wants of the eyewitness, so we are keen just to make sure that the eyewitness is getting the credit, whether that's financial or just a name credit," says Galvin.[34] If a uGc creator's life could be endangered if their identity were revealed, Storyful protects it, and that person will remain anonymous to clients.

On being hired at Storyful, journalists are trained in verification procedures, the use of proprietary technologies, and the use of custom tools and methodologies. The Newswire team has about sixty journalists working worldwide, including a director of news (frontline news coverage, final editorial decisions), lead standards editors (fact-checking and copyright), and duty editors (assignment editors).

A fascinating part of the Storyful newsdesk is called News Intelligence. This small team of journalists focuses on identifying fake news and disinformation.[35] News Intelligence emerged later than the Newswire service, in response to the growing problem of disinformation: journalists were wasting time trying to chase down false stories, and there was a risk that false stories would be posted to clients, thus damaging their reputation as news providers. Storyful journalists observed that fake news and disinformation in the online world often followed a pattern: it started in obscure places like 4Chan, GAB, and VOA and then migrated out to intermediary websites and blogs and, finally, to more mainstream platforms. News Intelligence monitors how false rumours and fake news stories migrate from fringe spaces to platforms like YouTube and Twitter.

As breaking news occurs, according to one team member, genuine UGC begins to emerge alongside misinformation and false reports. The News Intelligence team is on the lookout for the false information to prevent its use by clients. According to Thomson, "We know that there are now a lot of actors online who will use that news event, particularly if there's an information vacuum, arising from that news event to further their own points of view, so they will fill this space with unverified or demonstrably false claims and hope that that's the story that gets credit quickly."[36] False and misleading stories and visuals are identified by the News Intelligence team, and this information is shared with the Newswire team and clients.

According to Storyful's website, the News Intelligence service has potential value for *corporate* clients as well – it can forecast market trends, help clients stay clear of false news reports, aid in understanding actors and influencers, and assess market impact. "Assessment Reports provide comprehensive analysis of the customers, competitors and threat groups operating in the new information environment. We use pattern analysis and intelligence expertise to understand the issues and market trends that inform investment decisions and business strategy. Our framework allows our experienced analysts to forecast and track market trends, assess business impact and make detailed recommendations."[37]

An emerging service at the time of the interviews involved embedding Storyful journalists in client newsrooms, where they worked directly with client journalists to deliver reports and assist with UGC management and verification. Storyful also offers branding services, linking UGC to advertisers, as well as reputation risk management services, but this is, according to Galvin, an entirely separate operation with a completely different team. The Newswire team focuses on UGC for news agency clients. "That's a bit of a church–state thing," said Galvin. "We make sure that the editorial does not in any way influence the journalism."

Conclusion

Storyful and F24 represent two unique responses to the emergence of UGC as an increasingly integral element of contemporarily news practice. F24 perhaps demonstrates the most robust set of relations with UGC creators of all the examples discussed in this book, to the point in some cases of full collaboration with UGC providers; it has forged long-term bonds with untrained and non-professional people all over the world. Storyful offers the curation, verification, and contextualization support services necessary to make UGC a relevant facet of journalism for organizations that publish news. It transforms UGC into a commodity for sale and circulation to the highest bidders in a global media market. In Storyful's realm, the UGC creators remain at arm's length, although reliable creators may end up contributing again if their social media presence reveals relevant material for other news stories from their region. Storyful's relationship with UGC creators is respectful but maintains boundaries. F24, by contrast, nurtures talent by sometimes providing production assistance and opportunities for collaboration and in this way has helped launch a hybrid form of UGC that combines the proximal opportunities of eyewitness members of the public with the storytelling skills and production conventions of professionally trained journalists.

In the case of F24, that the corpus of this chapter comes from different years (2015, 2018, 2019, 2021) and various types of data (interviews, websites, a paper presented at a symposium, etc.) has allowed us to uncover the diverse ways in which the F24 website *The Observers* has worked over the years, and how it has been dependent on technological developments, among other things. The amateurs who provide UGC to F24 have unavoidably been influenced by these changes, not only in terms of the quality of the videos they provide but also, in some ways, in terms of their status in the labour structure. Some things, however, have not changed much over the years.

In each case, there is to be observed a new and unprecedented professional and commercial model for creating news discourse. The presence and importance of UGC has led to structural changes in newsrooms, entirely new business models, new routines and conventions of journalistic production, and new forms of collaboration between traditional journalists and UGC producers that have begun to challenge even the stability of such seemingly set categories of actor as "employee." As both these cases demonstrate, the implications of UGC for journalistic practice are and will be far-reaching as news organizations continue to grapple with the discursive significance and availability of UGC in today's digital mediascape.

Notes

1 A lack of response to our requests to the editors and journalists at France 24 for a summary of their unique *The Observers* system compelled the editors of this book to write an overview of the system based on the following: a long interview given to one of the editors by Julien Pain, the editor-in-chief of *The Observers* in July 2015; interviews given three years later (December 2018) by the head of France 24 News Magazines and Reports, Loïck Berrou, the deputy editor (French) Corentin Bainier, and the journalist Alexandre Capron, all attached to *The Observers* website; a paper presented by Derek Thomson, current editor-in-chief of *The Observers*, at the Symposium "Eye Witness Texture," to which he had been invited in May 2019, and which was simultaneously streamlined online; and the 2021 public website of *The Observers* (https://observers.france24.com/fr).

2 For a look at France 24's use of UGC, see chapter 7 (Lithgow and Martin).

3 Interview with Loick Berrou, Head of Picture Pool and Magazines, France 24, and Alexandre Capron, Journalist, *The Observers*, December 2018.

4 Conference presentation, MacEwan University, Edmonton, Alberta, 21 May 2019.

5 On the 2021 version of *The Observers* website, Derek Thomson mentions in his short biography that he developed the system with Julien Pain. The lack of communication from Thomson prevents us from clarifying this contradiction.

6 Information gathered during our interview with Julien Pain in July 2015.

7 Ibid.

8 Ibid.

9 Conference presentation, MacEwan University, Edmonton, Alberta, 21 May 2019.

10 Interview Loick Berrou, Head of Picture Pool and Magazines, France 24, and Alexandre Capron, Journalist, *The Observers*, December 2018.

11 Ibid.

12 *The Observers*, 2021, https://observers.france24.com/fr.

13 Ibid.

14 Interview with Pain, July 2015.

15 One must mention, however, that among the thousands of news clips examined in our survey of the data, none identified their authors.

16 An interesting aspect of comparing data from interviews given at different times is that it reveals the speed at which technology has developed. When we had the 2018 interview with France 24 journalists in December 2018, they found it amusing that offering a good camera was a way of recompensing an observer. With smart phones, there was no need of cameras, they said.

17 Interview with Pain, July 2015. Note: "Traditional reporters" is the term used by France 24 on *The Observers* website, in contrast to the expression "professional journalists," used by other organizations.

18 Actually, when we surveyed the 1,000 clips related to the Arab Spring and archived in the general archives of France 24, we indeed realized that all the UGCs integrated within the news clips were rather short and always part of a larger topic.

19 Ibid.

20 Conference presentation, MacEwan University, Edmonton, Alberta, 21 May 2019.

21 https://observers.france24.com/fr.

22 Ibid.

23 Retrieved 16 June 2021 from https://observers.france24.com/en/who-are-we.

24 *The Observers*, France 24, retrieved 16 June 2021, https://observers.france24.com/en/tag/verification-guide.

25 Interview with L. Berrou, Head of Picture Pool and Magazines, France 24, and A. Capron, journalist, *The Observers*, December 2018

26 Interview with Pain, July 2015.

27 Ibid.

28 The following brief description of Storyful comes from interviews conducted in 2018 at Storyful's head office in Dublin, with staff members Joe Galvin, Director of News, Alan O'Riordan, and a third journalist who preferred anonymity, as well as from Storyful's website as at June 2021.

29 For more on the use of UGC during the Arab Spring, see chapters 7 (Lithgow and Martin) and 9 (Lithgow).

30 O'Riordan, interview.

31 O'Riordan.

32 Galvin, interview.

33 O'Riordan, interview.

34 Galvin, interview.

35 For more on fake news, see the prologue and chapters 3 (Miller) and 4 (Rempel).

36 Thomson, "Les Observateurs, France 41."

37 Storyful website, https://storyful.com/intelligence/reporting.

Bibliography

Bainier, Corentin. Deputy Editor (French), *Les Observers*. Interview, Paris, 2018.

Berrou, Loïck. Head of France 24 News Magazines and Reports. Interview, Paris, 2018.

Capron, Alexandre. Journalist, *Les Observers*, France 24. Paris, 2018.

Galvin, Joe. Director of News, Storyful. Interview, Dublin, 2018.

Observers. 2021. https://observers.france24.com/fr.

O'Riordan, Alan. Standards Editor, Storyful. Interview, Dublin, 2018.

Pain, Julien. Editor-in-Chief of *Les Observers*. Interview, Paris, 2015.

Storyful. 2021. https://storyful.com/intelligence/reporting.

Thomson, Derek. "Les Observateurs, France 24." Presentation at Eyewitness Textures Symposium, 23–24 May 2019, MacEwan University. Edmonton, Alberta.

PART TWO

User-Generated Content and the Changing Landscape of News Outcomes

7

From Evidence to Affect

The Different Discursive Functions of User-Generated Content in Coverage of the Arab Spring

MICHAEL LITHGOW AND MICHÈLE MARTIN

The growing use of user-generated content (UGC) in newsrooms is one of the most challenging and important changes in the production of news in the twenty-first century. By UGC we mean any content that is produced by eyewitness non-journalists at news events and either sent to a particular news organization or posted on an Internet platform where journalists can source it for use in news production. During the Arab Spring uprisings in 2010–11, UGC producers captured dramatic events such as protesters being shot, beaten, and run down by military vehicles; spontaneous protests in public spaces; clashes between different groups; and street celebrations. These were often the only available visual records of events.¹ This chapter uses the events of the Arab Spring to examine UGC as a discourse of conflict produced by untrained and unpaid media users often at great personal risk, which is then taken up by and incorporated into news by various broadcast networks. This material can include tweets, cell phone videos and photographs, Instagram posts, YouTube footage, and so on. In this chapter, however, we focus on the ways UGC video recordings were used in news coverage by France 24 and the Canadian Broadcasting Corporation (CBC).²

How UGC was used at the time of the Arab Spring offers a unique window onto changing practices among professional journalists. In 2010–11, newsrooms were certainly aware of UGC as a possible source of news content, but few newsrooms had routinized procedures for sourcing, verifying, using, and crediting/labelling UGC that most newsrooms have today. As the corpus of our study reveals, a wide variety of approaches to using UGC were taken, including the prevalent use of unverified UGC, something far less common today.

A distinguishing feature of UGC has to do with picture quality and composition. The various semiotic elements comprising amateur images such as colour saturation, pixilation, image composition, blurriness, and shakiness create what we call an "eyewitness texture." At the time of the Arab Spring, that texture reflected the generally low-quality technologies in use and non-professional camera skills; it also fed the public's desire for proximity and immediacy. Thus, news organizations often used UGC not only for its evidentiary value but also as a means to authenticate their coverage.[3] "Eyewitness texture" describes aspects of imagery that influence meaning through other-than-rational means – for example, by creating a feeling of being there, of immediacy and proximity to events, even if the events depicted in the amateur footage are only indirectly related to the core subject of the news story.

Our study closely examines UGC from Tunisia, Egypt, and Libya that was used for news coverage by France 24 and the CBC during the first 100 days of the Arab Spring (17 December 2010 to 31 March 2011). Tunisia is where that uprising began, with the self-immolation of Tunisian fruit vendor Mohammed Bouazizi; Egypt was the second and arguably more affected country to which it spread; and Libya was the third. We focused on the early phase of the uprisings (the Arab Spring lasted at least until late 2012), a period when journalists from Western news organizations had the least access and were therefore more reliant on UGC, a pattern confirmed in the decreasing frequency of UGC use in news stories over the course of the first three months of coverage.

Our chapter takes a multilayered approach to discourse analysis, one that encompasses aesthetic qualities, narrative fragments and metanarratives, and justificatory conditions, thus revealing a range of priorities at work in the discursive function of UGC in early coverage of the Arab Spring. These priorities include the evidentiary value of the images as a visual record of the contents of news stories, and also at times their rhetorical value as eyewitness texture in response to a public desire to know through the immediacy of being there, even when the images appear to serve no direct evidentiary function. Our goal in focusing on this unique early example of the widespread uptake of UGC by large, professional news organizations at a time when routines of verification and handling of UGC had not been established is to better understand both intended and unintended news outcomes in the early use of UGC in television journalism.

UGC and the Production of News

Our research uses the term "UGC" as defined by some scholars, namely as textual or visual information made available online by amateurs witnessing important events in their part of the world. Traditional journalists are then able to access it through social media, blogs, independent websites, and other platforms.[4] UGC is an increasingly important element in journalism networks in part because it responds to consumer and market demands for "immediate" information and can enhance perceptions of "authenticity"[5] and proximity to events.[6] Nevertheless, in the period this research is covering, the often murky ontology of UGC also challenged the established values of "objectivity" and "trust" on which the business of journalism is based.[7] Lack of verification, however, was not and is still not an absolute barrier to UGC's use in professional reportage; our study observed that unverified UGC was sometimes used and labelled as such. As we have seen in previous chapters in this book, there have been more recent efforts to develop standards of UGC verification, such as the *Verification Handbook* published by the European Journalism Centre of the Poynter Institute.[8] Changing standards of verification reflect the increasing value of UGC to professional news organizations: it may be the only way some visual materials in relation to a story can be obtained.

UGC can be interpreted in various ways. For the audiences, its "eyewitness textures" can signify perceived proximities to the events they record and signal greater authenticity. However, UGC is often selected by professional journalists because of its affective impact: dead bodies, wounded and bloody protesters, horrific acts of violence, pools of blood on the sidewalk, and so on. Add to this the difficulties frequently encountered, particularly in the period studied here, in verifying where images have come from and why they were recorded, and the result can be images whose significance both exceeds and depends on contextual news narratives in the sense that UGC on its own can be suggestive of many possible meanings and rarely only one.

Methodology

Our research set out to identify the discursive impacts of UGC on news outcomes. While the use of digital technologies by amateurs in the production and distribution of information extends to various types of media – television, newspapers, magazines, audio, video, and so on – for this chapter, we target the impact on the television industry of UGC arriving through various social media. The originality of the research lies in an international comparative analysis of coverage of the Arab Spring uprisings by two television news networks, CBC (Canada) and France 24, operating in different countries. The time period of our study corresponds to the first 100 days immediately following the immolation of Bouazizi, who set himself on fire in the city of Sidi Bouzid in Tunisia on 17 December 2010. We chose the first three months of coverage as a timeframe after preliminary viewings of news footage indicated greater use of UGC in the early weeks of uprising coverage, likely due to the inability of Western news organizations to get journalists into affected areas.[9]

CBC and France 24 provided us from their archives all of the news stories during the first 100 days of the Arab Spring uprisings that incorporated amateur-produced images. We analyzed this corpus by taking a critical discourse analysis approach based on the broad category of "critical qualitative research" as defined by Kincheloe and McLaren.[10]

Aligning ourselves with a renewed interest among some scholars in textual analysis to excavate implied or contextualizing ideological and cultural assumptions,[11] we reviewed the corpus of news stories using amateur video and identified the following categories of significance in relation to the amateur video clips, each of which will be described briefly below: structural role, evidentiary value, narratives (including narrative fragments and metanarratives), aesthetic qualities (affect and picture quality), and degree of proximity to the events depicted.

The structural role of UGC refers to how amateur visuals are used within the broader structure of the news story.[12] Journalists sometimes refer to the narrative structure of a television news story as the "clothesline" on which news elements are "hung" when a story is presented.[13] The structural role of amateur clips has to do with how central or how peripheral they are to the overall visual structure of the story.

The evidentiary value of UGC has to do with its function in relation to a news story: is it visual filler (or B-roll), or is it visual evidence – that is, directly and specifically about the focus of the news story?

UGC as narrative fragments reflects what Georgakapoulou calls "small stories."[14] Such fragments have a less obvious and somewhat incomplete narrative structure but often emerge as events are unfolding and often reflect experiences discouraged or disallowed from cultural circulation. Recognizing that UGC has been created by individuals not employed by the news organizations that use them, our analysis sought to take into account any discursive implications of these "small stories."[15]

Narrative fragments are discursively interesting in this context when they imply other, larger narratives (i.e., metanarratives).[16] They can be understood as depending for their significance on metanarratives.[17] For example, UGC showing damaged property takes on particular significance within a larger metanarrative of the collapse of social order under the "democratic" pressures of protests in Arab states during the Arab Spring.

The aesthetic elements of amateur images play a role in shaping images' discursive significance even while falling outside the rational criteria generally brought to bear on news discourse.[18] Thus, the affective register of the clips in our sample often distinguished those clips from other images, especially in terms of shock, horror, and/or heightened anxiety or urgency.[19] In addition, the UGC we examined had unique pictoral qualities that distinguished it from professional images, almost always suggesting inferior picture quality in terms of resolution, composition, and colour. In some cases, the image distortion was so prevalent that it was difficult to determine what was being filmed (shaky camera, fast pans and zooms, blurriness).

And finally, there is the attribute of proximity, which reflects the camera operator's closeness to the events being depicted. Amateur images were often recorded from *within* the events taking place at extremely close proximity to people, actions, and dangers. This quality of amateur footage has important implications for viewers.[20]

With these seven categories of discursive significance as our analytic framework, we proceeded to examine the amateur-produced images in news coverage by CBC and France 24, considering the use of amateur images in each case, then comparing and contrasting the two news networks' use of those images.

CBC and France 24 Coverage of the Arab Spring

CBC APPROPRIATION OF UGC IN NEWS STORIES

In the first 100 days of CBC's coverage of the Arab Spring uprisings in Tunisia, Egypt, and Libya, twenty-two of its news stories incorporated UGC. Two referred to Tunisia, six to Egypt, and fourteen to Libya.

In only two of the stories that used UGC did it play more than a secondary role structurally; the great majority of news stories in which UGC appeared were comprised largely of professionally shot images, with amateur clips strategically woven in. The first exception was a news story dated 16 February 2011 about Libya, narrated by a news anchor, accompanied by UGC identified by the narrator as "amateur video." The second story was also from Libya, dated 20 February 2011. The journalist narrating the story says at the beginning: "Accurate reporting from Libya is complicated because the country has blocked access to foreign journalists."[21] Some of the images in the story are introduced with descriptors such as "with the postings online" and "these images are apparently of what's being called a massacre," or with graphic overlays stating "YouTube video"; others (unlabelled in any way) are so pixelated and of such poor quality that their contents are barely discernible – that is, they have the hallmark visual qualities of amateur footage and in this sense demonstrate the eyewitness textures suggesting "authenticity," but their meanings are ambiguous. Our observation is while it was used widely in Arab Spring coverage, especially in the early days of the unrest, when access to events was difficult or impossible for foreign journalists, the CBC mostly used UGC in news coverage in a subordinate way, as an addition to professionally produced video imagery. As Chouliaraki has pointed out,[22] the presence of ordinary voices in news network discourse is a phenomenon not often seen in the media, and the ratios of amateur to professional footage support this observation.

In terms of presentation, fifteen of the twenty-two stories explicitly identified amateur footage (UGC) either in voiceover narration or with a graphic overlay. In seven of those, the UGC was only indirectly related to the news story being told; that is, the specific events, places, and times recorded in the images were not the focus of the story. In other words, in one third of the cases examined, the UGC was used as secondary footage to fill in the visual narrative and was not the direct object or event under scrutiny.

Table 7.1 Strategies for indicating amateur-produced images in CBC news stories

Voiceover descriptors	Graphic tags
"Amateur video"	
"Postings online … these images are apparently…"	
"even with these shaky cellphone pictures"	
"Phone cams are still about the only way pictures are getting out of Libya"	
"these pictures purport to show …," "these images are from youtube. CBC cannot verify their authenticity"	"unsourced video"
"these are images in a closed country loaded onto social media"	"Youtube"
	"Amateur video"
"Images that cannot be verified"	
"Images of a citizens arrest … made its way onto a social media website"	
"This unverified video purportedly shows"	
"this video is unverifiable"	
"this video impossible to verify"	

An example may help illustrate this. In a news story dated 26 February 2011, UGC was used in a story about events on the previous day – fighting between Gadhafi's troops and rebel troops in Libya's Tripoli and the emergence of a citizen-run impromptu government to keep city infrastructure running in Benghazi.[23] The total story length is 1:54 minutes. The UGC is identified as "unsourced video" by a graphic overlay and by the narrator, who says: "what appears to be a citizen's arrest of one apparent mercenary has made its way onto a social media website." It is five seconds in length, showing a man in khaki uniform on the ground with his hands bound, lying in a pool of blood, pleading with people dressed in civilian clothing. The clip has an implied meaning in the context of the news story: that this was a scene from the previous day. In terms of its evidentiary value, however, most of the content of the images in the UGC remains factually ambiguous: who, where, when, and even why are uncertain. Moreover, the presence of mercenaries in the conflict is not discussed or examined in any substantive way; it is merely mentioned in passing (it was considered more substantively in another news story that used the same amateur clip two days later).[24] The images create a sense of urgency and immediacy (and in this case, the affective disturbance of witnessing brutality), while offering little in the way of traditional "facts." These hyperfactual sensibilities add what we are describing as "eyewitness texture" to the news narratives, while also challenging an existing hierarchy of places in the media by recognizing the voices of distant others, as Chouliaraki would say.[25]

When we looked more closely at what was being depicted in UGC (whether directly or indirectly related to the news story in which it appeared), we found that 90 per cent of the time, it evoked a strong affective state – of horror, revulsion, outrage – by depicting shocking, dramatic events such as protesters being injured or killed, physical clashes between police and protesters and between different factions of protesters, destruction of property, angry mobs, and the immolation of Bouazizi. Most of the amateur clips – 90 per cent – positioned the viewer in close proximity to the events being depicted, that is, amidst protesters being shot and injured, facing police retaliation, in conflict with other protesters, and so on. Together these qualities created a "proximal urgency" associated with most uses of UGC video.

In all cases, the images were of poor quality: washed-out colours, pixelated, shaky camera work, and poor composition. In at least one case, the image was virtually indecipherable in the sense that it was difficult to determine what was happening in one viewing; the meaning relied heavily on context and implication.

In the twenty-two news stories, there were eighty-six separate UGC clips. Whether or not they were used directly as evidence, the clips had their own narratives or what we describe as narrative fragments. For example, in a story about the president of Tunisia stepping down, one UGC clip depicts men carrying an injured man through the streets – that is, a narrative fragment of protesters being injured in the street.[26] The clips depict specific situations and actions, but their meanings and significance have been subsumed into the news stories in which they appear.

In descending order of frequency, the narrative fragments identified were of (1) citizens/protesters taking to the streets, (2) injuries to protesters, (3) state attacks against protesters, (4) protesters damaging property, (5) protesters clashing with police/military, (6) protesters clashing with one another, (7) the immolation of Bouazizi, and (8) ambiguous images. We next looked for metanarratives within which these narrative fragments potentially drew meaning and significance. We identified five broad themes, each of which requires some explanation.

The most common theme was the violent tyranny of Arab states, with clips suggesting that the protests were a response to tyrannical states that were violent toward their citizens or that tolerated police violence against citizens, or both. This was not always stated explicitly in the news stories, but it was clearly implied. For example, in one news story, the news narrative is about the significance of a video clip getting a lot of attention on YouTube. The newscaster describes the video (in which an Egyptian protester is shot, falls to the ground, and is helped away by another protester) with the following narration:

> Confrontations between protesters and police are being captured
> on camera and uploaded to the Internet. Today we came
> across one particular video on YouTube that's attracting a lot
> of attention, and it's easy to understand why. The video shows
> the man collapsing to the ground after the sound of gunshots.
> Another man runs to help him, and the victim is carried away.
> The person who posted the video claims it was filmed during the
> protests in the last five days.[27]

The news narrative about attention being attracted by graphic amateur video footage from Egypt and the narrative fragment about a civilian shot in the street both take on a deeper significance within a metanarrative about tyranny and violence by Arab states (in this case, Egypt) against their own citizens, something that is not mentioned explicitly in the news story.

The second most common theme suggested by amateur video clips was the collapse of social order as a result of the citizen uprisings. For example, in one news story the news narrative is about protests spreading to Iran, stating that the only images getting out are through social media and that in the face of protests the Iranian regime is organizing counter-protests whose participants chant death threats at students and protesters.[28] The news story is about the spreading Middle Eastern turmoil and uprisings. There are two amateur video clips: one shows crowds in streets covered in debris and rubble, with overturned objects on fire; the second shows crowds in the street, smoke in the air, and then the crowd turning and running. Over these images the narrator says: "Protesting in Iran takes something almost beyond courage, given the tendencies of the clerical authorities, and yet Iranians are doing it by the thousands, according to some reports, all over the country."[29] The property damage in the first clip and the smoke hovering in the air in the second clip take on particular significance within a metanarrative of the potential for social and political collapse.

The third most common metanarrative theme conveys public protest as a form of democratic uprising. For example, in one news story, the news narrative is about the importance of cell phone video in the Tunisian and Egyptian uprisings. One of the amateur video clips shows a group of demonstrators in the street in front of a municipal building in Tunisia. The narration says: "A day after Mohammed Bouazizi burned himself, friends and relatives went to the provincial office and loudly protested the injustice that drove him to such desperation. This cell-phone video of the event was instantly circulated to tens of thousands of Arabs through Facebook and Twitter ... shortly after that protest, far larger protests began to appear in the capital of Tunis."[30] The story is about technology being the cause of civic unrest in the Arab world. The amateur clip shows an example of this unrest, which takes on particular significance in the context of a growing movement of protest against unfair treatment by state officials.

The fourth metanarrative theme that emerged was the idea that the Arab Spring was caused by new media and digital technologies. This is a technological determinist narrative about Western technology being the cause of Middle Eastern democratic uprisings. For example, in one of the news stories the news narrative was about Egypt having blocked the Internet that day, as a result of the online circulation of voices of defiance that had grown louder in concert with the protests, the result of a sophisticated network of young people using social media to incite a revolution.[31] A UGC clip in the story shows a man lying prone in the street in a pool of blood, two people crouching to help. Although none of the images in the clip display a link with new technology, the narration mentions that "technology is nothing new to dissidents. Iran's failed uprisings two years ago were called the Cellphone Revolution after images of police brutality were captured that way." The clip takes on particular significance in the context of a narrative about digitally driven revolutions.

The final metanarrative theme observed had to do with the gendering of the Arab Spring uprisings as an expression of male Arab anger. This metanarrative emerged from UGC as a whole: 95 per cent of the clips featured men (and only men) who were screaming, chanting, in conflict with state forces, or firing weapons.[32]

What makes these themes interesting and significant is that UGC appeared to serve different discursive functions depending on the discursive context in which it appeared. UGC recorded by Arab nationals in Tunisia, Egypt, and Libya took on broader ideological motifs in Western mainstream news discourses.[33] For example, the theme of "male Arab anger" obfuscated many other realities of the Arab Spring, including the important role of women in organizing, supporting, and participating in all forms of protest,[34] as well as the many different kinds of activities and participants involved in Arab Spring protests. The theme that the Arab Spring uprisings were a product of new media obscured significant offline organizing efforts by activists and social movement leaders that both preceded and occurred during the uprising;[35] it also shifted causation to something emerging from a Western context, that is, digital technologies. The theme of social collapse obscured the ways Arab states, like Western states, have rich histories of social unrest.[36] And finally, the theme of tyranny oversimplified the many ways Arab states operated during the uprisings – for example, the UGC used did *not* show that tyrannical repressions were directed at some social groups more than others; that some aspects of despotism and tyranny in Arab contexts might have parallels in Western liberal contexts;[37] that Arab states were being routinely demonized in information campaigns tied to foreign policy strategies – strategies that obscured, among other things, cultural attributes Westerners tend to boast about among themselves such as their successes in science, education, fine arts, market economics, and so on.[38] Amateur videos in these instances appear to be doing discursive work, overreducing complexity in an arguably orientalist framework.[39] So while UGC used and recognized in some respects the voices of distant others, there remained limitations in the metanarratives that were ultimately supported by how these voices were incorporated into news narratives for a Western audience.

France 24

In the first 100 days of France 24's coverage of the Arab Spring, eleven of its news stories incorporated UGC: four, events in Egypt, and seven, events in Tunisia. In nine of those stories, UGC played a central structural role, that is, it provided most of the footage for the story or was its central organizing feature, or both. Eight stories opened with UGC, suggesting a strategic placement of those clips in terms of framing. Most uses of UGC by France 24 (80 per cent) seemed directly related to the story being told in terms of the time, place, and events depicted – that is, they served as visual evidence of the story's content.

Most of the UGC that was used (80 per cent) evoked a high affective state – of horror, revulsion, and outrage – by depicting shocking, dramatic events. All UGC located the viewer in close proximity to the events being depicted. Together, these qualities created the "proximal urgency" associated with most uses of UGC.

All of the images were of poor quality. In at least two, the images were almost indecipherable in the sense that it was difficult to determine what was happening, and their meaning depended heavily on context and implication, neither of which was clear. But in this sense, their meaning was all the more authentic for the viewers, in that those images were obviously, in Anden-Papadopoulos's and Pantti's words, "first hand recordings by individuals who witnessed or experienced an event while it was happening."[40] That is, they did not reflect the conventions of news institutions. The indecipherability in these instances was directly tied to their perceived authenticity.

The eleven news stories used thirty-eight separate UGC clips. The narrative fragments depicted in those clips (which were distinct from the narratives of the news stories being supported by the clips) broke down as follows (in decreasing order of frequency): (1) citizens taking to the streets (walking, shouting, throwing stones at barricades), (2) people in streets proximal to property destruction (destroyed cars and buildings, rubble, fires, etc.), (3) the self-immolation of Bouazizi, (4) state violence against protesters, (5) injured protesters, (6) ambiguous, (7) protesters clashing with police, and (8) protesters clashing with one another.

We examined these narrative fragments following the same approach as for the CBC stories, that is, we looked for metanarratives from which these narrative fragments might draw discursive significance and meaning. We identified five broad themes (described earlier): (1) the Arab Spring as an expression of male Arab anger, (2) the Arab Spring as a collapse of social order, (3) the Arab Spring protests as a democratic uprising, (4) the protests as a response to tyranny, and (5) the Arab Spring as an East–West clash of civilizations. We described each of these themes earlier, in detail.

Let us consider the UGC recording Bouazizi's self-immolation (figure 1 shows an image extracted from it). The story was shown on France 24 on 30 December 2010 and lasted 1:48 minutes. It begins with a clip showing a group of mostly male citizens taking to the streets in the city of Sidi Bouzid, where the self-immolation occurred. They are, the commentary tells us, protesting against high unemployment; there is no mention at this stage of the self-immolation or of the anger of the Arabs. After ten seconds, the story shows another ten-second clip about a demonstration happening in another city, where lawyers (again mostly men) are protesting against the corrupt legal system. The poor quality of both clips (washed-out colours, shaky camera work, poor composition) identifies these images as UGC. The commentary informs the viewers that in both demonstrations, the mood was tense but peaceful.

These two UGC clips are followed by professional and formal footage showing the president, Ben Ali, declaring that the demonstrations are damaging the country's reputation. The commentary translates the words of the president, who is saying that the protests are being fomented by a handful of evildoers who are trying to convince other people to follow them and thereby shatter the civil peace. The commentary asserts that Ben Ali blames the media for broadcasting false information that is hostile to the government and to Tunisia. Ben Ali, the commentary says, asserts that these people will be subjected to the law, which will be applied firmly and severely. There is no mention of the lack of democracy in Tunisia or the tyranny of the ruling government.

The commentary goes on to explain that the demonstrations began with the self-immolation by Bouazizi, "a jobless graduate," in response to the police confiscating the few fruit and vegetables he was trying to sell to earn a living. The video here shows, for nine seconds, fuzzy images of what appears to be a fire, which we are to believe is that self-immolation. It is followed by another video, this one showing a quiet crowd in front of a courthouse, with no explanation given for that assembly.

The video ends with views of streets with orderly cars; the commentary now states that protests in Tunisia are rare because the ruling institutions keep a firm lid on dissent; the implication here is that the uprisings are a democratic response to state tyranny (rather than, say, mob rioting or the work of radical activists).

The two UGC clips that open the story have structured the content in the sense that they show demonstrations against the government's weak and corrupt administration; however, this kind of structuring is not always used. As noted earlier, when TV news networks produce and distribute information, their use of UGC reflects a complex system of relationships generated by human interventions, often in unstructured situations that can be hard to explain.

For example, the UGC showing the self-immolation is of such poor quality that its representative value is limited; it could be depicting nearly anything. We can thus assert that its use in the story is indirectly related to the rational arguments in the explicit news narratives, suggesting possibly a gendered dimension to the uprising as a whole and a kind of chaos and breakdown of social order. Although the commentary is making some effort to explain the events, the images are not necessarily providing visual evidence of them. This suggests that excess meaning (i.e., in excess of the explicit news narratives) is perhaps being imported into the news discourse.

Other studies of Western ideological tendencies in the coverage of events in the Middle East support some of these findings.[41]

CBC versus France 24: Similarities and Differences in Use of UGC

In assessing the excess narrative content of individual UGC, we noted both similarities and differences in the themes represented. In terms of similarities, in both cases the most common theme was citizens taking to the streets, including crowds chanting, throwing stones, standing behind barricades, or just peacefully walking; these are "conventional" expressions of conflict between states and crowds of protesters. Moreover, at times, both France 24 and CBC used images that were *indecipherable*, due to the poor quality of the image or the lack of context. So one could say that in these cases, the effect of "heightening authenticity" was almost lost. Mortensen writes that amateur-produced images close the gap between *seeing* and *saying*, but when closing the gap also makes the image indecipherable, it is not saying anything.[42] So the question is this: why have the clips been included? Our answer is, in part, that they serve to create eyewitness textures that have less to do with who, what, where, why, and how and more to do with creating a sensibility suggesting proximity, immediacy, and authenticity. As well, most of the UGC used by both CBC and France 24 evoked a strong affective state by depicting shocking events. Finally, for both CBC and France 24, most UGC (90 per cent) located the viewer in close proximity to events being depicted.

However, there were important divergences between the two networks. While we found similarities in the ways that both France 24 and CBC strategically used UGC, the frequency of those themes differed for each network, as did some of the themes themselves. In France 24's coverage of events, the most common visual was of groups of Arab men expressing anger – shouting, throwing stones, and so on (six clips focused on these kinds of images). Overall, women were noticeably absent from the UGC;[43] they were represented in only two clips. One of these showed an Arab woman shouting angrily in a crowd in the street; the other, an Arab woman being dragged on her back through the street by police in Cairo, her shirt ripped open, and a soldier stomping violently on her chest. We have only these two very different female representations during the conflicts, one woman is defiant, the other a victim.

Yet on the CBC, male Arab anger featured in only around 10 per cent of the news stories. The most common theme in CBC coverage was the tyranny of the Arab state (which in France 24's coverage was fourth most common). On both networks, the second most common rhetorical theme was the collapse of social order, followed by the democratic uprising. France 24's second most common visual narrative was of crowds in the streets, proximal to property destruction, whereas the CBC focused on injured protesters. The third most common narrative for the CBC was state violence against protesters; for France 24, it was Bouazizi's self-immolation. In fact, perhaps to spare the feelings of viewers, the CBC was sparing in its use of the footage of Bouazizi's act. Then followed state violence against protesters for France 24 and, for the CBC, people in the streets, proximal to property destruction. Finally, France 24 only briefly mentioned police violence (even torture) against those it had captured, while it was mentioned several times by the CBC.

Table 7.2   Themes in excess of explicit news narratives

CBC	1. Arab Spring as the expression of the tyranny of Arab states 2. Arab Spring as collapse of social order 3. Arab Spring as democratic uprising 4. Arab Spring as expression of male Arab anger. 5. Arab Spring as the product of new media, i.e., technological determinism
France 24	1. Arab Spring primarily as an expression of male Arab anger (with minor representation of Arab Spring including angry women, and victimized women, and peacefully demonstrating male professionals) 2. Arab Spring as collapse of social order 3. Arab Spring as democratic uprising 4. Arab Spring as the expression of the tyranny of Arab states 5. Arab Spring as a clash of civilizations East v. West

The finding that these themes are not found at the same frequency between broadcasters supports the thesis that UGC is used for discursive work in excess of what is ostensibly its intended purpose. Audiences, journalists, and news editors should all be cognizant of this.

At the structural level, in about 80 per cent of the stories shown by France 24 (nine of the eleven), UGC was central to the news coverage in the sense of being at the core of the visual narrative. That makes it all the more important to understand how it is used. In contrast, for the CBC, UGC always played a secondary role; it was added into a much broader visual narrative as either visual evidence or eyewitness texture.

Another difference between the two networks related to how UGC was identified. France 24 never explicitly identified UGC; we had to discern it largely on basis of picture quality (from news stories identified by France 24 as containing UGC). On the CBC, by contrast, fully three quarters of the news stories specified when UGC was being used, either with a graphic overlay or in the voiceover narration. With both broadcasters, though, most of the UGC related directly to the main issue of the coverage.[44]

Worth noting is this final observation: CBC coverage linked the Arab Spring to social media; France 24 coverage[45] linked it to a clash of civilizations, East against West.

Discussion

At the time of the Arab Spring, the use of UGC in newsrooms was still relatively new; since then, it has become well integrated into news-gathering and production routines in many if not most news organizations. In this regard, the Arab Spring serves as a snapshot of a time when the journalism profession was changing, and no doubt our findings reflect some of those instabilities and inconsistencies.

What is important in our findings, from our perspective, is that UGC can at times import themes in excess of intended narratives, an outcome most crucially linked to the absence of verified facts in UGC. The clips often "float" free of verification procedures, thereby shaping news outcomes in subtle and unexpected ways. The affective qualities of UGC can at times offer an eyewitness texture that draws viewers into close proximity to urgent events that fit into larger historical narratives, while at the same time giving "distant others" a "voice into news network discourse."[46]

The selection of Arab Spring clips apparently was done within a highly compressed time frame, given that UGC is most relevant and useful to news organizations when news is just beginning to break. At the time of the Arab Spring, the protocols for using UGC, at least at the CBC, were in their formative stages, both technologically and in terms of news practice. To heighten the authenticity of the information they provide, most television newsrooms today have been restructured in whole or in part to incorporate UGC in many different forms into all production routines. In fact, the distinctions between television news production and production for other platforms are increasingly irrelevant in today's newsrooms, where content is gathered and packaged by a news team and then later circulated on different platforms.

One unexpected finding related to how UGC was integrated into news coverage. Specific rules seemed to be lacking, at least with France 24. It was a matter of seizing opportunities and adapting to the situation at hand, and this sometimes created decontextualized moments, as suggested by Mortensen.[47] One consequence of relying on opportunity is that, as the conflict prolongs itself, the use of amateur videos becomes less and less frequent, since most news organizations eventually are able to dispatch professional reporters to "the ground." It seems that

Figure 7.1   Still frame image taken from amateur footage of the immolation of Mohammed Bouazizi, a fruit vendor in Sidi Bouzhid, Tunisia, that appeared in multiple news stories by France 24.

after a few weeks, UGC was perceived as being useful only for adding authenticity to reports – that "eyewitness texture" mentioned earlier – in order to satisfys the public's desire for proximity and immediacy.

During the Arab Spring, specific rules also seemed to be lacking regarding the length of UGC used by France 24. As noted earlier, the time allotted to UGC in news coverage is generally longer at the beginning of a conflict, although usually limited to a minute or so. If the quality of the video is rather bad, which it was for the self-immolation (see figure 7.1), it is trimmed to a few seconds.

Another characteristic of the integration of amateur video into news coverage by France 24 is that very short clips are sometimes stacked together in a montage created by professional editors. This can be verified by the different qualities of the UGC and by the different backgrounds of the image. The idea behind this practice is not clear, as some UGC does not seem to add new meaning to the news; rather, it appears to be "filling" the space with "authentic" images that produce an eyewitness texture – not always successfully.

This sort of practice raises the question of whether UGC used in news coverage provides "immediate" information, as suggested by Ahva and Hellman.[48] Also, do some news editors reuse it at times? More than once, we have seen the same UGC used in news stories provided on different

Figure 7.2   Still frame from amateur footage used in a CBC news story about protests in Tunisia

dates. This diminishes, if not cancels, the effect of its immediacy. The silence of the commentators on this issue is suggestive and at the very least reflects unclear intentions.

Another important aspect of the UGC used in the Arab Spring coverage was its easily identifiable visual qualities, including shaky images (often close proximity to tumultuous events), desaturated colours, and pixelated forms (as is obvious in the self-immolation video in figure 7.1 and in another still frame from a UGC clip in figure 7.2). These images can provoke ambiguities in terms of their legibility; simultaneously, the poor quality of the UGC suggests immediacy of coverage and authenticity of the image. It satisfies the desire of news organizations and viewers alike to be "eyewitnesses" to events. When such a poor-quality video is part of a professional report – sometimes only for a few seconds – it discursively constitutes proof that what the reporter is discussing has really happened, or even better, is happening right now. It provides textures of authenticity, proximity, and immediacy.

Most intriguing of all, perhaps, are the narrative implications of UGC. When it has been stripped of any evidentiary value, UGC offers a fascinating visual palette. What do the images *mean*? And what do they mean within the tightly edited argumentation of a brief news story? Besides providing textures of authenticity, the images can evoke and invoke cultural themes, norms, and values. The eyewitness textures are not value-neutral and often challenge existing hierarchies, as Chouliaraki suggests.[49] For the CBC, the most common themes woven into news narratives included the Arab Spring as a public response to Arab state tyranny, as the collapse of social order in Tunisia and Egypt, and as forms of democratic uprising. For France 24, the most common themes woven into news narratives included the Arab Spring as an expression of male Arab anger, as the collapse of social order, and as a democratic uprising. To understand the significance of these themes, which routinely emerged in news stories, we can imagine other possibilities that could be produced by other kinds of images: the Arab Spring as a form of sedition or terrorism, as an aspect of Arab social order (which is largely how protest is understood in Western liberal democracies), as a tightly organized and peaceful attempt to shape political outcomes by men and women from all strata of society, and so on. UGC, at least sometimes, despite its heightened status as authentically "eyewitness" and neutral – does much of the heavy lifting, so to speak, in aligning news outcomes within hegemonic discourses.

Conclusion

A question we must ask is whether the different self-regulated systems through which the two distinct media organizations we examined incorporate UGC into their coverage resulted in divergent information conveyed by their coverage. France 24, with its system of a pool of "collaborators,"[50] had the opportunity to use more amateur-produced images than the CBC, yet as we have seen, it did not make much difference. Both organizations inserted only very short clips into their regular coverage.

We said earlier that the use of UGC organizes audience encounters with "reality," giving rise to news outcomes that exceed the intended results of professional conventions for verification and objectivity. So, how does UGC influence the coverage of conflicts? Is it truly a decentralized and unregulated way of producing authentic information about the conflicts covered? The fact is, the average length of the clips used in each of the news networks examined was very short (less than a minute), and they were used not only sparingly, albeit prudently and strategically. In a society in which news is consumed increasingly bit by bit on social media platforms (especially by young people),[51] a few seconds extracted from UGC may be long enough to give viewers the sense that they were there, which is no doubt good for the news production market.

Of particular interest in our findings is the idea that UGC can introduce discursive values based on the "voice of distant others" into news outcomes in excess of the news narratives intended. For example, the images we examined might suggest that the Arab Spring protests were almost exclusively male, that they were spontaneous outbursts of anger caused by new media forms of collectivity at a time when Islamic civilization was suddenly collapsing within the broader historical context of a clash of civilizations, East against West. But this outcome would elide many critically important aspects of the Arab Spring, including an active demographic of women protesters involved throughout the uprising and the significance of pre-existing grassroots networks of activists who had developed sophisticated skills for planning, organizing, and mobilizing large-scale public engagement.[52] It also obscures the complex and ongoing political, economic, and military relationships and alliances between Western governments and the Arab countries affected by the Arab Spring uprisings.[53] The eyewitness textures of UGC in some cases led to implied meanings that tied news narratives to these broader and largely ideological forms of discursive significance, something that, in our estimation, editors and journalists alike – and the public – should be aware of when navigating the complexities of incorporating UGC into news narratives.

Notes

There exists an earlier version of this chapter titled "Eye Witness Texture of Conflicts: Contribution of Amateur Videos to News Coverage of the Arab Spring," *Global Media Journal* (German ed.) 8, no. 1 (2018): 1–52.

1 For more on the use of UGC during the Arab Spring, see chapter 9 (Lithgow).
2 For an in-depth look at France 24, see chapter 6 (Lithgow and Martin); for a discussion of UGC at the CBC, see chapter 5 (Lau et al.).
3 For more on the perception of authenticity and proximity, see chapter 10 (Santos).
4 See Popple and Thornham, *Content*; Harkin et al., *Deciphering*; Duffy and Dhabi, "Networked"; Santos, "So-called"; and Beckett, *Value*.
5 See Ahva and Hellman, "Citizen"; and Wahl-Jorgensen et al., "Audience."

6 See Pantti, "Getting Closer?"
7 See Anden-Papadopoulos, "Media"; Mortensen and Kristensen, "Amateur"; and Singer, "Quality."
8 Silverman, *Verification Handbook* and *Verification Handbook for Disinformation.*
9 From an archive located at Carleton University.
10 Kincheloe and McLaren, "Rethinking."
11 See Fürsich, "In Defense."
12 Dahlgren, *Visual*, 5090.
13 See Hansen, "Reality."
14 Georgakapoulou, "Small Stories."
15 Small stories are not "highly tellable," but rather lack clearly marked beginnings, middles, and ends, often describing non-linear events situated within other forms of narrative-making, with an emphasis on the "detachability" of the narrative fragment and its ability to be recontextualized, and its use in the co-construction of meanings between teller and audience. Small stories are incomplete in context, often reflecting an immediacy of circumstance. "Sharing events as they are happening," writes Georgakapoulou, "completely changes the handling of a story's point: the point is not known to the teller (yet), but is emerging through the tellings in collaboration with the audience" ("Small Stories," 262). Furthermore, as with the amateur videos in the Arab Spring, small stories often reflect the narration of experiences not allowed or discouraged from circulation by hegemonic forces. In this sense, "small stories research serves as an epistemology rather than just an analytical toolkit. It becomes an ideological standpoint for the analyst who seeks to 'listen' to such counter-stories and make them hearable" (263).
16 The presence and significance of narratives in news reporting has been widely studied; see Adam, *Notes*; Bird and Dardenne, "Myth"; Carey, "Dark Continent"; Chalaby, *Invention*; and Roeh, "Journalism."
17 Metanarratives are structures of meaning that present assumed forms of knowledge and order of a time and place and that reinforce the status quo (Lyotard, *Postmodern*; "Metanarrative," New World Encyclopedia).
18 For more on the aesthetics of UGC, see chapters 9 (Lithgow) and 10 (Santos).
19 The importance of affect in connection with news images has been documented in various studies, including Brantner et al., "Effects"; Gray, "News"; Pfau et al., "Influence"; and Seib, *Global*.
20 As mentioned earlier, the proximity effect of amateur footage has also been explored by Pantti ("Getting Closer?").
21 AR 20110220.
22 Chouliaraki, "I Have a Voice" and "Witnessing."

23 AR 20110226 DUNN LIBYA TODAY.

24 AR 20110228 MACDONALD LIBYA DIPLOMACY.

25 Chouliaraki, "I Have a Voice."

26 AR 20110114 CBC NATIONAL AIR FRI 2300.

27 AR 20110129 CBC YouTube video.

28 AR 20110215 MACDONALD MIDEAST TURMOIL.

29 AR 20110215 MACDONALD MIDEAST TURMOIL 18 AR 20110216 MCKENNA ANATOMY PART I.

30 AR 20110216 MCKENNA ANATOMY PART I.

31 AR 20110128 CBC NATIONAL AIR FRI 2300.

32 Other studies of orientalism in news and Western moral panics about Muslims lend support to these findings. See Bonn, "Social"; Karim, "American"; Said, *Orientalism*; and Saeed, "Media."

33 For more on Western notions, discourses, and conventions with regard to news media, see the Prologue and chapter 8 (Burchell and Fielding).

34 See Al-Ali, "Gendering"; Al-Natour, "Role of Women"; Bargain et al., "Women's"; Hafez, "Revolution"; Johansson-Nogués, "Gendering"; Khamis, "Revisiting"; and Radsch, "Unveiling."

35 See Aourgh and Alexander, "Egyptian"; Hassan, "Making"; and Salvatore, "New Media."

36 See Bunce, "Rebellious"; Cole, "Egypt's"; and Hanafi, "Arab."

37 See Kroes, "Signs."

38 See Herland, "Western"; and Ventura, "Arab Spring."

39 Hanafi argues that the term "Arab Spring" itself is orientalist, preferring instead the regionally employed term "Arab revolutions." Hanafi argues that the Arab revolutions should be "read as continuities in a long history of protest in the region rather than a total rupture." "Arab," 41).

40 Anden-Papadopoulos and Pantti, *Amateur*, 12.

41 See note 29.

42 Mortensen, "Witnessing" and *Journalism*, 30.

43 One could infer, from this finding, that most UGCs were produced and provided by male citizens.

44 The question of unlabelled amateur video remained unanswered, in part due to the length of time that had passed and our inability to locate the people directly involved in the editing decisions at the time. The most likely explanation is that it had been verified to the satisfaction of the broadcaster.

45 Anecdotally, one of the researchers was in Rome at the beginning of February 2011, and watched the news coverage of the Arab Spring from France 24, since it was the only available channel there in French. She noticed that this technological deterministic argument was coming up regularly in the comments accompanying the visual narrative.

46 Chouliaraki, "I Have a Voice."
47 Mortensen, "Witnessing" and *Journalism*.
48 Ahva and Hellman, "Citizen."
49 Chouliaraki, "I Have a Voice" and "Witnessing."
50 For an in-depth look at France 24, see chapter 6 (Lithgow and Martin).
51 From a study carried by the American Press Institute, quoted in Emma Teitel, "Online bias a real concern," *Toronto Star*, 15 May 2016, A20.
52 See Al-Ali, "Gendering"; Al-Natour, "Role of Women"; Hafez, "Revolution"; Hassan, "Making"; Hirst, "One Tweet"; Newsome and Lengel, "Arab"; Radsch, *Unveiling*; and Warf, "Myths."
53 See Hamid, "Islamism."

Bibliography

Adam, S. *Notes towards a Definition of Journalism*. St Petersburg: Poynter Institute, 1993.

Ahva L., and M. Hellman. "Citizen Eyewitness Images and Audience Engagement in Crisis Coverage." *International Communication Gazette* 77, no. 7 (2015): 668–81.

Al-Ali, N. "Gendering the Arab Spring." *Middle East Journal of Culture and Communication* 5 (2012): 26–31.

Al-Natour, M. "The Role of Women in the Egyptian 25th January Revolution." *Journal of International Women's Studies* 13, no. 5 (2012): 59–76.

Anden-Papadopoulos, K. "Media Witnessing and the 'Crowd-Sourced Video Revolution.'" *Visual Communication* 12, no. 3 (2013): 341–57.

Anden-Papadopoulos, K., and M. Pantti. *Amateur Images and Global News*. Chicago: University of Chicago Press, 2011.

Aourgh, M., and A. Alexander. "The Egyptian Experience: Sense and Nonsense of the Internet Revolution." *International Journal of Communication* 5 (2011): 1344–58.

Bargain, O., D. Boutin, and H. Champeaux. "Women's Political Participation and Intrahousehold Empowerment: Evidence from the Egyptian Arab Spring." *Journal of Development Economics* 141 (2019): 102379.

Beckett, C. *The Value of Networked Journalism*. London: POLIS, London School of Economics, 2010.

Bird, E., and R. Dardenne. "Myth, Chronicle, and Story: Exploring the Narrative Qualities of News." In *Media, Myths and Narrative*, edited by J. Carry, 67–86. Newbury Park: Sage, 1988.

Bonn, S. "The Social Construction of Iraqi Folk Devils: Post-9/11 Framing by the G.W. Bush Administration and US News Media." In *Global Islamophobia Muslims and Moral Panic in the West*, edited by G. Morgan and S. Poynting, 83–100. Burlington: Ashgate, 2012.

Brantner, C., K. Lobinger, and I. Wetzstein. "Effects of Visual Framing on Emotional Responses and Evaluations of News Stories about the Gaza Conflict 2009." *Journalism and Mass Communication Quarterly* 88, no. 3 (2011): 523–40.

Bunce, V. "Rebellious Citizens and Resilient Authoritarians." In *The New Middle East: Protest and Revolution in the Arab World*, edited by F. Gerges, 446–68. Cambridge: Cambridge University Press, 2013.

Carey, J. "The Dark Continent of American Journalism." In *Reading the News*, edited by R. Manoff and M. Schudson, 146–96. New York: Pantheon, 1986.

Chalaby, J. *The Invention of Journalism*. London: Macmillan, 1998.

Chouliaraki, L. "I Have a Voice: The Cosmopolitianism and Ambivalence of Convergent Journalism." In *Citizen Journalism: Global Perspectives*, edited by S. Allan and E. Thorsen, vol. 2, 51–66. New York: Peter Lang, 2014.

– "Witnessing without Responsibility." Keynote talk at Eyewitness Textures Symposium, 23–4 May 2019, MacEwan University, Edmonton, Alberta.

Cole, J. "Egypt's Modern Revolutions and the Fall of Mubarak." In *The New Middle East: Protest and Revolution in the Arab World*, edited by F. Gerges, 60–79. Cambridge: Cambridge University Press, 2013.

Duffy, M.J., and A. Dhabi. "Networked Journalism and Al-Jazeera English: How the Middle East Network Engages the Audience to Help Produce News." *Journal of Middle East Media* 7, no. 1 (2011): 1–23.

Fürsich, E. "In Defense of Textual Analysis: Restoring a Challenged Method for Journalism and Media Studies." *Journalism Studies* 10, no. 2 (2009): 238–52.

Georgakopoulou, A. "Small Stories Research: Methods – Analysis – Outreach." In *The Handbook of Narrative Analysis*, edited by A. De Fina and A. Georgakopoulou, 255–72. Malden: Wiley Blackwell, 2015.

Gray, J. "The News: You Gotta Love It." In *Fandom: Identities and Communities in a Mediated World*, edited by C. Sandvoss, S. Harrington, and J. Gray, 75–87. New York: NYU Press, 2007.

Hafez, S. "The Revolution Shall Not Pass Through Women's Bodies: Egypt, Uprising, and Gender Politics." *Journal of North African Studies* 19, no. 2 (2014): 172–85.

Hamid, S. "Islamism, the Arab Spring, and the Failure of America's Do-Nothing Policy in the Middle East." *Atlantic*, 19 October 2015. https://www.theatlantic.com/international/archive/2015/10/middle-east-egypt-us- policy/409537.

Hanafi, S. "The Arab Revolutions: The Emergence of a New Political Subjectivity." *Contemporary Arab Affairs* 5, no. 2 (2012): 198–213.

Hansen, K. "Reality in TV Journalism: Dramaturgy of the Motor." *Nordicom* 25, nos. 1–2 (2004): 227–37.

Harkin, J., K. Anderson, L. Morgan, and B. Smith, eds. *Deciphering User-Generated Content in Transitional Societies: A Syrian Coverage Case Study*. Centre for Global Communication Studies, Annenberg School for Communication, University of Pennsylvania, 2012.

Hassan, K. "Making Sense of the Arab Spring: Listening to the Voices of Middle Eastern Activists." *Development* 55, no. 2 (2012): 232–8.

Herland, H.N. "The Western Demonization of Muslims." *Foreign Policy Journal*, 13 January 2017. https://www.foreignpolicyjournal.com/2017/01/13/the-western-demonization-of-muslims/#comments.

Hirst, M. "One Tweet Does Not a Revolution Make: Technological Determinism, Media, and Social Change." *Global Media Journal – Australian Edition* 6, no. 2 (2012): 1–11.

Johansson-Nogués, E. "Gendering the Arab Spring? Rights and (In)security of Tunisian, Egyptian, and Libyan Women." *Security Dialogue* 44, nos 5–6 (2013): 393–409.

Karim, K. "American Media's Coverage of Muslims: The Historical Roots of Contemporary Portrayals." In *Muslims in the News Media*, edited by E. Poole and J. Richardson, 116–27. New York: I.B. Tauris, 2006.

Khamis, S. "Revisiting Cyberactivism Six Years after the Arab Spring: Potentials, Limitations, and Future Prospects." In *Media in the Middle East*, 3–19. London: Palgrave Macmillan, 2017.

Kincheloe, J., and P. McLaren. "Rethinking Critical Theory and Qualitative Research." In *The Landscape of Qualitative Research*, edited by N.K. Denzin and Y.S. Lincoln. Thousand Oaks: Sage, 2003.

Kroes, R. "Signs of Fascism Rising: A European Americanist Looks at Recent Political Trends in the US and Europe." *Society* 54, no. 3 (2017): 218–25.

Lyotard, J.-F. *The Postmodern Condition: A Report on Knowledge*. Minneapolis: University of Minnesota Press, 1984.

"Metanarrative." *New World Encyclopedia*. 2014. http://www.newworldencyclopedia.org/p/index.php?title=Metanarrative&oldid=984936.

Mortensen, Mette. *Journalism and Eyewitness Images: Digital Media, Participation, and Conflict*. New York: Routledge, 2015.

– "Witnessing War: Proximity and Distance." Keynote talk at Eyewitness Textures Symposium, 23–4 May 2019, MacEwan University, Edmonton, Alberta.

Mortensen M., and N. Kristensen. "Amateur Sources of Breaking the News, Meta Sources Authorizing the News of Gaddafi's Death." *Digital Journalism* 1, no. 3 (2013): 352–67.

Newsom, V., and L. Lengel. "Arab Women, Social Media, and the Arab Spring: Applying the Framework of Digital Reflexivity to Analyze Gender and Online Activism." *Journal of International Women's Studies* 13, no. 5 (2012): 31–45.

Pantti, M. "Getting Closer?" *Journalism Studies* 14, no. 2 (2013): 201–18.

Pfau, M., M. Haigh, T. Shannon, and T. Tones. "The Influence of Television News Depictions of the Images of War on Viewers." *Journal of Broadcasting and Electronic Media* 52, no. 2 (2008): 303–21.

Popple, S., and H. Thornham. *Content Cultures: Transformations of User Generated Content in Public Service Broadcasting.* New York: I.B. Tauris, 2014.

Radsch, C. *Unveiling the Revolutionaries: Cyberactivism and the Role of Women in the Arab Uprisings.* Houston: Rice University James A. Baker III Institute for Public Policy Research Paper, 2012. http://ssrn.com/abstract=2252556.

Roeh, I. "Journalism as Storytelling: Coverage as Narrative." *American Behavioral Scientist* 33, no. 2 (1989): 162–8.

Saeed, A. "Media, Racism and Islamophobia: The Representation of Islam and Muslims in the Media." *Sociology Compass* 1, no. 2 (2007): 443–62.

Said, E. *Orientalism.* New York: Pantheon, 1978.

Salvatore, A. "New Media, the 'Arab Spring,' and the Metamorphosis of the Public Sphere: Beyond Western Assumptions on Collective Agency and Democratic Politics." *Constellations* 20, no. 2 (2013): 217–28.

Santos, M.L.B.D. "The 'So-Called' UGC: An Updated Definition of User-Generated Content in the Age of Social Media." *Online Information Review,* 46(1):95-113. https://doi.org/10.1108/OIR-06-2020-0258.

Seib, P. *The Global Journalist: News and Conscience in a World of Conflict.* Lanham: Rowman and Littlefield, 2002.

Silverman, C. *Verification Handbook: An Ultimate Guide for Digital Age Sourcing for Emergency Coverage.* Maastricht: European Journalism Centre, 2014.

Silverman, C., ed. *Verification Handbook for Disinformation and Media Manipulation: A Definitive Guide for Investigating Platforms and Online Accounts to Reveal Inauthentic Activity and Manipulated Content.* Maastricht: European Journalism Centre, 2019.

Singer, J. "Quality Control." *Journalism Practice* 4, no. 2 (2010): 127–42.

Ventura, L. "The 'Arab Spring' and Orientalist Stereotypes: The Role
    of Orientalism in the Narration of the Revolts in the Arab World."
    Interventions 19, no. 2 (2016): 282–97.
Wahl-Jorgensen, K., A. Williams, and C. Wardle. "Audience Views on User-
    Generated Content: Exploring the Value of News from the Bottom Up."
    Northern Lights 8, no. 1 (2010): 177–94.
Warf, B. "Myths, Realities, and Lessons of the Arab Spring." *Arab World
    Geographer* 14, no. 2 (2011): 166–8.

8

What Hits Me the Hardest ...
The Photojournalist Blog

Genres and Practices of Journalistic Witnessing

KENZIE BURCHELL AND STEPHANIE FIELDING

"To witness is to wish that the record of the past were more whole"[1]

War is a particular type of crisis. War reporting is a necessary and dangerous confrontation with numerous obstacles for journalists and witnesses alike. Calling attention to such an emergency, to peril and suffering amounts to a moral-political intervention: as the old adage goes, coverage of war and suffering brings us the first rough draft of history. Yet various state and non-state actors often seek to hinder, if not control, the work of that drafting. When journalistic practice is to a degree precluded and journalists are forced out of a conflict zone, what genres and practices of witnessing are turned to by those who stay behind, and what if they could tell that story again?

Witnessing and bearing witness: these stand at the moral apex of social and political practices. When faced with danger and inhumanity, the individual acts with an urgency tethered to the protection of human life and with the moral force of providing testament to crisis, to tragedy, and to suffering.[2] Witnessing is inherently bound up with temporalities of current and unfolding events, urgent calls for action, and contributions to the future construction – and at times correction – of collective historical memory. The ubiquity of mobile phones and digital cameras, their image-producing affordances, and the readied networked reach of social media platforms have, in their confluence, radically extended the possibilities for ordinary people to take on distinct roles as users, eyewitnesses, and producers of imagery.[3] Those images can in turn influence the present course of current events and serve as documents for posterity to reflect on. Political state and non-state actors, from the partisan to the malevolent, have learned to strategically stymy the conditions for bearing witness; they have appropriated the same technologies and genres of witnessing for their own ends. Journalists and journalistic practices have doggedly adjusted to this landscape in order to provide a platform for those eyewitnesses. Along the way, they have found new ways to witness and bear witness themselves.

This chapter analyzes user-generated content (UGC) production practices by examining an emerging type of non-traditional user-turned-journalist generated content, which borrows the personal authenticity and subjective formats from UGC-style witnessing via the genre of diaristic blog, as a means to reflect on the experience of war reporting. We focus on *AFP Correspondent*,[4] an online, publicly available blog produced by correspondents, photojournalists, and their editors, a journalistic genre that stands in contrast to the traditional newswire bulletin, stories, and multimedia subscriber content produced by international news agencies for media outlets worldwide.

Our "on the ground" focus will be on the Syrian war, more specifically, on how international news agencies have covered that conflict's military campaigns and humanitarian crises.[5] Burchell has written elsewhere that Agence France-Presse (AFP) has maintained a more consistent on-the-ground presence in Syria than other international news agencies such as Reuters, AP, ITAR-TASS, and RIA NOVOSTI; the latter have relied more consistently for their content on governmental releases reported on from international capitals; this reflects conventionalized sourcing practices as well as the well-documented danger to journalists covering the war.[6] AFP was able to maintain its presence in part by training local non-journalists, who have documented their experiences in *AFP Correspondent*. This case study, then, examines retrospective personal blog–style essays reflecting on realities of conducting agency work amid the Syrian war, a context otherwise defined by unreported, underreported, and the divergent reporting of events.

The ten blog posts examined here were published between September 2014 and March 2018. They were chosen because of their focus on the unique experiences of Syrian UGC producers turned agency freelancers ("stringers"), experiences that turned them into professional photojournalists who could report on the war from within Syria when others could not. We supplement our study with additional analysis of the *AFP*

Charter,[7] an update to the AFP *Editorial Standards and Best Practices* guidelines,[8] and the concurrent AFP Annual Reports that reflected on Syria coverage and/or the use of UGC.[9] This case study focuses on the analytical gap that arises in understanding diverging genres of war reporting in a landscape increasingly influenced by Western notions of citizen journalism and other UGC witnessing practices. We ask two questions: How does the photojournalist blog, as an emerging news genre, offer a critical vantage point for better understanding the conditions of war and crisis reporting? And in considering news-making practices, what are the conditions for UGC-style witnessing by local non-journalists when they not only stand in for but become professionalized within international agency workflows?

The Implication of Labels: User, Citizen, Journalist

We will focus on emerging *genres of witnessing* as they intersect with shifting *journalistic practices*. News-making is influenced by and must adjust to the wider landscape of UGC production practices that increasingly fulfil the reporting function of witnessing and bearing witness to conflict and crisis. In particular, the discussion that follows seeks to develop a framework for understanding the changing conditions for witnessing and bearing witness, distinct but temporally related practices that come together amid unfolding crises when conventional journalistic practice is obstructed.

Both UGC and the AFP *Correspondent* blog make the unseen available, but in different ways from each other and in different ways from traditional agency reporting. When journalists take to blogging, the practice is distinct from yet informed by the everyday social media and blogging practices of non-journalist UGC producers. Set up in 2012, the AFP *Correspondent* blog is framed as "taking readers behind the scenes at a global news agency ... to give the public a glimpse inside of the 24-hour operations of the world's third largest news agency, whose 1,500 text, video and photo journalists span the globe in a vast, multilingual network."[10] We argue, however, that the AFP *Correspondent* blog does more than this.

Because of the assumed totality of global reporting networks, which are erroneously understood as a universal field of potential surveillance, undocumented forms of coordinated and systemic violence remain outside of public consciousness.[11] Traditional news as a genre (or rather a set of genres) additionally prioritizes newsworthy events, with the result that the painful realities of daily life amid conflict go undocumented. Genres of UGC image production is a thing apart from traditional war reporting: "In photojournalism, nonevents tend to escape from representation; in amateur photography they are the rule ... condition[ing] the seen and unseen, the visible and invisible."[12] Ordinary people in proximity to danger can and do provide an "embodied authenticity" that is legible in the images they capture as eyewitnesses.[13] Yet the apparently unassailable veracity of the image exaggerates the automaticity and neutrality of recording technologies, displacing the witnesses themselves along with their subjective accounts, personal experiences, biases, and motivations.[14]

International media's emphasis on the authenticity of witness accounts in the news, represented in this case by the images captured by (journalist-verified) UGC producers, involves a number of elisions particular to the hegemonic influence of Anglo-American and Western media conventions in international reporting. The framing of UGC as "citizen journalism" carries Western connotations of what it means to be a citizen vis-à-vis a nation-state and what it means to be a journalist vis-à-vis specifically Western manifestations of democratic ideals.[15] Assumptions about the role of journalism do not always take into account the realities of news media under non-democratic governments or in Arabic or Islamic contexts. Where a state media apparatus is accompanied by partisan, religious, or sectarian-oriented news media and social media channels, divergent representations of conflicts and crises can leave diverse publics without a shared understanding of unfolding events.[16] When Western definitions of civic agency are universally applied in relation to UGC production, further tensions of misrepresentation are produced through the universalizing misapplication of Westphalian notions of the nation-state, thus collapsing opportunities for responsible representations of the diverse forms of socio-political collective identity that are encountered across Arab and Muslim contexts.[17] Western conceptions of witnessing have long drawn from disparate historically contingent domains of Western theology, law, and science,[18] each with its own field-specific mediations via conventionalized sets of practices and related procedures or technology. These traditions mingle thresholds of uncertainty with conventions of knowledge production that cannot always be transposed onto other domains. The domain of journalistic witnessing is intertwined with these traditions – borrowing from Western antiquity through to the Enlightenment and toward modernity – of testament, of evidence, and of verifiable proof. This asserts a particular tradition of Anglo-Saxon–style factual reporting; the conventions for international newswire reporting on distant events then evolved from these into contemporary performances of objectivity in the news.[19]

The overreliance on UGC and citizen journalism in international reporting extended this tradition by collapsing the contexts and experiences of content production toward journalistic goals. This has often translated into either an overemphasis on the non-journalistic origins of the material or an obscuring of its origins in order to maintain institutional claims of objectivity.[20] International news agencies similarly assert their gatekeeping role as they selectively remediate local voices to align with their transnational subscribers and audiences.[21] The institutional and editorial parameters for selecting and verifying UGC material represent a type of conventionalized arbitration between what is democratic witnessing and what could be politically motivated if not propagandistic. By applying a postcolonial framework to digital media in such contexts, Omar Al-Ghazzi unpacks the ideological assumptions captured in the Western discourses related to citizen journalism.[22] The very notions of citizenship and journalism therein are entangled in practices of verification and the use of non-journalistic materials by international – in particular, Western – media outlets. Practices of verification involve assessing whether the contexts and motivations of UGC production demonstrably align with the civic virtues and democratic aspirations that will make them palatable to Western audiences.

This stands in contrast to material that cannot be disentangled from political motives and is thus deemed antithetical to Western conceptions of citizenship and the nation-state, whether that material is couched within matrices of local cultural and religious difference that are less understood by foreign journalists themselves[23] or within acts of UGC witnessing deemed politically destabilizing and thus framed as antidemocratic and as possibly espousing ideologies of division, hate, or extremism.[24] AFP Correspondent addresses some of these imbalances by communicating the embodied and social experiences of Syrian correspondents and where they are situated relationally in the wider network of an international agency; this in turn contributes to temporal dimensions of bearing witness that extend beyond the institutionalized conventions of newsworthy events.

The Syrian Civil War

The war in Syria, which has gone on for over a decade at the time of writing, has seen unstable, changing constellations of regional and international military actors. State and non-state actors enter and exit the fray, continually redrawing the military map. This geopolitical matrix has seen a reduction of US presence and corresponding changes in territorial control. De-escalation efforts negotiated by Turkey, Russia, and Syria gave way to flashes of renewed conflict in 2020, just before the world's attention shifted away from the civil war and toward the emerging COVID-19 pandemic. Earlier in the Syrian conflict, the extremist militant group ISIS held varying degrees of military control over swathes of territory spanning Syria and Iraq.[25] The kidnapping and execution of foreign journalists led many agencies to withdraw from the country, and in their absence, ISIS undertook a strategic campaign of "not merely producing videos" but also "acting as competing media outlets."[26] At the same time, journalists were less and less welcome in rebel-held Syria, becoming "targets, or commodities to be traded for ransom," according to AFP Global News Director Michèle Léridon.[27] Most international news agencies had stopped sending their own staff to Syria by mid-2013, and only the largest outlets or agencies could afford the time or labour to independently verify the UGC that was then being uploaded to social media platforms. This, as Murrell argues, left "the various participants in the war to put out their own versions of the truth."[28]

A comparative study encompassing five international news agencies found that AFP coverage of the Syrian conflict did demonstrate a particular commitment to reporting on developments from the "event-space" of particular urban military sieges and reporting on the resulting humanitarian crises.[29] This paralleled their commitment to reporting breaking news at critical junctures of these assaults and turning points in the resulting crises. AFP accomplished this in part by working with locals turned stringers and then professionalized agency photojournalists, who reflected on their experience in the AFP *Correspondent* blog. In interviews with content producers variably described as activists, citizen journalists, journalists, and photographers of the Syrian conflict, Mollerup and Mortensen found three incongruities in their relations with international media outlets.[30] First, these various labels were often determined and applied by others, including the media organizations that depended on them as content producers and sources. Second, while the work of the local Syrian photographers shaped international news coverage of the war in Syria, it did so in conformity to Western reporting norms. These UGC producers had set out to produce "alternative images from their local conflict,"[31] but having been turned into professional photojournalists, they were compelled to adapt to a rhetoric of humanitarian photography, one that spoke specifically to Western audiences. Third, as they brought the realities of the Syrian conflict to global audiences through photography, they found that their witnessing pratices had to align not only with the reporting conventions of international agencies but also with the vagaries of international news cycles. That is, they could only hope that the international media would engage with Syria as a priority among other news items.[32]

Boundaries and the Field of Journalism

While much of this edited collection focuses on UGC rather than journalist-generated eyewitness content, the framework presented here offers a path toward understanding changing journalistic practices in relation to UGC-style media production, in particular the co-constitution or possibly cross-fertilization of media practices within organizational or institutional conventions of media outlets, in which formal and traditional news production increasingly learns from non-journalistic media practices. The need for such a framework hinges on the blurring of that divide: media production is difficult to distinguish from the everyday media practices of journalists, just as it is sometimes difficult to distinguish non-journalists' content (which news media depend on) from professionally produced content. The AFP Correspondent blog offers a unique site where Syrian UGC producers who have been trained as stringers can reflect on the experience of becoming seasoned photojournalists covering a war that divides and ravages their country to this day.

Specific definitions of UGC distinguish it clearly from the media production and publication practices enshrined as "traditional" journalism. It is plain from this that it is professionals in the field who are defining what is and is not journalistic work, and doing so in ways that emphasize the integrity of their own professional content.[33] Yet some of the more traditional sourcing and reporting practices are becoming difficult to differentiate from those used by journalists who inhabit social media; similarly, non-journalistic actors increasingly intervene in those same social media spaces, strategically seeking to amplify, counter, drown out, or discredit the more "institutional" content of news media outlets. According to Witschge and colleagues, there is little new about the hybridity and technological change that characterize journalism today: journalism has always been a heterogenous complex of practices bundled together at different times in different ways to define the boundaries of field.[34] Wahl-Jorgensen posits that as news organizations develop strategies for the "cooptation and segregation" of UGC, subtle shifts are occurring in the epistemological truth claims of journalistic practice.[35] Knowledge is being produced through diverging and multiplying forms of storytelling through which the moral-political acts of witnessing and bearing witness are performed.

Events, Witnessing, and Bearing Witness

Witnessing involves a set of practices that are intrinsically and categorically defined by the embodied presence or absence, temporal concurrence or remove, of the witnesses themselves vis-à-vis the space and time of an event. This matrix of spatial and temporal alignment constitutes different forms of witnessing, as well as diverse typologies of events and their framing, which when combined with particular media and modalities of journalistic address amount to distinct genres of witnessing. John Durham Peters outlines these types of witnessing as the paradigmatic witnessing of "being there" in the event-space at the time of the event; "live transmission" through forms of simultaneous or near simultaneous mediated witnessing at a distance; the "historicity" of being removed in time but visiting the locale of the events in question; and finally the most tangential form of witnessing: "recording" for audiences that are removed spatially and temporally but are engaging in these transcribed and captured historic accounts.[36]

Bearing witness is a practice that is distinct from but depends on witnessing, extending onwards from one's presence at historical or contemporary experiences or events. To bear witness is to bring an account of that presence-based witnessing to others; it is a social and political practice that mediates the opportunity for others to understand what has been or is being witnessed. Paul Frosh argues that "presence is not just told," it "is also telling – it makes a difference."[37] Witnessing fundamentally involves one's presence in the simultaneous "present" of an ongoing event; however, there is an additional future-orientation of bearing witness that evokes the past or present in the name of social change as well as the persistence of social memory with the future in mind.

There are genre-specific slippages between contexts and conditions of production specific to UGC, witness accounts, and professional photojournalism when incorporated into international agency reporting. These categories of content production are conflated, or not, depending on the boundaries drawn between who is considered a journalist and who is not. It also depends on what is considered an event and thus framable as "news" by international news agencies, and what is not and dropped from coverage for that reason. Wagner-Pacifici argues that this sociological engagement with events uncovers the "restless 'handoffs' from one genre to another."[38] Witnessing practices beget particular types of event-oriented communicative performances that keep newsworthy developments coherent and alive despite their remediation across the modalities of witnessing, memory, and history. There is an "inability of any one genre to contain or fix events,"[39] because these diverse witnessing practices involve mediations across time and space, highlighting how the conventions of genre are interwoven with the affordances of communication technology.

Acts of witnessing are communicative events with performative power. The event-defining and event-oriented quality of such practices – the "eventness" – is the hinge between witnessing and bearing witness that comes to contradistinguish between genres and practices of journalistic witnessing. The currency of journalistic witnessing relies not only on the framing of particular developments as newsworthy events but also on the eventness of the reporting itself. Reed sees the eventness of particular sets of concrete actions (such as professional reporting and photojournalism) as the source of a performative power that serves to determine how others will come to understand or define a situation, transforming the expectations, emotions, and possibly coordination of action by other actors.[40]

The *AFP Correspondent* blog brings into sharp relief the disconnect between the institutionalized genre of objective agency reporting and the personal genre of subjective blog essay, often more associated with UGC than journalistic output. Events within the Syrian war are mediated by these genres, yet there is a genre-specific eventness to these types of reporting as well. The currency of reporting on events relates to their newsworthiness as crises, experiences, voices, and accounts, which are remediated from the local context for global audiences. For example, "emergency" as a category of event operates in conjunction with particular temporalities relating to exceptionalism and urgency, as well as the possibility that action can still be taken in relation to the event.[41] Much of the traditional international agency reporting on the Syria conflict examines the temporalities of particular events with these event-oriented notions of emergency and intervention;[42] this stands in contrast to inescapable quotidian experiences of the conflict and conflict reporting examined in *AFP Correspondent*.

Case Study: The *AFP Correspondent* Blog

The *AFP Correspondent* blog has a chronological, multi-author format. It applies a reflective, diary-like mode of address related to the experiences of practising journalists. Its entries cover topics as diverse as the conflicts in Syria and Yemen, the Black Lives Matter and Gilet Jaunes protests in the United States and France, the Australian wildfires, and coronavirus restrictions in mainland China and Hong Kong. The "weblog," now called a "blog," has been defined as "a form of writing that is unique to the Web"[43] and that, despite a vast array of contemporary journalistic blogs, was at first characterized by its Web-specific functionality (e.g., hyperlinks or multimedia) or diary format. The diaristic mode of address in news blogs is organized as a form of commentary: a particular voice or set of voices is "expressing experiences which find no outlet in conventional reporting."[44] Individual reflection is largely incongruent with the editorial standards of news agency bulletins, stories, and visual imagery production for client and subscriber networks. *AFP Correspondent* is one of four blogs run by the agency; there are similar Spanish- and French-language blogs, as well as "AFP Photo" on the separate Tumblr blogging platform, once again highlighting the elisions between this genre of news blog and the content found on platforms typically associated with UGC.

Journalistic blogs are a form of personal commentary on news stories and news-making; they fall outside traditional journalistic conventions and the restrictive editorial standards of brevity, currency, and objectivity. Bloggers deem the personal to have value in the public sphere.[45] Interviewed about AFP Correspondent in the AFP 2017 Annual Report, the journalist Marion Lagardère commented: "The blog is a way of following a story from a different viewpoint. What gives it power is the use of the first-person and the reporter's subjectivity ... Whenever one reports from the group, one speaks from a point of view, whatever it may be."[46]

In contrast to the strict reporting standards and institutionalized (if not simply anonymized) voice of agency bulletins and stories, the AFP Correspondent blog takes on subjective and reflective forms, thus providing an institutionalized space for journalists to bear witness to their own experiences of reporting from Syria. The methodology used prioritizes journalistic practices to examine what correspondents do and what they say about what they do, operationalized here through the representations of practice and reflections on practice that are included within the reporting and blogging itself. Drawing from practice-based sociology,[47] this analytical lens situates journalistic practices across the embodied, social, and relational experiences of the practitioners, further complicating our understanding of what is and is not reporting in terms of the past-, present-, and future-oriented temporalities of witnessing and bearing witness, as we will explore. This methodological lens has been deployed by means of critical discourse analysis to code the relevant blog essays in relation to policy documents; in this way, we are able to examine the institutional context of reporting and production practices represented in both sets of texts.[48] Given that this is a photojournalist blog, there are additional degrees of intertextuality specific to the multimedia space of the Web. Fairclough assigns to intertextuality "the property texts have of being full of snatches of other [media] texts, which may be explicitly demarcated or merged in, and which the text may assimilate, contradict, ironically echo, and so forth."[49] The intertextual cues within the blog provide perspective on the experiential histories of producing other media texts, some in circulation and some not. In the AFP Correspondent blog, photojournalists are able to publish and discuss many more photos produced for the agency in particular contexts than would have been previously taken up in the business-to-business news ecosystem based on a breaking news and subscriber service business model.

AFP *Correspondent* is not simply a journalist blog, it is also a space where non-journalists turned photojournalists – who came to report for AFP amid the Syrian conflict – make sense of their experiences for the wider public. As Matheson argues, blogs represent a space of journalistic production where "writing authoritatively *for* a public and writing *to* a public is renegotiated constructively."[50] The AFP blog entries provide an account not only of what was witnessed but also of the relational complexity of photojournalism reporting practices – complexity that is bracketed out of primary agency coverage. The photojournalist blog as a genre provides a space for bearing witness, for reclaiming both the experience of everyday life that persisted despite the conflict and the hope for the future of Syria.

Reporting as Embodied Social Practices

Much of the journalistic experience – arguably more so for photojournalists – is edited out of traditional journalistic accounts, from the embodied and social experience of reporting on war and suffering, to the relational complexities of working within a professional network of individuals spread across the country, region, and world. Due to the well-documented risks to foreign journalists in Syria during the conflict, with the exception of two teams that covered the siege of Raqa at different points in 2017, AFP had not sent any special correspondents to Syria since 2013. Day-to-day and on-the-ground coverage was provided by stringers, some of whom had been trained by AFP during a photography workshop in Turkey in June 2013.[51] The conflict represented a challenge to exactly how AFP could maintain its mission statement, which was "to provide accurate, balanced and impartial coverage of news *wherever* and *whenever* it happens in the world *on a continual basis*."[52] As one journalist states in reference to the blog's utility for audiences, "I am journalist … When I read an article, I can pretty well see how it was written and how the information was obtained. But the reader or listener does not necessarily have the ability to understand that context."[53] The experience of these stringers turned correspondents is an account of the witnessing practices of UGC producers turned photojournalists yet also an account of the journalistic practice of bearing witness to adverse conditions of reporting on conflict.

All practices of witnessing are embodied and social, whether they are occurring on the ground and therefore alongside those you are covering or at a distance at the editing desk of a regional bureau. In Abdulmonam Eassa's essay "If I Remain Alive: The Ghouta Diaries," about the bombardment of eastern Ghouta, Eassa was constantly confronted with this moral and professional decision: "Should I help him or continue to take pictures? It's a question that I constantly ask myself."[54] He reflects on the time he took the son of friend from the arms of a "White Helmets" volunteer (officially the Syria Civil Defence), carrying him to the hospital: "The boy holds on tight to me, he doesn't want to let me go. When we get inside, I want to take a picture of him, but he doesn't want to let go of my hand. I manage to free my hand, but he keeps holding his hand towards me. I can feel myself crying."[55]

In another instance, he sees a man on the ground: "It's a friend of mine. He has a head injury. He is dead. But we have to just leave his body there because there are wounded children and they have to be taken to the hospital."[56] Yet in the photojournalist's engagement with the potential subject there is a moral requirement that this be a caring social interaction, as Abd Doumany explains: "I behave differently when I photograph child victims. I look for a way to ease their pain if possible. Sometimes I tell them jokes, sometimes I show them how they came out on a picture, sometimes I let them take some pictures."[57] Doumany similarly outlines the complexity of photographing suffering, which for these photographers is both personal and social: "What hits me the hardest is seeing the pain of those who have lost loved ones. Usually I avoid photographing those scenes out of respect for them. I know exactly how they feel: I've lost one of my brothers in this war."[58]

In their interviews with citizen journalists, photojournalists, and other image-makers during the conflict in Aleppo, Mollerup and Mortensen found a sense of care for the well-being of victims: suffering was a reason not to photograph people or their next of kin.[59] This stands in contrast to the othering of Syrians that is intertwined with the assumption of detached distance by foreign correspondents, who seek to construct opportunities for Western audiences to witness suffering at a distance. In each of the instances above, reporting practices are intimately tied to the embodied but also socially situated experiences of these individuals as both witnesses and photojournalists.

Networks of Relational Institutional Practices

The blog also provides insight into the journalists' relational networks through dialogues between actors who occupy distinct practitioner roles within the agency, who are often geographically dislocated from one another even while working closely together. In "Covering Syria Through Hunger and Fear" and "The Last Days in Aleppo," one of the UGC producers turned photojournalists who had been covering Aleppo, Karam Al-Masri, writes alongside Rana Moussaoui, who was the AFP deputy bureau chief in Beirut at the time. Moussaoui offers a personal but also procedural account of their news-making – "since February 2016, we've 'lived' daily life with Karam"[60] – as they communicate through the messaging platform WhatsApp. In the same post, Karam reflects on his induction into the workflow, from being managed as a source and UGC producer to being trusted as a professional journalist, as Moussaoui explains: "He started off by giv[ing] us little bits of information. But then, after impressing us [his Beirut colleagues] with his rigour and accuracy, we started asking him for full stories." This rigour was soon recognized as an emerging mastery of professional agency standards: "He gave us everything we needed to tell the story … His images didn't even have to be edited."[61] On the one hand, these are reflections on the processes and conventions of institutionalized professional practices; on the other, they speak to the technologically mediated networks of contemporary international reporting and news production practices.

When emptied of these reflections and of the experience of producing news content, conventional news production often entails typifying news as events. In a conflict like Syria, there is additionally a strategic planning of military events with political actors coordinating engagement with the media by announcing particular sieges or declaring crises. Unfolding events are declared to be historic turning points or thresholds, and this masks the ongoing reality of the protracted conflict.[62] In contrast to these pre-framed events, the blog communicates the ongoing routines that constitute practices of covering conflict, as well as the exhaustion and trauma as these are compounded over the weeks, months, and years of coverage. Doumany, who captured the famous photo of the young boy Omran Daqneesh in the back of an ambulance, writes about the thousands of people injured and the routine nature of his many photographs of people carrying wounded or dead children from the rubble of an airstrike or bombardment. He interjects, as if both to himself and to the blog reader, "That sounds harsh, doesn't it? But that's what it has become. It has become routine."[63]

This routine does not just affect those reporting from the conflict zones. It also impacts the wider network of journalists and editors. Moussaoui works as a regional deputy bureau chief; even so, her writing offers a subjective account of Aleppo's devastation, likely gleaned from her interactions with Karam but also through his embodied, situated experiences, as captured in the photos being edited, communicating an authenticity related to his proximity to suffering: she was moved to write in a similar embodied manner that "the smell of the hunger [in Aleppo] is frightening."[64] In a protracted conflict such as this, the ubiquity of mobile phones has meant that both ordinary people and a diverse range of militarized actors are on the ground in Syria producing UGC that captures scenes of violence, killings, kidnapping, and torture. Digital imagery and video itself have been weaponized, and the resulting political and ideological complexity is often collapsed in the ways that international media use UGC as well as by the projection of Western ideals through the trope of the citizen journalist.[65]

Making sense of this information glut goes beyond just verifying UGC for its use in news production. Across the transnational network of international agency bureaux and their subscribers, there are different degrees of political and religious literacy among journalists and editors in relation to Syrian society.[66] Between news agencies there are also differences in editorial conventions that are further complicated by conventionalized sourcing patterns, in the sense that international agencies often hold a "nationalistic bias" toward ideologically aligned state actors.[67] This contributes to a Balkanization of news narratives circulating globally, which in turn provides opportunities to disseminate conflicting governmental framings of the conflict based on the diverse interests of the foreign powers involved.[68]

In contrast, reflections on the working relationships of the UGC producers-turned-photojournalists set the *AFP Correspondent* content apart from both traditional reporting and other UGC being produced amidst the Syrian conflict. Christian Chaise, the AFP regional director for the Middle East and North Africa, writes in another post about the growing danger of "post-traumatic stress" among the editors who worked closely with the local stringers during the early phases of the Syrian conflict.[69] In the blog post "Covering the Islamic State," AFP journalists at the Nicosia and Beirut bureaux who examined footage coming from ISIS-controlled areas were "deeply affected" by the sheer volume and graphic nature of the footage.[70] (The impact of UGC on journalists who must view it as part of the production cycle is discussed in a number of chapters in part I of this book.) Distinct from the reporting practices that produce the images, these journalistic practices and practitioners were rendered invisible by the mediations inherent in media production. But these types of media workers are part of that relational network of journalistic practice, a set of workflow conventions and editorial processes contributing to the mediated witnessing of the Syrian conflict by global publics.

Communicating the Everyday

Beyond the experience of witnessing as a local Syrian and as a photojournalist, something else is captured in the AFP *Correspondent* blog and similar blogs, that is, corrective contributions to the historical record of the conflict. It is not just that readers and audiences lack access to the behind-the-scenes elements of news production, it is also that the traditional news audience is "bombarded with information that often lacks perspective and is not presented to them in the right order."[71] These blogs bear witness to the temporalities of experience and hope that are absent from the institutionalized conventions of traditional reporting. Practices of bearing witness offer testaments to the daily life that persists amidst conflict and reclaim the hope for a future in Syria – hope that rarely finds its way into breaking news agency coverage.

The multipart essay "Syria Shimmers of Hope" presents parallel descriptions of the conflict through the distinct voices and perspectives of three UGC producers turned photojournalists: Abd Doumany in Douma, Delil Souleiman in Qamishli, and Sameer al-Doumy, writing from Paris after leaving Syria.[72] Their reflective vignettes are accompanied by photographs that bear witness to everyday life under and despite the conflict, as well as to the persistence of hope, which is not covered in the politicized accounts of sieges and crises, so often framed by the comments of governmental sources. The photojournalists reflect on their experiences of covering a conflict as part of a community, but they also reflect on editorial processes. Al-Doumy writes that "in daily life situations people react positively to me, they show their happiness. When I am covering destruction and bombing, they react differently ... Daily life photography gets me closer to people and helps me share their happiness and pain."[73] Similarly, Karam Al-Masri pitched the story of an older man who stayed in Aleppo, keeping watch over his car collection despite the conflict. As the Beirut editor reflected, "the images were touching and I remember in particular a sequence of the man listening to a record on his gramophone."[74] Souleiman writes that "there isn't only war and destruction, there's also joy and happiness in the Syrian reality"; he adds that "when people see images like these, they get some comfort because it can become repetitive to constantly look at image[s] from war – death, destruction, killing."[75] The blog post does include the more institutional style of reporting that recounts timelines, attacks, and casualities; Souleiman notes that he has "become a witness to the life and death of so many people."[76] Doumany expresses the temporality and corrective record offered by reflections: "Everything in Syria will fade and change, but these images will remain, documenting the war and destruction. But I hope that my images will also bear witness to the happiness and joy in times of war, a war that will surely end someday."[77] In these photojournalist blogs, the authors strive to bear witness to the lives, not just the deaths, of Syrians, thus balancing the earlier traditional journalistic record that their photography helped produce.

Again, while the AFP Correspondent blog provides a window onto the everyday of conflict through the eyes of these UGC producers turned photojournalists, the selective gatekeeping capacity of international agencies reinforces existing imbalances. These imbalances often preclude quotidian perspectives that are so central to UGC-focused alternatives to traditional news stories about Syria. Dina Matar's examination of the alternative media spaces produced and maintained by Syrian women demonstrates how the event-driven orientation of traditional news – in conjunction with patterns of gender inequality in war reporting and in newsrooms more generally – prevents many stories of the everyday from achieving wider circulation beyond Syria; instead, it is representations of conflict that enjoy the internationally and institutionally vetted notion of newsworthiness.[78] Matar describes how during times of crisis and societal upheaval, the disruption of the norms of daily life creates liminal moments for renegotiating societal conventions. These examples of alternative media open a path for renegotiating gendered patriarchal hierarchies, for changing expectations within Syrian society at the intersection of religious, professional, and family life. Traditional media's overdependence on the currency of events overlooks the conditions endemic to everyday life in times of conflict, overlooking then also how norms are being renegotiated as, and through, liminal spaces of UGC and alternative media beyond institutionalized newsmaking. Unlike traditional agency coverage, the AFP Correspondent blog draws on everyday life. Yet even that blog is circumscribed by a focus on journalists' experiences, and thus fails to challenge the persistent omission of particular voices in both journalism and war reporting.

Performative Mediations upon the Future

Bearing witness is about more than recounting the past; it is also an inherently future-oriented practice. Traditional photojournalism is often a representation of the *aftermath* of newsworthy events as events in and of themselves.[79] In both traditional reporting and UGC, event or aftermath witnessing often involves a second time frame, specifically the interval of time within which future harm can be prevented through some sort of intervention.[80] The AFP Correspondent blog offers yet another time frame, one that testifies to the impact of tragedy beyond the interval for immediate intervention. And yet another: a testament that carries a particular form of futurity, one of hope, which persists during, beyond, and despite the crises.

In conventional reporting and editorial practice, especially in the times and spaces of war, events compete for newsworthiness. Having been strengthened by repetition throughout the news cycle and across myriad news organizations, negative developments are more often treated as newsworthy.[81] This negative valence is central to a particular mode of eventness that links bearing witness to crisis and the future.[82] Anderson examines how the process of bearing witness seeks to "forestall" or "curtail" the imminent future being represented within a present crisis.[83] Journalism's reliance on eventfulness binds this notion of urgency with that interval between bearing witness and preventing further destruction.

Photojournalism in particular often involves a subtle but important temporal shift away from UGC eyewitness imagery that can capture a crisis as it is unfolding toward professional photojournalism,[84] which more often than not consists of photography of the "aftermath-as-event."[85] The aftermath-as-event is an extension of an event, one often rooted in the practical realities of representing the event from the scene only after it has occurred. Aftermath photography captures the harm produced by an event (such as a siege or chemical weapon attack) as representative of an ongoing crisis; in doing so, it emphasizes causality and temporality: event and aftermath are the cause and effect of crisis, with the effects shown linked to the possibility of intervention before further harm can be done. In traditional aftermath reporting, peace is referenced by its absence and bearing witness to the aftermath can be understood as "a possible first step towards peace."[86] Both traditional photojournalism and UGC offer temporal apertures to show the everyday of conflict as discussed above, yet in that everyday there is also a possible representation of hope for the future.

Reclaiming the persistence of joy in everyday life is the first step toward bringing back memories of a future for Syria beyond the war; it is how hope can accompany reporting on crises and suffering. Writing about his escape and journey from rebel-held eastern Ghouta to Idlib, which active conflict had not yet reached, Eassa ponders this temporal bridge where bearing witness links a record of the past with the future: "Maybe I'll live and tell the story of what happened here, talk about the crimes committed against us, about the hard days we had, and the beautiful days."[87] These reflections capture fear for Syria's future: "With no end in sight to the conflict, many fear that this war will produce a 'lost generation' of children, who will lack basic necessities and who will not have access to education."[88]

The essay "Syria Shimmers of Hope," written by three of the UGC producers turned photojournalists, opens with this uncredited contextual note: "Photographers who document wars in their own countries … often say the same thing. Their best-known images – the heartbreak and destruction of their homelands – are not the ones of which they are most proud. The ones of hope are – this is the subject of the blog."[89] These sorts of reflections on hope amidst suffering find a voice through the photojournalist blog; as Souleiman writes: "When the war ends, I will photograph life after death, I will photograph the traditions and customs of my country, I will photograph places that are full of life and hope."[90]

Conclusion: Practice Theory and Genre Contribution

As a genre, the photojournalist blog wrests personal and subjective control from the austere conventions of traditional news. Embodied, social, relational, and temporal dimensions of the reporting emerge in the photojournalist blog, which stands outside of the cycle of breaking news, giving new legacies and new futures to communities struggling amidst conflict. Blogs devoted to reporting on crises like war, catastrophe, and civil unrest reflect back upon journalistic experience and practice. But the photojournalist blog adds an additional layer of reflection: as a genre it consists of written reflections on embodied experience and social contexts that cannot be disentangled from the conditions of journalistic work despite their invisibility in the imagery itself. Importantly, this includes the conditions for producing those lesser-known images, the ones that do not gain traction or go viral among a wide array of agency subscribers. This demonstrates the ways in which the genre is necessarily reflexive: the intertextual, multimodality of photojournalistic production and the multiple genres inherent to journalistic output are both reflected in the blog's format and reflected upon as its subject. Relationally, this case study also highlights the complicated reporting and editorial practices that are largely hidden within the mediations of traditional news production, which is subject to conventional editorial framings that bracket out the labour and the networked interpersonal workflows undergirding news production. War reporting practices are also constrained by the material realities of the situation on the ground across a landscape that is often manipulated if not controlled by political actors with their own strategic agendas regarding what stories can be told and how.[91] As a genre, the photojournalist blog makes the unseen of photojournalism visible, from the real danger and emotional labour of those reporting on the ground to the vicarious trauma of professionals working with their material and the interpersonal practices that infuse and connect both contexts.

These conditions for journalistic practice are invisible in traditional coverage, but they can emerge through a critical discourse analysis of text and language. In this case study, they have been identified from within the findings of a wider multilingual comparative study of international agency coverage, using a triangulated critical discourse analysis of blog entries, policy documents, and annual reports to reveal traces and cues that demonstrate the conditions, decisions, and experiences inherent to newsmaking practices. As a case study, AFP *Correspondent* represents a unique platform, one that allows UGC producers who have become professional photojournalists to reflect on their experiences and thereby address the gap between media studies literature on eyewitness image production and journalism studies' engagement with newsroom practices of sourcing, vetting, and framing UGC and other publicly circulating open-source information.

In format as well as practice – and therein genre – the AFP *Correspondent* blog is wholly distinct from the news agency bulletin, photo, and video content as accessed by the agency's subscriber network. From a stance outside that commercial and business-to-business ecosystem, it highlights the experiences of journalistic practice removed from the objective formalities of informational subscriber journalism, where practices of witnessing speak to the subjective experience of being an on-the-ground image producer welcomed into an international news agency's network of bureaux, correspondents, and professionalized stringers.

The AFP *Correspondent* blog gives voice to the subjective experiences of photojournalists; in the blog essays we have examined, of becoming a photojournalist in response to a war ravaging one's own country. Such experiences fall outside the institutional frame of traditional agency reporting; but paradoxically, the task of the local photojournalists is to ensure that the agency can continue to practice its *own* form of journalism. In that sense, the blog highlights the persistent gatekeeping function of international agencies, which extends beyond determining what is newsworthy, instead distinguishing events from non-events and through that lens determining who is and who is not a journalist. That is, the editorial power to determine newsworthiness extends to determining who is a *reporter in contradistinction to a witness*. This demonstrates the centrality of international news agencies as hegemonic global institutions, as well as how contexts of suffering can so easily be flattened when reported on from a distance.

Even in *AFP Correspondent*, the subjective reflections on what it means to be reporting on the Syrian war remain circumscribed as an institutionalized form of UGC, specifically user-turned-photojournalist content: a traditional media institution remains the gatekeeper of the stories being told, the Western gatekeeper of who can tell the story of Syria, of which locally produced UGC can stand in for international journalistic content and which UGC producers will be accepted as international journalists. Even when expanding the breadth of traditional news to include the reflections of news practitioners, an international institution remains the arbiter of what is and is not war reporting and of who is and who is not a journalist. The vast complexities of local everyday experiences amidst the Syrian conflict remain outside the institutionalized news blog as a platform for witnessing. Among other collective bases for individual agency, the plurality of partisan, ethnic, religious, or pan-Arab identities are often flattened within representations of war and crisis when they are packaged for Western audiences,[92] while the myriad intersectionally varied voices of women and women journalists in Syria continue to be systematically excluded from spaces where traditional war reporting is happening, whether in the newsroom or in the field.[93]

AFP Correspondent is an important renegotiation of UGC into an institutionalized platform for reflecting on reporting and newsmaking practices; yet as a genre, the journalists' war blog often runs roughshod over possibilities for renegotiating societal norms amidst conflict. More specifically, the photojournalist blog offers a space for practices of bearing witness, where these UGC producers turned photojournalists can wrest the recent past back from the first draft of institutionalized reporting. It is where they can tell the stories of photographs that did not circulate worldwide and write down the lives of everyday Syrians as they are lived between, despite, and throughout the waging of war by others. The subjective and personal recounting of media work in the *AFP Correspondent* blog reclaims the embodied, social, and relational experience of war reporting by reasserting the subjective temporalities of witnessing and bearing witness. Drawing from the diarist genre of blog and UGC eyewitness practices, the photojournalist blog is a genre of journalistic witnessing that transcends the austere and limiting conventions of objective agency reporting while also wresting control of the narrative from military and governmental actors, whose decisions, commentary, and actions intervene in and inflect formal journalistic accounts. Through witnessing and bearing witness, the past and future of Syria are given life in reflective accounts of those who were there to capture the stories that others could not.

In the words of Abd Doumany, "I did my best to try and show their pain through my lens. You do your best to save them."[94]

Notes

1 Peters, "Witnessing," 722.
2 For more on the act of witnessing, see the prologue and chapter 9 (Lithgow).
3 See Mortensen, "Eyewitness."
4 As of the time of publication, AFP Correspondent is publicly available online at. https://correspondent.afp.com.
5 This case study, the wider project, the principal investigator, and the team of graduate researchers were funded by an Insight Development Grant (2017–2019) of the Social Sciences and Humanities Research Council of Canada and the JHI-UTSC Digital Humanities Fellowship (2019–20) awarded by the Jackman Humanities Institute and the University of Toronto Scarborough.
6 See Burchell, "Reporting."
7 AFP, AFP Charter.
8 Wishart and Léridon, "AFP Editorial," April 2016 and June 2016.
9 AFP, "AFP 2017 Annual Report."
10 See AFP, "About."
11 See Cottle, "Global"; Burchell, "Reporting."
12 Möller, "Peace," 36.
13 See Blaagaard, "Post-human."
14 See Peters, "Witnessing"; Burchell, "Take My Picture"; Hutchings and Burchell, "Media Genre."
15 See Al-Ghazzi, "Citizen."
16 See Powers and O'Loughlin, "Syrian."
17 Al-Ghazzi, "Citizen," 444–445.
18 See Peters, "Witnessing," 720; Frosh, "Telling Presences."
19 See Boyd-Barrett and Rantanen, Globalization.
20 See Sjovaag, "Amateur."
21 For more on gatekeeping, see chapter 5 (Lau et al.).
22 Al-Ghazzi, "Citizen."
23 See Powers and O'Loughlin, "Syrian."
24 Al-Ghazzi, "Citizen," 438.

25 ISIS is known colloquially as Daesh in Arabic and is frequently referred to by its claimed moniker "Islamic State," "IS," or the "Islamic State of Syria and Iraq" in international media.

26 Simon and Libby, "Broadcasting Murder."

27 Léridon, "Covering."

28 Murrell, "Global," 270.

29 See Burchell, "Reporting."

30 Mollerup and Mortensen, "Proximity."

31 Ibid., 9.

32 See Hutchings and Burchell's policy reports ("Comparative" and "Approaches") comparing the representation of Islam in public service media and state media broadcasters in the UK, France, and Russia for a detailed analysis of how the Syria conflict, among other security-focused issues, was represented in flagship broadcast news shows.

33 Wahl-Jorgensen, "Resisting," 166.

34 Witschge et al., "Dealing."

35 Wahl-Jorgensen, "Resisting," 169.

36 Peters, "Witnessing," 720.

37 Frosh, "Telling," 266.

38 Wagner-Pacifici, "Theorizing," 1383.

39 Ibid., 1383.

40 Reed, "Power," 31.

41 Anderson, "Emergency," 463.

42 See Burchell, "Reporting."

43 Matheson, "Weblogs," 445.

44 Ibid., 451–2.

45 See Matheson, "Weblogs"; Wishart and Léridon, "AFP Editorial," June 2016.

46 AFP, "AFP 2017 Annual Report."

47 See Schatzki, "Introduction"; Couldry, "Theorising"; Burchell et al., "Practicing."

48 See Fairclough, *Discourse*.

49 Ibid., 84.

50 Matheson, "Weblogs," 453.

51 See Chaise, "Behind."

52 AFP, "AFP Charter," my emphasis.

53 AFP, "AFP 2017 Annual Report."

54 Eassa, "If I Remain."

55 Ibid.

56 Ibid.

57 Doumany and Dlugy, "Others."

58 Doumany, "Syria's 'Hospital.'"
59 See Mollerup and Mortensen, "Proximity."
60 Al-Masri and Moussaoui, "Covering."
61 Ibid.
62 Burchell, "Reporting."
63 See Doumany and Dlugy, "Others."
64 Al-Masri and Moussaoui, "Covering"; Al-Masri and Moussaoui, "Last Days"
65 See Al-Ghazzi, "Citizen"; Matar, "Syrian."
66 See Powers and O'Loughlin, "Syrian."
67 See Horvit, "International."
68 See Burchell, "Reporting."
69 See Chaise, "Behind."
70 Léridon, "Covering."
71 AFP, "AFP 2017 Annual Report."
72 See Doumany et al., "Syria."
73 Ibid.
74 Al-Masri and Moussaoui, "Covering."
75 Doumany et al., "Syria."
76 Ibid.
77 Ibid. Ellipses included in original text.
78 Matar, "Syrian."
79 See Möller, "Peace."
80 See Anderson, "Emergency."
81 Möller, "Peace," 35.
82 While we use the terms "eventness" and "crisis" here, in Anderson's (2017) writing the near-equivalent terms are "eventfulness" and "emergency."
83 Anderson, "Emergency," 465, 468.
84 See Burchell, "Take My Picture"; Hutchings and Burchell, "Media Genre."
85 See Möller, "Peace."
86 Möller, "Peace," 37–38.
87 Eassa, "Escape."
88 Doumany and Dlugy, "The Others."
89 Doumany et al., "Syria."
90 Ibid.
91 See Burchell, "Reporting."
92 See Al-Ghazzi, "Citizen"; Powers and O'Loughlin, "Syrian."
93 See Matar, "Syrian."
94 Doumany and Dlugy, "The Others."

Bibliography

AFP. "AFP charter." 4 April 2016. https://www.afp.com/sites/default/files/paragraphrich/201604/12_april_2016_afp_charter_1.pdf.

– "AFP 2017 Annual Report." May 2018. www.afp.com/en/annual-report-2017.

– "About." *AFP Correspondent*. 2019. https://correspondent.afp.com/about.

Al-Ghazzi, O. "'Citizen Journalism' in the Syrian Uprising: Problematizing Western Narratives in a Local Context." *Communication Theory* 24, no. 4 (2014): 435–54. https://doi.org/10.1111/comt.12047.

Al-Masri, K., and R. Moussaoui. "Covering Syria through Hunger and Fear." *AFP Correspondent*, 26 September 2016. https://correspondent.afp.com/covering-syria-through-hunger-and-fear.

– "The Last Days in Aleppo." *AFP Correspondent*, 8 February 2017. https://correspondent.afp.com/last-days-aleppo.

Anderson, B. "Emergency Futures: Exception, Urgency, Interval, Hope." *Sociological Review* 65, no. 3 (2017): 463–77. https://doi/org/10.1111/1467-954x.12447.

Blaagaard, B.B. "Post-Human Viewing: A Discussion of the Ethics of Mobile Phone Imagery." *Visual Communication* 12 no. 3 (2013): 359–74. https://doi/org/10.1177/1470357213483056.

Boyd-Barrett, O., and T. Rantanen. *The Globalization of News*. London: Sage, 1998.

Burchell, K. "Reporting, Uncertainty, and the Orchestrated Fog of War: A Practice-Based Lens for Understanding Global Media Events." *International Journal of Communication* 14 (2020): 2905–27.

– "'Take My Picture': The Media Assemblage of Lone-Wolf Terror Events, Mobile Communication, and the News." In *The Routledge Companion to Media and Humanitarian Action*, edited by R. Andersen and P.L. de Silva, 465–76. New York and London: Routledge, 2017. https://doi/org/10.4324/9781315538129.ch38.

Burchell, K., O. Driessens, and A. Mattoni. "Practicing Media – Mediating Practice: Introduction." *International Journal of Communication* 14 (2020): 2775–88.

Chaise, C. "Behind AFP's Syria Coverage." *AFP Correspondent*, 16 March 2018. https://correspondent.afp.com/behind-afps-syria-coverage.

Cottle, S. "Global Crises in the News: Staging New Wars, Disasters, and Climate Change." *International Journal of Communication* 3 (2009): 494–517.

Couldry, N. "Theorising Media as Practice." *Social Semiotics* 14 no. 2 (2004): 115–32.

Doumany, A. "Syria's 'Hospital' of Horrors." *AFP Correspondent*, 12 November 2014. https://correspondent.afp.com/syrias-hospital-horrors.

Doumany, A., and Y. Dlugy. "The Others." *AFP Correspondent*, 30 August 2016. https://correspondent.afp.com/others.

Doumany, A., D. Souleiman, and S. Al-Doumy. "Syria Shimmers of Hope." *AFP Correspondent*, 30 September 2016. https://correspondent.afp.com/syria-shimmers-hope.

Eassa, A. "Escape from War." *AFP Correspondent*, 30 March 2018. https://correspondent.afp.com/escape-war.

– "If I Remain Alive: The Ghouta Diaries." *AFP Correspondent*, 26 February 2018. https://correspondent.afp.com/if-i-remain-alive-ghouta-diaries.

Fairclough, N. *Discourse and Social Change*. Cambridge: Polity Press, 1992.

Frosh, P. "Telling Presences: Witnessing, Mass Media, and the Imagined Lives of Strangers." *Critical Studies in Media Communication* 23, no. 4 (2006): 265–84. https://doi/org/10.1080/07393180600933097.

Horvit, B. "International News Agencies and the War Debate of 2003." *International Communication Gazette* 68, nos. 5–6 (2006): 427–47. https://doi/org/10.1177/1748048506068722.

Hutchings, S., and K. Burchell. "Approaches to the Reporting of Islam in Russian Television News" [Original title in Russian: Подходы к освещению ислама в российских телевизионных новостях]. Policy Report. Moscow: SOVA Center for Information and Analysis, 2015. http://www.sova-center.ru/files/religion/islam-media.pdf.

– "Comparative Approaches to Islam, Security, and Television News: Implications for the Editorial Policies and Practices of Public Sector Broadcasters." Policy Report. University of Manchester, 2014. http://www.alc.manchester.ac.uk/medialibrary/subjects/rees/projects/tvrepresentations/reports/comparative-approaches-to-islam-report.pdf.

– "Media Genre, Disrupted Memory, and the European Securitization Chronotope: Transnationalizing the Lee Rigby Murder." In *Memory and Securitization in Contemporary Europe*, 155–85. London: Palgrave Macmillan, 2018. https://doi/org/10.1057/978-1-349-95269-4_7.

Léridon, M. "Covering the 'Islamic State.'" *AFP Correspondent*, 17 September 2014. https://correspondent.afp.com/covering-islamic-state.

Matar, D. "The Syrian Regime's Strategic Communication: Practice and Ideology." *International Journal of Communication* 13 (2019): 2398–416.

Matheson, D. "Weblogs and the Epistemology of the News: Some Trends in Online Journalism." *New Media and Society* 6, no. 4 (2004): 443–68. https://doi.org/10.1177/1461444804044329.

Möller, F. "Peace Aesthetics: A Patchwork." *Peace and Change* 45, no. 1 (2020): 28–54. https://doi.org/10.1111/pech.12385.

Mollerup, N.G., and M. Mortensen. "Proximity and Distance in the Mediation of Suffering: Local Photographers in War-Torn Aleppo and the International Media Circuit." *Journalism* 21, no. 6 (2020): 729–45. https://doi/org/10.1177/1464884918793054.

Mortensen, M. "The Eyewitness in the Age of Digital Transformation." In *Amateur Images and Global News*, edited by K. Andén-Papadopoulos and M. Pantti, 61–75. Bristol: Intellect, 2011.

Murrell, C. "The Global Television News Agencies and Their Handling of User-Generated Content Video from Syria." *Media, War, and Conflict* 11, no. 3 (2018): 289–308. https://doi/org/10.1177/1750635217704224.

Peters, J.D. "Witnessing." In *Media Witnessing: Testimony in the Age of Mass Communication*, edited by P. Frosh and A. Pinchevski, 23–41. Houndmills: Palgrave Macmillan, 2009.

Powers, S., and B. O'Loughlin. "The Syrian Data Glut: Rethinking the Role of Information in Conflict. *Media, War, and Conflict* 8, no. 2 (2015): 172–80.

Reed, I.A. "Power: Relational, Discursive, and Performative Dimensions." *Sociological Theory*, 31, no. 3 (2013): 193–218.

Schatzki, T.R. "Introduction: Practice Theory." In *The Practice Turn in Contemporary Theory*, edited by T.R. Schatzki, K. Knorr-Cetina, and E.V. Savigny, 1–14. London and New York: Routledge, 2001.

Simon, Joel, and Samantha Libby. "Broadcasting Murder: Militants Use Media for Deadline Purposes." *Committee to Protect Journalists*, 27 April 2015.

Sjovaag, H. "Amateur Images and Journalistic Authority." In *Amateur Images and Global News*, edited by K. Anden-Papadopoulous and M. Pantti, 80–95. Bristol: Intellect Books, 2011.

Wagner-Pacifici, R. "Theorizing the Restlessness of Events." *American Journal of Sociology* 115, no. 5 (2010): 1351–86. https://doi/org/10.1086/651299.

Wahl-Jorgensen, K. "Resisting Epistemologies of User-Generated Content?" In *Boundaries of Journalism: Professionalism, Practices and Participation*, edited by M. Carlson and S.C. Lewis, 169–85. London and New York: Routledge, 2015.

Wishart, E., and M. Léridon. "AFP Editorial Standards and Best Practices." 12 April 2016. https://www.afp.com/communication/chartes/12_april_2016_afp_ethic_final.pdf.

– "AFP Editorial Standards and Best Practices." 6 June 2016. https://www.afp.com/sites/default/files/paragraphrich/201701/22_june_2016_afp_ethic.pdf.

Witschge, T., C.W. Anderson, D. Domingo, and A. Hermida. "Dealing with the Mess (We Made): Unraveling Hybridity, Normativity, and Complexity in Journalism Studies." *Journalism* 20, no. 5 (2019): 651–9. https://doi/org/10.1177/1464884918760669.

9

User-Generated Ethical Audiences

*On the Discursive Significance of the Abject
in Amateur Video during the Arab Spring*

MICHAEL LITHGOW

The use of amateur content by journalists is no longer a novelty. Amateur content in the news is ubiquitous as news organizations have come to rely more and more on public use of digital technologies to record and share content. It is hard to imagine news today without the low-resolution, shaky, hastily recorded images created by non-expert members of the public, or what is often referred to as user-generated content (UGC).

As others in this volume have discussed, the term "UGC" encompasses the multimodal ways that members of the public create mediated content – cell phone photographs, audio recordings, texts, tweets, blogs, and so on.[1] Arguably, its most dramatic and commonly used form in news narratives is amateur video. The use of amateur video in the news dates back to at least the 1991 video recording of Rodney King being assaulted by Los Angeles police officers, but it is the Boxing Day tsunami in Sumatra, Indonesia, in 2004, that is often identified as the tipping point for professional journalists' use of amateur video to cover an event.[2] In its immediate aftermath, visual images of tsunami damage were only available via amateur video from people in places directly affected, and news organizations around the world snapped up amateur videos and photographs to incorporate into their coverage. As the journalist chapters in this volume point out, most newsrooms today have dedicated staff for sourcing and verifying UGC, and amateur video appears routinely in the output of most major news organizations.[3]

A key tension surrounding the use of UGC is that the amateur images are not recorded by journalists – they are not made for use in the news stories in which they appear, and they are not made by the news organizations that use them. The origin of news content is no small matter when its discursive value as "news" is being determined. In a historic period defined in part by the proliferation of "fake news" and growing public doubt about whether the news they watch is "real," objectivity, news value, and evidence are still essential to professional news organizations if they hope to distinguish their output from entertainment, opinion, propaganda, and marketing. The legitimacy of a news story, that is, its discursive significance as "truth," has long been grounded in journalistic training that produces professionals taught to test information using an objective method that corroborates information, relies on sources, is intellectually fair-minded to the many sides of a story, and reduces as much as possible the impact of the journalist's own inherent biases and opinions.[4] Objectivity, however battered that notion is, still suggests a severability between subject/journalist and object/news that *de facto* interpellates the audience in a similarly uninvolved way. In a sense, the claim that the information in a news story is presented by a trained journalist is a key part of the covenant between the audience and traditional news organizations, even if that trust has broken down considerably in the past two decades.[5]

My goal in this chapter, however, is not to unravel the philosophy of "truth" behind news discourse; rather, it is to draw attention to the importance of the journalist's role as journalist in the production of news and to what happens when that role is fulfilled by someone else. Content produced within the workflows of a news organization by journalists is assumed by audiences to have been produced using objective methodology to filter information in order to present verified (i.e., as verified as possible) versions of the truth. By definition, UGC is not produced by journalists and thus is not produced within this value framework. It can be created for many reasons. Sometimes video is captured by a startled bystander. The tragic images of George Floyd being assaulted by police that proved one of the catalysts for accelerating and amplifying the Black Lives Matter movement were recorded by a seventeen-year-old bystander on her way to a nearby corner store. She saw Mr Floyd's distress at being detained by the police and "knew it wasn't right."[6] But as often as not, especially in political crises, the bystander is there because they have an interest in events. The UGC images of police assaulting protesters during the Arab Spring were often captured by fellow protesters. Images of the Boxing Day tsunami damage were captured by residents in the neighbourhoods where the flood waters were wreaking havoc. And recent images of unrest in Iran over the death of Mahsa Amini at the hands of state police are being gleaned from the social media accounts of private citizens, who share their perspectives of events from within the protesting crowds.[7] UGC emerges from a different set of ontological conditions than traditional content created by journalists. If journalistic methodologies play a role in the discursive significance of traditional news content, what kinds of discursive significance, if any, are harboured by the "methodologies" and contexts of amateur video?

One of the difficulties in assessing these kinds of questions is that UGC rarely if ever appears on its own. That is to say, most viewers only ever encounter UGC in the context of a news story where a journalist has placed it at the discursive service of a news narrative. UGC (in the case of amateur video) is captioned by the news narrative within which the amateur video appears. One of the primary questions put forward in this chapter is, what is the discursive significance of amateur video independent of the news narratives in which it is generally encountered?

The UGC I have chosen for my case study comes from coverage of the Arab Spring of 2010–11, another relatively early example of sudden and widespread use of amateur footage at a time when most newsrooms had yet to develop standards and guidelines for handling UGC.[8] My corpus is the amateur video used by the Canadian Broadcasting Corporation (CBC) in news stories that appeared during its nightly 11 p.m. newscast in the first 100 days of the uprising. The Arab Spring as a historical event was key to UGC's emergence as an important element in global journalism. Its significance in coverage of the Arab Spring story was undeniable, as was the volume of material available and journalists' lack of standardized procedures for handling UGC – something discussed in chapter 7 of this volume. What emerged in the present study was that – as distinct from traditional news narratives – amateur video during the Arab Spring interpellated viewers as empathetic participants in the scenes of upheaval recorded. In other words, the unique ontological conditions out of which UGC emerged (i.e., distinct from the ontologies of conventional journalism) had the potential to constitute engaged, empathetic, and collectively oriented audiences in response to the events depicted, an altogether different subjectivity from the passive, uninvolved observer traditionally constituted through conventions of journalism.

The Aesthetics of Unrest: Understanding the
Discursive Significance of Arab Spring UGC

The use of UGC (in particular, amateur video) by Western news outlets during the Arab Spring has been widely studied – for its impact on gendered participation in events,[9] for the ways it imposed Westernized ideas onto local conditions of media practice,[10] for the different and unique ways news organizations handled UGC during the Arab Spring,[11] as symptom and cause of changing journalistic practices,[12] for the ways the creation of UGC was transformed by Western news outlets' editorial expectations,[13] for its role in supporting and extending Western ideological narratives implicit in some news reporting,[14] and for its role in expanding global audiences for the Arab Spring movement through established mass media outlets.[15] A particularly prevalent narrative of analysis, especially in the West, has been to describe the Arab Spring in terms of practices of unrest inextricably tied to social media.[16] The technological determinism that a "social media revolution" implies has also been critiqued as a form of orientalism that occludes local and more complex and longer-term efforts at collective action and organizing.[17] The Arab Spring has attracted considerable attention from scholars around the world.

But despite this attention, what has often been overlooked are the video clips themselves separate from the analytic and polemic narratives that accompany them. Just as televisual reports created by journalists purport to reflect the world from within particular relations (i.e., relations of trust between news organizations and audiences that the narratives and analysis presented reflect accurate versions of reality rather than special interests), it seems plausible that amateur video clips might also perform unique discursive work. Or to phrase this as a question: do the particular ontological conditions of amateur video have any lingering effects on their discursive significance in excess of those generated through conventional news values?

A few studies point in encouraging directions. The social media sharing of UGC during the Arab Spring has been observed as both a communicative tool for political organizing and as a "revolutionary contagion" through regional and international (subsequently accessed by local audiences) broadcast and circulation.[18] But the discursive significance of the amateur footage itself and how exactly it made revolution "contagious" in other regions is addressed only in passing, the implication being that audiences seeing dissidence and repression in a neighbouring state were inspired to be dissident locally. Even more encouraging, in the study of a single UGC video clip from Libya during the Arab Spring, Snowdon has argued that the aesthetics of that particular amateur video redistributed sensibilities of subjectivity – that they instantiated "a certain dissolution of the self" and "refusal of individual authorship," which in turn presented a "collective audio-visual language, a vernacular which exists to embody and project the desires and values of the people on their own terms."[19] In other words, the amateur video in question, Snowdon argues, asserted not an individual subjectivity, but an emergent collective subjectivity. This is the territory I want to explore further in this chapter: how amateur images circulating in news narratives affected subjectivities. If the images acted as a contagion for revolution, how might we better understand the dynamics between circulation of amateur video and interpellated subjectivities during the Arab Spring? And how might we approach the discursive significance and legitimacy of amateur video itself?

Photographic images in journalism hold a special, if controversial, place in the making of meaning in discourses of news. Many thinkers have commented on the role of text in reducing the complexities of images. Roland Barthes interpreted the photograph as a "floating chain of signifieds," by which he meant a polysemic presentation of possibilities for meaning, which only become fixed by language, a process he called "anchorage."[20] Accompanying text (or the caption) serves to direct attention to some signs while ignoring others, serving what Barthes described as a "repressive" function.[21] Messaris and Abraham claim that images in news narratives have three distinctive (i.e., distinct from text) qualities: their analogical quality, their indexicality, and their lack of explicit propositional syntax.[22] A photograph's indexical qualities (i.e., the recording of actual physical light waves and thus empirical link to the analogue world) make it easier for audiences to overlook its human-made ontology; this indexicality imputes it with a "closer to truth" quality than text, and its limited syntactic propositions[23] shift the burden of sense-making onto the viewer, whether they know it or not. Historically, photography in journalism has served news narratives as icons, evidence, and sensation(al) (i.e., affective) content.[24] This ambiguous status of images in the news as compared to language has been described as a lingering form of iconoclasm, one that shies away from the complexities of visual meaning.[25] Photographs, Anden-Papadopoulos writes, "speak a language of their own. They are complexly coded cultural artifacts that to some extent 'place' us in specific viewing positions and convince us to see matters in a certain way ... We consequently need to note the possibility of resistance of the visual image to the dominant news narrative, and the potential of certain persistent images to invade and even help reframe that narrative."[26] In a similar fashion, perhaps there are complexities being reduced in the amateur video footage incorporated into news narratives that harbour their own kinds of information – this is the central tension explored in this chapter.

Methodology

To better understand the discursive significance of amateur images in news outcomes, I examined amateur video that appeared on the CBC's 11 p.m. nightly news program during the first 100 days of the Arab Spring.[27] In total, 665 seconds of amateur video appeared in thirty-two different news stories covering events in Tunisia, Egypt, Libya, Syria, and Yemen. A content analysis of these video clips was undertaken that revealed the following categories of content depicted in the images: 46 per cent (of 665 seconds of video) showed images of crowds in streets – crowds walking, running, chanting, milling in public spaces; 38 per cent showed images of bodies in some kind of trauma: injured and wounded bodies, blood-covered bodies, people screaming in pain, injured people being carried through the streets, and dead bodies; 8 per cent showed conflict – people in conflict with other protesters, clashing with the police and military forces, and throwing stones; and, finally, 6 per cent showed property damage, either happening in the moment or as aftereffects – fires in the street, cars burning, buildings burning, statues and posters being torn down, and so on. How best, then, to make sense of events and images depicted in amateur footage that are then circulated and made available for viewing through news narratives?

Home Movies: An Insider's Perspective

A unique feature of amateur video clips is their intimacy to events depicted. They offer a kind of access usually only available to an insider, someone already there and close to events. Another genre of moving images that shares some of these attributes is home movies and home video: people documenting their own lives and the lives of friends and family with film and video. "Home video," writes James Moran, "closes the gap between production and reception. Its images may be viewed ... while the event being recorded is still in progress, imbuing its artifacts with a self-conscious reflexivity foregrounding the theatricality inherent in the *home mode*."[28] A "home mode" of mediation, Moran argues, is less dependent on where a video is recorded (e.g., in the home, at the beach, on vacation) than it is on the way mediation is used by practitioners to "explore and negotiate the competing demands of their public, communal, and private, personal identities."[29]

Identity production is key here, as are the implications of identities within relations of power. The home mode has been observed as a resource for self-narrativizing, generational continuities, and articulating ties to places and landscapes.[30] Home movies have also been shown to evidence relations of power shaping a time and place – for example, the function of the nuclear family within the logics of capitalism, the instrumentalization of leisure time, and bourgeois social reproduction.[31] In this sense, home movies and videos have drawn legitimacy from their role in service of wider social and ideological contexts. And as this suggests, there may be contradictory forces at work in the home mode: the intentions of users and how those intentions shape and are (re)shaped by discourses in service of social reproduction.

Digital technologies in particular have destabilized structures of privilege, affordability, and expertise that regulated amateur use of home filmmaking practices. Among these destabilizing affordances are the unique conditions of digital circulation and exhibition. Images available for immediate exhibition can become a discursive resource for self-reflexive exploration, and easy and wide circulation of digital materials allows amateur video to communicate texts with wider groups in ongoing processes of identity formation.[32] Digital exhibition and circulation of home movies introduced what Rascaroli and colleagues describe as the "testimonial mode" of home movie making.[33] "The most significant trait of the testimonial mode," they write, "is that it requires a fundamental evaluation of identity (who are you in bearing witness to this event?), of doing (where were you at the moment of the events?), and of truth, a truth for which the author of the testimonial is held accountable."[34] The "home mode" in this light has been and is being irretrievably altered through new and emerging digital practices that situate the recordings of intimate, subjective experiences in wider social contexts. Of particular significance for the current discussion is the observation that amateur video recording functions discursively in complex ways, reflecting the legitimacies of hegemonic norms regulating social reproduction, articulating senses of self and identity in wider social contexts, articulating senses of self in family and social contexts, and as archival records of subjective experiences. As we will see, many if not all of these discursive functions are reflected in the UGC produced by participants and observers of the Arab Spring.

Eyewitness to Trauma:
Wounding the Body of National Identity

The discursive complexity of amateur video will of course be grounded in part by the images recorded. As mentioned, the content of the amateur images used by the CBC in the first 100 days of the Arab Spring fell into three broad categories. The largest category of images (46 per cent) was of crowds occupying public spaces in unusual and collective ways, that is, of protesters gathering in the streets, chanting, and so on. I will return to the significance of these kinds of images later on. But for now, I want to focus on the second-largest category of images (38 per cent), those of the human body experiencing or evidencing physical trauma. (Together, bodies in public spaces [i.e., crowds] and bodies in trauma made up 84 per cent of images, and if we include images of conflict and people clashing as a kind of hybrid of the two, these categories collectively account for 92 per cent of UGC imagery in the corpus.)

Elaine Scarry in *The Body in Pain* argues that pain obliterates language: "The moment language bodies forth the reality of pain," she writes, "it makes all further statements and interpretations seem ludicrous and inappropriate."[35] This describes in a sense why images of trauma can have such affective impact: as language becomes less relevant, embodied understanding becomes more relevant. An image of atrocity, write Wolf and Grindell, renders language unintelligible in the sense that the photo cannot describe what is shown or interpret it.[36] The image of a wounded body, says Gita Chandra, is witness to an unutterable event. Images of trauma transcend in certain ways any attempts to caption them.[37]

But amateur video of traumatized bodies introduces another layer – perhaps "circuit" is a better metaphor – of discursive significance. In the first instance, the amateur video creates a "permanent" visual record of the traumatized body. In news discourse, this is often its evidentiary value, as news narratives describe events and the visual images of UGC provide the evidence for claims made about those events. But the amateur video clips also record the act of witnessing.[38] This speaks to the unique ontology of UGC as a form of witnessing from *outside* the professional contexts of journalism. Journalists are paid to be in close proximity to news events, they choose to be there as part of professional practice and privilege, and they are often accorded privileges of security (from harassment, arrest, other legal repercussions, etc.) not accorded to non-journalists caught up in an event.[39] But even with this, journalists rarely get as close to events as the people who are involved in them. The journalist remains an outsider; the amateur video maker is an insider, first in terms of temporal and physical intimacy to events, but also often in terms of social and cultural relationality. Amateur video makers, certainly the ones in the Arab Spring, often have a direct relation to the events being recorded. Amateur video clips of traumatized bodies in this instance are an indelible record of someone seeing first-hand, up-close damage done to people with whom the witness with a camera has relations.

Holocaust researchers have identified three kinds of witnessing to trauma: (1) first-person witness to one's own trauma, (2) witness to others' testimonies about their trauma, and (3) witness to the process of witnessing itself, or in other words, the self-reflexivity of a researcher.[40] Curiously, witnessing the trauma of others is not explicitly addressed in this typology; however, the fifth edition of the *Diagnostic and Statistical Manual of Mental Disorders* (DSM–5) defines events that qualify as "traumatic" (i.e., direct trauma) as the experience of trauma to an individual *or their witnessing trauma as it occurs to others*.[41] UGC suggests the potential for a hybrid form of witnessing trauma: the record of direct trauma to others (through the lens of the camera), and also a self-reflexive gesture of making a record of witnessing.

Holocaust survivors who documented their experiences of trauma often tried to ensure that their testimony would survive their own demise – by burying diaries for imagined future audiences, scratching messages in secret on prison walls, smuggling messages out of prisons and labour camps, and so on.[42] Laub argues that this urge was more than an urge to tell the stories; the process of telling became a survival tactic, both during the war and after, for those who survived. "One has to know one's buried truth," she writes, "in order to be able to live one's life."[43] We can imagine that the amateur videographers recording traumas of protest during the Arab Spring were sharing in this task of survival. As ones among many in an event that provoked trauma for some, they helped with the task of ensuring that certain truths did not remained buried.

This "shared" quality to the creation of UGC – the act of witnessing the trauma of others and of ensuring that these experiences do not remain buried (as Laub says) – is important, in fact central to understanding why UGC is so qualitatively different from images produced by journalists, but more importantly to understanding UGC's unique ontological status as an act rooted in collective identity building. Trauma has two structures of legitimacy, writes Hal Foster: the social context producing the trauma, and its assumed authenticity as experience.[44] In the case of wounded and dead bodies in amateur images from the Arab Spring, the social context is a collective response to state authority through embodiment in public spaces. The collective is asserting transgression (of public norms), demands (for meaningful political response), and a new collective identity (that encompasses alliances with community members and a willingness to explicitly and physically challenge authority). The articulation and instantiation of new collective civic identities falls into what Bob Kurik describes as prefiguration of subjectivities through protest, an embodied process of "constructing alternative selves, decision-making processes, infrastructures, and worlds, here and now."[45] Prefiguration is the political space created through protest out of which new subjectivities are expected to emerge. Trauma in this context is collective trauma, which describes "a blow to the basic tissues of social life that damages the bonds attaching people together."[46] The cell phone recorder has not been traumatized physically like the bodies recorded, but shares with the bodies this experience through proximity of collective appeal and co-presentation of new shared civic demands. The traumatized body could have been theirs, and in this sense, the images record injury to the collective sense of self.

In other work, I have examined how aesthetic experience can shape discourse legitimacies.[47] One way aesthetic experience manifests discursively is through a sense of belonging, an orientation to others inherent in the construction of meaning that implies a particular range of expectations and obligations. For example, the phrase "protesters in the Arab Spring" implies a set of relations among a group of people that includes some and excludes others, and within this group will exist expectations and obligations of alliance, security, support, and so on. The phrase "protesters in the Arab Spring" is not a simple fact, but shorthand for a fluid set of relations. A sense of belonging is an imprecise and subjective array of sensibilities to be sure, and especially in a context in which the expectations and obligations are explicitly being challenged; this is in part why a sense of belonging emerges as a facet of discursive aesthetics.[48] It is precisely these relationships of expectation and obligation – as among and between citizens and the state – that come under assault in the kinds of public traumas witnessed in amateur video. Collective trauma reflects the realization that the communal body is under attack.

In his insightful and complex study of one particular amateur video clip from the Libyan war mentioned earlier, Snowdon also suggests that these kinds of emergent political subjectivities result from the aesthetics of amateur video.[49] Using Jacques Rancière's approach to aesthetics as a (re)distribution of the sensible, Snowdon argues that the discursive significance of the amateur video lies in part in its aesthetic (re)organization of sensibilities. The amateur images recorded during the Arab Spring reflect in part an aesthetics of no longer belonging to a certain collective, a national identity, while at the same time – through the act of recording/witnessing the trauma – also making claim to this disruption and the damage the disruption has caused.

National Identity as Abject:
Revealing the Horror of the Status Quo

The amateur video recorded during the Arab Spring as witness to the rending of national identity, as described above, often depicts scenes that are difficult to watch – images of protesters being run over, beaten, sprayed with water cannon, tear gassed, and shot. What has been observed and recorded are state forces trying to stop, render silent and non-existent, eliminate something from the public spaces under their authority. Julia Kristeva writes that stable identities depend on the elimination of the perception of the abject, by which she means that a coherent and whole identity depends on the elimination of those elements that destabilize and contradict a unified sense of self.[50] Kristeva identifies these elements as the abject: as what fills us with a sense of horror when perceived because of the threat of breakdown in meaning, especially a sense of coherent identity/subjectivity. For example, the horror and distaste most of us feel at the sight of what is inside our bodies – the chaotic and uncontrollable messiness of fluids, internal organs, slippery tissues, and so on – is the state of abjection in response to these hidden parts of ourselves suddenly spilling out.[51] This separation of controllable exterior and uncontrollable interior is necessary, Kristeva argues, to maintain a "clean and proper body,"[52] that is, a docile and submissive subject that won't disturb "identity, system, order."[53] The amateur images of wounded, traumatized bodies reveal a number of ostensibly hidden aspects of Egyptian, Libyan, Syrian, and Tunisian social reality. One possibility is the foundation of violence to bodies on which these societies have built senses of national identity: a requirement for civic submissiveness at risk of physical punishment that belies the state's legitimacy as caretaker of the people. It might also reveal the violence to individual bodies required to reinscribe alternative nationalisms, new national identities. "The nation inscribes its needs and demands on the body through national identities [and] senses of belonging in nationhoods," Elaine Scarry writes.[54] The goal presumably in recording and witnessing national civic trauma such as that captured by amateurs during the Arab Spring is in part to demonstrate the possibility and presumably the urgency of rewriting the collective identity.

Benedict Anderson in *Imagined Communities* argued that nation-states are created by shaping collective imaginations, which is a way of describing public sensibilities of belonging to a national culture.[55] To the extent that these identities are adopted by members of the public, the nation-state functions to achieve its aims. But when they are rejected, as happened during the Arab Spring, the imagined community – and what it means to belong to it – must be reimagined, and this reimagining must be enacted by the stakeholders in the national project. John Di Stefano suggests that the concept of a nation describes a performative accumulation of citizens exploring "roles and relationships of belonging and foreignness."[56] Performances describe embodied gestures iterating subjectivities of possibility within social relations, some complicit with existing relations of power, some challenging them and possibly drawing censure, a kind of regulating disapproval – or "policing," as Judith Butler puts it[57] – aimed at guiding stray performances back to accepted norms. For marginalized groups, command and ownership of the body is often the only real sense of power they direct.[58] Social movements like the ones enacted during the Arab Spring use their collective control over their bodies to perform in different ways: enacting new forms of citizenship and collectivity, a demand and rejection of limitations on where they can be and with whom they can gather, stopping the routines of urban life to declare and impose that *something different is happening.* "Bodies, and subsequently identity," writes Hohle, "are the effects not cause of performance."[59] The largest group of UGC images in the CBC's first 100 days of coverage was of bodies (protesters) moving in large groups in the street cheering and chanting, physically confronting police and military, sometimes brandishing and shooting guns. The third-largest group of images was of protesters vandalizing private or civic property. In both kinds of image the performances are evidence of unconventional behaviour challenging expectations of authority. "Social movements attempt to overcome the limits imposed on the body by using and manipulating civic norms," Hohle writes.[60] The amateur images record the performances and in their circulation perform again the challenging enactments of new civic identities.

A performance is defined, at least in part, by its anticipation of publicity, that is, enactments for audiences. Social movements are public events that in order to succeed require audiences that will be moved to accept new relations, that is, audiences that will accept the new relationalities and subjectivities being enacted.[61] In fact, the "success" of a civic performance depends on the reintegration of performers with their audiences through symbolic message(s) that are understood as both intended and received.[62] Social movements as performance have at least three different kinds of audience wherein to seek their success: within the social movement itself, within forces of opposition, and within the general public.[63] In the case of the Arab Spring, social movement bodies confronted the state, arguably its first audience. And rather than integration, as we have seen in the amateur footage, it was a violent rejection. Another way to think about these images of violence and trauma is as a kind of unmasking of the brutal "policing" mechanisms – in the Butlerian sense – used to maintain civic identities within accepted bounds. The performances of protesters were not successful in the sense described, certainly not at first. They attracted the kind of trauma that breaks bonds of social belonging. The bonds of belonging as they break also break the bodies that have not conformed to the expectations of, in this case, the state. The trauma of not belonging can be read in the wounded and dead bodies of Arab Spring protesters captured in amateur video.

That is the first audience. But who is the audience for the (video) record of these traumas? This is where the idea of bearing witness to witnessing trauma becomes so important. Photography mimics the human experience of witness, but clearly photography and video are not the same thing. Photography and by extension video extend the duration of witnessing; witnessing is enabled to continue long past the actual moment or event of witness. The act of witnessing is objectified, after which all sorts of things can happen – for example, it can be turned into a commodity, or circulated in places far and wide, and certainly far away from where the original event took place. One of the results of these kinds of media flows, certainly in a digital context, is the constitution of new audiences. The objectification and circulation of the act of witnessing new civic identities expressed in Arab Spring amateur footage constituted an audience(s) other than the state. In a sense, these acts of recording these performances were in anticipation of the performance to the state failing to succeed, that is, failing to reconcile protesters with the state in a shared sense of collective identity.

In summary, civic performances of protest enact new collective identities, thereby revealing the abject, the (physical) horror on which national identities depend for their stability. Participants in protests both witness the traumatic events that unfold and sometimes record their acts of witness on mobile phones. These objectified acts of witnessing trauma circulate far and wide through digital ecologies and in part through the news narratives into which they are incorporated, and in doing so constitute new audiences. But what about these audiences? Or more specifically, what kinds of subjectivities are anticipated by the amateur images of the civic abject?

Squirming Our Way to Engaged Subjects

The audiences for amateur video clips are geographically and temporally removed from the events recorded (both from within nearby regional contexts and beyond), yet they can still be deeply moved by the images. Amateur images of wounded bodies present the traumatic process of articulating new collective identities in all its abject unpleasantness. These images, comprising 38 per cent of those studied, are the ones that have the most affective impact – the images of bodies being shot, run over, beaten, or torn open, the ones that shock us and make us squirm. Jill Bennett describes the squirm of audiences to performances of trauma as "the condition of continued participation, the sensation that works with and against the deeper-level response, which on its own is unbearable. The squirm lets us feel the image, but also maintain a tension between self and image."[64] The squirm is what allows the spectator to assimilate, perhaps endure, the abject. This allowance is the foundation for what she calls "empathic vision," a way of seeing that evokes empathetic identification. Sophie Oliver argues that the squirm is what can enable an audience to echo the trauma physically. Oliver, too, is writing in a performing arts context, but her observations draw attention to the significance of the body in spectatorship. The flinch of an audience exposed to the abject "is an empathy in and of the body that, as in the psychological definition of the term, suggests the capacity to put oneself in the place of the other while always returning to the self."[65] Another term used to describe the bodily responses of spectators to performances of trauma is "kinesthetic empathy," the process by which "performance can give the effect of the trauma's presence" in an audience.[66] Kinesthetic empathy describes an echo of trauma experienced in a spectator's own body, and the spectator need not be present physically; that is, affective and embodied echoes of trauma can also manifest themselves in mediated audiences.[67] In fact,

Auslander suggests that notions of "liveness" are better understood as "built primarily around the audience's affective experience."[68] Our own experiences watching film and television – the ways we flinch, squirm, and startle, and all the other affective and embodied responses we have to mediated texts – would seem to support such a thesis.

The voyeuristic potential of such sensation/al viewing has been widely studied. Audiences can watch with fascination images of trauma without experiencing moral culpability; audiences entertained by the suffering of others rather than moved to action have been well documented.[69] By contrast, ethical spectatorship suggests that viewers understand their own relationality to the plight being witnessed and/ or are interpellated into collective responses to difficulties viewed.[70]

An ethical response to viewing trauma has been described in different ways. "Slow looking" describes opportunities that can arise for new subjectivities to emerge in the dissonance of aesthetic ambiguity.[71] "Empathic vision" similarly describes a response to aesthetic complexities and contradictions that invites audiences to negotiate meaning and value.[72] And reflexivity or recursive viewing invites audiences to take into account the implications of witnessing within larger historical processes of privilege, power, and violence.[73] The squirm – kinesthetic empathy – suggests a foundation and precursor for one of the ways subjectivity can shift audiences from passive to active.

As other studies have suggested, mass media discourses, including news outcomes, can act as hailing mechanisms for subjectivities – for the production of racialized identities, gendered identities, civic and national identities, ethnic identities, and so on.[74] News discourses have specifically been implicated in the production of passive forms of citizenship either through the demonization of active participation in civic events or by leaving citizen engagements out of the news altogether – in other words, citizens solving the social and political problems depicted in the news either are absent or are a problem to be corrected.[75] The physiological flinching or squirming produced by UGC during the Arab Spring did not, of course, in and of itself produce ethical spectatorship; however, the empathic and engaged subjectivities being interpellated through amateur images during the Arab Spring echoed exactly the subject positions of the amateurs who produced the video, who were engaged and active participants in the events depicted. In contradistinction to the passive and dissociated subjectivities traditionally associated with journalistic conventions of objectivity, whose subject–object orientation is one of radical separation and deracination of the witness from events, it seemed that UGC in the case of the Arab Spring harboured a very different subjectivity altogether, one that not only depended on the interconnection between observer and observed but also was rooted in the kinds of ethical spectatorships that acknowledge proximity and involvement with the traumas on display. UGC in such instances is more than just hastily shot, relevant accidental visual content; it hails an emergent condition of news values that encompass being witness to events while actively engaging in them. To be informed in this setting is to be involved.

Conclusion

The interpellation of an emergent engaged subjectivity is presumably – at the very least – as plausible as its more commonly assumed opposite, the interpellation of passive voyeurs. But what happens when the relations of power shaping subject positions – or, perhaps more incisively, shaping the conditions of possibility for subject positions – are challenged through the interpellating process itself? The UGC images during the Arab Spring reflected embodied performances of new subject relations at great cost. As with home movies, the intimate recording of what happened to fellow protesters mediates identity reflexively through the public negotiation of private trauma. The body in pain is both public – witnessed – and private in the sense that a body is being unspeakably violated. The amateur videos of these events record the traumatized body and acts of witnessing, which become objectified (through digital technologies), opening uniquely mediated possibilities for circulation and archiving. As with Holocaust survivors burying diaries of atrocities witnessed, the archive of trauma emerges as an act of survival. Or to say it differently, the act of witnessing trauma in such close proximity is inextricably linked to the conditions of subjectivity of the witness and her urge to record trauma as evidence to force accountability. It is a distinctly political act, one that reflects or expresses an engagement with events at great personal risk. What is being archived in these political acts of engagement are emergent civic identities, which in turn evidence a structure of violence perpetrated by the state on citizens inherent in the status quo. As the images reveal, it is a gory process. Challenges to the status quo during the Arab Spring revealed the abject foundation of civic identity. The UGC images that make us squirm – the bloody bodies, the bodies trampled and run over, bodies falling to the ground – show what cannot be shown under the old order, which is the foundation of violence required to maintain the relations desired by the state.

But the images that make us squirm also reveal our own potential for empathetic spectatorship. It is hard not to be horrified for the right reasons when your vantage point is from within the group traumatized. UGC emerges from a sense of belonging, it is an insider's perspective – the proximities are obvious and in many ways defining of UGC and often why UGC harbours such dramatic impact – so when one of our own, so to speak, is traumatized, we are implicated. At least, the interpellation of an engaged, proximal, and interconnected subjectivity is on offer, and our flinching at the scenes before us suggests an embodied, if not yet cognitive, willingness to join in.

We rarely encounter UGC without caption, and the UGC in CBC coverage of the Arab Spring was no exception. In other work included in this book (Chapter 7), I have examined the same corpus of amateur video to better understand the discursive function of UGC in the context of the news stories in which they appear. A close reading of the news stories reveals that UGC clips woven into news narratives serve multiple discursive functions, not least among which is in service of a variety of narratives (see Chapter 7). The potential for new subjectivities described in this chapter inherent in amateur video images must contend for significance and relevance with the contextualizing narratives found in the news stories in which they appear. The extent to which this kind of civic interpellation is accessible to audiences, or the extent to which UGC is handled in news production so as to mask or obscure these kinds of civic potentials, remains an area in need of further study.

Notes

1 Allan, *Citizen Witnessing*.
2 Cooper, "Boxing Day." For more discussion on the Boxing Day tsunami, see chapters 3 (Miller) and 12 (Escudero).
3 Wardle, et al., "Amateur Footage."
4 Kovach and Rosenstiel, "The Elements of Journalism."

5 Robinson, "Crisis," 56–9.
6 Associated Press, "Darnella Frazier." For more on anti-Black racism and the Black Lives Matter movement, see chapter 5 (Lau et al.).
7 Tabrizy and Willis, "What Video Footage Reveals."
8 For more on the use of UGC during the Arab Spring, see chapter 7 (Lithgow and Martin).
9 Zarnmina, "Women, Arab Spring and Social Media."
10 Al-Ghazzi "Citizen Journalism."
11 Robertson, "Connecting in Crisis," 325–41.
12 Belair-Gagnon, "'Getting It Right,'" 235; Bosio, "How Al Jazeera Reported the Arab Spring"; Van Leuven et al., "Are Twitter and YouTube?"; Russell, "The Arab Spring," 10.
13 Hänska-Ahy and Shapour, "Who's Reporting the Protests?"
14 Lithgow and Martin, "The Eyewitness Textures of Conflict."
15 Aday et al, "Watching," 899–919.
16 Allagui and Kuebler, "The Arab Spring"; Comunello and Anzera, "Will the Revolution," 453–70; Eltantawy and Wiest, "The Arab Spring," 18; Howard et al., "Opening"; Khondker, "The Role," 675–9; Lotan et al., "The Revolutions," 1375–407; Tudoroiu, "Social Media," 346–5; Wilson and Dunn, "The Arab Spring," 25; Wolfsfeld et al., "Social Media and the Arab Spring."
17 Hirst, "One Tweet Does Not a Revolution Make"; Fuchs, "Behind the News," 383–91; Moussa, "From Arab Street"; Post and Crone, "Reporting Revolution"; Warf, "Myths, Realities, and Lessons."
18 Tudoroiu, "Social Media."
19 Snowdon, "The Revolution Will Be Uploaded."
20 Barthes, Image, 39.
21 Ibid., 40.
22 Messaris and Abraham, "The Role."
23 Syntactic propositions are the connective claims such as causality, comparison, generalizations, and so on that explain the relationships between objects and aspects of focus.
24 Bednarek and Caple, "Images."
25 Andén-Papadopoulos, "Abu Ghraib"; Zelizer, About to Die.
26 Andén-Papadopoulos, "Abu Ghraib," 9.
27 On 17 December 2010, Mohamed Bouazizi set himself on fire in Tunisia in response to being arrested for not having a permit to run a vegetable stall. This event initiated protests in Tunisia, which were followed by protests in Egypt, Syria, Morocco, and Libya. My corpus is made up of UGC video used by CBC in its 11 o'clock news from 10 December 2010 to 31 March 2011.
28 Moran, There's No Place Like Home Video, emphasis added.
29 Ibid., 60.

30 Chalfen, *Snapshot*.

31 Zimmermann, "Hollywood, Home Movies, and Common Sense."

32 Van Dijck, " Digital Photography"; Lange, "Video-Mediated Nostalgia."

33 Rascaroli et al., *Amateur Filmmaking*.

34 Rascaroli and Monahan, *Amateur*, 20.

35 Scarry, *The Body in Pain*.

36 Wolf and Grindell. 2007. "The Tears of Photography."

37 Chandra, *Narrating Violence*.

38 For more on the act of witnessing, see the prologue and chapter 8 (Burchell and Fielding).

39 Despite historical protections from local risks while covering news events, there has been a trend in recent years toward growing violence, harassment, and state persecution of journalists. See Jamil and Muschert, *Risks*; Jamil and Sohal, *Reporting*; Posetti et al., *Online*; Walulya and Nassanga "Democracy."

40 Laub, "Truth."

41 American Psychiatric Association, *Diagnostic and Statistical Manual of Mental Disorders: DSM-5* (vol. 5, no. 5). Washington, DC: American Psychiatric Association. The definition of direct trauma (experienced first-hand or witnessed first-hand) is described in the criteria established for Post Traumatic Stress Disorder (PTSD).

42 Laub, "Truth."

43 Ibid., 63.

44 Foster, "Obscene, Abject, Traumatic."

45 Kurik, "Emerging," 59.

46 Alexander, "Toward a Theory of Cultural Trauma," 4.

47 Lithgow, "Defying"; Lithgow, "Aesthetics." For more on the aesthetics of UGC, see chapters 7 [Lithgow and Martin] and 10 (Santos).

48 Lithgow, "Defying"; Lithgow, "Aesthetics."

49 Snowdon, "The Revolution Will Be Uploaded."

50 Kristeva, *Powers of Horror*. Kristeva's work builds on Jacques Lacan's theory of the mirror stage, according to which humans develop a unified sense of self and identity (symbolized by a reflection in the mirror) that masks a more fragmented and incoherent fundamental experience.

51 Campbell, and Spackman, "With/out An-aesthetic."

52 Kristeva, *Powers of Horror*, 101.

53 Ibid., 4.

54 Scarry, *The Body in Pain*, 112.

55 Anderson, *Imagined Communities*.

56 Di Stefano, J., "Moving images of home," *Art Journal* 61, no. 4 (2002): 38–53, 38.

57 Butler, *Gender Trouble*.

58 Hohle, "The Body and Citizenship."
59 Ibid., 287.
60 Ibid., 286.
61 Ibid.; Eyerman and Jamison,. *Social movements*. Focusing on the performance aspects of social movements "calls attention to corporeality and presence, to acting and acting out, to the role of drama and the symbolic in movement activity. It turns our attention to the performance of opposition and the aesthetics of movement, to the choreography of protest, as well as to the moral and emotional in mobilization" (207).
62 Hohle, "The Body and Citizenship."
63 Ibid..
64 Bennett, *Empathic Vision*, 37.
65 Oliver, "Trauma," 127.
66 Duggan, "Feeling," 56.
67 Auslander, "Live."
68 Ibid., 112.
69 Rothe, *Popular Trauma Culture*; Oliver, "Trauma"; Hohle, "The Body and Citizenship"; Thussu, *News as Entertainment*.
70 Interpellation of subject positions through discourse describes the hailing of subjects into already predetermined subjectivities defined within parameters of legitimacy set by existing relations of power (see Althusser, "Ideology"; Fiske, "Culture"). The idea is that news discourses are produced with audiences in mind, and as news is decoded in the ways intended, audiences are to a greater or lesser extent interpellated into particular subject positions.
71 Hohle, "The Body and Citizenship"; Shapiro, "Slow Looking.".
72 Bennett, *Empathic Vision*.
73 Kozol, "Witnessing," 222.
74 Anderson, *Imagined Communities*; Fiske, "Culture," 1268–71; Hall, "Spectacle," 324–44; Hohle, "The Body and Citizenship"; Hariman and Lucaites, *No Caption Needed*; Lind, *Race*; Maitra, *Identity*; Mohanty, "Under Western Eyes," 6188; Said, *Orientalism*.
75 Lewis et al, "Images."

Bibliography

Aday, S., H. Farrell, D, Freelon, M. Lynch, J. Sides, and M. Dewar. "Watching from Afar: Media Consumption Patterns around the Arab Spring." *American Behavioral Scientist* 57, no. 7 (2013): 899–919.

Allagui, I., and J. Kuebler, "The Arab Spring and the role of ICTs: Introduction." *International Journal of Communication* 5, no. 8 (2011).

Alexander, J.C. "Toward a Theory of Cultural Trauma." In *Cultural Trauma and Collective Identity*, ed., J.C. Alexander, R. Eyerman, B. Giesen, N.J. Smelser, and P. Sztompka, 620–39. Berkeley: University of California Press, 2004.

Al-Ghazzi, O. "'Citizen journalism' in the Syrian Uprising: Problematizing Western Narratives in a Local Context." *Communication Theory* 24, no. 4 (2014): 435–54.

Althusser, Louis. "Ideology and Ideological State Apparatuses." In *Lenin and Philosophy and Other Essays*, 127–86. London: New Left Books, 1971.

Allan, S. *Citizen Witnessing: Revisioning Journalism in Times of Crisis*. John Wiley and Sons, 2013.

American Psychiatric Association. *Diagnostic and Statistical Manual of Mental Disorders*, 5th ed. Arlington: American Psychiatric Association, 2013.

Andén-Papadopoulos, K. "The Abu Ghraib Torture Photographs: News Frames, Visual Culture, and the Power of images." *Journalism* 9, no. 1 (2008): 5–30.

Anderson, Benedict. *Imagined Communities*. New York: Verso, 1983.

Associated Press. "Darnella Frazier, Teen Who Recorded George Floyd's Arrest, Murder, Wins Pulitzer Citation." Canadian Broadcasting Corporation, 11 June 2021. https://www.cbc.ca/news/world/darnella-frazier-george-floyd-video-pulitzer-1.6062709.

Auslander, P. "Live and Technologically Mediated Performance." In *The Cambridge Companion to Performance Studies*, edited by Tracy Davis, 107–19. Cambridge: Cambridge University Press, 2013.

Barthes, Roland. *Image. Music. Text*. London: Fontana Press, 1977.

Bednarek, Monika, and Helen Caple. "Images in the News." In *News Discourse*, edited by Monika Bednarek and Helen Caple, 111–26. A&C Black: 2012.

Belair-Gagnon, V. "'Getting It Right!': How Did Social Media Transform BBC News Journalism?" In *Communiquer dans un monde de normes. L'information et la communication dans les enjeux contemporains de la mondialisation*, 235. March 2012. https://hal.univ-lille3.fr/hal-00839288 document.

Bennett, J. *Empathic Vision: Affect, Ttrauma, and Contemporary Art*. Stanford: Stanford University Press, 2005.

Bosio, Diana. "How Al Jazeera Reported the Arab Spring: A Preliminary Comparative Analysis." *Media Asia* 40, no. 4 (2013): 333–43.

Butler, Judith. *Gender Trouble*. New York: Routledge, 1990.

Campbell, P. and H. Spackman. "With/out An-aesthetic: The Terrible Beauty of Franko B." *The Drama Review* 42, no. 4 (1998): 56–74.

Chalfen, Richard. *Snapshot Versions of Life*. Bowling Green: Bowling Green State University Popular Press, 1987.

Chandra, G. *Narrating Violence, Constructing Collective Identities: "To witness these wrongs unspeakable."* Springer, 2008.

Comunello, F., and G. Anzera. "Will the Revolution Be Tweeted? A Conceptual Framework for Understanding the Social Media and the Arab Spring." *Islam and Christian–Muslim Relations* 23, no. 4 (2012): 453–70.

Cooper, Glenda. "Boxing Day Tsunami Heralded New Era of Citizen Journalism." *The Conversation*, 28 December 2014. https://theconversation.com/boxing-day-tsunami-heralded-new-era-of-citizen-journalism-35730.

Di Stefano, J. "Moving images of home." *Art Journal* 61, no. 4 (2002): 38–53.

Duggan, P. "Feeling Performance, Remembering Trauma." *Platform* 2, no. 2 (2007): 44–58.

Eltantawy, N., and J.B. Wiest. "The Arab Spring: Social Media in the Egyptian Revolution: Reconsidering Resource Mobilization Theory." *International Journal of Communication* 5, no. 18 (2011). 1207-1224.

Eyerman, R., and A. Jamison. *Social Movements: A Cognitive Approach*. University Park: Pennsylvania State University Press, 1991.

Fiske, John. "Culture, Ideology, Interpellation." In *Literary Theory: An Anthology*, edited by Julie Rivkin and Michael Ryan, 1268–73. Malden: Blackwell, 2004.

Foster, H. "Obscene, Abject, Traumatic." *October 78* (1996): 107–24.

Fuchs, Christian. "Behind the News: Social Media, Riots, and Revolutions," *Capital and Class* 36, no. 3 (2012): 383–91.

Hall, S. "The Spectacle of the Other." In *Discourse Theory and Practice: A Reader*, edited by Margaret Wetherell, Stephanie Taylor, and Simeon Yates, 324–44. London: Sage, 2001.

Hänska-Ahy, M.T., and R. Shapour. Who's Reporting the Protests? Converging Practices of Citizen Journalists and Two BBC World Service Newsrooms, from Iran's Election Protests to the Arab Uprisings." *Journalism Studies* 14, no. 1 (2013): 29–45.

Hariman, R., and J.L. Lucaites. *No Caption Needed: Iconic Photographs, Public Culture, and Liberal Democracy*. Chicago: University of Chicago Press, 2017.

Hirst, M. 2012. "One Tweet Dpes Not a Revolution Make: Technological Determinism, Media and Social Change." *Global Media Journal – Australian Edition* 6, no. 2 (2012): 1–11.

Hohle, R. "The Body and Citizenship in Social Movement Research: Embodied Performances and the Deracialized Self in the Black Civil Rights Movement, 1961–1965." *Sociological Quarterly*, 50, no. 2 (2009): 283–307.

Howard, P.N., A. Duffy, D. Freelon, M.M. Hussain, W. Mari, and M. Mazaid.
"Opening Closed Regimes: What Was the Role of Social Media during
the Arab Spring?" Project on Information Technology and Political Islam,
Working Paper 2011.1 (2011). http://pitpi.org/?p=1051.

Jamil, S., and G.W. Muschert. "Risks to Journalists' Safety and the
Vulnerability of Media Freedom in the US." In *Agenda for Social Justice*,
135–42. Bristol: Policy Press, 2020.

Jamil, S., and P. Sohal. "Reporting under Fear and Threats: The Deadly Cost
of Being a Journalist in Pakistan and India." *World of Media: Journal of
Russian Media and Journalism Studies* 2 (2021): 5–33.

Khondker, H.H. "The Role of the New Media in the Arab Spring."
Globalizations 8 (2011): 675–9.

Kovach, Bill, and Tom Rosenstiel. *The Elements of Journalism* (rev. ed.).
New York: Three Rivers Press, 2007.

Kozol, Wendy. "Witnessing Genocide and the Challenges of Ethical
Spectatorship." In *Politics in Visual Autobiography*, edited by Sarah Brophy
and Janie Hladki. Toronto: University of Toronto Press, 2014.

Kristeva, J. *Powers of Horror: An Essay on Abjection*. Translated by Leon. S.
Roudiez. New York: Columbia University Press, 1982.

Kurik, B. "Emerging Subjectivity in Protest." In *The SAGE Handbook of
Resistance,* edited by David Courpassan and Steven Vallas, 51–77.
New York: Sage, 2016.

Lange, P.G. "Video-MediatedNostalgia and the Aesthetics of Technical
Competencies." *Visual Communication* 10, no. 1 (2011): 25–44.

Laub, Dori. "Truth and Testimony: The Process and the Struggle." In
Explorations in Memory, edited by in Cathy Caruth. Baltimore: Johns
Hopkins University Press, 1995.

Lewis, J., K. Wahl-Jorgensen, and S. Inthorn. "Images of Citizenship on
Television News: Constructing a Passive Public." *Journalism Studies* 5,
no. 2 (2004): 153–64.

Lind, R.A. *Race/Gender/Class/Media : Considering Diversity across
Audiences, Content, and Producers*, 4th ed. London: Routledge, Taylor and
Francis Group, 2019.

Lithgow, Michael. 2013. "Aesthetics of Legitimacy: Resisting the Effects
of Power with 'Grassroots News' and Queer Sasquatches." *American
Communications Journal* 15, no. 1 (2013).

– "Defying the News: New Aesthetics of Truth in Popular Culture."
Canadian Journal of Communications 37, no. 2 (2012): 279–302.

Lithgow, Michael, and Michèle Martin. "The Eyewitness Textures of Conflict:
Contributions of Amateur Videos in News Coverage of the Arab Spring."
Global Media Journal 8, no. 1 (2018).

Lotan, G., E. Graeff, M. Ananny, D. Gaffney, I. Pearce, and D. Boyd. "The Revolutions Were Tweeted: Information Flows during the 2011 Tunisian and Egyptian Revolutions." *International Journal of Communication* 5 (2011): 1375–407.

Maitra, A. *Identity, Mediation, and the Cunning of Capital.* Evanston: Northwestern University Press, 2020.

Messaris, Paul, and Linus Abraham. "The Role of Images in Framing News Stories." In *Framing Public Life: Perspectives on Media and Our Understanding of the Social World,* edited by S.D. Reese, O.H. Gandy Jr, and A.E. Grant, 215–26. New York and London: Routledge, 2001.

Mohanty, C. "Under Western Eyes: Feminist Scholarship and Colonial Discourses." *Feminist Review* 30, no. 1 (1988): 61–88.

Moran, J.M. *There's No Place Like Home Video: Questions of Medium Specificity.* Los Angeles: University of Southern California, 1998.

Moussa, M.B. "From Arab Street to Social Movements: Retheorizing Collective Action and the Role of Social Media in the Arab Spring." *Westminster Papers in Communication and Culture* 9, no. 2 (2013). 47-68.

Oliver, Sophie Anne. "Trauma, Bodies, and Performance Art: Towards an Embodied Ethics of Seeing." *Continuum* 24 (2010): 119–29.

Posetti, J., N. Aboulez, K. Bontcheva, J. Harrison, and S. Waisbord. *Online Violence against Women Journalists.* Paris: UNESCO, 2020.

Post, J., and V. Crone. "Reporting Revolution: Technological Determinism in Journalistic Reports on Social Media and Movements." *Digital Journalism* 3, no. 6 (2015): 871–87.

Rascaroli, L., G. Young, and B. Monahan, eds. *Amateur Filmmaking: The Home Movie, the Archive, the Web.* New York: Bloomsbury, 2014.

Robertson, A. "Connecting in Crisis: 'Old' and 'New' Media and the Arab Spring." *International Journal of Press/Politics* 18, no. 3 (2013): 325–41.

Robinson, Sue. "Crisis of Shared Public Discourses: Journalism and How It All Begins and Ends with Trust." *Journalism* 20, no. 1 (2018): 56–9.

Rothe, Anne. *Popular Trauma Culture.* New Brunswick: Rutgers University Press, 2011.

Russell, A. "The Arab Spring: Extra-National Information Flows, Social Media, and the 2011 Egyptian Uprising." *International Journal of Communication* 5, no. 10 (2011). 1238–1247.

Said, E.W. *Orientalism.* New York: Vintage: 1979.

Scarry, E. *The Body in Pain: The Making and Unmaking of the World.* New York: Oxford University Press, 1985.

Shapiro, M.J. "Slow Looking: The Ethics and Politics of Aesthetics." In Jill Bennett, *Empathic Vision: Affect, Trauma, and Contemporary Art.* Stanford: Stanford University Press, 2008.

Snowdon, P. "The Revolution Will Be Uploaded: Vernacular Video and the Arab Spring." *Culture Unbound* 6, no. 2 (2014): 401–29.

Tabrizy, Nilo, and Haley Willis. "What Video Footage Reveals about the Protests in Iran." *New York Times*, 4 October 2022. https://www.nytimes.com/2022/10/04/world/asia/iran-protest-video-analysis.html.

Thussu, D. *News as Entertainment: The Rise of Global Infotainment.* Sage, 2007.

Tudoroiu, T. "Social Media and Revolutionary Waves: The Case of the Arab Spring." *New Political Science* 36, no. 3 (2014): 346–65.

Van Dijck, J. "Digital Photography: Communication, Identity, Memory." *Visual Communication* 7, no. 1 (2008): 57–76.

Van Leuven, S., A. Deprez, and K. Raeymaeckers. "Are Twitter and YouTube the New Networked News Wires? A Quantitative Content Analysis of Journalists' Sourcing Practices during the Arab Spring." *Etmaal van de Communicatiewetenschappen, Abstracts.* Presented at the Etmaal van de Communicatiewetenschap, Rotterdam, 2013.

Walulya, G., and G.L. Nassanga. "Democracy at Stake: Self-Censorship as a Self-Defence Strategy for Journalists." Media and Communication 8, no. 1 (2020): 5-14.

Wardle, C., S. Dubberley, and P. Brown. "Amateur Footage: A Global Study of User-Generated Content in TV and Online News Output." New York: Tow Center for Digital Journalism, Columbia Journalism School, 2014.

Warf, B. "Myths, Realities, and Lessons of the Arab Spring." *Arab World Geographer* 14, no. 2 (2011): 166–8.

Wilson, C., and A. Dunn. "The Arab Spring: Digital Media in the Egyptian Revolution: Descriptive Analysis from the Tahrir Data Set." *International Journal of Communication* 5, no. 25 (2011): 1248–72.

Wolf, Herta, and Nicholas Grindell. "The Tears of Photography." *Grey Room* 29, *New German Media Theory* (Fall 2007):. 66–89.

Wolfsfeld, G., E. Segev, and T. Sheafer. "Social Media and the Arab Spring: Politics Comes First." *International Journal of Press/Politics* 18, no. 2 (2013): 115–37.

Zarnmina, Israr.. "Women, Arab Spring, and Social Media: Effects of Social Media on Egyptian Women's Participation in the Revolution." *Research Review Journal* 4, no. 4 (2019): 402–6.

Zelizer, B. *About to Die: How News Images Move the Public.* Oxford University Press, 2010.

Zimmermann, P.R. "Hollywood, Home Movies, and Common Sense: Amateur Film as Aesthetic Dissemination and Social Control, 1950–1962." *Cinema Journal* 27, no. 4 (1988): 23–44.

PART THREE

User-Generated Content Journalism around the World

10

User-Generated Content Narrates #ForaTemer on Twitter

Patterns of Citizen Media as Users Document an Anti-impeachment Protest in Brazil

MARCELO SANTOS

The pervasive recording of extraordinary events by people and organizations outside the mainstream media industry has been an issue of interest for a while now. Still, there are not many studies dedicated to systematically gathering and analyzing empirical data on user-generated content (UGC) as a source for understanding or narrating those events.

This chapter sets out to do so, based on a Twitter dataset from a street protest in Brazil, following (and questioning) the controversial impeachment of President Dilma Rousseff in August 2016. A lot has happened in Brazilian politics since, but the relevance of the impeachment process has only grown.[1] As for the street protests that took place at that time, frequent accusations of mainstream media's active role against Rousseff during the impeachment process[2] – accusations that echoed those made during the "Jornadas de Junho" protests in 2013[3] – could help explain *why* citizens protesting the impeachment took matters into their own hands and documented the demonstrations – it was to prove that media accounts were unreliable. How accurate, though, can a UGC-based patchwork-like narrative be? Is UGC created, published, and shared equally during different moments of a long protest, or do distinctive patterns emerge? Finally, how relevant is UGC for the regular user who is following a topic on Twitter – for instance, as it mingles with mainstream media content as well as that of celebrities and public figures, and even content created or amplified by bots and trolls, among other sources?

The Rise of UGC

The twentieth century was the pinnacle of broadcast mass media. After the popularization of radio and television, respectively in the first and second halves of the century, by the end of the century there were some clear signs that massification was in crisis as the rise of cable TV and the first possibilities of the Internet as a platform for media channels began to challenge traditional business models in the media as well as mass-media consumption habits. Within a decade of its commercialization, the Internet went from a digital telecommunication network to a publishing technology, to a media-rich environment massively occupied by user-generated information systems, or UGISS.[4] In such systems – blogs at first, and now the various social media platforms – users are able to publish content without needing to know how to program. Such user-friendly publishing platforms lower the technological barrier for participation by users outside the mainstream media, who can then populate the digital realm with self-generated, self-directed content, and at the same time self-select the sources to which people are exposed.[5]

The catharsis that led to the wide cultural adoption of UGC, exemplified these days by the success of social media sites and/or apps like Facebook and Twitter, is better explained by observing the different drivers that facilitate or, better yet, trigger such social catharsis. Wunsch-Vincent and Vickery claim there are four drivers that account for this "rapid growth and pervasiveness" of UGC:[6]

1 *Technological*, such as increased broadband access, more powerful technologies, and software to create and share content, including for non-professional users. The result is the circulation of not only more UGC but also more *complex* UGC (such as high-quality photos, videos, and livestreams).
2 *Social*, such as the rise of the "digital natives" and a cultural acceptance of the logics of expressing oneself and of sharing, opening the possibility for more open and interactive platforms for personal expression and for collaborative projects or community building through digital media and information and communication technology (ICT) tools.

3 *Economic*, referring to less expensive broadband access as well
   as cheaper devices and software for producing, editing, and
   distributing content, such as smart phones and business models
   monetizing UGC.

4 *Institutional*, including new permissive licences such as creative
   commons that allow for reuse or distribution of content and
   specific licences for UGC-like content.

Croteau earlier pointed to many of the same factors as Wunsch-Vincent and Vickery but also outlined other aspects that can be aligned with the same general drivers: decentralized data distribution services and the convergence of the PC and the TV, bringing the former to the living room (technological driver); the growth of DIY culture among young people (social driver); the growing accessibility of digital devices to capture, create, and manipulate audio or imagery; and the emergence of services that allow the distribution and promotion of self-produced media content (economic driver).[7]

Van Dijck writes that the possibility of answering traditional media in their own language is facilitated by low costs and ease of access to digital technologies. He highlights the importance of UGC sites for enhancing user engagement and agency: "a more important driver is the many internet channels, particularly UGC sites, that allow for do-it-yourself distribution."[8]

Approaches to the definition and operationalization of UGC vary. Moreover, its growth as a communicative practice embedded in contemporary society is not a technological phenomenon isolated from other variables. The convergence of technological, technical, economic, social, and institutional/legal drivers has created a fertile environment for the expansion of UGC into digital media. Still, as the years pass and the aforementioned drivers keep evolving, different possibilities for instrumentalizing UGC have emerged as a result of the ongoing domestication of the technologies, so as to allow for an even more significant appropriation of the devices, which can lead to, for instance, the creation of politically charged UGC – the sort that is the focus of this chapter.[9]

Taking Matters in One's Own Hands:
The Value of Testimonial Tweets

What then is the value, if any, of UGC that documents extraordinary events such as the protest against Rousseff's impeachment? Is there anything new to it? Chris Walton, a BBC journalist, offers his view of what is and what is not new regarding UGC in the realm of journalism: "The thing about user-generated content is that it's not new ... What's new is that it's coming very fast, instantaneously, and the volume is absolutely huge and coming via devices like the Internet and mobile phones."[10]

But UGC is not confined to the realm of major media, such as the BBC. Especially since the advent of social media platforms, the user behind the creation of the content may as well be her own publisher, using a regular user channel such as those provided by YouTube, Twitter, Facebook, and so on, bypassing broadcast media. As Harrison and Barthel contend, what is novel about "Web 2.0" is "the now-widespread recognition and acknowledgement that users actively apply the affordances of new technologies *in the service of their own creative and instrumental objectives.*" This highlights how non-savvy users can instrumentalize digital media in these publishing environments.[11] Van Dijck explains how the ability to respond empowers users, highlighting the relevance of UGC distribution channels: "What is different in the digital era is that users have better access to networked media, enabling them to 'talk back' in the same multi-modal language that frames cultural products formerly made exclusively in studios."[12]

This chapter discusses the creation and diffusion of UGC in the context of political mobilization. UGC's capacity to "talk back" to mainstream media is essential for understanding the impact of the users who created content during the anti-impeachment protest in Brazil. This case is especially relevant since it has been argued elsewhere that participants' main motivator for creating content during the protests was perceived media bias, to which they were reacting.[13]

UGC can refer to content in areas such as tourism (e.g., hotel evaluations) and sports (e.g., fan commentary), but UGC can also document extraordinary events and, in so doing, offer an expressive relevance, in that events are followed in real time. Mortensen refers to this sort of UGC as "eyewitness images"; according to her, they "provide counter-narratives to officially sanctioned narratives."[14] Bruns (2018) highlights the role played by Twitter when acute events break out: "social media (and here especially Twitter) are now without doubt the space where acute events break first and are tracked in the greatest detail."[15] The immediacy allowed by Twitter creates a live and lively channel on which users can broadcast and narrowcast competing accounts of events that users are experiencing live. This chapter aims to shed some light on whether this content is able to effectively narrate or even "counter-narrate" an event.

Distinctive Traits of UGC

According to Polydoro, UGC's "amateur aesthetics" hold an enhanced perception of authenticity, "free from the plastic membrane of the spectacular."[16] Its sense of freshness is based on an "emotional proximity"[17] as opposed to the aesthetics of professional journalism. Silverstone refers to the latter as *proper distance*: "We [media] need to be close but not too close, distant, but not too distant."[18] The powerful perception of closeness, even obtrusiveness, contained in unconstructed, sometimes even embodied, first-person UGC that documents an extraordinary event creates an affective engagement that contrasts radically with the coldness embedded in the *proper distance* of professionally produced and institutionally disseminated media content.[19] Wahl-Jorgensen and colleagues describe the value of UGC as perceived by news audiences: "It adds drama, human emotion; it is seen as more 'real' and less 'packaged,' providing different perspectives and insights on events."[20]

The question of obtrusiveness and perceptions of UGC's authenticity become even more important in the case studied here, for three reasons: (1) Brazil's classic social institutions of liberal democracy, from political parties to mainstream media, faced a severe crisis of legitimacy;[21] (2) there was a historical distrust in Brazil's national media systems, which were perceived as having been "captured" by economic and/or political elites,[22] along with a growing distrust since the controversial media coverage of the 2013 protests in Brazil, widely evaluated as biased;[23] and (3) there was sharply rising need for honest information during Rousseff's impeachment process in 2016.[24] In such a scenario of extraordinary political crisis, alternative sources of information like UGC are likely to play an important role.

As we will see in this chapter, it is predictable that users of UGC-capable technology, be they journalists, activists, alternative media collaborators, or ordinary citizens, can feel compelled to take representation into their own hands and document events of the kind that are often ignored or criminalized by the mainstream media (i.e., protests). As if all of these factors were not enough, on the day before the street demonstration studied in this chapter, Brazilian president Michel Temer in an interview on mainstream media – *O Globo*, the newspaper outlet of Brazil's main media group, Globo – minimized and disparaged the protests that had been going on. He downplayed not only their relevance but also their attendance figures, contending that "there were no more than forty, fifty, one hundred people."[25] As we will see, those "forty" people definitely heard him.

Method

CASE: ROUSSEFF'S IMPEACHMENT

In 2016, Brazil was the site of political turmoil that to this day has left scars on the country's democratic skin, owing to growing polarization.[26] On 17 April of that year, an impeachment process against President Rousseff of the left-wing Workers' Party (PT), was supported by the House of Representatives, sustained by an accusation that she had mismanaged public finances. She would later be convicted and impeached after an almost year-long judicial process; this paved the way for her vice-president, centre-right politician Michel Temer, to inherit her office, under myriad accusations of having conducted a coup d'état,[27] "parliamentary coup,"[28] betrayal,[29] or, as Noam Chomsky referred to it, a "soft coup."[30] The whole process deepened an ongoing political crisis that in turn sparked a series of street protests in 2016, both for and against the impeachment.

This chapter asks to what extent UGC created and disseminated during an extraordinary street demonstration in Brazil on 4 September 2016 against Rousseff's impeachment provided a comprehensive account of the event. It was the first organized mass protest against the president's impeachment since her official ousting on 31 August, a few days earlier. The case studied is relevant for answering such a question since there were multiple accusations of media bias: van Dijk detected a different treatment by each of the political poles and concluded that a "massive manipulation" had taken place.[31] Both analysts and citizen activists perceived that the media had criminalized the protests when they did not simply ignore them, and this did much to drive participants to document and disseminate UGC of the protests on Twitter.[32]

This chapter also explores the different patterns of UGC creation and dissemination during different stages of the protest, given that various external factors mediated the creation of UGC, such as daylight, police brutality, landscapes, landmarks, and so on. Furthermore, this chapter tests the correlation between UGC creation and dissemination on Twitter and the total tweets in the selected dataset, in order to explore the possibility that UGC helped set the agenda for the conversation around the #ForaTemer hashtag.

DATA: TWITTER AS A SOURCE

UGC is present in many different forms and on many different platforms. This study relies on Twitter as its sole entry point for data, for many reasons. It was chosen because of how its characteristics fit the needs of the research, such as its quality of being an "event-following tool."[33] Bail highlights the importance of Twitter as a source of data in a natural environment, which for this research implies a better quality of analysis when examining spontaneous UGC creation: "it is naturally occurring – unlike survey research or cross-sectional qualitative interviews – and therefore critical to understanding the evolution of meaning structures *in situ*."[34] In fact, the content used in this research was mostly generated spontaneously, without any sort of prompting, except perhaps for activists, public figures, and alternative media present at the protest, who did plan to document their participation as part of their professional activity or public political commitment. Additionally, Bruns and Stieglitz state that "large amounts of data might be used to *better understand issues or events retrospectively*, detect issues or events at an early stage, or even to predict certain real-world developments,"[35] a process applied to the present case, analyzed retrospectively. Risse and colleagues also defend Twitter's value as a source: "As a side effect of its active and pervasive usage, Twitter documents contemporary society in rich detail. Tweets give valuable insights into individuals, groups, and organisations, and enable an understanding of the public perception of events, people, products, or companies, including the flow of information."[36]

Bail also refers to the "real time" characteristics of Twitter, which for this research is paramount, as it means to assess to what extent UGC on Twitter can be said to tell the story of the event in real time. In the same vein, Bruns points out the perceived immediacy of Twitter – that is, its lack of mediation – arguing that more than 95 per cent of its accounts are public, which means that the flows of information are more direct and publicly accessible than those offered by Facebook, for example, on which the processes of breaking news "are relatively slower [than on Twitter] and take more circuitous routes."[37] This chapter aims to empirically apply these assertions as to evaluate to what extent they are also accurate for UGC published on Twitter.

DATA COLLECTION AND CONTENT ANALYSIS

The data used in the analysis were obtained ex-post from Sifter.[38] Two criteria were adopted to build the dataset: (1) time, which here meant between 4:30 p.m. and 11:30 p.m., local time, on 4 September 2016; and (2) adoption of #ForaTemer, the main hashtag used during the protests. The initial dataset of 52,554 tweets was then processed and screened with the analytics software Tableau[39] in order to select only original tweets (not retweets or quoted tweets) with media content (images, videos, URLs, etc.) for content analysis.

The context of the images was verified by the author using various digital forensics techniques: (1) geo-checking content with geo-referenced images from Google Street View, street signs (as "Av. Rebouças/Pinheiros"), and previously known landmarks, such as buildings, as well as the tunnel entrance that played a significant part in the day's events; (2) identifying commonalities such as signs, flags, and the like; (3) checking the daylight conditions according to the hour in that place at that time (almost dark, in this case); and (4) checking other content from the user, including available biography and links. Nevertheless, it should be noted that when an abundance of imagery has been produced by a crowd, it becomes much easier to verify the content by superimposing the group of images as a sort of patchwork.

#FORATEMER

A hashtag on Twitter works as an aggregator of content, making it possible to create – intentionally or not – *ad hoc* publics: "Twitter's user-generated system of hashtags condenses such processes [emerging issues and acute events] to an instant, and its issue publics can indeed form virtually ad hoc, the moment they are needed."[40] At the same time its adoption can be considered as a performative statement with political intent:

> including a hashtag in one's tweets signals a wish to take part in a wider communicative process, potentially with anyone interested in the same topic. Where used in such a way, hashtags can aid the rapid assembly of ad hoc issue publics (Bruns & Burgess, 2011b), *especially also in response to breaking news or other sudden developments ... tweeting to a topical hashtag resembles a speech at a public gathering* – a protest rally, an ad hoc assembly – of participants who do not necessarily know each other, but have been brought together by a shared theme, interest, or concern.[41]

It must be acknowledged that we use Twitter as the *only* data source. It offers a dataset around a hashtag deemed to be relevant to our case. Such an approach has limitations in terms of representativeness, given that a hashtag is not a fair representation of what happens on Twitter, and Twitter is not a robust representation of what happens around an event. These limitations, though, do not affect the main purpose of this chapter, which is to explore a set of data as an alternative means of telling a story about an acute social event. The hashtag, in this instance, adds a common nexus to the narrative of users who were likely previously unknown to one another.

CONTENT ANALYSIS

This research aims to shed some light on the patterns of creation and diffusion of testimonial media content published on Twitter, which we will refer to as *testimonial tweets*. To perform the present analysis, three criteria were applied to *testimonial tweets*, within the previously defined initial dataset:

1   Content must be *original*. Retweets and replies were
    therefore excluded.
2   Tweets must contain *media*. This is based on the assumption that
    media content (mainly video and photographs) has a more power-
    ful ability to represent the event since it holds an inevitable physical
    connection to the event.[42] Thus, text-only tweets were discarded.
3   Content must be *testimonial* – that is, refer to the event at hand,
    not to past events or other issues – and be supported by the
    above-described digital forensics techniques.

After performing the above-described coding process, the data were
analyzed on their own merits and then folded back into the original
complete dataset to assess the role its content played within the whole
conversation around #ForaTemer.

Results and Discussion

UGC NARRATES #FORATEMER

The first research question examines the extent to which UGC can be
relied upon as a valid depiction of the event. An important characteristic of Twitter is its real-time affordance, which is both technically
allowed for and culturally expected. At the same time, UGC is hard to
verify, and social media have been overwhelmed by misinformation and
manipulative content.[43] Even so, this research found just one relevant
example of disinformation, which will be addressed below.

The timeline in figure 10.1 tells the story of the protest through the
lenses of testimonial content on Twitter, depicting each stage of the protest during the period at hand. The individual contents are as follows:

1   16:30. The first testimonial content of the dataset shows the
    gathering stage, when people got together prior to the march. The
    meeting point is MASP (the São Paulo Art Museum), an iconic
    building and traditional meeting point for protests.
2   18:03. First accounts of marching, at twilight. People "walking,"
    according to the tweet's author. In the dataset, this was the first
    testimonial account of people moving toward Largo da Batata,
    where the final act would take place.

3 19:16. A very popular tweet shows people using mobile phones as flashlights after a blackout in a tunnel through which they are walking. The National Students Union (UNE), among others, would use this image to falsely accuse the state government of intentionally sabotaging the demonstration.

4 19:32. Peak minute of testimonial tweets (total of eighty). A major contributor was Mídia NINJA,[44] which published almost half the testimonial content that was tweeted or retweeted during the period. The depicted example was the most retweeted content at that precise minute (twelve times).

5 20:14. Testimonial tweets show that there were speeches for at least half an hour (19:45–20:15) after the march ended. The original plan was to end the protest at 20:30. This picture focuses on one of most important social movement leaders of the protest, Guilherme Boulos, from MTST,[45] later a presidential candidate for the leftist party PSOL in the 2018 national elections.

6 21:09. From 20:51 on, according to the data, there is various testimonial evidence of excessive use of tear gas by police in closed places like bars, the subway (see photograph), and other places, even though there are no reports of mob violence or any other signs of a citizen-sparked riot.

7 22:21–22:30: Seven posts in nine minutes, with different lighting conditions, by the same user, These are examples of a demonstrator arriving home and publishing her perspective of the protest, engaging in conversation through #ForaTemer. This is a kind of asynchronous mediated form of protest I have called the stage of *mediated conversation.*

When compared with the real-time documentation by the main media outlet in Brazil, Globo, on its digital news outlet G1,[46] there seem to be enough similarities to validate the crowd-sourced depiction of the event. Table 10.1 compares some key moments as depicted by both sources.

G1 did not rely on UGC, for it had people on the ground as well as helicopter images from the event. It published information on its website in a special section called "Real Time" (which emulates the Twitter timeline); some of this content was replicated on Twitter. It seems that content published on Twitter is automatically redirected to G1's website

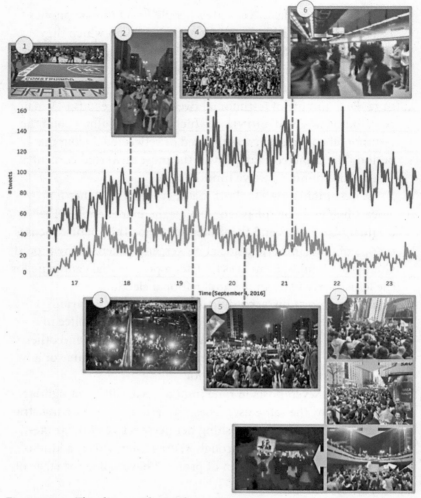

Figure 10.1   This diagram depicts how citizenry portrayed the events on a near real-time basis up to its end, when some of the users publish their images in an all-in-one format, supposedly after getting home. The top line are testimonial tweets while the bottom line are the total tweets within the dataset for the period. Source: Author with images from Twitter.

but not the other way around. An analysis of G1's coverage of the event does not seem to corroborate the suggestion that it was biased; indeed, the major complaints tended to be directed at TV news and printed press, as widely documented by scholars.[47] Such appreciation, though, is beyond the scope of this research.

Table 10.1   Comparative of testimonial tweets against mainstream media

Key event	Testimonial tweets	G1 live coverage
Protesters start to move towards destination	18:03	18:00
Entering Av. Rebouças	18:41	18:40
Final act	19:45–20:50	19:46–20:33
Police hostility and tear gas thrown into the crowd	20:51	20h49

Source: Author with data from Twitter and G1.

There was a clear intent by some users to respond to or counter the mainstream media through testimonial tweets. That intent extended to the mainstream coverage of the former president Temer, provoked by the above-mentioned interview in which he had downplayed the relevance and the attendance of the protests.[48] This suggests two things: first, the mainstream media are a prominent agenda setter. Even as technology enables the creation of original, independent content, between 7 and 8 per cent of the content created and retweeted, and of the testimonial media content created, contained some reference to the president's "40 people protest" statement. Also, it showed that people took matters into their own hands and used interactive media to, as Wolton proposes, "negotiate" the meaning and even the validity of the mainstream media narrative, to assess public spokespersons,[49] and to dispute the meaning of political events.[50] It seems, though, that magnifying the effects of such engagement, even within Twitter, does not come easy for ordinary people.[51]

As we will see, some moments of the protest were more attractive for Twitter users to record and share, but all of the relevant episodes were documented to some extent. Still, the story the testimonial tweets tell about the event, when contrasted with eyewitness accounts and media reports, seems rather accurate.[52] A lot of UGC is created during an event like this, and when looking at it in sequence, a swarm-like thread is found to connect it all.

From a digital forensics perspective, though, UGC could turn out to be problematic, due to what Mortensen calls "decontextualization," which is one trait of eyewitness images. According to Mortensen, "information about the producers as well as the depicted individuals,

Roberta Prescott
@robertaprescott

Following ⌄

Acho que tem mais que 40 pessoas
#foratemer

🌐 Translate from Portuguese

6:37 PM - 4 Sep 2016

28 Retweets **27** Likes

Figure 10.2   Irony in the tweet that references the previous
day's president interview: "I'm guessing there's more than
40 people"

circumstances, locations, etc., is frequently neither volunteered nor
easily available through journalistic research."[53] Nevertheless, this work
shows that when media content abounds, social media may become the
canvas for a patchwork of fragmented images that validate themselves
through repetition rather than unity, as a result of the persistence of
the crowd rather than the verification of experts. Figure 10.3 illustrates
this phenomenon with a highly documented moment of the protest,
when people were marching through the tunnel connecting two of the
most important streets in São Paulo: Avenida Paulista and Avenida
Rebouças. The constructed image is an attempt to superimpose the
flow of images that pop up on Twitter's timeline when such an event
happens and (1) is documented by different users, (2) is shared on a
quasi-real-time basis on a common channel, such as Twitter, and (3) is

Figure 10.3   Patchwork of UGC perspectives over one scene during a lapse of around 30 minutes.

shared under a socio-technical aggregator, such as #ForaTemer, which acts as the nexus connecting the content, thus creating an illustrated "*ad hoc* public."[54]

STAGES OF THE PROTEST

The protest lasted roughly seven hours (4:30 p.m.–11:30 p.m.), with different dynamics taking place during those hours. Tilly says that although there are no "universal forms" for collective action, it "usually takes well-defined forms already familiar to the participants"; this refers to his well-known concept of a repertoire of collective action.[55] At the same time, the forms that street demonstrations take depend invariably on context.[56]

The seven hours of the protest's dataset were mapped onto five stages, based on media reports, interviews, qualitative analysis of the data, and, especially, the testimonial tweets.[57] The intention here is not to generalize for other demonstrations; the focus is solely on this particular protest. The goal is to develop insight into how these different stages reflect different patterns of creation of testimonial content. The stages are (1) gathering, (2) the march, (3) the final act, (4) the repression, and (5) mediated conversation. Table 10.2 sums up the descriptive data for each of these stages within the analyzed dataset, distinguishing testimonial from non-testimonial tweets. Although more testimonial content per minute was created during the gathering (2.8) and march(2.6) stages than during the repression stage (1.1), the testimonial tweets during this repression stage are the most retweeted, with an average 22.6 retweets per tweet. This contradicts evidence regarding patterns of the retweeting of media news content, for which depictions of conflict are less shared not only on Twitter but also on Facebook.[58] This suggests that UGC testimonials of repression mobilize users in a different way than mainstream media news.

Figure 10.4 shows the timeline for the total number of testimonial tweets published during the analyzed period, as per the classification of stages proposed. One of the key takeaways here relates to the peak within the march stage, particularly between 19:15 and 19:45 or thereabouts. That was precisely when the protesters were passing through the tunnel. The echo of the chants inside the tunnel, the darkness versus the mobile phone lights illuminating the tunnel (see figure 10.5), and the framing of

Table 10.2 Descriptive data for each stage of the protest as per the present classification

Stage	Time-lapse (hh:mm:ss)	Interval (min)	All total tweets	TESTIMONIAL				NON TESTIMONIAL			
				Total tweets	Original tweets	RT	AVG RT rate	Total tweets	Original tweets	RT	RT rate
Gathering	16:30:00–18:00:00	90	8,063	2,166	249	1,917	7.7	5,897	2,013	3,884	1.9
March	18:00:01–19:45:00	105	14,523	4,438	277	4,161	15.0	10,085	3,387	6,698	2.0
Final act	19:45:01–20:50:00	65	9,529	2,169	96	2,073	21.6	7,360	2,037	5,323	2.6
Repression	20:50:01–22:20:00	90	12,708	2,262	96	2,166	22.6	10,446	2,988	7,458	2.5
Mediated conversation	22:20:01–23:30:59	71	7,731	1,171	62	1,109	17.9	6,560	1,697	4,863	2.9
	16:30:00–23:30:59	7 hours	52,554	12,206	780	11,426	14.6	40,348	12,122	28,226	2.3

Source: Author.

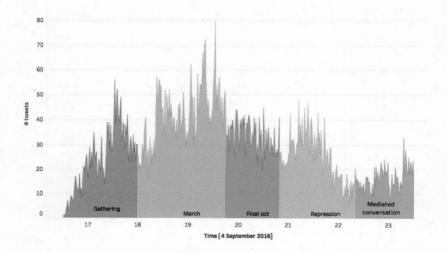

Figure 10.4   Testimonial tweets' reach (i.e., including retweets) per stages of the protest over time.

Figure 10.5   Picture taken during the protest while crossing the lightless tunnel. Source: Mídia NINJA, Twitter.

Original tweets per stage

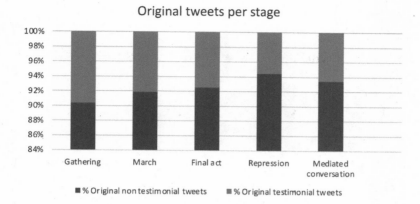

■ % Original non testimonial tweets   ■ % Original testimonial tweets

Total tweets per stage

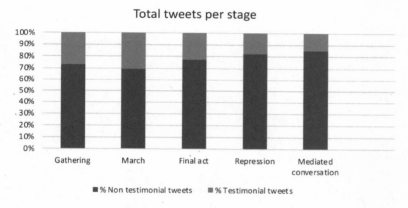

■ % Non testimonial tweets   ■ % Testimonial tweets

Figure 10.6   Original versus total tweets per stage

the crowd from above, among other features, were strong simultaneous aesthetic and emotional elements that seem to have engaged both the content creators and the audience.

Figure 10.6 displays the differences in patterns of original creation of testimonial content versus other original content (left side of the graph) and the same difference in the amount of testimonial content within the whole of the data, including retweets (right side of the graph). Although all the testimonial content is relatively diffused across the stages, the second stage, the march, features a noticeably higher amount of content in the conversation around #ForaTemer during the period of time it covers, jumping from 8 per cent (original content) to 31 per cent (total tweets), an almost fourfold difference.

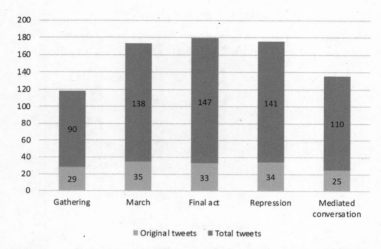

Figure 10.7 Number of tweets (original × total) per minute per stage of protest

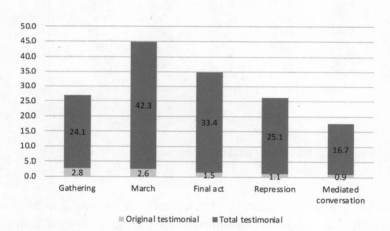

Figure 10.8 Number of testimonial tweets (original × total) per minute per stage of protest

Figure 10.7 shows the number of original and total tweets created per minute[59] for #ForaTemer during the period analyzed, divided into the stages identified earlier. Total activity grew through the final act (figure 10.7), but there was also a lot of activity during the repression stage.

Analyzing only the testimonial tweets (figure 10.8), it seems that the stage that encouraged this kind of content was the march. Such data

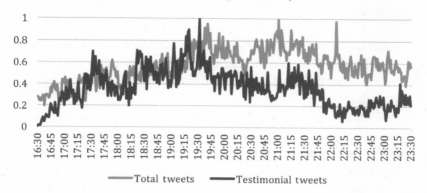

Figure 10.9   Normalized timeline for the whole period (7 hours)

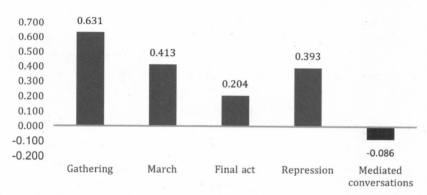

Figure 10.10   Correlation coefficient per stage of protest

could be linked to the time of day, to the aesthetic images of the crowd, or to the impulse to contradict biased information by the media and the words of the president, who belittled the protest (as discussed earlier).

Looking at the normalized correlation (figure 10.9) as divided by stage (figure 10.10), we see some important differences that help explain the general curve variations in the creation of testimonial content. Curve correlation is medium to high in the beginning and diminishes as time passes and the stages of protest advance. This could be interpreted as the agenda of the conversation tagged with #ForaTemer becoming less related to the testimonial content being created the later the content is posted (below 0.3 means there is no linear relationship, as during the final act and mediated conversation stages). That trend is broken, though, by the stage of repression: it seems that, as would be expected, testimonial content of police brutality attracts attention, and its creation and publication correlates more closely with the trends in general conversation around #ForaTemer, generating a weak to moderate positive relationship (0.393).

The final stage, mediated conversations, displays a slightly negative indicator that points to the absence of correlation between the two curves during this last period. Since the retweeting rates are still relatively high during this period (17.9 retweets per tweet), it is more probable that the trend reflects that the testimonial content has less relevance to the whole conversation. This perhaps suggests that it is important, on Twitter, to publish content immediately instead of afterwards, and that the protest itself focuses conversation around #ForaTemer as night falls and people return to their homes. Also evident in figures 10.4 and 10.10 is the counter-tendency triggered by the repression stage: it seems that the trend of testimonial content creation was steadily going down when police brutality caused it to spike back for about half an hour.

Conclusion

This research points to the possibility of using UGC as a potentially reliable alternative to broadcast media for documenting and even following large and extraordinary events in real-time. The method developed to identify testimonial tweets seems to generate a coherent and numerous enough set of content to do so. The motivation to create this kind of content is pivotal to the generation of enough testimonial tweets, as its legitimacy comes mainly from abundance, not from expert validation or selection. In other words, your knowledge of the event would not be very different if you followed "real time" coverage by, in this case, either the mainstream outlet G1 or the testimonial tweets tagged with #ForaTemer on Twitter. In the case at hand, the trigger was a generalized perception of media bias regarding the coverage of previous protests by Rousseff's sympathizers, boosted by a mainstream media interview with the president in which he offered an infamous and inaccurate account of the protests.

Note well that a certain set of conditions must be present to enable the documentation of extraordinary events in the form of UGC. In terms of this case study, when police conducted repressive measures, it was Mídia NINJA, an emerging digital alternative media outlet with a strong prsence on Twitter and Facebook, that documented what was happening, instead of ordinary people, since the media outlet was equipped to face the intensity of tear gas and other collateral violence of institutional repression against street demonstrations.

It is clear that even within one event, there are different triggers for the creation and diffusion of UGC. The data analyzed suggest that different stages of the protest presented different patterns of creation and dissemination (as measured by average retweeting and percentage of testimonial content within the whole dataset, for instance). Testimonial tweets accounting for the event were more or less relevant within the whole conversation according to different stages and hours of the day. There are some likely reasons for this: on the one hand, contextual factors such as the landscape, acoustics, architecture, and time of day (lighting conditions) may work as catalysts for UGC creation; on the other, the competition for audiences' attention with other activities, as Sunday evening, begins. Also, perhaps the nearly live tweets were perceived as more relevant compared to tweets of the lived experience that were posted a few hours later, in the aftermath of the protest.

The interplay between news media and social media is evidenced in this study in some respects. First, the main news media outlet in Brazil used both Twitter and its own platform in an integrated way, but privileged its own. Also, when we compare the traditional journalistic account of the event and the collective fragmented account of testimonial tweets, the timeline is surprisingly similar. Finally, mainstream media's influence as a motivating factor for content creation is clear; note the high volume of content responding to the news published one night before the event: the "40 people protest."

There are a number of limitations to the interpretation of the results, however, as Twitter is not representative of all of the Brazilian population, nor of the entire constituency of the protest. Moreover, one single hashtag is far from producing the perfect sample with which to analyze the content and reach definitive conclusions. Further work could take as a starting point a more comprehensive dataset around a topic, with sets of keywords and hashtags to validate whether the patterns observed repeat or differ. Still, the analysis does shed some light on ways that UGC may serve social sciences, journalism, and even ordinary users: social media can act as a source of this content and as a channel on which to publish self-created content documenting an extraordinary event. Although the impact of such publication is obviously more limited for those with fewer followers, the patchwork of fragmented UGC images adds up to a mosaic with different angles, which not only increases the chances of general users stumbling upon similar content but also simultaneously delivers different angles and allows for easier verification by professional journalists, as well as by other users.

Note, however, that there are a (growing) number of problems related to such practice, such as disinformation, automated or semi-automated networks of bots and trolls that create or amplify news, the challenges of verifying and contextualizing content, and so on. All of these must be considered when designing UGC research or adopting it as a source for narrating events. Still, there is no doubt about the potential value of UGC as a complementary communicative practice for documenting events and providing an alternative registry to compare to or even confront traditional media accounts, especially when the "what" or "where" being depicted could be biased.

Acknowledgments

This research was funded by the Chilean PhD Scholarship CON-ICYT-PCHA/Doctorado Nacional/2016-21160426. It focuses on a subset of the entire dataset analyzed for the PhD research.

Notes

1 The impeachment process, as we will see, has been interpreted by many scholars as a *coup d'état*. It was followed by other important landmarks in recent Brazilian political history – first and foremost, the allegedly politically motivated arrest of ex-President Lula da Silva, which restrained him from running for president in 2018. It could be argued that this was a key event that set the conditions for the election of radical right politician Jair Bolsonaro that year. For an account of these events, refer to Santos and Guarnieri, "From Protest"; Conci. "Lula"; and Avritzer, "Pêndulo."

2 Albuquerque, "Protecting Democracy"; T. van Dijk, "Globo Media."

3 Santos and Guarnieri, "From Protest."

4 DesAutels, "UGIS."

5 Castells, *Comunicación*.

6 Wunsch-Vincent and Vickery, *Participative Web*, 27.

7 Croteau, "The Growth."

8 J. van Dijck, "Users," 43–4.

9 Proulx, "Techno-Activism."

10 Walter, in Williams et al., "Have they got news," 89.

11 Harrison and Barthel, "Wielding," 161; emphasis added.

12 J. van Dijck, "Users," 43–4.

13 Santos, "Testimonial Tweeting."

14 Mortensen, "Connective Witnessing."

15 Bruns, *Gatewatching*.

16 Polydoro, *Vídeos Amadores*, 29. For more on the aesthetics of UGC, see chapters 7 (Lithgow and Martin) and 9 (Lithgow).

17 Pantti, "Getting Closer?"

18 Silverstone, "Regulation," 444.

19 Pantti, "Getting closer?"

20 Wahl-Jorgensen et al., "Audience Views," 181.

21 Jinkings et al., *Por que*.

22 Guerrero and Márquez-Ramírez, "'Captured-Liberal.'"

23 de Araújo et al., "Mídia, Movimento Passe Livre e cidadania"; Fontanetto and Cavalcanti, "A cidade."

24 Weaver, "Audience Need."

25 Oswald, "Na China."

26 Golstein, "La tormenta"; Ortellado et al., "Uma sociedade."

27 Jinkings et al., *Por que*.

28 Ansell, "Impeaching"; Albuquerque, "Protecting."

29 Hirata, "PT compara Temer."

30 Chomsky, interview.

31 T. van Dijk, "How Globo media."

32 Santos, "Testimonial tweet."

33 Rogers, "Debanalizing Twitter," ix.

34 Bail, "The cultural environment," 467.

35 Bruns and Stieglitz, "Metrics," 70; emphasis added.

36 Risse et al., "Documenting," 208.

37 Bruns, *Gatewatching*, 9.

38 Sifter, originally hosted at https://sifter.texifter.com and connected to Twitter's Firehose, presumably delivered the complete group of tweets with the search criteria used. It has been decommissioned as of

30 September 2018, and Twitter Firehose also is no longer available. Instead, Twitter offers a "Premium" API connection for commercial partners.

39 Tableau Desktop is a commercial software (www.tableau.com) that defines itself as a "business intelligence and analytics" tool.

40 Bruns and Burgess, "Use of Twitter Hashtags," 7.

41 Bruns and Moe, "Structural Layers," 18; emphasis added.

42 Though there are obvious interpretive dimensions to the audio, visual, or audiovisual creation of content (such as intentional framing), whenever they are verifiable, they are intrinsically connected to the depicted event, whereas a textual description depends heavily on the reputation of the author. In the words of Barthes, *Lo obvio,* the photo is an "iconic uncoded message" (34, my translation), more purely denotative than a text, which relies heavily on connotation – that is, symbolism and code.

43 Wardle and Derakhshan, "Information Disorder"; Bastos and Mercea, "The Brexit Botnet."

44 Mídia NINJA is an alternative activist media. Its acronym stands for "Independent Narratives, Journalism, and Action" in its Portuguese acronym.

45 MTST stands for Movimento dos Trabalhadores sem Teto (Roofless Workers Movement), an important social organization that fights for the habitational rights of roofless city workers, more or less the urban parallel with much more famous rural MST landless movement.

46 Retrieved from http://g1.globo.com/sao-paulo/ao-vivo/2016/protestos-em-sp.html on 20 November 2020.

47 See Albuquerque, "Protecting democracy"; T. van Dijk, "Globo Media"; and Damgaard, "Cascading."

48 Oswald, "Na China."

49 Wolton, *Informar.*

50 De Moraes, *A batalha da mídia.*

51 Santos, *From Testimony.*

52 Santos, "Testimonial Tweeting."

53 Mortensen, "Conflictual," 541.

54 Bruns and Burgess, "Use of Twitter Hashtags."

55 Tilly, "From Mobilization," 51.

56 van Stekelenburg, Klandermans, and Van Dijk, "Context Matters."

57 Santos, "Testimonial Tweeting."

58 Valenzuela et al., "Behavioral Effects."

59 This was done to normalize activity over time since the duration of stages was not uniform.

Bibliography

Albuquerque, Afonso. "Protecting Democracy or Conspiring against It? Media and Politics in Latin America: A Glimpse from Brazil." *Journalism*, 20, no. 7 (2017): 906–23. https://doi.org/10.1177/1464884917738376.

Ansell, Aaron. "Impeaching Dilma Rousseff: The Double Life of Corruption Allegations on Brazil's Political Right." *Culture, Theory, and Critique* 59, no. 4 (2018): 312–31. https://doi.org/10.1080/14735784.2018.1499432.

Avritzer, L. "O pêndulo da democracia no Brasil: uma análise da crise 2013–2018." *Novos Estudos CEBRAP* 37, no. 2 (2018): 273–89.

Bail, Christopher. "The Cultural Environment: Measuring Culture with Big Data." *Theory and Society* 43, nos. 3–4 (2014): 465–82. https://doi.org/10.1007/s11186-014-9216-5.

Barthes, Roland. *Lo obvio y lo obtuso: Imágenes, gestos, voces*. Barcelona: Paidós, 1986.

Bastos, Marco T., and Dan Mercea. "The Brexit Botnet and User-Generated Hyperpartisan News." *Social Science Computer Review* 37, no. 1 (2017): 38–54. https://doi.org/10.1177/0894439317734157.

Bruns, Axel. *Gatewatching and News Curation: Journalism, Social Media, and the Public Sphere*. New York: Peter Lang, 2018.

Bruns, Axel, and Jean E. Burgess. "The Use of Twitter Hashtags in the Formation of Ad Hoc Publics." In 6th European Consortium for Political Research General Conference, 25–27 August 2011, University of Iceland, Reykjavik, 2011.

Bruns, Axel, and Hallyvard Moe. "Structural Layers of Communication on Twitter." In *Twitter and Society*, edited by Katrin Weller, Axel Bruns, et al., 15–28. New York: Peter Lang, 2014.

Bruns, Axel, and Stefan Stieglitz. "Metrics for Understanding Communication on Twitter." In *Twitter and Society*, edited by Katrin Weller, Axel Bruns, et al., 69–82. New York: Peter Lang: 2014.

Castells, Manuel. *Comunicación y Poder*. Madrid: Alianza Editorial, 2009.

Conci, Luiz Guilherme Arcaro. "The Lula da Silva Case: Background and the Effects of His Conviction." *DPCE Online* 35, no. 2 (2018): 425–39.

Croteau, David. "The Growth of Self-Produced Media Content and the Challenge to Media Studies." *Critical Studies in Media Communication* 23, no. 4 (2006): 340–4.

Damgaard, Mads. "Cascading Corruption News: Explaining the Bias of Media Sttention to Brazil's Political Scandals." *Opinião Pública* 24, no. 1 (2018): 114–43.

de Araújo, L.V., M.H. de Sousa Alves Filho, and M.V. Nunes. "Mídia, Movimento Passe Livre e cidadania: a cobertura do estado de São Paulo durante as manifestações de junho de 2013." *Revista Mídia e Cotidiano* 5, no. 5 (2014): 1–18. https://doi.org/10.22409/ppgmc.v5i5.9723.

de Moraes, Denis. *A batalha da mídia: governos progressistas e políticas de comunicação na América Latina e outros ensaios.* Rio de Janeiro: Pão e Rosas, 2009.

DesAutels, Philip. "UGIS: Understanding the Nature of User-Generated Information Systems." *Business Horizons* 54, no. 3 (2011): 185–92. https://doi.org/10.1016/j.bushor.2010.12.003.

Fontanetto, Renata M., and Cecilia Cavalcanti. "A cidade em narrativas: jornalismos tradicional e cidadão durante as 'Jornadas de Junho' de 2013 no Brasil." (Informe). *Chasqui* 131 (2016): 349–62.

Goldstein, Ariel. "La tormenta perfecta: crisis e impeachment en el segundo mandato de Dilma Rousseff." *Análisis Político* 29, no. 88 (2016): 90–104.

Chomsky, Noam. "Noam Chomsky: Brazil's President Dilma Rousseff 'Impeached by a Gang of Thieves.'" Interview by Amy Goodman. *Democracy Now!,* 17 May 2016. Video, 30:28. https://www.democracynow.org/2016/5/17/noam_chomsky_brazils_president_dilma_rousseff.

Guerrero, Manuel A., and Mireya Márquez-Ramírez. "The 'Captured-Liberal' Model: Media Systems, Journalism, and Communication Policies in Latin America." *International Journal of Hispanic Media* 7 (2004): 1–12.

Harrison, Teresa M., and Brea Barthel. "Wielding New Media in Web 2.0: Exploring the History of Engagement with the Collaborative Construction of Media Products." *New Media and Society* 11, nos. 1–2 (2009): 155–78. https://doi.org/10.1177/1461444808099580.

Hirata, Lucas. "PT compara Temer a traidor da inconfidência mineira." *Estado de São Paulo,* 21 April 2016. https://politica.estadao.com.br/noticias/geral,pt-compara-temer-a-traidor-da-inconfidencia-mineira,10000027423.

Jinkings, Ivana, Kim Doria, and Murilo Cleto, eds. *Por que gritamos golpe.* São Paulo: Boitempo Editorial, 2016.

Mortensen, Mette. "Conflictual Media Events, Eyewitness Images, and the Boston Marathon Bombing (2013)." *Journalism Practice* 9, no. 4 (2015): 536–51. https://doi.org/10.1080/17512786.2015.1030140.

– "Connective Witnessing: Reconfiguring the Relationship between the Individual and the Collective." *Information, Communication, and Society* 18, no. 11 (2015): 1393–406. https://doi.org/10.1080/1369118X.2015.1061574.

Ortellado, Pablo, Esther Solano, and Márcio Moretto. "Uma sociedade polarizada?" In *Por que gritamos golpe,* edited by Ivana Jinkings, Kim Doria, and Murilo Cleto. São Paulo: Boitempo Editorial, 2016.

Oswald, Vivian. "Na China, Temer minimiza protestos contra impeachment." *O Globo,* 3 September 2016. https://oglobo.

globo.com/brasil/na-china-temer-minimiza-protestos-contra-impeachment-20047094.

Pantti, Mervi. "Getting Closer? Encounters of the National Media with Global Images." *Journalism Studies* 14, no. 2 (2013): 201–18. https://doi.org/10.1080/1461670X.2012.718551.

Polydoro, Felipe S. *Vídeos Amadores de Acontecimentos: Realismo, evidência e política na cultura visual contemporânea*, PhD diss., Escola de Comunicação e Artes, Universidade de São Paulo, 2016.

Proulx, Serge. "Techno-Activism as Catalyst in Promoting Social Change." *COST Action 298 Conference*, Moscow, 2007, 1–10.

Risse, Thomas, Wim Peters, Pierre Senellart, and Diana Maynard. "Documenting Contemporary Society by Preserving Relevant Information from Twitter." In *Twitter and Society*, edited by Karin Weller, Axel Bruns, Jean Burgess, Merja Mahrt, and Cornelius Puschmann, 207–20. New York: Peter Lang, 2014.

Rogers, Richard. "Debanalizing Twitter: The Transformation of an Object of Study." In *Twitter and Society*, edited by Karin Weller, Axel Bruns, Jean Burgess, Merja Mahrt, and Cornelius Puschmann, ix–xxvi. New York: Peter Lang, 2014.

Santos, Marcelo. "Testimonial Tweeting: People's Voice (and Eyes) on Anti-impeachment Protests in Brazil." *Inmediaciones de la Comunicación* 13, no. 1 (2018): 215–39. https://doi.org/10.18861/ic.2018.13.1.2834.

– *From Testimony to Testimonial: A Proposal for the Conceptualization of Testimonial User-Generated Content (tUGC) on Twitter Applied to the Case of the Protests against Dilma Rousseff's Impeachment.* PhD diss., Pontificia Universidad Católica de Chile, 2018. https://repositorio.uc.cl/handle/11534/22328.

Santos, Fabiano, and Fernando Guarnieri. 2016. "From Protest to Parliamentary Coup: An Overview of Brazil's Recent History." *Journal of Latin American Cultural Studies* 25, no. 4 (2016): 485–94. https://doi.org/10.1080/13569325.2016.1230940.

Silverstone, Roger. "Regulation, Media Literacy, and Media Civics." *Media, Culture, and Society* 26, no. 3 (2004): 440–9. https://doi.org/10.1177/0163443704042557.

Tilly, Charles. "From Mobilization to Revolution." *CRSO Working Paper 8156*, University of Michigan, 1977. https://deepblue.lib.umich.edu/bitstream/handle/2027.42/50931/156.pdf.

Valenzuela, Sebastián, Martina Piña, and Javier Ramírez. "Behavioral Effects of Framing on Social Media Users: How Conflict, Economic, Human Interest, and Morality Frames Drive News Sharing." *Journal of Communication* 67, no. 5 (2017): 803–26. https://doi.org/10.1111/jcom.12325.

van Dijck, José. "Users Like You? Theorizing Agency in User-Generated Content." *Media, Culture, and Society* 31, no. 1 (2009): 41–58. https://doi.org/10.1177/0163443708098245.

van Dijk, Teun. "How Globo Media Manipulated the Impeachment of Brazilian President Dilma Rousseff." *Discourse and Communication* 11, no. 2 (2017): 199–229. https://doi.org/10.1177/1750481317691838.

van Stekelenburg, Jacquelien, Bert Klandermans, and Wilco. W. Van Dijk. "Context Matters: Explaining How and Why Mobilizing Context Influences Motivational Dynamics." *Journal of Social Issues* 65, no. 4 (2009): 815–38. https://doi.org/10.1111/j.1540-4560.2009.01626.x.

Wahl-Jorgensen, Karin, Andy Williams, and Claire Wardle. "Audience Views on User-Generated Content-Exploring the Value of News from the Bottom Up." *Northern Lights: Film and Media Studies Yearbook* 8, no. 1 (2010): 177–94.

Wardle, Claire, and Hossein Derakhshan. "Information Disorder: Toward an Interdisciplinary Framework for Research and Policy Making." Council of Europe report DGI(2017)09, 2017. https://rm.coe.int/information-disorder-toward-an-interdisciplinary-framework-for-researc/168076277c

Weaver, David H. "Audience Need for Orientation and Media Effects." *Communication Research* 7, no. 3 (1980): 361–73. https://doi.org/10.1177/009365028000700305.

Williams, Andy, Claire Wardle, and Karin Wahl-Jorgensen. "Have They Got News for Us?': Audience Revolution or Business as Usual at the BBC?" *Journalism Practice* 5, no. 1 (2011): 85–99. https://doi.org/10.1080/17512781003670031.

Wolton, Dominique. *Informar no es Comunicar: contra la ideología tecnológica*. Barcelona: Gedisa, 2010.

Wunsch-Vincent, Sacha, and Graham Vickery. *Participative Web and User-Created Content Web 2.0, Wikis and Social Networking*. Paris: OECD, 2007. https://www.oecd.org/sti/ieconomy/participativewebanduser-createdcontentweb20wikisandsocialnetworking.htm.

Making Room for Citizen Journalism against User-Generated Content

Situating South Korea's OhmyNews in the History of Journalism

INKYU KANG

Citizen journalism is a contested concept. Some have welcomed the idea of swinging open the door of journalism to everybody, hailing it as a "democratization of media" or "democratic journalism."[1] A majority of people with a journalism background, however, have expressed serious concerns about citizen journalism. Samuel Freedman has denounced it as an "attempt to degrade, even to disenfranchise journalism."[2] David Hazinski has dismissed the possibility of citizen journalism, stating that "it really isn't journalism at all."[3] He even argues that the practice of citizen journalism needs to be regulated, citing "the strong probability of fraud and abuse." And this negative view of citizen journalism is not limited to professional journalists. Entrepreneur and author Andrew Keen has painted an equally unflattering picture of citizen journalists:[4] "Most amateur journalists are wannabe Matt Drudges – a pajama army of mostly anonymous, self-referential writers who exist not to report news but to spread gossip, sensationalize political scandal, display embarrassing photos of public figures, and link to stories on imaginative topics such as UFO sightings or 9/11 conspiracy theories."

More than two decades have passed since Web-based citizen journalism began to take root, but perceptions of it have not significantly improved, as evinced by recent studies. When asked to describe citizen journalists, the answers given by the largest percentage of mainstream journalists focused on their "lack of training."[5] They see citizen journalists as "non-trained members contributing information ... without regard to the accuracy and fairness of their contributions." In the same vein, the news editors who participated in the survey defined citizen journalism in terms of "opinion" and "bias." They perceive citizen journalism as "typically inaccurate info from misinformed people who write based on their opinions."[6] If citizen journalism means inaccurate information provided by misinformed people, then it is the *opposite* of journalism.

Quite a few media scholars have a similar attitude. Molina and her colleagues, for example, set citizen journalism against "real news."[7] In their search for ways to detect problematic content through machine learning, the authors categorize citizen journalism as "fake news," bundling it with false news, polarized content, satire, misreporting, commentary, and efforts to persuade. Their categorization is part of an apparent attempt to amplify the reliability and credibility of news sources rather than disparage non-traditional form of journalism; this approach, however, reveals the generalized assumption that citizen journalism is not "real journalism." Citizen journalism has yet to earn a legitimate place in journalism, although it has been discussed extensively and passionately for years.

A review of the literature reveals that the unbridgeable disagreement derives not only from different attitudes toward the changing role of citizens in journalism but also from the lack of a working definition of citizen journalism. For all the dramatic responses mentioned above, the concept lacks a consistent definition. For this reason, its theoretical boundaries have yet to be delineated, and this has added to the confusion and controversy.[8] The term "citizen journalism" is applied to wildly different practices, from the uploading of unedited video footage, to crudely crafted pseudo-reporting, and even to quality journalism in its fullest sense. For Freedman, citizen journalism is synonymous with uploading "raw material" to websites like YouTube.[9] Fred Brown equates citizen journalism with blogging, which he thinks consists at best of "finding the flaws in others' information," in contrast to traditional journalism, which finds and reports "new, accurate information."[10]

More recently, citizen journalism has been associated with social media. Lynn Clark and Regina Marchi, for instance, view "mediated storytelling" through social media as "citizen journalism."[11] They define citizen journalism broadly to include "socializing practices" such as "sharing links to humorous political satire and commentary" as well as "videos or photos of the events unfolding around them."

They investigate what they call "youth citizen journalism" in a positive light, but this conceptualization misses a key aspect of journalism: verification.[12] It would be a fatal omission to ignore this fundamental journalistic filtering process, which is "what separates journalism from entertainment, propaganda, fiction, or art."[13]

Contrary to conventional wisdom, citizen journalism has always taken seriously the core values of journalism, such as accuracy, reliability, and independence. OhmyNews, which spearheaded Internet-based participatory journalism, has been fact-checking all of its stories before publication since its launch in 2000. OhmyNews's citizen reporters work closely with the professional editorial staff and indeed are required to abide by the organization's code of ethics and journalistic standards. Many critiques amount to straw man arguments by failing to consider journalistic integrity – a crucial aspect of citizen journalism – and this has resulted, unfortunately, in a missed opportunity for a constructive discussion of a potentially beneficial way to practise journalism. Citizen journalism can help address the issue of relevance, which has been pointed out as one of the most significant problems facing journalism today.

A common mistake in these discussions is to examine citizen journalism in terms of "user-generated content" (UGC) or "Web 2.0." A notable example is a 2007 report by the Organisation for Economic Co-operation and Development (OECD), which defines citizen journalism as a type of user-created content (UCC).[14] Even recent studies routinely conceptualize citizen journalism along the same lines, defining it as "UGC," "user-submitted stories (USS)" or the "new genre of user-generated content."[15] If that were accurate, then citizen journalism could include any type of content, regardless of quality, as long as it had been generated by non-professionals. Is it fair to criticize citizen journalism for its inaccuracies after defining it so broadly and vaguely and without any regard for accuracy?

To construe UGC as a technology-oriented business discourse is to ignore the elements of truth, intention, morality, and social responsibility that constitute the essence of journalism. By ignoring the fundamental tenets of journalism, those using the language of UGC have reinforced misunderstandings of citizen journalism.[16] This chapter explores the possibility of developing citizen journalism into a public forum "by and of the people, rather than merely for the people."[17]

The Public Sphere, Journalism, and "Pointless Babbling"

Journalism plays a fundamental role in democracy, which depends on deliberation. An independent press is an integral part of public debate; without an accurate understanding of what is happening around us, we, the public, cannot make informed decisions about issues that matter. In the nineteenth century the emergence of a powerful, profit-driven, entertainment-focused media system started undermining public debate.[18] The media became unrepresentative and non-participatory (Curran 1991).[19] Jürgen Habermas, who conceptualized the public sphere, wrote: "By 'the public sphere' we mean first of all a realm of our social life in which something approaching public opinion can be formed. Access is guaranteed to all citizens. A portion of the public sphere comes into being in every conversation in which private individuals assemble to form a public body."

Journalism is supposed to function as a public sphere, but to that end, it should be open to all citizens. Habermas does not mean, of course, that all news stories should be written by average citizens. Even so, to involve citizens in the public debate, journalists must report things deemed important to the general public. Journalism today faces many challenges, and one of the most serious is that it is losing its relevance for the public. Today, nearly half of all journalists (46 per cent) think they are extremely or very connected with their audiences, yet only about one quarter of the public (26 per cent) think they are connected to journalism.[20]

This disconnect between professional journalists and the public is also evident in the discrepancy in perceptions of how well news organizations are doing in terms of journalism's core functions. In particular, the public has been critical of journalists' capacity to give voice to the voiceless. Even journalists themselves admit that news organizations do a poor job at this essential task (35 per cent), and the public's evaluation is even harsher. Less than one quarter of the surveyed public say that news organizations are doing well (24 per cent), and a whopping 45 per cent say they are doing poorly.[21] Given that the job of the press is seen as being "to comfort the afflicted and afflict the comfortable," the public's decidedly negative response raises questions about the health of journalism. Unfortunately, news outlets are not trusted by their audiences in terms of accuracy, either. A strong majority of journalists think they are accurately reporting the news (65 per cent), but only a little over one third of the American public agree (35 per cent). And distrust in news outlets is not limited to the United States; it is a global issue.[22]

Fred Brown, an early critic of participatory journalism, contended that "a professional journalist's No. 1 obligation is to be accurate" while "a citizen journalist's No. 1 obligation is to be interesting."[23] Without defining citizen journalism, he asserted that, since many blogs are not fact-checked, citizen journalism must be riddled with errors and misinformation. When Hazinski warned of the dangers of citizen journalism and called for its regulation, some professional journalists took issue with his claim.[24] For example, Chuck Simmins lamented, "we're the real danger here," citing "little sign that ethics and standards are practiced" among professional journalists: "Anonymous sources, misstatements of fact, misquoting, staging photographs, outright falsifying of documents, and lack of fact checking are rife in journalism today. I, and those like me, could hardly do worse."[25]

That is a scorching criticism of journalism, but the disappointing performance of journalists does not in itself establish the legitimacy of citizen journalism. Indeed, many professionally trained journalists do not properly carry out their tasks, but that does not mean that every journalist deserves harsh condemnation. The same can be said about citizen journalism. No doubt, citizen journalists commit errors and inaccuracies, but this is not because average citizens are destined to disseminate misinformation, nor is it because citizen journalism cannot develop a verification system. Both professional and citizen journalism need an editorial filtering process, and both have one, as seen in the OhmyNews case. Although the principle of verification does not guarantee the fulfillment of the ideals and promises, it is still a necessary feature of journalism.

The American Press Institute (API) makes a clear distinction between journalism and other forms of communication – such as social media posts, emails, and text messages – which it refers to as "pointless babble." Journalism is only a tiny fraction of the information that is now increasingly available: "Journalism occupies a much smaller space than the talk, entertainment, opinion, assertion, advertising and propaganda that dominate the media universe."[26] According to the API, what separates journalism from the "stuff out there" is the discipline of verification. If the production and dissemination of information does not involve this essential process, it cannot be called journalism. Many of the practices and products that have been criticized as part of citizen journalism are not even meant to be journalism, so they must not be referred to as citizen *journalism*. In other words, "pointless babble" does not account either as professional journalism or as citizen journalism.

Many journalists and researchers have criticized citizen journalism for its inaccuracy, but it is a matter of verification, not a feature per se of citizen journalism. Nevertheless, associations between non-traditional journalism and inaccuracy and bias have come to be unquestioned. Whatever its form and content, journalism involves ongoing efforts to go one step further toward the unattainable yet necessary goal of the ultimate truth.[27] Again, journalism involves the gathering and distribution of verified information that can help society's members make informed decisions about their public and private lives. Journalism can be entertaining, but it must be entertaining within the boundaries of journalism "as a utility to empower the informed."[28]

Journalism and the Rhetoric of UGC and Web 2.0

Today, ordinary people are generating more information than professionals. Hollywood churns out about 700 hours of feature films every year; ordinary people upload roughly 100,000 hours of videos to YouTube every *day*.[29] The performance of Facebook is equally impressive: more than 1 billion stories are shared every day on that social network.[30] On Instagram, about 95 million pictures and videos are uploaded every day.[31] Twitter cannot be ignored; it is estimated that 500 million tweets are sent each day. TikTok, a popular short-form video platform, has become an important part of the media mix. There are also more than 600 million blogs, which publish 4.4 million new posts each day.[32]

The implication of these statistics is clear: the promise of UGC and Web 2.0 has already been fulfilled, at least in terms of quantity. The interactive nature of digital media is recasting the relationship between producer and audience, and journalism is not immune from this. Those who have traditionally been called "news consumers" can do more than simply read, watch, or listen to the news; they can distribute, comment on, and debate it. They can also create their own content, equipped with easy-to-use, affordable, but professional-grade tools and with always-on connectivity. There remains the question, however, of whether all the blog posts and social media feeds can be called "journalism."

If evaluated solely in terms of quantity, the media content created and used by end users is simply astonishing. The prevalence of digital devices is turning the information problem from a quantity issue into a quality one. In the past, when information was scarce, the main issue was how to make it available to the public. The barriers to physical access and technology have been drastically lowered in recent decades. For example, in 2021 about 85 per cent of Americans used a smart phone – a notable leap from 2011, when a mere 35 per cent did so.[33] According to the same survey, about three quarters of American adults now own a desktop or laptop computer, and roughly half have a tablet computer (a device that did not even exist until 2010). These handheld devices have contributed both to Internet penetration and to digital literacy in the conventional sense. Nowadays, thanks to graphical user interfaces (GUI) and voice user interfaces (VUI), combined with always-on connectivity, people can not only search and consume information easily but also create and distribute it freely.

The power of citizens is growing as the barriers to creating and distributing information are weakening, but quality remains a fundamental issue. As Lacy and Rosenstiel point out, "the question of why we should be concerned with the quality of journalism begins with the question of why we should be concerned with journalism."[34] Journalism is a matter of quality, not quantity. When it comes to journalism, the public's role is closer to that of citizens rather than customers. A traditional role of the press is to serve as a watchdog for the people; watchdog journalism has been advocated not just by liberal theorists but by the public and journalists themselves "as a mechanism for strengthening accountability in democratic governance."[35]

Of course, there is a business aspect to journalism, and building and maintaining a sustainable revenue model is crucial for any news organization. Journalism as a business, however, is meant to ensure its continued role, which is to provide a public service and function as a watchdog. To achieve those ends, it requires financial independence. Holding the powerful accountable is an indispensable element of journalistic practices. Almost three out of four American adults (73 per cent), for instance, believe that journalists should act as watchdogs over elected officials.[36] This role is inseparable from quality reporting. The more accurate the information the press provides, the better the decisions citizens can make, and the more accountable the government will be:

> If one accepts the definition that quality represents the ability
> of journalism to fulfill its functions, then improving quality of
> journalism would improve the ability of citizens to use
> the journalism to make better decisions and provide a check
> against abuse and malfeasance by people in power. This notion
> may be most memorably embedded in the famous aphorism
> of Joseph Pulitzer: "our Republic and its press will rise or fall
> together." The simple equation becomes – increasing quality of
> journalism will lead to better decisions by citizens and more
> accountability of government.[37]

In the same vein, the API defines journalism as "the activity of gathering, assessing, creating, and presenting news and information," and its purpose is "to provide citizens with the information they need to make the best possible decisions about their lives, their communities, their societies, and their governments."[38] Thus, for something to be called journalism – regardless of whether it is citizen or professional – it should meet specific qualifications: motive and intent, as well as a conscious, systematic process for producing "functional truth." The notion of UGC is routinely employed in discussions of citizen journalism, but as a business discourse that has developed based on the industry/consumer framework, it is unsuitable for conceptualizing any form of journalism meant to provide information to citizens for self-governance.

The term "Web 2.0" is closely associated with UGC: it is often asserted that "in the era of Web 2.0, user-generated content has somehow displaced mass media in the cultural lives of everyday people."[39] As celebratory rhetoric of user participation, Web 2.0 has been criticized along with UGC as a deceptive, self-serving discourse that masks free labour and inequalities. José van Dijck and David Nieborg see Web 2.0 as "an odd combination of grass roots values of commonality and hardcore capitalist value."[40] Christian Fuchs criticizes the utopian discourse as a "capital accumulation model" that has been actively promoted to convince investors to support new Internet startups since the dot.com crisis of 2000.[41] He suggests that Web 2.0 has functioned as a techno-deterministic ideology to disseminate the misconception that social media provide "new opportunities for participation" and enable "new forms of political struggle" and "more democracy."[42]

Anna Jönsson and Henrik Örnebring critically analyzed actual UGC, exposing the illusory nature of UGC discourse.[43] They showed that the participation of "users-as-consumers" tends to be addressed in the context of consumption. The utopian rhetoric assumed that users would be co-creators, but things have turned out differently, especially in the realm of journalism. As the authors demonstrate, "The 'we write, you read'-principle still rules the newsroom and UGC is placed within this framework."[44] Their study sheds harsh light on the misguided use of the concepts of UGC and Web 2.0. "Previous research on UGC/journalism has primarily focused on hard news journalism," Jönsson and Örnebring conclude. "However, in actual practice in online newspapers, UGC has very little to do with hard news journalism."[45]

Users have been empowered to some degree, but their participation is limited to the creation of culture-oriented content; their involvement in news production is rare. In addition, their content is predominantly personal and life-oriented, which deviates from the Habermasian notion of the public sphere as a place for "critical public debate" about "matters of general interest" rather than private affairs.[46] One critical problem with the UGC/Web 2.0 rhetoric is that it erases the rights and responsibilities of citizens, situating them as "users-as-consumers."[47] It is a category mistake to apply this techno-deterministic, business-centric framework to the discussion of journalism, regardless of the type.

OhmyNews and Citizen Journalism Redefined

The previous sections critically evaluated the notion of "citizen journalism." A particular focus has been on the industry discourse of UGC and Web 2.0 as umbrella terms encompassing a wide range of Web-based services, including blogs, wikis, and social media.[48] Although commonly used interchangeably with citizen journalism, the concepts emerged from very different socio-economic contexts and are thus incompatible with a specific type of communication called "journalism." Nonetheless, many studies have failed to distinguish between UGC/Web 2.0 and journalism (e.g., Keen 2007; Allan 2013; Nah et al. 2015; Nah and Chung 2020; Zeng et al. 2019).[49] What, then, is citizen journalism, and how should it be defined?

Some scholars trace the history of citizen journalism back to the San Francisco earthquake of 1906 or the assassination of John F. Kennedy in 1963.[50] The aftermath of the disaster in the Bay Area was captured by the residents in black and white, and the president's killing was captured on a dress manufacturer's shaky home-movie camera. Since then, the number of prominent cases of citizen reportage has increased significantly due to the widespread use of video-enabled mobile phones, as seen in the 9/11 attacks, the 2005 London bombings, and Hurricane Katrina. For this reason, Stuart Allan refers to citizen journalism as "accident journalism."[51] He suggests that what distinguishes professional journalism from "citizen witnessing" is the reporter's ability to "be dispassionately impartial when documenting what they see and hear":

> For the ordinary individual, however, any sense of journalism
> is likely to be far from their mind, should they find themselves
> unexpectedly caught-up in disturbing events rapidly unfolding
> around them. Nevertheless, they may well strive to engage in
> a form of eyewitness reportage, perhaps using their mobile
> telephone to capture an image, generate a video, or craft a tweet
> in order to record and share their personal experience of what is
> happening in front of them.[52]

The above description reflects the conventional view that citizen journalism is a product of chance rather than daily practice. Citizen journalism is often regarded as "accidental participation by those who happen to be on site when natural disasters, terrorism, and political turmoil take place."[53] This viewpoint is prevalent even in studies that explore the journalistic role of citizens in a positive light.[54] Within this framework, citizens can hardly play a central and systematic part in news-making. Most often, their role is limited to that of being an eyewitness lucky enough to have access to a recording device. It may be no surprise that Freedman argues that citizen journalism is "less journalism than the raw material" submitted by "anybody with a video camera or cellphone or blog."[55]

Albarado writes that "both the term and the practice [of citizen journalism] crystallized in South Korea," where Oh Yeon-ho launched OhmyNews in 2000, declaring that "every citizen is a reporter."[56] This motto is often confused with the rhetoric of UGC or Web 2.0, as seen in the criticism made by Keen: "Wikipedia is far from alone in its celebration of the amateur. The 'citizen journalists,' too – the amateur pundits, reporters, writers, commentators, and critics on the blogosphere – carry the banner of the noble amateur on Web 2.0."[57] Note carefully that the founder of OhmyNews created a professional editorial team and a code of ethics *before* recruiting its "news guerrillas." OhmyNews has let citizens play a central role in news gathering and reporting, but journalistic integrity has always been a pillar of the news service.

OhmyNews's emphasis on journalism ethics and standards had a significant impact on early studies of citizen journalism. For example, Shayne Bowman and Chris Willis viewed OhmyNews as "one future of online news [that] has arrived a few years early." Note that they define participatory journalism in terms not only of the active role of citizens but also of credibility, accuracy, and relevance, which constitute the core principles of journalism: "The act of a citizen, or group of citizens, playing an active role in the process of collecting, reporting, analyzing and disseminating news and information. The intent of this participation is to provide independent, reliable, accurate, wide-ranging and relevant information that a democracy requires."[58]

Likewise, Mary Joyce conceptualizes citizen journalism based on OhmyNews, which is "a pioneer in this field, not only for being an early player, but for having created a successful model with citizens as journalists and professional editors to filter content."[59] What makes OhmyNews stand out from other news organizations is its nearly 100,000 citizen reporters, who contribute the vast majority of the articles published on the site. The citizen reporters are from all walks of life; they include students, teachers, homemakers, farmers, factory workers, college professors, lawyers, lawmakers, and so forth. When citizens participate as news producers rather than consumers, it is inevitable that the criteria of news value change. They tend to find social issues in their own intimate surroundings: teachers write about the problems of standardized testing, while workers deal with job insecurity and unsafe working conditions, and so on.

What distinguishes OhmyNews from most online media or practices miscategorized as "citizen journalism" is that every story it publishes goes through strict verification procedures. Brown claimed that "a citizen journalist is usually a lone crusader," unlike professional journalists,

who have "layers of editors checking [their] facts."[60] If someone called a
"citizen journalist" wilfully ignores this fundamental step and distributes
questionable information, we need to blame the mislabelling, not the
label itself. The contributors to OhmyNews are never "lone crusaders"
of the sort alluded to earlier. They work closely with "layers of editors
checking their facts" while enjoying ready access to various resources,
including press releases, official sources, legal advice, and a wide range
of training opportunities such as in-house writing workshops. They can
also learn from more experienced citizen reporters while socializing
with them online and offline.

We can learn two important things from the OhmyNews model. One
is that citizens play a major role in the news-making process, aided by
editorial staff whose main responsibility is to support citizen reporters.
At OhmyNews, citizens go beyond being simply accidental observers
"who find themselves on the scene of events before journalists arrive"
to provide pictures, videos, and first-hand accounts, which journalists
may or may not use in their stories.[61] Another important feature of the
OhmyNews model is that citizen journalists are not meant to replace
their professional counterparts. Although they are significantly fewer in
number than citizen journalists, OhmyNews does have a professional
reporting team. Professional journalists and citizen reporters play
different roles: the former take care of comprehensive news coverage,
while the latter handle very specific topics that they know well or in
which they have first-hand experience.

Journalists routinely interview experts when writing a story about a
topic in which they have no expertise. Although most citizen journalists
do not have a degree in journalism, their lack of training is limited
to writing and reporting. Most of them have their own expertise in
specific domains. If a semiconductor engineer has worked in his field for
decades, would it be amateurish for that person to write a critical piece
on specific details of a government policy to promote the semiconductor
industry? If a Korean Japanese has operated a business in Tokyo, is it
unimaginable for that person to contribute an investigative report about
the post-COVID economic situation of Japan? These are the real cases of
Bongryul Lee and Chulhyun Park, respectively, who recently wrote top
stories about the aforementioned topics. Citizens can be both reporters
and experts. As Dan Gillmor admitted, "as a group, my readers know
more about any given topic than I ever could."[62]

Since its launch, OhmyNews has inspired many similar experiments around the world, but none have been able to replicate its success. Most of the numerous attempts, including Bayosphere (United States), NowPublic (Canada), and OhmyNews Japan, to name a few, shut down after a few years. Why are success stories so rare? As discussed, UGC has prevailed; citizen journalism has not. Their contrasting statuses make it clear that citizen journalism and UGC cannot be the same thing.

Conclusion: Call Gossip "Gossip"

The year 2020 marked the twentieth anniversary of the birth of OhmyNews. It was one of the first attempts at citizen journalism and today is one of the oldest organizations of its kind. Most of the stories it publishes are from non-professional journalists, but all of them are carefully checked and copy edited. In its analysis of OhmyNews, which is a collaborative effort between professional journalists and citizen reporters, this study has warned against equating citizen journalism with UGC or Web 2.0. Journalism involves creating and delivering validated information purposefully created to help people make deliberative decisions about their society and lives.

It is ironic that some of the most constructive ideas for citizen journalism have been provided by some of its earliest and harshest critics, including Brown, Hazinski, and Keen.[63] Brown's discussion of citizen journalism was preoccupied with blogs; he did, however, grasp the potential of citizen journalists as watchdogs: "They provide a much-needed new layer of checks on the accuracy of the mainstream. Everybody needs a watchdog. It encourages higher standards." His main concern related to the credibility of citizen reports. Yet the absence of journalistic standards and proper verification is not an inevitable aspect of citizen journalism, as proven by OhmyNews.

Some call OhmyNews a "hybrid model" in which amateur and professional journalists work together, but that does not seem to be the correct terminology; "a team of seasoned editors with years of training" is indispensable to any journalistic institution or organization.[64] So any practice that lacks this fundamental element is disqualified as journalism, whether it is conducted by professional reporters or citizen journalists. Even Hazinski, who finds the term citizen journalist as nonsensical as "citizen surgeon" or "citizen lawyer," admits that citizen reports can be a valuable addition to the news and information flow, provided that some protections are in place: "Major news organizations must create standards to substantiate citizen-contributed information and video and ensure its accuracy and authenticity. They should clarify and reinforce their own standards and work through trade organizations to enforce national standards so they have real meaning."[65]

As Hazinski suggests, it is crucial to establish journalistic standards as well as systems to ensure the accuracy and authenticity of every submission. It is unfortunate that he did not realize that OhmyNews already had these. It was not because of the obscurity of the new medium. In fact, the first successful attempt at citizen journalism attracted global media attention as "the world's first interactive online newspaper," and it grew rapidly into one of the most influential news media in South Korea.[66]

Despite all the praise it attracted, the OhmyNews model has not altered the trajectory of the academic discussion of citizen journalism as "amateur journalism." This is partly due to the widespread failure of the OhmyNews model outside the Korean peninsula. Most importantly, the discussion of citizen journalism has been dominated by misguided notions that it is equivalent to UGC and Web 2.0. By ignoring key aspects of journalism, Web 2.0 has contributed to the misunderstanding that citizen journalism is merely UGC. The term "amateur journalism" is often employed to criticize citizen journalism, but it is an oxymoron; "journalism" means a specific type of writing or reporting that meets a certain standard of quality and professionalism – even in citizen journalism.[67]

Citizen journalism needs to be limited to more narrow types of journalistic practices involving rigorous fact checking and copy editing. Journalism is an activity, not a profession; it should be judged by what is done rather than who does it.[68] More specifically, citizen journalism needs to be redefined so as to meet the conditions for both "citizen" and "journalism." First, to be called *citizen* journalism, it should be open to the all citizens so that they can play an important part in the news-making process. As Jönsson and Örnebring point out, however, "'users-as-citizens' are placed in a mostly reactive position" in the realm of journalism.[69] Citizens' empowerment can best be described as "pseudo-power." If it was "we write, you read" in the past, now it is "we write, you read and possibly comment." Citizen journalism can help address the imbalance.

Second, to be citizen *journalism*, verification is necessary. Citizen journalism is still journalism. Only information that has come through the journalistic filtering process that Freedman calls "mediating intelligence" or "editorial gate-keeping" can be categorized as such, regardless of the contributor. As Hazinski rightly puts it, "information without journalistic standards is called gossip."[70] A major pitfall in studies of citizen journalism is that "gossip" and citizen journalism are too often lumped together. Habermas emphasizes the significance of the editors in news organizations, quoting Karl Bücher: "A new element emerged between the gathering and the publication of news: the editorial staff. But for the newspaper publisher it meant that he changed from a vendor of recent news to a dealer in public opinion."[71]

Editorial staff do more than check facts and improve readability. The debate between reporters and editors serves as a microcosm of the public sphere. Even well-trained journalists and editors work within constraints, including limited time, resources, experience, and knowledge, as well as prejudices and social norms. That explains why a pioneering participatory medium, which declared that "every citizen is a reporter," started by hiring editors. Perhaps it is time to clarify that decades-old adage. Can every citizen be a reporter? Yes – as long as the reporting goes through a rigorous process of verification.

Notes

1 Baase, *A Gife of Fire*; Bowman and Willis, "We Media"; Nduhura and Prieler, "Citizen Journalism."
2 Profita, "Outside Voices."
3 "A License to Blog?," CNET, 17 December 2007. https://www.cnet.com/tech/tech-industry/a-license-to-blog.
4 Keen, *The Cult of the Amateur*, 47.
5 Chung et al., "Conceptualizing," 1702–4.
6 Ibid., 1703.
7 Molina et al., "Fake News."
8 Miller, "Citizen Journalism."
9 Profita, "Outside Voices."
10 Brown, "Citizen's Journalism."
11 Clark and Marchi, "Youth Citizen Journalism."
12 For more on the verification process, see chapters 2 (Bowler) and 3 (Miller).

13 Kovach and Rosenstiel, *The Elements of Journalism*, 101.
14 OECD, *Participative Web*.
15 Nah et al., "Modeling"; Zeng et al., "New Perspectives."
16 Kang, "Web 2.0."
17 Wahl-Jorgensen, "Ensuring Richness," 28.
18 Habermas, *The Structural Transformation*, 165.
19 Curran, *Media and Democracy*.
20 Gottfried et al., "Journalists Sense Turmoil."
21 Ibid.
22 Toff et al., "Depth and Breadth."
23 Brown, "Citizen's Journalism."
24 "A License to Blog?" CNET.
25 Harshaw, "Revenge."
26 API, "What Is the Purpose."
27 Mort, "Truth and Partisan Media," 99.
28 API, "What Is the Purpose."
29 Potter, *Media Literacy*, 3.
30 Connell, "33 Latest Facebook Statistics."
31 Wise, "How Many Pictures."
32 Byers, "How Many Blogs"; Jones, "How Many Blogs."
33 Pew Research Center, "Mobile Fact Sheet."
34 Lacy and Rosenstiel, *The Elements of Journalism*, 9.
35 Norride, "Watchdog Journalism," 525; Pew Research Center, "Striking the Balance."
36 Jurkowitz and Mitchell, "Most say journalists should be watchdogs."
37 Lacy and Rosenstiel, *Defining*, 9.
38 API, "What Is the Purpose."
39 Jenkins et al., *Spreadable Media*, 15.
40 Van Dijck and David Nieborg, "Wikinomics," 858.
41 Fuchs, *Digital Labour*.
42 Ibid., 81.
43 Jönsson and Örnebring, "User-Generated Content."
44 Ibid., 128.
45 Ibid., 135.
46 Habermas et al., "The Public Sphere"; Habermas, *The Structural Transformation*.
47 Jönsson and Örnebring, "User-Generated Content," 140.
48 Anderson, *Web 2.0*, xxvii.
49 Keen, *The Cult of the Amateur*; Nah et al. "Modeling the Adoption"; Nah and Chung, *Understanding Citizen Journalism*; Zeng et al., "New Perspectives."
50 Muthukumaraswamy, "When the Media Meet."

51 Allan, *Citizen Witnessing*.
52 Ibid.
53 Kang, "Web 2.0."
54 Antony and Thomas, "This Is Citizen Journalism."
55 Profita, "Outside Voices."
56 Albarado, "Citizen Journalism."
57 Keen, *The Cult of the Amateur*, 46.
58 Bowman and Willis, "We Media."
59 Joyce, "The Citizen Journalism Web Site," 3.
60 Brown, "Citizen's Journalism."
61 "Citizen Journalism."
62 Fioretti, "Citizen Journalism."
63 Brown, "'Citizen" Journalism"; Keen, *The Cult of the Amateur*; "A License to Blog?" CNET.
64 Keen, *The Cult of the Amateur*, 53.
65 "A License to Blog?," CNET.
66 Veale, "Seoul Searching," 94.
67 Kang, "Web 2.0."
68 Reynolds, *An Army of David*.
69 Jönsson and Örnebring, "User-Generated Content," 140.
70 "A License to Blog?" CNET.
71 Habermas et al., "The Public Sphere."

Bibliography

Albarado, Sonny. "Citizen Journalism." *Encyclopedia Britannica*, 21 November 2018. https://www.britannica.com/topic/citizen-journalism.

Allan, Stuart. *Citizen Witnessing: Revisioning Journalism in Times of Crisis.* Cambridge: Polity, 2013.

Anderson, Paul. *Web 2.0 and Beyond: Principles and Technologies.* Boca Raton: Chapman and Hall/CRC, 2016.

Antony, Mary Grace, and Ryan J. Thomas. "'This Is Citizen Journalism at Its Finest': YouTube and the Public Sphere in the Oscar Grant Shooting Incident." *New Media and Society* 12, no. 8 (2010): 1280–96. https://doi.org/10.1177/1461444810362492.

API. "What Is the Purpose of Journalism?" American Press Institute, 24 August 2022. https://www.americanpressinstitute.org/journalism-essentials/what-is-journalism/purpose-journalism.

Baase, Sara. *A Gift of Fire: Social, Legal, and Ethical Issues for Computing and the Internet.* Upper Saddle River: Prentice Hall, 2008.

Bowman, Shayne, and Chris Willis. "We Media: How Audiences Are Shaping the Future of News and Information." The Media Center, July 2003. https://wemedia.com/we-media-how-audiences-are-shaping-the-future-of-news-and-information.

Brown, Fred. "'Citizen's Journalism Is Not Professional Journalism." *Quill*, 2005. https://www.quillmag.com/2005/08/01/citizen-journalism-is-not-professional-journalism.

Byers, Kyle. "How Many Blogs Are There? (and 141 Other Blogging Stats)." GrowthBadger, 14 January 2022. https://growthbadger.com/blog-stats.

Chung, Deborah S, Seungahn Nah, and Masahiro Yamamoto. "Conceptualizing Citizen Journalism: US News Editors' Views." *Journalism* 19, no. 12 (2017): 1694–712.

"Citizen Journalism – Technology, Conventions, and Modern Journalism – GCSE Journalism (CCEA) Revision – BBC Bitesize." BBC News. https://www.bbc.co.uk/bitesize/guides/zy4rfrd/revision/5#.

Clark, Lynn Schofield, and Regina Marchi. "Youth Citizen Journalism: The Connective Journalism Practices of Participation and Making the Story." In *Young People and the Future of News: Social Media and the Rise of Connective Journalism*, 136–62. Cambridge: Cambridge University Press, 2017. doi:10.1017/9781108116015.007.

Connell, Adam. "33 Latest Facebook Statistics and Facts for 2022." *Blogging Wizard*, 29 August 2022. https://bloggingwizard.com/facebook-statistics.

Curran, James. *Media and Democracy*. London: Routledge, 2011.

– "Rethinking the Media as a Public Sphere." In *Communication and Citizenship: Journalism and the Public Sphere*, edited by Peter Dahlgren and Colin Sparks, 27–56. London: Routledge, 1997.

Fioretti, Natascha. "Citizen Journalism as an Alternative?" *European Journalism Observatory*, 15 November 2011. https://en.ejo.ch/digital-news/citizen-journalism-as-an-alternative.

Fuchs, Christian. *Digital Labour and Karl Marx*. London: Routledge, 2014.

Gottfried, Jeffrey, Amy Mitchell, Mark Jurkowitz, and Jacob Liedke. "Journalists Sense Turmoil in Their Industry amid Continued Passion for Their Work." Pew Research Center, Journalism Project, 25 August 2022. https://www.pewresearch.org/journalism/2022/06/14/journalists-sense-turmoil-in-their-industry-amid-continued-passion-for-their-work.

Habermas, Jürgen. *The Structural Transformation of the Public Sphere: An Inquiry into a Category of Bourgeois Society*. Cambridge, MA: MIT Press, 1989.

Habermas, Jürgen, Sara Lennox, and Frank Lennox. "The Public Sphere: An Encyclopedia Article (1964)." *New German Critique* 3 (1974): 49–55. https://doi.org/10.2307/487737.

Harshaw, Tobin. "Revenge of the 'Citizen Journalist.'" *New York Times*, 14 December 2007. https://archive.nytimes.com/opinionator.blogs. nytimes.com/2007/12/14/revenge-of-the-citizen-journalist.

Jenkins, Henry, Sam Ford, and Joshua Green. *Spreadable Media: Creating Value and Meaning in a Networked Culture*. New York: NYU Press, 2013.

Jones, Brandon. "How Many Blogs Are Published per Day? (2021 Update)." Envisage Digital, 8 February 2022. https://www.envisagedigital.co.uk/number-blog-posts-published-daily.

Jönsson, Anna Maria, and Henrik Örnebring. "User-Generated Content and the News." *Journalism Practice* 5, no. 2 (2011): 127–44. https://doi.org/10.1080/17512786.2010.501155.

Joyce, Mary. "The Citizen Journalism Web Site 'OhmyNews' and the 2002 South Korean Presidential Election." Berkman Center for Internet and Society, Harvard University. https://cyber.harvard.edu/sites/cyber.harvard.edu/files/Joyce_South_Korea_2007.pdf.

Kang, Inkyu. "Web 2.0, UGC, and Citizen Journalism: Revisiting South Korea's OhmyNews Model in the Age of Social Media." *Telematics and Informatics* 33, no. 2 (2016): 546–56. https://doi.org/10.1016/j.tele.2015.07.007.

Keen, Andrew. *The Cult of the Amateur: How Blogs, Myspace, YouTube, and the Rest of Today's User-Generated Media Are Destroying Our Economy, Our Culture, and Our Values*. New York: Doubleday, 2007.

Kovach, Bill, and Tom Rosenstiel. *The Elements of Journalism: What Newspeople Should Know and the Public Should Expect*. New York: Crown, 2021.

Lacy, Stephen, and Tom Rosenstiel. *Defining and Measuring Quality Journalism*. News Measures Research Project. New Brunswick: School of Communication and Information, 2015.

Miller, Serena. "Citizen Journalism." *Oxford Research Encyclopedia of Communication*, 2019. https://doi.org/10.1093/acrefore/9780190228613.013.786.

"Mobile Fact Sheet." Pew Research Center: Internet, Science and Tech. Pew Research Center, 23 November 2021. https://www.pewresearch.org/internet/fact-sheet/mobile.

Molina, Maria D., S. Shyam Sundar, Thai Le, and Dongwon Lee. "'Fake News' Is Not Simply False Information: A Concept Explication and Taxonomy of Online Content." *American Behavioral Scientist* 65, no. 2 (2019): 180–212.

Mort, Sébastien. "Truth and Partisan Media in the USA: Conservative Talk Radio, Fox News, and the Assault on Objectivity." *Revue française d'études américaines* 133, no. 3 (2013): 97–112. https://doi.org/10.3917/rfea.133.0097.

Muthukumaraswamy, Karthika. "When the Media Meet Crowds of Wisdom." *Journalism Practice* 4, no. 1 (2010): 48–65. https://doi.org/10.1080/17512780903068874.

Nah, Seungahn, and Deborah S. Chung. *Understanding Citizen Journalism as Civic Participation.* New York and London: Routledge, Taylor and Francis Group, 2020.

Nah, Seungahn, Masahiro Yamamoto, Deborah S. Chung, and Robert Zuercher. "Modeling the Adoption and Use of Citizen Journalism by Online Newspapers." *Journalism and Mass Communication Quarterly* 92, no. 2 (2015): 399–420. https://doi.org/10.1177/1077699015574483.

Nduhura, Dominique, and Michael Prieler. "Citizen Journalism and Democratisation of Mainstream Media in Rwanda." *African Journalism Studies* 38, no. 2 (2017): 178–97. https://doi.org/10.1080/23743670.2017.1332659.

OECD. *Participative Web and User-Created Content: Web 2.0, Wikis, and Social Networking.* Paris: OECD, 2007.

Pew Research Center. "Mobile Fact Sheet." Pew Research Center: Internet, Science and Tech. 7 April 2021. https://www.pewresearch.org/internet/fact-sheet/mobile.

Potter, W. James. *Media Literacy.* Thousand Oaks: Sage, 2021.

Profita, Hillary. "Outside Voices: Samuel Freedman on the Difference between the Amateur and the Pro." CBS Interactive, 9 August 2006. https://www.cbsnews.com/news/outside-voices-samuel-freedman-on-the-difference-between-the-amateur-and-the-pro.

Reynolds, Glenn H. *An Army of Davids: How Markets and Technology Empower Ordinary People to Beat Big Media, Big Government, and Other Goliaths.* Nashville: Thomas Nelson, 2007.

Toff, Benjamin, Sumitra Badrinathan, Camila Mont'Alverne, Amy Ross Arguedas, Richard Fletcher, and Rasmus Kleis Nielsen. "Depth and Breadth: How News Organisations Navigate Trade-Offs around Building Trust in News." Reuters Institute for the Study of Journalism, 2 December 2021. https://reutersinstitute.politics.ox.ac.uk/depth-and-breadth-how-news-organisations-navigate-trade-offs-around-building-trust-news.

Van Dijck, José, and David Nieborg. "Wikinomics and Its Discontents: A Critical Analysis of Web 2.0 Business Manifestos." *New Media and Society* 11, no. 5 (2009): 855–74. https://doi.org/10.1177/1461444809105356.

Veale, Jennifer. "Seoul Searching." *Foreign Policy,* January 2007, 94–6.

Wahl-Jorgensen, Karin. "Ensuring Richness and Diversity of Representation in the Public Sphere: Mass Media as Forums for Democratic Debate." *Journal of the Northwest Communication Association* 27 (1999): 24–52.

Wise, Jason. "How Many Pictures Are on Instagram in 2022?" *Earth Web*,
    28 July 2022. https://earthweb.com/how-many-pictures-are-on-instagram.
Zeng, Xin, Savyasaachi Jain, An Nguyen, and Stuart Allan. "New
    Perspectives on Citizen Journalism." *Global Media and China* 4, no. 1
    (2019): 3–12. https://doi.org/10.1177/2059436419836459.

12

Media and User-Generated Content Images during the Terrorist Attacks in Catalonia

Recommendations and Remediation

CAROLINA ESCUDERO

When analyzing the user-generated content (UGC) created following an act of terrorism, which includes selecting and characterizing the material, it is important to understand that those who were exposed to the event (as well as the journalists exposed to the UGC) may have been traumatized and in shock while producing the videos or taking photos; at such times, the mobile phone often becomes a tool allowing them to better process and assimilate what is happening in front of them. So in this chapter, when we discuss remediation and make recommendations, it is in reference to the images shown to the public. Those images lead to fear and insecurity and have a negative impact on those who did not directly witness the incident – Nacos refers to this as "mediatized terrorism."[1] Yet we also find creative actions within the media process in response to acts of terrorism – acts of remediation carried out by social media users and disseminated by media organizations.

The terrorist attacks perpetuated by Daesh in Barcelona and Cambrils on 17 August 2017 happened at a time when the Islamic State was about to lose control of the Syrian city of Raqqa, the *de facto* capital of the caliphate. Daesh's forced withdrawal from that important city would have diverse effects, including a decline in its daily production of propaganda, whose main objective had been to recruit more young people, whose numbers fell by 77 per cent from their previous high.[2] Yet at the same time, the decrease in official IS propaganda in the last quarter of 2017 spurred IS supporters to produce more – and translate older – UGC, thus blurring the boundary between official and unofficial activism.[3]

According to Torres-Soriano, the attacks in Catalonia by Daesh signalled that the terrorist group was weakening, for the terrorists were able to produce only a single video about the attacks. By comparison, after the attacks in Paris on 13 November 2015 and Brussels on 22 March 2016, the organization had followed up by broadcasting a dozen high-quality videos produced by various *wilayas* (provinces) of the caliphate.

Media and Terrorism

Gulyas notes that journalists' attitudes toward social media differ from one country to the next.[4] One result is that diverse actions to reduce the impact of terrorists' attacks – such as censorship – are carried out in countries where the perception is that terrorists want/need to be present in the media and social media in order to further their cause. This "need/want" of terrorists has been analyzed by authors such as Paletz and Boiney, who write that "the bulk of the literature on the relationship between media and terrorism is dismaying."[5]

Various scholars have observed a close relationship between terrorism and the media.[6] Thanks to the skills acquired by terrorists, acts of terrorism become media events, and this challenges liberal democracies to respond effectively to their violent deeds without suppressing fundamental human rights and civil liberties, among them free expression and freedom of the press.[7] In turn, within the framework of freedom of expression, news characterized by drama and accompanied by personal stories of the victims can be found.[8] In response to public anxiety, even democratic governments are tempted to and at times actually do curb direct terrorist communication, including news and social media that facilitate terrorist messages. Such efforts in themselves can have a negative emotional impact on the public that is not always easy to repair.[9] As a consequence, the emotional factor grows stronger.[10] This is what Weimann calls the "theatre of terror."[11]

With regard to what Nacos calls "mediatized terrorism,"[12] many authors agree that terrorists view the media as a bullhorn for publicizing their violent acts, their hopes, and their very existence.[13] Indeed, when carrying out their attacks, they take into account journalistic routines and publication styles.[14] In killing and maiming civilians, terrorists are also attacking fundamental human rights,[15] and diverse arguments have been made as to what information in what form should be published about terrorist acts. That debate includes how to address the effects of

UGC. The news media contend that information about terrorist acts generates interest and that their obligation is to inform, which means that silence is not an option.[16]

Terrorist Attacks in Europe

A precedent for media use of UGC was set during the London bombings in 2005, when the BBC showed images that had not been filmed by their employees.[17] After this experience, the BBC established a permanent UGC Hub.[18]

In 2017, a total of 205 terrorist attacks – foiled, failed, and completed – were reported by nine EU member-states: France (54), Spain (16), Italy (14), and Greece (8). Belgium and Germany reported two attacks each; Finland and Sweden noted one attack each. Spain, Finland, and Sweden all reported jihadist terrorist attacks after a long period without being affected by this phenomenon. In 2017, 68 people died as a result of terrorist attacks and 844 were injured. Much as in 2016, nearly all reported fatalities and casualties were the result of jihadist terrorism.[19] The number of jihadist terrorist attacks more than doubled between 2016 and 2017, from thirteen in 2016 to thirty-three in 2017.[20] By 2017, more than 150 social media platforms had been identified as being abused by terrorists for propaganda dissemination.[21]

UGC Precedents

Various authors agree that the attack on the Twin Towers in 2001 marked the beginning of UGC, as people went onto the Internet looking for information and witnesses on various blogs recounted their experiences and shared with the world what had happened.[22] Another event that has since served as a reference point in the use of UGC was the Southeast Asian tsunami of December 2004.[23] In that case, many correspondents were not actually present, as they had already gone on holiday for Christmas; another difficulty was that journalists in Thailand could not get to the area hit by the tsunami for security reasons. The photos and videos of the catastrophe that were taken on mobile telephones or with video cameras would later be uploaded onto blogs.

The use of UGC by mainstream media outlets has risen dramatically, especially during crisis events and humanitarian disasters. At such times, dramatic photos and videos taken by onlookers are often considered "more newsworthy than professional content."[24]

Soft Power

Earlier studies of social media did not anticipate the security implications of the online space – specifically, its capacity to radicalize and recruit audiences. This sort of impact is a clear illustration of "soft power," which refers here to the ability to attract followers through persuasion rather than coercion. Bloom and Daymon maintain that soft power entails processes of radicalization/recruitment[25] and that the same concept can be applied to the study of UGC materials disseminated in the hours after a terrorist attack. Images of fear, terror, and death underscore the terrorists' power and demonstrate that cities are vulnerable spaces. This type of UGC material becomes "soft power" when, without coercion, it makes us aware of our vulnerability – a state of mind whose fostering is a principal objective of the terrorist attack. Not everyone was on Las Ramblas in Barcelona on 17 August, but the images transported people to a well-known place. Awan writes that cyber-terrorism as presented on the Internet and in social media has been utilized by extremists to set in motion a "process of online hate."[26]

The Message: Censored or Regulated

The 9/11 attacks in the United States set a new precedent for coverage of this type of terrorism, for its international dimension led to greater news interest.[27] Global interest in terrorism was then renewed with later attacks. In addition to this, we may observe the active role of audiences[28] as well as how UGC led to a revision of the media's ethical principles.[29]

A number of scholars have concluded that the press too easily bought the administration's hard sell of its hawkish counterterrorism agenda[30] and that the "largely complacent mainstream media were essentially covering for Big Brother by allowing elites to frame the issue of terrorism around individual exemplars while the pendulum swung out toward national security."[31]

After reviewing free speech and anti-terrorism laws in Europe, Barak-Erez and David Scharia concluded that "European countries have consistently acknowledged the legitimacy of anti-incitement law, subject to judicial methods of balancing the government interest in prohibiting terrorist incitement with the right of free speech, in the particular context."[32] Because contemporary terrorist organizations "utilize advanced communication technology and especially social media to radicalize, recruit, plan and coordinate horrific acts of terrorism, top legal scholars in the US also discussed the pro and con of limiting free speech of terrorist entities, most of all ISIS."[33]

For Marthoz, news coverage of terrorism is particularly complex because journalists must try to provide the public with truthful, accurate, and comprehensive information while also respecting fundamental personal rights such as the presumption of innocence and the right to privacy.[34] Various media take the line that information about terrorism is of great interest for their audiences and that their duty is to inform them.[35]

According to Marthoz, informing the public becomes even more complicated when citizens, neighbours, and bystanders film the scene and freely post videos or information on social networks, thus circumventing the rules set up for journalists and confronting traditional media with serious ethical dilemmas. The media cannot ignore these information flows but must view them critically. The blunders of "news amateurs" do not exonerate professionals from the principles of caution they must uphold.[36] Marthoz also points out that during a terrorist attack, the media go "live," with continuous coverage of the incident, even without editing, in order to satisfy an audience that is anxious to know more. This sort of coverage may be full of drama and lead to fear, paranoia, and vicarious trauma among the populace, with UGC material having the most influence.

In addition, the treatment of victims, and the filming of them, are priorities when deciding which information is the most appropriate for broadcast during and after a terrorist attack.

Sourcing and Verifying When Covering Terrorism

The sourcing and verifying of UGC has become an important part of journalism.[37] This represents a challenge, because journalists must not only verify the sources they have selected and justify those choices but also differentiate journalism from other forms of public communication.[38] In addition, media coverage of terror faces challenges related to the spread of misinformation and "fake news."[39]

Also, journalists who are sent to the scene of a terrorist incident are subject to a greater impact than the general public. Faced with scenes of terror, reporters, like anyone else, can suffer stress and in some cases PTSD,[40] just as those exposed to these situations like the neighbours and shopkeepers on Las Ramblas in Barcelona and the neighbours in Cambrils who, from behind their mobile phones, witnessed acts of violence. First responders exposed to these situations – firefighters, doctors, police officers – have also had to deal with post-traumatic stress disorder[41] or vicarious trauma.[42]

Salvat and Paniagua write that users no longer simply consume information that is served to them but also become broadcasters as they post photos, videos, and information on social media and blogs.[43] In this sense, Redondo writes, verification can be carried out today thanks to free tools and traditional journalistic techniques.[44]

Authorship, and Asking the Right Question

The 2016 terrorist attacks in Brussels launched a discussion about UGC and intellectual property within journalism and news media. Anna Ahronheim, a defence correspondent with the Middle East TV channel, shared a video on Twitter of the explosions at the airport. It was retweeted nearly 27,000 times. Ahronheim was credited with that video even though she had taken the video from a WhatsApp group. She insisted at the time: "Just FYI, this is NOT my video. I am not in #Brussels. It was shared with me on WhatsApp. I do not have a name for credit but please DON'T use mine."[45]

Consent

According to Cooper, consent, as applied to journalism practice, goes beyond legal constraints and raises particularly difficult problems, especially in the aftermath of disasters, when an eyewitness/survivor/victim's ability to fully comprehend the consequences of what they are doing may be diminished. Terrorism is an international issue, but it is up to each country to establish its own legal regime for treating these types of events.

Nissenbaum suggests that the fundamental problem with social media is "contextual integrity." That is because privacy means different things in different situations and is violated when two types of contextual norms are not respected: those of suitability (the type of information that is shared) and flow and distribution (with whom the information is shared).[46]

The contextual integrity of UGC material during a terrorist attack and in the hours after the event should receive special attention. During this study, the integrity of and respect for the victims was at times problematic. An example was the cries of children in the background of images of the terrorist attack on Las Ramblas in Barcelona; those children could not be seen, but their suffering could clearly be heard. Thus, while their privacy was respected, their integrity did not appear to be (discussed below).

Along the same lines as Nissenbaum, Cooper has studied these aspects of UGC, arguing that all too often the focus is on obtaining copyright approval rather than engaging in a conversation with a (possibly) traumatized individual. Rarely, it seems, do journalists think about what it is like for an eyewitness to be repeatedly contacted on Twitter or Facebook after being caught up in a disaster. Journalists should also bear in mind the situation in which creators of content find themselves, even when meeting them online rather than face to face.[47]

The Dart Center offers the following advice in highlighting the importance of treating victims appropriately: "Realize that victims may be in shock or severely injured when you first approach them. Calmly introduce yourself and then ask whether they need any medical help. If they do, seek medical help immediately."[48]

Methodology

For this chapter we have conducted a qualitative analysis of UGC material that allows us to interpret systematically how audiovisual images produced by users were later disseminated by the media. The content published by two newspapers, *El País* and *La Vanguardia*, has been analyzed in terms of the recommendations offered by *Guidelines on News Coverage of Terrorism*, crafted by the Catalan Audiovisual Council and the Association of Journalists of Catalonia.[49] Section 3.8 of the guidelines, "Media Use of Amateur Material," points out that amateur footage is created *for* the media but not *by* the media. This raises certain dilemmas when it comes to broadcasting. Out of that section's five recommendations, we will focus on the second and fourth: "Cite the source: if known, the owner of amateur footage given to the media";[50] and "Respect the rights of victims and the audience: the same criteria for professional footage must be used for amateur videos. The rights of victims and the audience are the same in both cases and the recommendations made above therefore also apply."[51] In the latter recommendation, reference is made to the protection of victims' identities, as well as to respect for the privacy of those killed and any survivors; and emphasis is placed on special protection for minors and vulnerable people. Regarding the audience, it calls for warning to be given about distressing images. Also, sensational audiovisuals and sensational language are to be avoided, and the same goes for repeated or excessive exposure to certain images. It notes that "references to other acts of terrorism for no justifiable reason can stir up pain, hatred and anger among surviving victims and the public at large," and therefore a distinction ought to be drawn between "live coverage, documentary reconstruction and fictional recreation"[52] (CAC–CPC 2016, 7–9).

The UGC selected was published in the two newspapers on 18 August 2017, one day after the first attack carried out on Las Ramblas. The material was found on the Web using the Google search engine; ten videos published by *El País* and five by *La Vanguardia* were analyzed (see below).

Media Regulations in Spain

Several countries, among them Spain, Germany, and Greece, have outlawed the publication of statements and other materials deemed to encourage or glorify terrorism. In Spain, at the national level, it is a crime "to support and praise terrorist organizations or the deeds or commemorative dates of their members by publishing or broadcasting via the mass-media opinions, news reports, illustrations and other forms of dissemination."[53]

In Spain, around a dozen professional media outlets and collectives have adopted ethical regulations, expressed in a more or less precise manner and laid down in codes, editorial statutes, collective conventions, and style manuals. Most of these were established during the 1990s, and they all address ethical and deontological issues affecting professional groups, including the Association of Journalists of Economic

Information (APIE), the Catalan Journalists' College, the Federation of the Press Associations in Spain (FAPE), and mass media including *El País*, *El Mundo*, ABC, *El Periódico de Catalunya*, and Europa Press.[54]

It is noteworthy that countries like Ireland and Spain have taken a different path in response to attacks by extremist separatists. As stated earlier, this study is based on the *Guidelines on News Coverage of Terrorism* crafted by the CAC–CPC, as this was one of the most up-to-date documents relating to the journalistic coverage of acts of terrorism in Catalonia at the time of the 2017 attacks.[55]

Newspapers Analyzed

The two Spanish newspapers selected for this study both have a global reach, but they also have different identities. *La Vanguardia* (founded in 1881) is the newspaper of record for Catalonia: it heads the readership ranking for the region and has the third-highest circulation in Spain, behind *El País* and *El Mundo*. It is published both online and as hardcopy (in Castilian and Catalan), has its head editorial office in Barcelona, and is distributed throughout Spain.[56] As for *El País* (founded in 1976), its head office and main editorial department are in Madrid, with branches in Spain's main cities and correspondents in various capitals around the world. It has the highest circulation in Spain,[57] and its online version is the most-read Spanish-language publication in the world. Given that it is the Spanish and international newpaper of record, we thought it appropriate to analyze the UGC material it has published.

Criteria

To organize our qualitative analysis of the UGC material, we developed a table showing publication date, hour, analyzed media, story headline, number of videos, video duration, authorship/source, analysis criteria, and content link. Another column specifies how the UGC material answers the two criteria used for the analysis: "Source" and "RVA," where Source refers to the recommendation to "Cite the source – if known, the owner of amateur footage given to the media should be stated," and RVA refers to the recommendation to "Respect the rights of the victims and the audience: the same criteria for professional footage must be used for amateur videos" (see Methodology). The answer can be "Yes," "No," or "Unclear" (UNC).

La Vanguardia UGC

La Vanguardia gave the most space to coverage of the terrorist attacks in Barcelona and Cambrils, publishing twenty-nine articles on 18 August 2017, three of which used UGC material to illustrate the news, with a total of five videos analyzed for this study.

Regarding *La Vanguardia*, audiovisual material containing UGC images and using the newspaper's logo are viewable on YouTube. In the video titled "The terrorists killed in the attack on Cambrils," we can hear the following comments made by witnesses and the people recording the video: "Sons of bitches. Sons of bitches, man, they were carrying explosives!" The same material was used by *El País*, which informs us that the images belong to a neighbour in Cambrils. *La Vanguardia* does not specify authorship.

El País UGC

El País published twenty-four articles on 18 August 2017, using UGC material in nine of the stories, with a total of ten videos analyzed for this study. A significant number of the videos published by *El País* are part of El País Video (EPV), and this content may also be seen via its YouTube channel. The EPV team is part of a separate department of the newspaper. Bernal and Carvajal write that

> EPV works as an integral part of the editorial department, in fact the directors of each section act as "motivators and facilitators" and take part in certain videos. Hence, the Director of Digital Development at the media explains that, besides the professionals who carry out the reports and interviews, the "most mediatic" journalists have their own sections, between five and ten minutes long, which they upload onto the channel.[58]

We also observed extremely violent videos, such as the UGC material published alongside the news "Shooting and death of the fifth terrorist in Cambrils." This UGC material was filmed by an English-speaking neighbour in Cambrils,[59] who exclaims "What the fuck" and shows the police shooting at a terrorist. In this footage, the cries and comments of witnesses can be heard. While the source is not clearly cited, in the body of the news item can be read "made by a neighbor in the area." So in this case, respect for the source is considered "Unclear" (UNC).

The criteria of *El País* vary: at times information as to the authorship of the video can be found in the body of the news item – for example, "The authorship of the video is a neighbor in Cambrils." This can lead to confusion as to the specific source of the material. The video, published at 14:43 with a duration of 2:12 minutes and accompanying the article "The Islamic State accepts responsibility for the terrorist attack in Barcelona," does not comply with the criteria of respect for the victims, as blurred images can be seen of dead people on Las Ramblas, and of a woman with a haunted gaze running in flight, and children can be heard crying plaintively. The children cannot be seen. As for the bodies, while the images are blurred, the sizes of the bodies scattered on the ground can be seen and it can be deduced that children are among the victims. It is questionable whether this material is actual news. Moreover, based on these characteristics of the video, one might argue that this material does not comply with respect for the victims and the audience, based on the section "Minors and vulnerable people: in news coverage of terrorism, special attention must be paid to protection and best practices regarding minors. Privacy and fundamental rights must be specifically respected."[60]

On certain occasions, *El País* warns that "the images may be considered offensive." This warning does not appear in all UGC images – only in those in which the bodies of fatalities can be seen in which there is shooting or images of people fleeing. The longest video, published by *El País* with a duration of 02:58 minutes and whose authorship is Reuters/Quality, titled "Eight terrorist hit-and-run attacks in Europe in the last year," does not comply with the analysis criteria of respect for victims. The recommendation in times of a terrorist attack is to not use archive material from other attacks, yet that is what has been done in this video, which illustrates one by one the eight attacks. Also, we found that the UGC material published in *El País* has not always been uploaded to its YouTube channel.

Similarities

Of the fifteen UGC videos published in the two media, none lasts longer than three minutes, and all were published as part of a news item. The times of publication for this material are highly varied, and there is no overlap.

Furthermore, of the UGC materials selected, edited, and published multiple times in both media, each has undergone a standard verification process when Twitter has been used as a source. Media outlets have started to rely on UGC sourced by news agencies (agencies such as Reuters/Quality, EFE, and NacióDigital), as they can guarantee verification.[61]

Differences

We observed differences in criteria between the two media outlets: *El País* published UGC live, as well as direct images of the shooting of one of the terrorists, with an introduction of "Warning." *La Vanguardia* did not show these images, although the shots fired that killed the terrorist can be heard. Also, there is no "Warning" given at the beginning of the video. Neither newspaper edited the voices of certain users who were hurling insults at the terrorists, with "sons of bitches" being the predominant insult used. However, in the UGC material analyzed, no comments, either seen or heard, hurt or disrespected the victims.

Views

Most of the UGC videos from both newspapers have been uploaded to YouTube. The video with the most views is of Cambrils, published by *La Vanguardia* at 09:13 and updated at 13:07, in which the shots fired by the police and the terrorists being killed can be heard, with 2,413,183 views; the second most viewed is another video published at the same time of day in which the bodies of the four terrorists who have been killed can be seen lying on the ground, with 1,209,720 views. The UGC material with the most views in *El País* is one that uses various UGC images of the terrorist attack on Las Ramblas, ending with the bodies of the four terrorists killed in Cambrils. This final section of the video is the same as the one provided by *La Vanguardia* that is the second most viewed. Of the videos published on 18 August, those with the most views are the ones showing the terrorists who have been killed. In both *El País* and *La Vanguardia*, the comments and insults of those watching can be heard, which is something that could have been edited out.

Remediation

After analyzing the UGC material and its presence in the media, we studied the messages and hashtags that went viral following the terrorist attack. They pointed to a change in communication strategy, with messages highlighting assistance and collaboration rather than the terrorist attack itself. We present these messages as acts of remediation, giving rise to corrective actions in which humour was key.

In this section, we examine the reporting on these "acts of remediation" by the Spanish media *El País*, *La Vanguardia*, and *El Confidencial*. People followed the recommendations of the police to not share content about the terrorist attacks, and the content that went viral instead was a result of collaborative actions aiming to repair the situation and to damper the violence and fear, based on a desire for remediation. It will be seen that this remediation was followed by a process of "corrective actions" (among media, institutions, and the audience), which resulted in "creative actions" (here images were prioritized, such as those of cats), culminating in the equally creative use of irony and humour as an empowering response to the threatening messages and images sent by the ISIS terrorists. Through this process, people, organizations, and communities took back control over their lives.[62]

Bolter and Grusin write that the logic of remediation is similar to Derrida's account of mimesis,[63] in terms of the reproduction of the feeling of imitation or resemblance in the perceiving subject: "Mimesis here is not the representation of one thing by another, the relation of resemblance or identification between two beings, the reproduction of a product of nature by a product of art. It is not the relation of two products but of two productions. And of two freedoms ... True mimesis is between two producing subjects and not between two produced things."[64]

In our study we observe that the two producing subjects were the people who were producing the UGC, on the one hand, and the journalists who decided to use it (edited or not), on the other. Both subjects produced and reproduced the UGC, and, as analyzed, this content highlighted the victims on Las Ramblas and the execution of the terrorists in Cambrils. During the night of 17 August when the Spanish police requested that false news and information on the police not be shared, those two producing subjects, both the audience (as potential producer of UGC material) and the journalists, followed this request, giving rise to new messages and new images no longer linked to terror and vulnerability. This ability of the "two producing subjects" to modify tone and visual identity reflects a process of remediation, one that carves out an artistic and creative space for the new production and reproduction of images, as explained by Bolter and Grusin. Messages and images appeared that both deflected attention (from a visual stance) and attempted to improve a complex situation, making use of freedoms in which the "two producing subjects" were part of both the institutions and other users.

After the first images and videos were posted on social media, the Spanish National Police and the Mossos Police advised: "We are now working in Cambrils, please do NOT share the images, they could hinder our job"; "Do not share images of Las Ramblas";[65] "DO NOT believe everything you receive on #WhatsApp, even if it says that your cousin police officer confirms it. Only official sources! #StopBulos."[66] For the National Police, it was clearly extremely important that people not contribute to the viralization of this content. "We always advise people to report them to the platform and block these users. If it is a tweet that could be considered a crime, it must be reported. We have specific Internet units that investigate this type of publication to detect any type of criminal content."

"We usually repeat this message during situations like this," states Carolina González, in charge of social media at the National Police. "But what happened in Barcelona spread enormously through Twitter, with more than 100,000 retweets and over 5 million impressions."[67]

This was how a period of remediation began and little by little gained strength in social media from the night of 17 August, leading to various creative actions by the "two producing subjects," from offering refuge to people (such as #BedInBarcelona and #BedInCambrils) to sharing images of cats with animated messages or creatively modifying the threatening images of a Spanish member of ISIS, as can be seen below.

Corrective Actions

The resort to social media during an act of terrorism involves high levels of emotion and expressions of compassion and solidarity as well as the sense that when shared, pain is easier to bear.[68] It is apparent that after the terrorist attacks in Catalonia, users understood that sharing UGC and related material could hamper the work of the police. So they instead undertook corrective action in a process of remediation, in accordance with Benoit's conceptualization.[69]

Five categories of image repair strategies were identified: denial, evasion of responsibility, reduction of offensiveness, corrective action, and mortification.[70] The content published and shared in response to the terrorist attacks corresponds to "corrective action," the fourth strategy put forward by Benoit, which has two types: an organization can try to correct the damage, or it can take small steps to prevent the act from happening in the future. These two types of action can occur together or separately. In this case, the media forwarded the requests of the police and also reproduced the creative actions of users – a process that continued throughout the month of August.

Creative Actions

On the night of 17 August 2017 at 19:53, *El País*, in its supplement "Verne," published: "Twitter replies with cats to the police request of not posting information on the terrorist attack in Barcelona," referring to the Brussels attacks in 2016, when people also responded by posting images of cats on Twitter; at 23:22 the newspaper *La Vanguardia* published a request that users not post images of the attack on Las Ramblas, also citing as a precedent the Brussels strategy of using cats.

For her part, the mayor of Barcelona made public one of the phrases trending on social media: #Notenemosmiedo ("we are not afraid").[71]

Humour in Response to Terrorism

After the Manchester attacks on 22 May 2017 and the attacks in Barcelona and Cambrils in August 2017, ISIS media (channels, publications, and chat rooms) showed memes with the hash tag #JUSTTERROR. As already stated, many scholars maintain that the media can actually assist terrorists by amplifying the drama of their actions.[72]

Figure 12.1   Don Pimpon Cat

Figure 12.2   Nando López Cat

Figure 12.3   Ada Colau, #Wearenotaffraid

On Telegram, ISIS propagates jihadi publications such as *Dabiq* (the Islamic word for Armageddon), *al-Naba'* (a weekly magazine/ pamphlet), and *Rumiyab* (Rome). After the Barcelona attack, posts began appearing on Amaq (a sort of Daesh news agency), which were then disseminated through Telegram: "Amaq agency: those responsible for the attacks on Barcelona were soldiers of the Islamic State, who responded to the calls to attack the countries of the coalition."[73]

The second message from the group no longer attempted to establish a link between the events in Barcelona and Cambrils but rather set out to spread false news. This is why the only audiovisual product made from these terrorist attacks in Catalonia was a video by the Wilaya Khayr titled: "The beginning of the torment: the conquest of Barcelona," which appeared on the Internet almost a week after the first attack.[74] And in order that this message have greater impact on Spanish public opinion, for the first time the Islamic State used two Spanish-speaking soldiers as their spokespersons.[75] The few sentences used in this short video are pronounced in a Spanish difficult to understand for a Spanish-speaking audience, and this led to reactions such as jokes and memes.

On Twitter, the best-known hashtags were #Tomasa and #ElCordobés, referring to the mother and the nickname of one of the jihadists.

Conclusions

In most cases, the information about the UGC material used by the two Spanish newspapers in this analysis was clear in terms of authorship and respect for the victims and the audience. Some of this UGC material was among the most violent, specifically a live broadcast of a police officer killing a terrorist, with the screams of nearby people in the background. This material corresponds to the images of fear and terror from Nacos's argument that "architects of terrorism exploit the media for the benefit of their operational efficiency, information gathering, recruitment, fund raising, and propaganda schemes."[76] This material could have been presented in a different manner.

This is also in accordance with the argument put forward by Altheide that reporting on terrorism, including the images used in that reporting, is often linked to victimization narratives that tend to spread fear.[77] Future research on this subject should analyze these UGC images in greater depth in order to develop more and better tools for studying audiovisual material related to terrorism, so as to evaluate to what degree it benefits the audience (keeping in mind vicarious trauma) and the police forces, and whether in fact it empowers the terrorist groups. Along the same lines, we agree with Zimmer, who argues that "just because personal information is made available in some fashion on a social network, it does not mean it is fair game for capture and release to all."[78] Cooper examines this same point, stating that all too often the (journalist's) focus is on obtaining copyright approval rather than engaging in conversation with a (possibly) traumatized individual. Hence it is important for new protocols and recommendations to be implemented for UGC material used by the media and related to acts of terrorism, in which clear rules are laid down as to, for example, sound editing (avoiding insults and the cries of children in the midst of the tragedy). Also, the media should keep in mind the point made by the CAC–AJC as to the need to avoid using stock images of previous terrorist attacks, as this makes no positive contribution to the audience and especially to the victims. Different sorts of messages could benefit people in the midst of a tragedy who are attempting to reduce their anxiety and fear.

In turn, it is necessary to analyze the possibility of creating trans-disciplinary[79] teams when covering these sorts of tragedies: teams made up of psychologists, specialists in media psychology, positive psychology, and trauma, who join the efforts of journalists when decisions are being made about images, video editing, and news items. It is also necessary to make progress in the constitution of transdisciplinary teams, which are activated during a crisis and take part in the selection and editing of UGC material to be published by media. In this way, concrete changes in the production and dissemination of images of terrorist attacks can be promoted and tangible recommendations can be made for users who produce this type of material, warning them of the effects of vicarious trauma, among other things.

Regarding the actions of institutions like the Spanish police as they relate to posting information for citizens or recommendations to social media users, and the responses of the population to these requests, we observe what we have called a remediation that corresponded to a corrective and committed action: to stop posting images of the terrorist attacks and to redefine the actions of citizens. These actions allowed the police to make progress in their investigations and to observe and corroborate the support of citizens on social media.

Finally, faced with the messages of confirmation and threats from the terrorist group weeks after the terrorist attacks, citizens took a unified and active stance on social media, mainly using humour and in some cases irony as a way of demonstrating that they had no fear of the threats. This type of response could serve as the basis for a compre-hensive analysis of the possible resilient reactions of a society faced with terrorism via social media – reactions that merit study in greater depth.

Appendix

Note: RVA: Respect for the Victims and the Audience; UNC: Unclear

EL PAIS NEWSPAPER

Date	18 August 2017
Hour	11:09:00
Analyzed media	EL PAÍS
Story headline	Eight outrageous attacks in Europe in the last year
Number of videos	1
Video length	00:02:58
Views	0:02:58: 28,741 views on Youtube El País.
Authorship	Toby Melville (REUTERS) Reuters-Quality
Criteria analysis	It does not meet the criteria for victims as it takes stock videos of previous terrorist attacks.
Link	https://elpais.com/politica/2017/08/17/actualidad/1502984651_363806.html?autoplay=1
Criteria analyses	Sources: YES; RVA: NO

Date	18 August 2017
Hour	11:11:00
Analyzed media	EL PAÍS
Story headline	The first images of La Rambla after the massive outrage in Barcelona
Number of videos	2
Video length	First video: 00.01.11; Second video: 00:00:14
Authorship	First video: No source in the first; Second video: @JORDIPC, @DELTA_CEROO, @OLIVERYANES
Views	00.01.11: No views registered/available online; 0:00:14: No views registered/available online
Criteria analysis	The first video is about the Rambla in Barcelona; the van and police personnel are observed. In the second video, people are seen walking in the areas surrounding the Rambla.
Link	https://elpais.com/elpais/2017/08/17/videos/1502985217_019303.html?autoplay=1
Criteria analyses	First video: Sources: NO; RVA: YES; Second video: Sources: YES; RVA: YES

Date	18 August 2017
Hour	11:50:00
Analyzed media	EL PAÍS
Story headline	Press review, the terrorist attack in Barcelona goes around the world
Number of videos	1
Video length	00.02:00
Authorship	Reuters/Quality
Views	00.02:00: 27,729 views on Youtube El País
Criteria analysis	The video shows the main buildings in the world lit up with the colors of the Spanish flag. Messages from leaders showing solidarity and people interviewed. It is a mix of UGC images and media.
Link	https://elpais.com/politica/2017/08/18/actualidad/1503023961_785254.html?autoplay=1
Criteria analyses	Sources: YES; RVA: YES

Date	18 August 18 2017
Hour	12:33:00
Analyzed media	EL PAÍS
Story headline	"What I've seen is a real disaster"
Number of videos	1
Video length	00.02:28 mins
Authorship	David Armengou, EFE
Views	0:02:28: 139,735 views on Youtube El Pais
Criteria analysis	On this day, this message appears for the first time WARNING: "This video may hurt your sensitivity." "The images have been processed to preserve the identity of the victims." 00.00:22 a group of people is observed in the Rambla after the attack (blurred images of the victims) and children crying. 00:02:04 UGC images of Cambrils, terrorists shot down on the floor at dawn; "Mother fuckers" says one of the users.
Link	https://elpais.com/ccaa/2017/08/17/catalunya/1502988257_907304.html?autoplay=1
Criteria analyses	Sources: YES; RVA: NO

Date	18 August 2017
Hour	14:43:00
Analyzed media	EL PAÍS
Story headline	The Islamic State assumes responsibility for the Barcelona attack
Number of videos	1
Video length	00:02:12
Authorship	Andrés Dalmaou EFE / EPV
Views	0:02:12: No views registered/available online
Criteria analysis	00: 00:14/15 families run in search of a relative and are looking at the bodies lying on the floor trying to recognize them. A man is heard shouting "Ignacio !!" 00:01:34 A family with children, the woman assists on the ground a person who could be her companion. 00.01:42 account of a person who experienced the attack on the Rambla: "there were fatal victims covered in blood."
Special note	
Link	https://elpais.com/politica/2017/08/17/actualidad/1502998376_827427.html?autoplay=1
Criteria analyses	Sources: YES; RVA: NO

Date	18 August 2017
Hour	16:08:00
Analyzed media	EL PAÍS
Story headline	ISIS kills 14 people in the attacks in Barcelona and Cambrils
Number of videos	1
Video length	00:02:24
Authorship	
Views	0:02:24: 24,346 views on Youtube El País
Criteria analysis	On this day, this message appears for the first time WARNING: "This video may hurt your sensitivity." "The images have been processed to preserve the identity of the victims." It uses many UGC images previously published; we again hear children crying, people running desperately down the Rambla in search of a relative.
Notes	This repetition (of certain UGC images) could play a role in revictimizing the victims.
Link	https://elpais.com/politica/2017/08/18/actualidad/1503057015_975618.html?autoplay=1
Criteria analyses	Sources: UNC; RVA: NO

Date	18 August 2017
Hour	16:57:00
Analyzed media	EL PAÍS
Story headline	A terrorist attack in Barcelona causes at least 13 deaths
Number of videos	1
Video length	00:02:28
Authorship	Andreu Dalmau
Views	0:02:28: 139,735 views on Youtube El Pais
Criteria analysis	WARNING: "This video may hurt your sensitivity." "The images have been processed to preserve the identity of the victims."
Notes	It is the same audiovisual material published at 12:33 but it accompanies another type of news.
Link	https://elpais.com/ccaa/2017/08/17/catalunya/1502982054_017639.html?autoplay=1
Criteria analyses	Sources: YES; RVA: NO

Date	18 August 2017
Hour	18:26:00
Analyzed media	EL PAÍS
Story headline	The Mossos kill five terrorists who planned a new massacre in Cambrils
Number of videos	1
Video length	00:01:50
Authorship	AP Video:EPV
Views	0:01:50: No views registered/available online
Criteria analysis	Some images have already been published before about Cambrils attacks. 01:28 "Mother fuckers, they carried explosives," in references to the terrorists already killed by the police
Special note	Parts of edited videos that were also published by La Vanguardia are observed.
Link	https://elpais.com/ccaa/2017/08/18/catalunya/1503014552_393278.html
Criteria analyses	Sources: YES; RVA: NO

Date	18 August 2017
Hour	21:40:00
Analyzed media	EL PAÍS
Story headline	A single agent of the Mossos killed four of the terrorists in Cambrils
Number of videos	1
Video length	00:01:13
Authorship	A neighbor from Cambrils
Views	0:01:13: No views registered/available onlin
Criteria analysis	The video begins with the message: WARNING: "This video may hurt your sensitivity" "The images have been processed to preserve the identity of the victims." The authors of the videos are not specified but the body of the note reads "Video recorded by a Cambrils neighbor." Inappropriate vocabulary: "What the fuck."
Link	https://elpais.com/politica/2017/08/18/actualidad/1503059332_365185.html
Criteria analyses	Sources: UNC; RVA: UNC

LA VANGUARDIA NEWSPAPER

Date	18 August 2017
Hour	5:18:00
Analyzed media	LA VANGUARDIA
Story headline	A massive accident leaves 13 dead and a hundred injured in an attack on the Rambla in Barcelona
Number of videos	2
Video length	First video: 00:02:03; Second video: 00:00:14
Views	First video: 0:02:03: 548,429 views on Youtube LV; Second video: 0:00:14: 539,688 views on Youtube LV
Authorship	LA VANGUARDIA
Criteria analysis	In the first video at 00:00:54 the camera gets very close to the surviving victims who are on the floor receiving assistance from other passers-by, invasive. There is no message of "Warning" advising the public of sensitive material. If the video is observed on Youtube, the warning of the "Youtube Community" appears. The second video is a general view of the scene of the attack.
Note	According to CAC AJC "The surviving victims of an act of terrorism are intitled to privacy (…) images must be edited to ensure that nobody can be recognised." If the video is observed on Youtube, the warning of the "Youtube Community" appears.
Link	https://www.lavanguardia.com/sucesos/20170817/43611025471/atentado-barcelona-rambla.html
Criteria analyses	First video: Sources: YES; RVA: NO. Second video: Sources: UNCL; RVA: YES

Date	18 August 2017
Hour	9:13:00 / Updated at 13:07:00
Analyzed media	LA VANGUARDIA
Story headline	Mossos kill five terrorists in Cambrils trying to cause another massacre.
Number of videos	2
Video length	First video: 00:00:42; Second video: 00:00:43
Views	First video: 0:00:52: 1,209,720 views on Youtube LV; Second video: 0:00:43: 2,413,183 views on Youtube LV
Authorship	LA VANGUARDIA
Criteria analysis	First video, 00:00:27 "Sons of bitches; 00:00:29 "Sons of of bitches, they were carrying explosives!" While showing the image of the 4 bodies of the terrorists killed on the floor. Innapropriate vocabulary. No "Warning" message about the images. If the first video is observed on Youtube, the warning of the "Youtube Community" appears. Second video, 00:00:18 the first shot is heard, followed by others, screams, sirens. No "Warning" message about the images.
Link	https://www.lavanguardia.com/sucesos/20170818/43622086026/cambrils-atentado-barcelona.html
Criteria analyses	First video: Sources: UNCL; RVA: NO. Second video: Sources: UNCL; RVA: NO

Date	18 August 2017
Hour	18:09 updated 19:06
Analyzed media	LA VANGUARDIA
Story headline	Josep Anglada attacks a Vic councilor during the minute of silence for the attacks
Number of videos	1
Video length	00: 00:51
Authorship	NacióDigital
Views	0:00:51: 281,966 Views on Youtube NacióDigital
Criteria analysis	The tension between two people is observed. One takes a sign away from the other that says "Jihadists get out of Catalonia."
Link	https://www.lavanguardia.com/politica/20170818/43633583556/josep-anglada-agrede-regidor-vic-durante-minuto-silencio-atentados.html
Criteria analyses	Sources: YES; RVA: YES

Notes

1 Nacos, *Mass-Mediated Terrorism.*
2 Torres-Soriano, *El estado de la yihad online.*
3 Europol, *European Union Terrorism Situation*, 31.
4 Gulyas, "The Influence of Professional Variables."
5 Paletz and Boiney, "Researchers' perspectives"; Nacos, "Media, Terrorism, and Freedom of Expression," 497.
6 See Bassiouni 1981 *Terrorism, Law Enforcement*; Wilkinson, *Terrorism versus Democracy*; Schmid and de Graf, *Violence as Communicarion*; Nacos, *Terrorism and the Media*; Nacos, *Mass-Mediated Terrorism*; Weimann 1987 "Media Events"; Weimann and Winn, *The Theater of Terror*; Weimann, *Terrorism in Cyberspace.*
7 Nacos, "Media, Terrorism and Freedom of Expression," 503.
8 Yarchi et al., "Rallying or Criticizing?"
9 Nacos, "Media, Terrorism and Freedom of Expression."
10 Shoshani and Slone, "The Drama."
11 Wiemann and Winn, *The Theater of Terror.*
12 Nacos, *Mass-Mediated Terrorism.*
13 Merolla and Zechmeister, *Democracy at Risk*; Nacos, *Terrorism/ Counterterrorism.*
14 Matthews, ""Media performance"; Seib and Janbek, *Global Terrorism*; Spencer, *The Tabloid Terrorist.*
15 Nacos, "Media, Terrorism and Freedom of Expression," 503.s
16 Houston, "Media Coverage of Terrorism"; Rivas-Nieto and Plaza, "Pautas para la cobertura periodística," 1359.
17 Wardle, *Amateur Footage.*
18 For more on the UGC Hub, see the discussion in chapter 3 (Miller).
19 Europol, *European Union Terrorism Situation*, 9.
20 Ibid.
21 Europol, *Internet Organized Crime*, 53.
22 Lavin de las Heras and Vadillo-Bengoa, *Los Medios del Futuro*; Redondo, *Verificación digital.*
23 For more discussion on the Boxing Day tsunami, see chapters 3 (Miller) and 9 (Lithgow).
24 Hermida and Thurman, "A Clash of Cultures," 344.
25 Bloom and Daymon, "Assessing the Future Threat," 377.
26 Awan, "Cyber-Extremism," 139.
27 Cali, "Journalism after September 11"; Sánchez-Duarte, "Narrativas y Portavoces."
28 Díaz Campos et al., "Los atentados terroristas."

29 Cooper, "Rights and Responsibilities."

30 Bennett et al., *When the Press Fails*; Nacos et al., "Prevention of Terrorism."

31 MacLeod and Shah, "News Frames and National Security;" Nacos, "Media, Terrorism, and Freedom of Expression," 499.

32 Barak-Erez and Scharia, "Freedom of Speech," 26.

33 Nacos, "Media, Terrorism, and Freedom of Expression," 501.

34 Marthoz, "Covering an Attack."

35 Houston, "Media Coverage of Terrorism."

36 Marthoz, "Covering an Attack," 5.

37 Heravi and Harrower, "Twitter Journalism in Ireland."

38 Zeller and Hermida, "When Tradition Meets."

39 Patel, "Media and Terror."

40 CAC-CPC, *Recomanacions sobre la cobertura informativa d'actes terroristes*, 10.

41 In terms of mental health, PTSD relates to how an event can "pierce" a person's psyche. PTSD is a psychiatric disorder that can occur in people who have experienced or witnessed a traumatic event such as a natural disaster, a serious accident, a terrorist act, war/combat, rape, or some other violent personal assault.

42 The term vicarious trauma (Perlman and Saakvitne, *Trauma and the Therapist*), sometimes also called compassion fatigue, is the most recent term that describes the phenomenon generally associated with the "cost of caring" for others (Figley, "Tramatization"). Other terms used for compassion fatigue are secondary traumatic stress (Stamm, *Secondary Traumatic Stress*; Stamm, "Work-Related Secondary Traumatic Stress") and secondary victimization (Figley, "Traumatization").

43 Salvat and Paniagua, "¿Es este Periodismo Ciudadano?"

44 Redondo, *Verificación digital*.

45 WAN-IFRA, "Mass misattribution of viral Brussels vieo."

46 Nissenbaum, "Privacy," 138.

47 Cooper, "Rights and Responsibilities," 264–5.

48 Hight, "First Responders."

49 CAC-CPC, *Recomanacions sobre la cobertura informativa d'actes terroristes*, 8.

50 Ibid., 6.

51 Ibid., 8.

52 Ibid., 7–9.

53 Wilkinson, *Terrorism versus Democracy*, 156.

54 The Federation of Press Associations in Spain (FAPE) is one of the most representative bodies of journalism at the national level. FAPE was the first professional journalists' organization in the country and has forty-nine federated associations and seventeen associated bodies that together represent about 19,000 journalists (FAPE, 2020). FAPE's Code of Conduct

was approved in 1993 and updated in 2017. At a regional level, the Declaration of Principles of the Profession of Journalism, comparable to the Code of Catalan Journalists, was approved on 1 November 1992 by the Catalan Journalists' College and the Advisory Council of the organization, on which the various communications media in Catalonia are represented. They agreed on the need for the profession of journalism to promote a collective initiative aimed at reasserting the right to freedom of expression and information and defending the existence of a free and responsible press within a plural and democratic society.

55 Other studies and guidelines for the media coverage of terrorist acts in Spain can be found, such as the one put forward by Rivas-Nieto and Plaza, "Pautas para la cobertura periodística 1208), aimed at contributing to reducing the margin of error "through the drawing up of a renewed and concise list of principles for those covering terrorism," to which other work published on the media and terrorism can be added (Torres, "El tratamiento»; Sánchez-Duarte, "Narrativas y portavoces"; Sánchez-Duarte and Sampedro "Visibilidad mediática"; Caminos et al., "Jerarquización"; Armentia and Caminos, "The Basque Press"; Caminos et al., "El asesinato"; Caminos et al., "Los diarios vascos"; although analytical studies on how to inform about terrorist attacks are fewer (Soria and Giner, *El secuestro terrorista*; Soria, *Prensa, paz, violencia*; Díaz-Campos et al., "Los atentados terroristas.

56 EGM-AIMC, "Newspaper Ranking."

57 Ibid.

58 Bernal and Carvajal, "Presence," 33.

59 *El País*, "Así fue abatido."

60 CAC-CPC, *Recomanacions sobre la cobertura informativa d'actes terroristes*, 8.

61 Matthews, "Media Performance"; Wardle et al., *Amateur Footage*.

62 Rappaport, "Studies in Empowerment."

63 Derrida, "Of Grammatology," in Bolter and Grusin.

64 Bolter and Grusin, "Mediation and Remediation," 54.

65 Otto, Carlos, "Por qué no debes difundir imágenes."

66 Policía Nacional, "La Policía Nacional alerta."

67 *El Plural*, "Así se gestionó."

68 Schudson, "What's Unusual." Keinan et al., "Attitudes and Reactions."

69 Benoit, "Image Repair Discourse."

70 Ibid.

71 *El País*, "Así fue abatido."

72 Barnett and Reynolds, *Terrorism and the Press*.

73 MAITIC, "Analysis of ISIS's Claims of Responsibility.".

74 Torres-Soriano, *El estado de la yihad online*.

75 One of them presented himself as Abu Lais al-Qurdubi (Abu Lais el
    Cordobés), although his real name is Muhammad Yasin Ahram Pérez,
    the son of a Spanish mother and Moroccan father, who left for Syria
    in 2013 to join the jihadist ranks. The other member of the terrorist
    network appeared with his face hidden and presented himself as Abu
    Salman al Andalusi (O'Connor, *Isis Calls on Muslims*).
76 Nacos, *Terrorism/Counterterrorism*. In Bilgen, "Terrorism and the
    Media," 1.
77 Altheide, *Terror Post 9/11*.
78 Zimmer, "'But the data is already public,'" 323.
79 Transdisciplinarity concerns "what is both between disciplines,
    through various disciplines and beyond any discipline. Its aim
    is the comprehension of the present world in which one of the
    imperatives is the unity of knowledge" (Nicolescu, "Methodology of
    Transdisciplinarity," 23).

Bibliography

Altheide, David. *Terror Post 9/11 and the Media*. New York: Peter Lang, 2009.
Armentia, Ignacio, and José María Caminos. "The Basque Press and
    Terrorism, 1990–2009: From Telling the Facts to Complicity against ETA."
    In *Violence and Communication*, edited by José Antonio Mingolarra,
    Carmen Arocena, and Rosa Martín, 145–70. Reno: Center for Basque
    Studies, University of Nevada, 2012.
Awan, Imran. "Cyber-Extremism: Isis and the Power of Social Media."
    Society 54, no. 2 (March 2017): 138–49. https://doi.org/10.1007/s12115-
    017-0114-0.
Barak-Erez, Daphne, and David Scharia. "Freedom of Speech, Support for
    Terrorism, and the Challenge of Global Constitutional Law." *Harvard
    National Security Journal* 2 (5 January 2011): 1–30. https://ssrn.com/
    abstract=1735007.
Barnett, Brooke, and Amy Reynolds. *Terrorism and the Press: An Uneasy
    Relationship*. New York: Peter Lang, 2009.
Bassiouni, Cherif. "Terrorism, Law Enforcement, and the Mass Media
    Perspectives, Problems, Proposals." *Journal of Criminal Law and
    Criminology* 72, no. 1 (1981): 1–51. Northwestern University School of Law.
Bennett, Lance W., Regina Lawrence, and Steven Livingston. *When the Press
    Fails*. Chicago: University of Chicago Press, 2007.
Benoit, William L. "Image Repair Discourse and Crisis Communication."

Public Relations Review 23 (Summer 1997): 177–87. https://doi. org/10.1016/S0363-8111(97)90023-0.

Bernal, Luisa, and Miguel Carvajal. "Presence, Formats, and Video Production Strategy on YouTube: Case Analysis of the Newspaper *El País.*" *Estudios sobre el Mensaje Periodístico* 26, no. 1 (January 2020): 25–35. https://dx.doi.org/10.5209/esmp.67283

Bilgen, Arda. 2012. "Terrorism and the Media: A Dangerous Symbiosis." July. Clark University. https://www.researchgate.net/publication/326489293_Terrorism_and_the_media_A_dangerous_symbiosis.

Bloom, Mia, and Chelsea Daymon. "Assessing the Future Threat: Isis's Virtual Caliphate." *Foreign Policy Research Institute* 62, no. 3 (Summer 2018): 372–88. https://doi.org/10.1016/j.orbis.2018.05.007.

Bolter, Jay D., and Richard Grusin. "Mediation and Remediation." In *Remediation: Understanding New Media*, Chap. 2. Cambridge, MA: MIT Press, 2000.

Caminos, José María, José Ignacio Armentia, and Flora Marín. "El asesinato de Miguel Ángel Blanco como ejemplo de key event en el tratamiento mediático de los atentados mortales de ETA" (The Assassination of Miguel Ángel Blanco as an Example of a Key Event in the Media Coverage of Fatal Attacks by ETA). *Ad Comunica. Revista Científica de Estrategias, Tendencias e Innovación en Comunicación*, no. 6 (2013): 139–60.

– "Los diarios vascos frente al terrorismo (1990, 2000, 2008 y 2009). Análisis de los editoriales sobre los atentados mortales de ETA" (Basque Daily Newspapers Faced with Terrorism [1990, 2000, 2008 and 2009]. Analysis of Editorials on Fatal Attacks by ETA). *Revista Latina de Comunicación Social* 68 (2013): 126. https://verne.elpais.com/verne/2017/08/17/articulo/1502987962_573043.html.

– "Jerarquización en el tratamiento periodístico de los asesinatos de ETA en los medios de comunicación vascos (1996–1998)" (Hierarchical Organization of the Journalistic Coverage of the ETA Assassinations in Basque Media [1996–1998]). ZER 17, no. 33 (2012): 119–42.

CAC, Catalan Audiovisual Council and the Association of Journalists of Catalonia (CAC-CPC). "Guidelines on News Coverage of Terrorism." First digital publication, November 2016. https://www.cac.cat/sites/default/files/2018-04/Recomanacions_terrorisme_EN.pdf.

Cali, Dennis D. "Journalism after September 11: Unity as Moral Imperative." *Journal of Mass Media Ethics* 17, no. 4 (2002): 290–303. https://doi.org/10.1207/S15327728JMME1704_04.

Cooper, Glenda. "Rights and Responsibilities When Using User-Generated Content to Report Crisis Events." In *The Routledge Companion to Media and Human Rights*, edited by Howard Tumber and Silvio Waisbord, pt 3. London and New York: Routledge, 2017.

Díaz-Campo, Jesús, María-Ángeles Chaparro-Domínguez, Ruth Rodríguez-Martínez. "Los atentados terroristas de Barcelona y Cambrils en la prensa online. Tratamiento informativo en *El Periódico, El País* y *The Guardian*" (The Terrorist Attacks in Barcelona and Cambrils in the Online Press: News Coverage by *El Periódico, El País*, and *The Guardian*). *El Profesional de la Información* 27, no. 6 (2018): 1358–67. https://doi.org/10.3145/epi.2018.nov.18.

EGM-AIMC. "Newspaper Ranking." 2020. http://reporting.aimc.es/index. html#/main/diarios.

El Confidencial. "Por qué no debes difundir imágenes del atentado en Barcelona en las redes sociales" (Why You Should Not Spread Images of the Barcelona Attack on Social Networks). 17 August 2017. https://www. elconfidencial.com/tecnologia/2017-08-17/atentado-barcelona-mossos-difundir-imagenes-redes-sociales_1430019.

El País. "Así fue abatido el quinto terrorista de Cambrils" (This Is How the Fifth Cambrils Terrorist was Killed). *El País*, 18 August 2017. https:// elpais.com/elpais/2017/08/18/videos/1503057854_819526.html.

El Plural. "Así se gestionó la información en Twitter tras los atentados de Barcelona" (This Is How Information Was Managed on Twitter after the Barcelona Attacks). 23 August 2017. https://www.elplural.com/ comunicacion/asi-se-gestiono-la-informacion-en-twitter-tras-los-atentados-de-barcelona_108222102.

Europol. *European Union Terrorism Situation and Trend Report 2018. Te-Sat.* 2018. https://doi.org/10.2813/00041.

–. *Internet Organized Crime Threat Assessment. IOCTA 2017.* 2017. https:// doi.org/10.2813/55735.

Federación de Asociaciones de Periodistas de España [Federation of the Press Assocations in Spain]. https://fape.es/home/quienes-somos.

Figley, Charles R. "Traumatization and Comfort: Close Relationships May Be Hazardous to Your Health." Keynote presentation, Families and Close Relationships: Individuals in Social Interaction, Texas Tech University, Lubbock. February 1982. https://doi.org/10.13140/RG.2.1.1973.8324. http://www.understandingwar.org/sites/default/files/ISW%20The%20 Virtual%20Caliphate%20Gambhir%202016.pdf.

Gulyas, Agnes. "The Influence of Professional Variables on Journalists' Uses and Views of Social Media." *Digital Journalism* 1, no. 2 (2013). https://doi. org/10.1080/21670811.2012.744559.

Heravi, Bahareh R., and Natalie Harrower. "Twitter Journalism in Ireland: Sourcing and Trust in the Age of Social Media." *Information, Communication, and Society* 19 (May 2016): 1194–213. https://doi.org/10.1080/1369118X.2016.1187649.

Hermida, Alfred, and Neil J. Thurman. "A Clash of Cultures: The Integration of User-Generated Content within Professional Journalistic Frameworks at British Newspaper Websites." *Journalism Practice* 2, no. 3 (September 2008): 343–56. https://ssrn.com/abstract=1262749.

Hight, Joe. "First Responders." *Dart Center*, 24 March 2009. http://dartcenter.org/content/first-responders.

Hoskins, A., A. Akil, and B. O'Loughlin. *Legitimising the Discourses of Radicalisation: Political Violence in the New Media Ecology.* Wiltshire: Economic and Social Research Council, 2009.

Houston, Brian. "Media Coverage of Terrorism: A Meta-Analytic Assessment of Media Use and Posttraumatic Stress." *Journalism and Mass Communication Quarterly* 86, no. 4 (2009): 844–61.

Keinan, Giora, Avi Sadeh, and Sefi Rosen. "Attitudes and Reactions to Media Coverage of Terrorist Acts." *Journal of Community Psychology* 31, no. 2 (2003): 149–65. https://doi.org/10.1002/jcop.10040.

Lavín de las Heras, Eva. "Los hitos que marcaron el inicio del periodismo ciudadano" (The Milestones of the Beginning of Citizen Journalism). In *Los Medios del Futuro y los Espectadores 2.0 (The Media of the Future and the Audience 2.0)*, edited by Eva Lavín de las Heras and Nerea Vadillo Bengoa, 99–122. Sociedad Latina de Comunicación Social, 2015.

Marthoz, Jean Paul. "Covering an Attack." In *Terrorism and the Media. A Handbook for Journalists*, edited by Mirta Lourenço, 71–4. Paris: UNESCO, 2017. https://unesdoc.unesco.org/ark:/48223/pf0000247074.

Matthews, Julian. "Media Performance in the Aftermath of Terror: Reporting Templates, Political Ritual, and the UK Press Coverage of the London Bombings, 2005." *Journalism* 17, no. 2 (2014): 173–89. https://doi.org/10.1177/1464884914554175.

McLeod, Douglas, and Dhavan Shah. "News Frames and National Security: Covering Big Brother." In Brigitte Nacos, "Media, Terrorism and Freedom of Expression," 499.

Meir Amit Intelligence and Terrorism Information Center (MAITIC). "Analysis of ISIS's Claims of Responsibility for Terrorist Attacks Carried Out Abroad," 15 August 2017. http://www.terrorism-info.org.il/app/uploads/2017/08/HF_159_17.pdf.

Merolla, J., and E. Zechmeister. *Democracy at Risk:. How Terrorist Threats Affect the Public.* Chicago Studies in American Politics. Chicago: University of Chicago Press, 2009.

Nacos, Brigitte L. *Mass-Mediated Terrorism*. Lanham: Rowman and Littlefield, 2002.

– *Mass-Mediated Terrorism: Mainstream and Digital Media in Terrorism and Counterterrorism*. Lanham: Rowman and Littlefield, 2016.

– "Media, Terrorism, and Freedom of Expression." In *The Routledge Companion to Media and Human Rights*, edited by Howard Tumber and Silvio Waisbord. London and New York: Routledge, 2017.

– *Terrorism and the Media*. New York: Columbia University Press, 1994.

– "Terrorism/Counterterrorism and Media in the Age of Global Communication." Presentation, United Nations University Global Seminar, Second Shimame-Yamaguchi Session, "Terrorism – A Global Challenge," 5–8 August 2006. https://archive.unu.edu/globseminar/files/shimane06/Nacos_text_en.pdf.

Nacos, Brigitte L., Yaeli Bloch-Elkon, and Robert Y. Shapiro. "Prevention of Terrorism in Post-9/11 America: News Coverage, Public Perceptions, and the Politics of Homeland Security." Terrorism and Political Violence 20, no. 1 (2008): 1–25. https://doi.org/10.1080/09546550701734028.

Nicolescu, Basarab. "Methology of Transdisciplinarity – Lives of Reality, Logic of the Included Middle and Complexity." *Transdisciplinary Journal of Engineering and Science* 1, no. 1 (2010): 19–38.

Nissenbaum, Helen. "Privacy as Contextual Integrity." *Washington Law Review* 79 (February 2004): 119–57. https://nyuscholars.nyu.edu/en/publications/privacy-as-contextual-integrity.

O'Connor, Tom. "Isis Calls on Muslims to Attack Spain, Becomes Top Twitter Meme." *Newsweek* , 25 August 2017. https://www.newsweek.com/twitter-blows-isis-militant-promising-more-attacks-spain-655242.

Otto, Carlos. "Por qué no debes difundir imágenes del atentado en Barcelona en las redes sociales" (Why You Should Not Spread Images of the Barcelona Attack on Social Networks). *El Confidencial*, 17 August 2017. https://www.elconfidencial.com/tecnologia/2017-08-17/atentado-barcelona-mossos-difundir-imagenes-redes-sociales_1430019.

Paletz, D., and J. Boiney. "Researchers' Perspectives." In *Terrorism and the Media*, ed. D. Paletz and A. Schmind. London and New York: Sage, 1992.

Patel, Sofia. "Media and Terror in the Age of Social Media." *The Strategist* (February 2018). https://www.aspistrategist.org.au/media-terror-age-social-media.

Pearlman, Laurie A., and Karen W. Saakvitne. *Trauma and the Therapist: Countertransference and Vicarious Traumatization in Psychotherapy with Incest Survivors*. New York: W.W. Norton, 1995.

Policía Nacional. "La Policía Nacional alerta de un nuevo bulo de WhatsApp sobre el atentado de Barcelona." *El País*, 18 August 2017. https://cincodias. elpais.com/cincodias/2017/08/18/lifestyle/1503047817_295650.html.

Rappaport, Julian. "Studies in Empowerment: Introduction to the Issue." *Prevention in Human Services* 3 (1984): 1–7.

Redondo, Myriam. *Verificación digital para periodistas. Manual contra bulos y desinformación internacional (Digital Verification for Journalists: Manual against Fake News and International Disinformation)*. Barcelona: Editorial UOC, 2018. https://www.universitarialibros.com/ebook/verificacion-digital-para-periodistas_E0002657277.

Rivas-Nieto, Pedro, and Juan F. Plaza. "Pautas para la cobertura periodística de actos terroristas. Propuesta de un modelo informativo de responsabilidad democrática." *Estudios sobre el mensaje periodístico* 21, no. 2, (2015): 1207–23. https://doi.org/10.5209/rev_ESMP.2015.v21.n2.50911.

Salvat Martinrey, Guimar, and Pedro Paniagua-Santamaria. "¿Es este periodismo ciudadano?" (Is this Citizen Journalism?). *Estudios sobre el Mensaje Periodístico*, no. 13 (2007): 227–46. https://revistas.ucm.es/index.php/ESMP/article/view/ESMP0707110227A.

Sánchez-Duarte, José Manuel. "Narrativas y portavoces del terrorismo mediatizado" (Narratives and Spokespersons of Mediatized Terrorism). *Revista Latina de Comunicación Social* 64 (2009): 481–90. https://doi.org/10.4185/RLCS-64-2009-839-481-90.

Sánchez Duarte, José Manuel, and José Luis Sampedro. "Visibilidad mediática y terrorismo: el caso de las víctimas de ETA" (Media Visibility and Terrorism: The Case of the Victims of ETA). *Textual and Visual Media*, no. 4 (2011): 183–210. https://www.academia.edu/1596440/Visibilidad_medi%C3%A1tica_y_terrorismo_el_caso_de_la_v%C3%ADctimas_de_ETA.

Seib, Philip, and Dana Janbek. *Global Terrorism and New Media: The Post Al-Qaeda Generation*. London: Routledge, 2010.

Schmidt, Alex, and Janny de Graf. *Violence as Communication*. Beverly Hills: Sage, 1982.

Schudson, Michael. "What's Unusual about Covering Politics as Usual." In *Journalism after September 11*, edited by Barbie Zelizer and Stuart Allan, 36–47. London: Routledge, 2002.

Shoshani, Anat, and Michelle Slone. "The Drama of Media Coverage of Terrorism: Emotional and Attitudinal Impact on the Audience." *Studies in Conflict and Terrorism* 31, no. 7 (2008): 627–40. https://doi.org/10.1080/10576100802144064.

Soria, Carlos. *Prensa, paz, violencia y terrorismo (Press, Peace, Violence, and Terrorism)*. Pamplona: Eunsa, 1990.

Soria, Carlos, and Juan Antonio Giner. *El secuestro terrorista de los medios de información (The Terrorist Kidnapping of Information Media)*. Pamplona: Eunsa, 1987.

Spencer, Alexander. *The Tabloid Terrorist: The Predicative Construction of New Terrorism in the Media*. London: Palgrave Macmillan, 2010.

Stamm, Beth Hudnall, ed. *Secondary Traumatic Stress: Self-Care Issues for Clinicians, Researchers, and Educators*. Lutherville: Sidran Press, (1995.

– "Work-Related Secondary Traumatic Stress." PTSD *Research Quarterly* 8, 1–8.

Torres, Emma. "El tratamiento de la imagen en los atentados del 11M. Terrorismo y violencia en la prensa» (Image Treatment in the 11M Terrorist Attacks : Terrorism and Violence in the Press). *Revista Latina de Comunicación Social* 9, no. 61 (2006). http://revistalatinacs.org/200603torres.htm.

Torres-Soriano, Manuel R. *El estado de la yihad online un* año después de los atentados de Barcelona y Cambrils (The State of Jihad Online One Year Aafter the Attacks in Barcelona and Cambrils). Instituto de Seguridad y Cultura, 2018. https://seguridadycultura.org/wp-content/uploads/2018/08/Yihad-online.pdf.

WAN-IFRA. "Mass misattribution of viral Brussels video." *World Association of News Publishers,* 24 March 2016. https://wan-ifra.org/2016/03/mass-misattribution-of-viral-brussels-video.

Wardle, Claire, Sam Dubberley, and Peter D. Brown. *Amateur Footage: A Global Study of User-Generated Content*. Tow Center for Digital Journalism, Columbia University, 2014. https://doi.org/10.7916/D88S526V.

Weimann, Gabriel. "Media Events: The Case of International Terrorism." *Journal of Broadcasting and Electronic Media* 31, no. 1 (1987): 21–39. https://doi.org/10.1111/j.1460-2466.1983.tb02372.x.

– *Terrorism in Cyberspace: The Next Generation*. New York: Columbia University Press, 2015.

Weimann, Gabriel, and Conrad Winn. *The Theater of Terror. Mass Media and International Terrorism*. New York: Longman, 1994.

Wilkinson, Paul. *Terrorism versus Democracy: The Liberal State Response*. London and New York: Routledge, 2006.

Yarchi, Moran, Yair Galily, and Ilan Tamir. 2015. "Rallying or Criticizing? Media Coverage of Authorities' Reaction to Terror Attacks Targeting Sporting Events." *Studies in Conflict and Terrorism* 38, no. 12 (2015): 1008–21. https://doi.org/10.1080/1057610X.2015.1076644.

Zeller, Frauke, and Alfred Hermida. "When Tradition Meets Immediacy and Interaction: The Integration of Social Media in Journalists' Everyday Practices." *Sur le Journalisme, About Journalism, Sobre Jornalismo* 4 (March 2015): 106–19. http://surlejourmalisme.com/rev.

Zimmer, Michael. "'But the data is already public': On the Ethics of Research in Facebook." *Ethics and Information Technology* 12 (2010): 313–25. https://doi.org/10.100/s10676-010-9227-5.

13

What's Trending?

The Influence of Twitter and Instagram Agendas on Online News Portals in Ghana

EUGENE BROWN NYARKO AGYEI AND SARAH AKROFI-QUARCOO

After a photo of a primary school teacher who used a blackboard version of Microsoft Office to teach his students information and communication technology (ICT) went viral in January 2018, the news dynamics in Ghana related to education changed for several weeks. The entire conversation had started with a tweet from a person who had copied the post from Facebook and tagged international organizations and brands like Microsoft and Google. The tweet became a news item on major news networks like the British Broadcasting Corporation (BBC), *The Guardian* (UK), Cable News Network (CNN), Tech Crunch, and Joy News Channel in Ghana. Social media agendas may have played a key role in influencing mainstream media in this period. The story subsequently raised a lot of issues regarding Ghana's education system.

Ghana is a multiparty democracy with an executive form of government. This means that several political parties struggle for power every four years. They do this by campaigning on various issues, including education. In the absence of a clear national policy on education, successive governments have relied on promises made in their party manifestos to address the issues relating to the sector, often ignoring pertinent discussions and reforms that could transform it. A major challenge in Ghana's education sector is poor infrastructure.

Ghana's return to democratic governance in the early 1990s after two decades of military rule has led to immense changes in the country's media landscape. Under the military, the traditional media (radio and television) and a few newspapers were state-owned; they were the primary sources of news as well as the main agenda setters. A return of democratic governance brought about media deregulation and liberalization, freedom of expression, rule of law, and greater access to international news. The new media landscape saw a proliferation of traditional and new media outlets, media technologies, and devices such as mobile telephony. In tandem with expanded ownership of media, a new public sphere emerged that enabled greater participation in news production/content through phone-in and talk-back programs on which citizens could engage with political and social discourses. This in turn influenced agenda-setting processes through social media platforms such as Facebook and Twitter.

The rise of new media platforms such as social media and online portals has lent an entirely new dimension to intermedia agenda setting. Today, social media tend to influence mainstream media, and vice versa.

Intermedia Agenda Setting in Ghana

Before the emergence of news websites and social media, the concept of intermedia agenda setting existed in the thick of mainstream media such as newspapers, television, and radio. Private and government-owned newspapers played a critical role in setting the news agenda. The advent of new technology is changing these dynamics.

The rise of social media coupled with the rise of online news platforms that deliver information more quickly has led to an intermedia agenda-setting relationship between online news websites and social media in Ghana. This chapter asks the following key questions:

1 What agendas dominate Twitter, Instagram, and online news portals in Ghana?
2 Do the issues discussed on Twitter and Instagram influence the content of the news portals?
3 How can we determine the issue categories (or agendas) that dominate Twitter, Instagram, and online news portals in Ghana?

Review of the Literature

Many recent empirical studies have lent support to the idea that issues that form the mainstream media's agenda may influence the public agenda.[1] This is what we refer to as "agenda setting." That concept has been further explored by Dearing and Rogers in an attempt to understand what influences the media's agenda.[2] This in turn has led to another aspect of the theory: *intermedia* agenda setting. Over time, issues picked up by some media outlets tend to influence what other news media put out.[3]

In Ghana, it is assumed that media influence has shifted: it no longer comes solely from the mainstream media; since the liberalization of Ghana's media landscape, it has also been coming from online and social media platforms[4]. Traditional media seem to be giving way to a variety of online media platforms that publish news more quickly. Additionally, social media have been emerging that enable ordinary citizens to create and share content and to network with other people.[5] Social media platforms like Facebook, Twitter, Instagram, and YouTube have positioned themselves as part of the public sphere, as important news sources, and as platforms for public debate. In Ghana, the growth of online media – social media in particular – has impacted the agenda-setting function of the media in Ghana, with anecdotal evidence suggesting an intermedia agenda-setting relationship between the two.

Data from the International Telecommunications Union indicate that the Internet adoption rate in Ghana increased substantially between 2014 and 2019, from 7.9 million users in 2014 to an estimated 10.3 million, representing about 35 per cent of Ghana's population. This suggests that more people are using various social media platforms, which have become a fundamental component of the Internet. Statistics compiled by Global Stats Counter indicate that 82.57 per cent of Ghanaians use Facebook and 9.41 per cent use Twitter. YouTube and Instagram follow with 2.66 per cent and 1.1 per cent, respectively. Users are now tweeting and posting about musical concerts happening on the weekend, in addition to trolling and lashing out at politicians. Twitter and Instagram are gradually taking on the form of newsrooms, albeit without the supervision of human editors. Some of the statistics presented here may not be significant enough for scholars to easily assume that these platforms are having an impact on the national discourse; that said, these platforms enjoy considerable engagement, with discussions ranging from criticism of politicians, to economic and social issues, to entertainment. Hashtags are increasingly employed by social media users as they engage in particular conversations, whether they are fighting for a cause or drawing the attention of media organizations to particular issues. The hashtag #DoSomething, for example, was used on Twitter and Instagram to advocate for a four-year-old girl who was the victim of sexual assault; this prompted the media to call on authorities to act quickly and provide justice for the girl. Every day, people tweet their opinions, share news stories, and engage with other tweets and posts.

Twitter and Instagram accounts or handles are not limited to individuals in Ghana. The desire to engage with consumers of news has led media organizations to create their own user accounts. Several media organizations in Ghana monitor the Twitter and Instagram accounts of newsmakers and prominent personalities. Tweets and Instagram posts of celebrities and ordinary users are used in news stories. For instance, during the 2016 presidential elections in Ghana, media organizations monitored the Twitter and Facebook accounts of all the presidential candidates for days, up to the declaration of the results. Some of their posts were written as scripts and used for radio and television news stories, complete with screenshots of the messages. Currently, almost all media organizations in Ghana that operate online have active social media pages through which they share content such as live news feeds, photos, and short clips. The reporters for the online media in turn monitor what their followers are discussing to get fresh leads on stories.

Several traditional media organizations that operate television, radio, and newspapers have vibrant online portals that publish stories before they are disseminated on other platforms. In the process, they have become more interactive, incorporating live blogs of events, social media user posts, and amateur videos into their online feeds. Links to and excerpts from stories are usually shared on social media for further discussion among and reaction from social media users. Sometimes these interactions give online media organizations other leads to follow. They also connect reporters to other offline sources, besides providing quotes to include in news stories.[6] In view of all this, and given how much engagement takes place on social media, journalists are constantly looking to tap into social media's news-gathering potential, seeing it as a new tool for engaging audiences and distributing the news more quickly. Issues that are trending on social media are eventually developed from different angles as major news stories for online news websites. In light of all this, social media today have some influence over the content online media outlets produce. All of this has raised the old question of who sets the media's agenda.

Methodology and Data Collection

This study takes a mixed-method approach, making use of quantitative content analysis for tweets, Instagram posts, and news stories as well as qualitative content analysis for interviews. In addition to Twitter and Instagram, this chapter has sampled the top five online news portals based on rankings by Alexa, an online platform that measures a website's popularity based on available data by region or category. These websites are Myjoyonline.com, Yen.com.gh, Ghananewsagency.org, Pulse.com.gh, and Citinewsroom.com, in no particular order. Also, editors from two of the five news websites were interviewed about the quantitative data gathered. The study spanned a two-week period from 17 to 31 March 2019. The study period was divided into four time spans, with a time lag of one day. Several studies have shown that a one-day time lag interval is appropriate for online intermedia agenda setting to occur. The time spans are as follows: 17 to 18 March 2019, 21 to 23 March 2019, 25 to 27 March 2019, and 29 to 31 March 2019.

The daily time frame was from 6:00 a.m. to 6:00 p.m. An extended daily time frame was chosen because online media mostly publish throughout the day. Additionally, social media do not have starting and closing times, like offical newsrooms.

Taking a daily monitoring approach, all the trending tweets and Instagram posts that appeared on the two social media platforms during the time span and the daily time frame were collected. For Twitter, the tweets included in the dataset were part of the top ten trending topics within the time frame under consideration and had been retweeted or liked more than twenty times. At any time, Twitter gives users the opportunity to see the top trending topics being discussed in their country on the platform. Under these trending topics were various tweets that pointed to the same issue. For Instagram, the posts were items that appeared in the "explore" section within the time period.

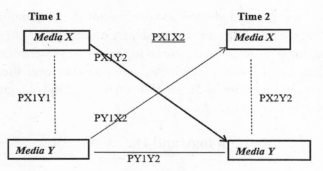

Figure 13.1   Cross-lagged correlation panel

Quantitative data were analyzed using Statistical Packages for Social Sciences (SPSS) to identify frequencies in data for the first level. On the second level, a cross-lagged time-series correlation with the Rozelle-Campbell baseline analysis was conducted on the data. This helped us explore the intermedia agenda-setting influences across the four main time spans. The Rozelle-Campbell baseline analysis helped measure the transfer of salience across the two-week period on the various media platforms. Basically, the analysis focused on how salience was transferred among Twitter, Instagram, and the selected online news portals during the time frame. The cross-lagged correlation also helped us investigate how the three media platforms influenced one another on specific issues within different time spans.

The assumption made by the cross-lagged correlation is that if media X (Twitter, for example) influences media Y (online news websites) more than media Y influences media X, then media X at time 1 (Monday and Tuesday) correlated with media Y at time 2 (Thursday and Friday) should be higher than media X at time 2 and media Y at time 1.[7] If there is a positive correlation, then intermedia agenda setting has occurred. In our study, various media were sampled across four time spans to calculate for correlation.

For the qualitative aspect of this study, two editors from the sampled news websites were interviewed. Transcripts of the semi-structured, in-depth interviews of the two editors were analyzed thematically to find patterns in the data that were of interest to the study and that contributed new dynamics to the quantitative data.

Findings and Discussion

Overall, twelve themes were identified from the Twitter and Instagram posts in the relevant time frames and categorized as the issue topics in a pre-study data collection over forty-eight hours. Some related themes were merged to give the issues a wider scope. Below are the issue categories:

1 *Elections, electoral violence, and vigilantism.* News articles, tweets, and posts related to electoral violence; for example, the Ayawaso by-election violence, political party vigilantism, the electoral commission, and presidential polls.

2 *Politics, corruption, and governance.* News articles, tweets, and posts related to corrupt officials, local governance, misappropriation of funds, ministries, new government projects, etc.

3 *Economy, depreciation of the cedi (the Ghanaian currency), and employment.* News, tweets, and posts related to the economic crisis, businesses, new economic policies, labour strikes, unemployment issues, the fall of the cedi, the government's promises to rescue the cedi, the cedi/dollar rate, etc.

4 *Security, kidnapping, and crime.* News and posts related to kidnappings, violence, robbery, mobile money scams, etc.

5 *Electricity, energy, and transport.* News, tweets, and posts related to power cuts, PDS, ECG, "dumsor" (intermittent power cuts that happened in Ghana between 2013 and 2016), accidents, road issues, traffic problems, energy, etc.

6 *Entertainment and celebrity scandals.* News, tweets and posts related to entertainment, celebrity scandals, celebrity lifestyles, gossip, music, etc.

7 *Education, youth, and technology.* News, tweets, and posts related to free SHS, law school and teacher trainee licensure exams, the double-track system, teacher association strikes, education policies, etc.

8 *Foreign and local sports.* News, tweets, and posts related to football, athletics, foreign sports, local league, football stars, Ghana Football Association committee reports, African Cup of Nations, etc.

9 *Social issues.* News, tweets, and posts related to women's and men's issues, children, domestic violence, empowerment of women, sex, relationship issues, etc.
10 *Religion and spirituality.* News, tweets, and posts related to church issues, religious views by prominent people, controversial spiritual issues, etc.
11 *Foreign news commentary.* News, tweets, and posts about other countries, crises in other countries commented on by Ghanaians, etc.
12 *Health, lifestyle, and sanitation.* News, tweets, and posts about health issues, lifestyle, sanitation, flooding, and sanitation-related matters.

At the end of the two-week period (four time spans), a total of 1,796 items were coded from Twitter, Instagram, and the selected online news websites.[8] Of the 1,796 units analyzed, 845 were posts from the selected online news websites, representing 42.7 per cent of the entire number of items. Twitter followed closely with 42 per cent. Instagram had the lowest number of posts. Generally, the frequency of issue coverage from one time span to another tended to fluctuate. The table below offers insight into the frequency of the various issue categories on all three media.

What Agendas Dominate on Social and Online Media in Ghana?

One objective of this chapter is to determine the issue categories (agendas) that dominate Twitter, Instagram, and online news websites in Ghana. Findings based on the frequency distribution table in table 13.1 show that even though some issue categories overlapped on the agendas of Twitter, Instagram, and the news websites, their ranking differed completely on each of the platforms. Agendas related to "entertainment and celebrity scandal," however, were at the top of the agenda for all three media. Those issues on the three media constituted 19.3 per cent of the total data collected within the period. Brannock Cox's 2014 study[9] found that online news media were more interested in topics such as legal issues and crime, accidents and disasters, politics, the economy, governance, and international events; the sampled online media in

Table 13.1 Frequency distribution table of issue categories on various media across the four time spans

Issue category	Twitter					Instagram					News websites				
	T1	T2	T3	T4	TTL	T1	T2	T3	T4	TTL	T1	T2	T3	T4	TTL
Elections, electoral violence and vigilantism	1	4	4	18	27	0	1	0	1	2	7	14	5	6	32
Politics, corruption and governance	3	13	56	12	84	1	1	3	11	16	14	45	19	15	93
Economy/Cedi depreciation/ employment	12	34	18	2	66	4	2	5	3	14	21	41	15	19	96
Security, kidnapping and crime	16	15	12	13	56	0	4	3	0	7	23	36	15	7	81
Electricity (Dumsor) and transport	20	31	105	3	159	0	3	5	1	9	2	20	21	5	48
Entertainment/ celebrity scandals	5	24	30	123	182	7	5	23	17	52	18	52	24	18	112
Education, youth and technology	3	15	22	4	44	9	1	1	0	11	17	37	17	22	93
Local and foreign sports news	0	47	8	24	79	0	1	1	0	2	12	29	13	11	65
Social issues	12	12	22	2	48	15	0	4	2	21	19	32	22	7	80
Religion and spirituality	0	7	0	0	7	0	0	1	1	2	3	10	4	1	18
Foreign news commentary	3	15	7	1	26	0	4	1	0	5	23	30	9	10	72
Health, lifestyle and sanitation	0	11	16	0	27	0	1	2	2	5	6	20	14	15	55
TOTAL	75	228	300	202	805	36	23	49	35	146	165	366	178	136	845

Note: T1=Time 1, T2=Time 2, T3=Time 3, T4=Time 4. TTL=TOTAL

Ghana did not follow that pattern. This indicates that online media, although still focused on "conventional" news categories, are becoming more inclined to cover unconventional news such as celebrity scandals and gossip, health, and lifestyle topics. As has been suggested by anecdotal evidence, this means that online news media have become more of a business venture in which the owners rely on revenue from pay-per-view and pay-per-click advertising to maintain their websites. Typically, the only way to keep a site running and to gain more advertising revenue is to get more clicks and views. To do this, a site must cover trending issues on social media in addition to its regular content to get more views, which will translate into revenue.

The findings also indicate that of the two sampled social media, Twitter has a greater interest in issues relating to politics, corruption, governance, economy, electricity, and transportation. This finding corroborates a 2016 conclusion by a How Africa Tweets report that argued that Africans on Twitter were more likely to discuss or share regular news topics such as those relating to politics and governance than Twitter users in some parts of the West. However, in contrast to previous studies by Bakan and Melek,[10] who concluded that attention on social media is likely to follow the online news media agenda during significant events such as elections, natural disasters, or anything of national interest, this study finds that Ghanaian users of social media platforms like Twitter were still concerned about regular news issues on "routine" news days. Interestingly, the "social issues" category received a relatively large amount of attention on Instagram. The most discussed topics on Instagram during the same period were related to gender, sex, and relationships, a departure from the existing notion that Instagram was used mainly to share glamorous photos and videos. This means that Instagram is gradually joining Twitter in becoming a social discussion platform on which people do more than update their pages with photos of what is happening in their lives. The comment section, as identified by this chapter, is a major field of discourse for several users. This ties in with Towner and Munoz's 2017 study,[11] which found that political candidates in the 2016 US presidential elections used Instagram, posting many of their campaign messages in the form of images.

The implication for future research is that new social media platforms that operate differently from Twitter and Facebook should be paid more attention in agenda-setting research. Aside from these findings, the number of social issues that received attention on the two social media platforms suggests that more people were willing to discuss issues relating to sex, gender, and relationships on the Internet. This finding supports previous research findings by Roberts and colleagues,[12] who argue that people are likely to discuss issues they view as sensitive (e.g., domestic violence) on the Internet even when such issues are not receiving attention on other mainstream media.

Do Twitter and Instagram Influence the Agendas of Online News?

To ascertain the influence of Twitter and Instagram on the agendas of online media, which is the major objective of this study, cross-lagged correlations were conducted to measure the influence among all the media sampled. The cross-lagged correlation established that the agenda on social media – Twitter and Instagram – influenced the agenda of the news websites most of the time. Analysis of the data provided evidence that some of the influences were reciprocal, while others were direct and clear, suggesting that within some time spans, a particular media's agenda clearly predicted the agenda of the other. Twitter's influence on the news websites was usually stronger than Instagram's except for some time periods in the cross-lagged panels, in which Instagram also exerted some influence. For instance, the correlation coefficient between Twitter at time 1 and the news websites at time 2 ($r = .951$, ...01, indicated in figure 13.2) showed a very strong influence of Twitter, whereas it showed a rather weak correlation of the reverse, that is between the news websites at time 1 and Twitter at time 2 ($r = .008$, ...01).

The cross-lagged correlations seem to suggest that the "Twitter-sphere" in Ghana has a strong intermedia agenda-setting capability; its online actors' activities such as tweeting, retweeting, and commenting direct reporters' attention to issues on various topics. Their activity, although somehow passive, directs online news editors regarding the various angles they can use to cover certain issues while giving them a sense of what the public agenda may be directed toward at any given time. In one of the interviews with an online editor at Yen.com.gh, the editor indicated that social media trends can influence reporting schedules for the day in their newsroom. Journalists are given new beats based on Twitter trends in the morning: "Sometimes you have

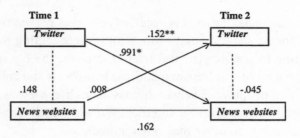

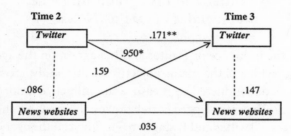

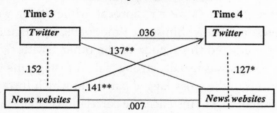

Figure 13.2   The transfer of salience between Twitter and the news websites across the various time spans

your plans for the next day, but you wake up in the morning and you realize there is something trending and then you push aside whatever you have and cash in on what is trending."

Respondent 2 (R2GNA), an editor with the Ghana News Agency, admitted that social media influenced some of their reporting activities. She added that the Ghana News Agency – the country's official news agency – only pays attention to social media trends that are of public interest: "We don't necessarily say that we are checking social media for news, but if an issue is trending on social media and it is of

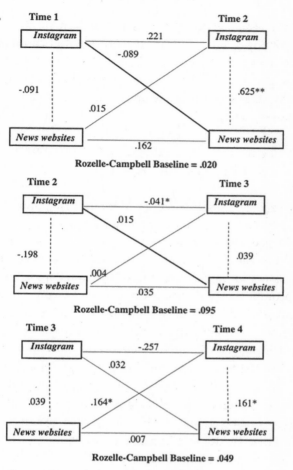

Figure 13.3 The transfer of salience between Instagram and the news websites across all time spans

public interest, yes, my news organization will always be interested in following up."

Twitter showed a strong influence on the news websites; Instagram's influence on the news websites was low. However, there was slightly higher influence of the news websites on Instagram between time 3 and time 4, as seen in figure 13.3. The influence was not strong enough to have affected all the discussions on Instagram at the time. However, contrast this finding with that of a study by Towner and Munoz,[13] who found that the Instagram posts about the 2016 US presidential elections predicted the issue agenda in newspapers. Even so, they concluded that the posts by Hilary Clinton, the presidential candidate for the Democratic Party, more readily influenced and predicted the mainstream newspaper agenda. This suggests that even though Instagram is in its early stages, its influence on mainstream media may depend on context and issues.

Twitter and Instagram a Greater Force of Intermedia Agenda Setting

When analyzed as a single force, Twitter and Instagram together displayed a stronger influence on the news websites, except for one of the cross-lagged panels, in which the news websites seemed to have influenced the agenda on social media slightly between time 3 and time 4. This could be because not all the news websites in Ghana, however prompt they are at breaking the news, run a full-time 24/7 cycle, so social media networking platforms will inevitably be first in breaking news. Weimann and Brosius's study argues that due to the pace at which many social media networking sites operate, they may have the potential to influence the agenda of traditional news outlets as well.[14] This returns us to the idea of intermedia agenda setting, in which the news media, while busily influencing the public agenda, are themselves being influenced by the agendas of other media. The study found that Twitter and Instagram are beginning to play the role of regular news media, whose activities influence the news selection preferences of online media. As has been argued by McCombs and colleagues,[15] new dynamics are developing in intermedia agenda setting, especially with the diffusion of new and social media. Technological advances have allowed public discussion of issues that would usually have occurred offline to appear on social media – a new platform for public debate – subsequently influencing the agendas of other media. The original agenda-setting theory itself did not anticipate the rapid growth of social media.

After looking at the influence of both Twitter and Instagram on the news websites, it was prudent to consider whether the two social media platforms exert the same influence on each other. The research found that Twitter and Instagram did in fact do so, although Twitter's influence was stronger most of the time. It is interesting that during some of the time spans, users on the two social media platforms were interested in different issues. This may be because Twitter lends itself to more "serious" public debate among highly active users. Twitter users are more diverse than Instagram users. Anecdotally, in Ghana, a lot of politicians, celebrities, religious leaders, heads of civil society organizations, and others are more likely to be found on Twitter. Instagram seems more likely to encourage people to share personal experiences and opinions. Other people can only comment on the main post on the original poster's feed, whereas on Twitter, users can retweet to their own timeline, comment under the tweet, or share and comment at the same time (this called a "quote retweet"). Another factor could be that on Instagram, all posts are images rather than text.

Conclusion

With the growing use of Twitter and Instagram in Ghana, coupled with the rise of online news websites, the findings and discussions in this chapter clearly indicate the importance of social media to mainstream media activities. A key finding in this chapter is that in Ghana, most of the issue agendas on Twitter and Instagram reflected the agendas of the online news websites. Another key finding is that issues relating to the economy, politics, electricity (power), governance, and corruption, which were seen as conventional topics for online news websites, dominated the agendas on Twitter and Instagram. This challenges existing studies suggesting that social media users are only concerned about trivial issues. Entertainment and celebrity scandals, which were once viewed as "specialty" topics for social media, are gradually gaining a bigger share in online media.

Interestingly, the study found that Instagram is gradually becoming a news-gathering platform. Interviews with the two editors suggested that they sometimes look to that platform for news content. This chapter recommends that reporters explore Instagram as a new venue for gathering leads for news stories, from the perspective of the ordinary person. Although the agenda found on social media is ephemeral by nature, this chapter suggests that journalists and editors could pay more attention to social media for leads and sources.

Furthermore, this study found that Twitter and Instagram together had a strong intermedia agenda-setting influence on news websites. The findings also indicate that of the two social media platforms, Twitter's influence was greater, although the two platforms were sometimes concerned about different issue agendas at the same point in time.

This chapter has demonstrated that the news media no longer wield the sole power to set the news agenda and that audiences have become more active and less passive, as some early communication theories have suggested. The power of the news media lies in their ability to refine and propagate the agendas of Internet users and bring to light more angles on particular issues by further engaging users as a result of their activity on social media platforms. Through social media, ordinary citizens are contributing to and shaping media content through their online activities.

Notes

1   See McCombs & Shaw, "Agenda-Setting."
2   Dearing and Rogers, *Agenda-setting*.
3   See Agyei, "Intermedia."
4   See Sikanku, "Ghana."
5   See Kaplan and Haenlein, "Social."
6   See Agyei, "Intermedia."
7   The inverse is also presumed: that if media Y affects media X at time 2 more than media X at time 2 affects media Y at time 1, then media Y should be higher than media X at time 1 and media Y at time 2. In this study, therefore, three cross-lagged correlations can be performed, that is, between time 1 and time 2, time 2 and time 3, and between time 3 and time 4 among the various media sampled. For instance, if Twitter (media X) issues affect the selected online media (media Y), then the issue agendas of Twitter at time 1 when correlated with the issue agendas of the online media at time 2 should have a higher correlation comparing the issues on Twitter at time 2 and the online media at time 1. In simple terms, for instance, intermedia agenda-setting occurs if the correlation of issues discussed on Twitter (media X) between Monday and Tuesday, and the correlation of issues published on the selected online news portals (media Y) between Thursday and Friday was higher than the correlation of issues published on the news websites between Monday and Tuesday (media Y) and the issues discussed on Twitter between Thursday and Friday. In this example, the issues being discussed on Twitter have had an effect on the topics published by the news websites.

8 The various number of issues were 276 in time 1, 617 in time 2, 527 in time 3 and 376 in time 4. Out of the four time spans, time 2 (21 March–23 March) received the highest number of items (n=617) from all three media, making up one third or 31.2 per cent of the data. Time 1 had the least number of items (n=276).
9 Cox, "News You Need to Know."
10 Bakan and Melek, "First and Second Level."
11 Towner and Munoz, "Picture Perfect?"
12 Roberts et al., "Agenda Setting."
13 Towner and Munoz, "Picture Perfect?"
14 Weimann and Brosius, "A New Agenda."
15 McCombs et al., "New Directions."

Bibliography

Agyei, Eugene B. "The Intermedia Agenda-Setting among Twitter, Instagram, and Online News Websites in Ghana." MA thesis, University of Ghana, 2019.

Bakan, Uğur, and Gizem Melek. "First and Second Level Intermedia Agenda-Setting between International Newspapers and Twitter during the Coverage of the 266th Papal Election." *Akdeniz Üniversitesi İletişim Fakültesi Dergisi* 26 (2016): 155–77.

Cox, J. "News You Need to Know: Examining the Prioritization of News Content in Print and Online Publications." *Journal of Mass Communication and Journalism* 4 (2014): 210.

Dearing, James W., and Everett M. Rogers. *Agenda-setting*, vol. 6. Thousand Oaks: Sage, 1996.

Kaplan, Andreas M., and Michael Haenlein. "Social Media: Back to the Roots and Back to the Future." *Journal of Systems and Information Technology* 14, no. 2 (2012): 101–4. https://doi.org/10.1108/13287261211232126.

McCombs, Maxwell E., and Donald L. Shaw. "The Agenda-Setting Function of Mass Media." *Public Opinion Quarterly* 36, no. 2 (1972): 176–87.

McCombs, Maxwell E., Donald L. Shaw, and David H. Weaver. "New Directions in Agenda-Setting Theory and Research." *Mass Communication and Society* 17, no. 6 (2014): 781–802.

Roberts, Marilyn, Wayne Wanta, and Tzong-Horng Dzwo. "Agenda Setting and Issue Salience Online." *Communication Research* 29, no. 4 (2002): 452–65.

Sikanku, Etse Godwin. "Inter-Media Agenda-Setting Effects in Ghana: Newspaper vs. Online and State vs. Private." PhD diss., Iowa State University, Ames, 2008. https://dr.lib.iastate.edu/handle/20.500.12876/69045.

Towner, Terri L., and Caroline Lego Muñoz. "Picture Perfect? The Role of Instagram in Issue Agenda Setting during the 2016 Presidential Primary Campaign." *Social Science Computer Review* 36, no. 4 (2018): 484–99.

Weimann, Gabriel, and Hans-Bernd Brosius. "A New Agenda for Agenda-Setting Research in the Digital Era." In *Political Communication in the Online World*, edited By Gerhard Vowe and Philipp Henn, 26–44. London: Routledge, 2015.

14

We Are Not Parasites

Intergroup Differentiation in the User-Generated Content of Nigerian News Media

BABATUNDE RAPHAEL OJEBUYI AND ABIODUN SALAWU

The Internet has created a digital space that enables not only traditional journalists but also citizens to create content and interact with other members of the online community.[1] There is now more freedom of expression and an expanded public space for citizens' participation in the political campaigns,[2] protests,[3] and overall democratic projects of their country.[4] But studies have shown that while there is now freedom of content creation and political participation,[5] the digital space has also provided platforms for negative discourse relating to race, civil rights, harassment, and discrimination. The notion that prevailed in the early days of the new media, either that race does not exist on the Internet or that cyberspace represents some sort of halcyon realm of "colour blindness," has turned out to be a myth.[6]

Scholars in a number of countries have long been examining harassment, crimes, defamation, hate speech, and ethnocultural stereotypes in cyberspace.[7] In Nigeria, a number of studies have focused on the influence of social media on how Nigerian youth use traditional mass media;[8] Nigerians' online stances, civic engagement, and responses to domestic terrorist attacks;[9] citizenship, participation, and computer-mediated discourse;[10] new media and negative rhetoric (Ojebuyi 2016); the uprising of Boko Haram (a Nigerian terrorist group based in the northeast of the country)[11] and online pragmatic acts by Nigerians in response to Boko Haram;[12] ideology in the tweets of Boko Haram;[13] and social media and political campaigns in Nigeria.[14] Nigeria is prone to crises arising from its cultural, ethnic, social, religious, and political diversity,[15] yet negative online comments reflecting inter-group prejudices – especially when they converge in response to political news stories at critical times such as general elections – have not received adequate scholarly attention. This study aims to address that gap. The core question we set out to answer is this: What forms of inter-group differentiation do Nigerians express in their online reactions to political stories reported by Nigerian news media? This study, then, analyzes hateful comments posted by the online audiences of Nigerian news media and proposes a theoretical interpretation that relates to the idea of inter-group differentiation. The specific focus is on readers' comments on political news stories.

Nigeria has Africa's highest rate of Internet use; globally, it is the eighth most "wired" country.[16] Since 2001, Nigeria has been one of the fastest-growing markets in Africa, with triple-digit growth rates. It is also one of the biggest and fastest-growing telecom markets in Africa, attracting huge amounts of foreign investment, and overtook Egypt and Morocco in 2004 to become the continent's second-largest mobile market after South Africa.[17] According to Internet World Stats, as of 25 May 2022, Nigeria recorded the second-highest number of Facebook users (31.9 million) in Africa, and total Internet users stood at 154.3 million, accounting for 73 per cent of the population (by comparison, Egypt had 54.7 million users, Kenya 46.9 million, and South Africa 34.5 million).[18] Given these impressive numbers, the nature of the discourse expressed by Nigerians when they interact in online communities must have implications for their social networking and coexistence.

Literature Review

NIGERIAN POLITICAL HISTORY AND GROUP IDENTITY

Like many other West African countries, Nigeria was a creation of its European colonial masters. More than 400 ethnic groups, including the three dominant ethnic nationalities – Hausa, Yoruba, and Igbo – were forced to coexist as a single nation.[19] The amalgamation of the Northern and the Southern protectorates in 1914 through the Native Authority System[20] brought different nationalities and ethnic groups together in a marriage of strange bedfellows, as described by Hodgkin (1960), who contended that Nigeria is a product of the complex histories of various people and civilizations.

Ajetumobi posits that the emergence of the Nigerian Colonial State was a by-product of a "fraudulent social contract" and not of a "'negotiated will' of the welded parts."[21] All of this means that Nigeria is a heterogeneous entity comprising many ethnic groups and nationalities that were yoked together to form a single artificial nation. This resulted in a complex web of religiously, culturally, and politically diverse communities. Consequently, Nigeria since it gained independence in 1960 has been on a turbulent journey marked by episodes of grave crisis driven by divergent interests among different nationalities, religious groups, and political alliances. Examples of such crises are the coup d'état of 1960; the counter-coup of 1966; the civil war of 1967 to 1970 between the Igbos and the rest of the country; the 12 June 1993 political impasse that set the Yorubas of the southwest against other ethnic groups, especially the predominant Hausa and Fulani of the north; the Kaduna religious crises in the early 2000s, in which Christians mostly from southern Nigeria were the targets; the Nupe–Yoruba conflict in Kwara state in 2000; the agitation for resource control in the Niger Delta region; the emergence of Boko Haram Islamists in the north; and recurrent outbreaks of electoral violence.[22] Thus it could be inferred that Nigeria is not a nation, but a geographical entity comprising different groups with different identities that find their roots in religious and ethnic differentiations, among other dividing factors such as political and social alignments. The late literary giant from Nigeria, Chinua Achebe, reflecting on his Igbo identity, captured how he believed his ethnic group had struggled to survive being a target of ethnic discrimination among the various nationalities in Nigeria:

> The origin of national resentment of the Igbo is as old as Nigeria and quite as complicated ... The Igbo culture being receptive to change, individualistic and highly competitive, gave the Igbo man an unquestioned advantage over his compatriots in securing credentials for advancement in Nigerian colonial society. Unlike the Hausa/Fulani he was unhindered by a wary religion and unlike the Yoruba unhampered by traditional hierarchies ... Although the Yoruba had a huge historical and geographical

head-start the Igbo wiped out their handicap in one fantastic
burst of energy in the twenty years between 1930 and 1950 ...
Had the Igbo been a minor ethnic group of a few hundred
thousand, their menace might have been easily and quietly
contained. But they ran in their millions![23]

The ethnic resentment and discrimination outlined by Achebe several years ago persists and is gathering intensity in Nigerian society, and
it targets all nationalities, not just the Igbo. Members of every ethnic
group, religious affiliation, social class, and political party see themselves
as distinct from others or as part of a disadvantaged minority that
has been marginalized, despised, or dominated by larger and stronger
groups. Right from independence, the Nigerian project has reflected a
social structure that promotes conflicts and inter-group discrimination
based on ethnicity, politics, religion, and social class. This phenomenon
has been captured by Chiluwa, who writes that "in Nigeria, social crises
have been as a result of religious intolerance, boundary disputes, resistance to a perceived injustice/exploitation and other political reasons."[24]
The formation of political parties in Nigeria has been driven not by real
ideology but rather by patronage[25] and ethnic sentiment; during most
elections, the articulation of public issues and voting patterns often
reflects religious and ethnic biases.

DEFINING THE "OTHER"

The concept of the Other can be traced back to Frantz Fanon's postcolonial writings,[26] especially his theory of racialization, which "provides
a starting point for bringing conversations of race and racism into
globalization theories."[27] Quoting Fanon, Al-Saidi writes that "the Other
is the 'not me,' he is the Other."[28] Al-Saidi then defines the Other as
the one "who lacks identity, propriety, purity, literality. In this sense
he can be described as the foreign: the one who does not belong to a
group, does not speak a given language, and does not have the same
customs; he is the unfamiliar, uncanny, unauthorized, inappropriate,
and the improper."[29]

Further delving into the concept of Otherness, Al-Saidi, citing different authors, submits that "the concept of Otherness sees the world
'as divided into mutually excluding opposites: if the Self is ordered,

rational, masculine, good, then the Other is chaotic, irrational, fem-
inine, and evil." Thus, we can describe the Other as the part outside
that group which sees itself as the standard, ordered, ideal, and good.
Those who do not reflect the identities and the norms of that group are
considered the Other, the outsider, who is always perceived and treated
as lesser, substandard, unfortunate, or disadvantaged. The Other, be it
an individual or a group, is considered different in terms of religion,
culture, nationality, race, social class, gender, or political orientation.[30]
The concept of Otherness also extends beyond the group or individual
level to the international level, in terms of how one nation perceives
another or how one continent is portrayed by another.

As Ibeleme explains, Otherness is "evident in the portrayal of
Africa [by most of the Western press] as a place that is removed from
modernity."[31] In the same way, other nations may perceive Nigeria as
a nation of Boko Haram, militancy, and corruption, or South Africa
as a nation of xenophobia, until such vices are eliminated from those
respective countries. In Nigeria, the concept of Otherness manifests
itself in how members of different ethnic groups, political parties, social
classes, or religious sects treat and relate to others who are not from
their own ethnic, religious, social, or political groups. As noted earlier, Nigeria is a pluralistic, politically and culturally complex country.
The various ethnic groups (Igbo, Hausa, and Yoruba, among others),
religious sects (e.g., Islam, Christian, African traditional), and social
and political groups express Otherness and discrimination in terms of
these constructs.[32] Linguistic and semiotic resources play a significant
role in the discursive construction of Otherness.[33] So in this study, we
have focused on how the online audiences of Nigerian news media
employ language to discriminate against those they view as "Others"
on the bases of religion, ethnicity, social class, and political affiliation."

Theoretical Framework

This study employs the social identity theory (SIT) as its theoretical
framework. That theory, developed in the early 1970s in Britain by Henri
Tajfel,[34] is a psychological analysis of how self-conception shapes group
membership, group processes, and inter-group relations. The theory
describes self-conception as the core cognitive factor to be considered
in defining a group.[35] That is, "a group exists psychologically if three

or more people constitute and evaluate themselves in terms of shared attributes that distinguish them collectively from other people."[36] The import of this is that the basis of social identity is group membership. Being a member of a group that has a comparatively positive identity in relation to other groups (out-groups) strengthens a person's self-esteem; furthermore, a person may decide to quit a group that seems less favourable in order to join or identify with a more favourable group.[37] Concepts such as prejudice, discrimination, ethnocentrism, stereotyping, inter-group conflict, conformity, group polarization, group cohesiveness, and deviance are the primary concerns of SIT.[38]

Applying SIT to the evaluation of Others, Tajfel and Turner proposed three mental processes that must take place: social categorization, social identification, and social comparison.[39] Social categorization has to do with using various social categories, such as Black, White, Christian, Muslim, student, bus driver, Yoruba, Igbo, Hausa, *okada* (motorcycle) rider, academic staff, non-academic, to categorize people into different groups. It is, however, possible for someone to belong to more than one group. Next, the characteristics of the group(s) to which individuals have been assigned are used to identify or label them. Emotion and self-esteem are affected by group identity.[40] Finally, the identity (characteristics) of one group is used to compare the group with another group in terms of favourability (or not). These competing identities usually breed inter-group hostility, conflict, antagonism, and prejudice.[41] As summarized by Brown, SIT contends that group members are likely to express inter-group differentiation by declaring that their own group is superior to other groups; thus, they readily express prejudice toward other groups and laud their own group, and themselves.[42] These claims make SIT relevant to our study, whose objective is to investigate inter-group prejudice in the comments made by the online audience of Nigerian news media.

Methodology

METHODS AND MATERIALS

Qualitative design through textual analysis was adopted for this study. Data for the study were extracted from the user-generated content (UGC) found on the online platforms of select Nigerian news media: *The Punch*,

The Vanguard, Sahara Reporters, and *Channels Television.* These news media were selected through a purposive sampling technique guided by the criteria of online presence, an active readers' comment section, and wide readership. In this study, we considered only UGC that used words or iconography (images) offered by online users of the news media selected. On the assumption that Nigerian politics is always driven by ethnic, religious, and social sentiments rather than by clear ideologies,[43] we focused solely on significant political news stories about Nigeria's presidential elections of 28 March 2015. We assumed that stories relating to politics, and readers' comments about those stories around this period (March/April 2015), would reflect these sentiments. By UGC, also known as consumer-generated media (CGM) or conversational media, we refer to online content created by users of online media and posted to the digital platforms of those media.[44] UGC includes chats, posts, tweets, comments, digital images, videos, audio files, and blogs.

We considered UGC that was responding to prominent political stories – for example, about the postponement of the elections, an alleged plot to scuttle the election by sponsoring a new political party, General Muhammadu Buhari's certificate controversies, the alleged distribution of foreign currencies to groups and Yoruba traditional rulers by former President Goodluck Jonathan, an alleged plot to assassinate Reverend Father Mbaka (a prominent Nigerian pastor and social critic), and reactions to the election results. We focused solely on the feedback comments on online platforms of Nigerian news media because a focus on *all* social media platforms would have been too wide. We assumed that media representation of issues of public interest would attract a high intensity of interaction and discussions among Nigerians. All users' comments (UGC) available on stories about the selected issues at the time we visited the sites were retrieved for sorting and textual analysis.

DATA ANALYSIS

We adopted qualitative content analysis to explore the corpus of UGC drawn from the selected online news media. As explained by Catanzaro[45] and Marshall and Rossman,[46] qualitative content analysis is appropriate when the main purpose of the study is to retest existing data in a new context or when the researcher aims to test concepts, constructs, categories, themes, models, or hypotheses. Thus, qualitative content analysis is relevant to this study because we used the constructs of SIT's inter-group prejudice as the guiding themes for the textual analysis. After rounds of reading the corpus of the UGC retrieved from the online platforms of the Nigerian news media we had chosen, we removed those comments we considered irrelevant; that reduced the corpus to 583 comments. We then randomly selected fifty-two samples accounting for about 10 per cent of the total corpus. The fifty-two comments were then textually analyzed based on the sub-constructs of ethnicity, political orientation, religion, and social class in order to extract the discourse of inter-group differentiation from the audience comments. In the samples, "COMT" represents "comments." To satisfy the principles of credibility and transferability,[47] we use extracts from the corpus of the UGC to illustrate and discuss the manifest categories of inter-group discrimination in the UGC of the selected Nigerian news media.

Findings and Discussion

Findings from the study show that the UGC sections of the select Nigerian news media contain inter-group differentiations (ethnicity, political affiliation, religion, and social class) as identified by SIT.[48] Online users of the selected news media displayed group identities along the taxonomies of ethnicity, politics, social abuse, and religion as they responded to the political news stories about Nigeria's general elections. Typically, instead of discussing the issues raised in the stories, the users referred to or directly expressed sentiments that reflected discrimination along ethnic, political, religious, or social lines. From the structures of the UGC, we identified the Igbo, the Yoruba, the Hausa, and the South-South minorities as the construct of ethnicity (COMTs 1–17); the Peoples Democratic Party (PDP) and the All Progressive Congress (APC), the two prominent and rival political parties, as the construct of politics (COMTs 18–32); Islam, Christianity, and atheism (although not obviously expressed) as the construct of religion (COMTs 33–45); and level of civilization, education, or literacy as the construct of social differentiation (COMTs 46–52).

The users, as evident in their comments, showed intra-group bias[49] by extolling the favourable characteristics of their own groups and presenting them as the best or as better than another group. Also, they expressed prejudices, discrimination, ethnocentrism, and stereotyping[50] toward the out-groups. The UGC analyzed in this study reflected that each user had a self-conception[51] of belonging to a group that was ordered, superior, standard, good, and ideal, while seeing others who belonged to the out-groups as inferior, uncivilized, backward, disadvantaged, substandard, and unfortunate. These inter-group discriminations are further explicated with textual evidence from the following corpus of the analyzed UGC in COMTS 1 to 52.

ETHNIC DIFFERENTIATION

One of the most prevalent inter-group prejudices expressed by online users was ethnicity-based. They blatantly favoured their own ethnic group or tribe and attached negative labels to other tribes. Nigeria is divided among diverse ethnic groups, with the Yoruba, the Hausa, the Igbo, and the South-South minorities featuring most prominently in the UGC analyzed in this study. The extracts in COMTS 1 to 17 from UGC on the websites of *The Punch*, Channels Television, and *Sahara Reporters* reflect obvious discrimination by different ethnic groups directed at one another. The UGC comments were retrieved from stories about the alleged bribing of Yoruba traditional rulers with foreign currencies by President Goodluck Jonathan, an alleged plot to scuttle or postpone the elections, and the results of the presidential election.

COMT 1: The Igbos again! What is wrong with these hyenas? Must they scrape and suck Nigeria to the bone? Four out of 6 zones are implacably opposed to their candidate, Jona (President Goodluck Jonathan), whose mother is Igbo.

COMT 2: Why does the Igbos' congenital greed blind him so? 419 [money transfer fraud], cocaine, human parts, fake drugs, career armed robbery, murder-for-hire, Okija necrophilia, human baby farms supplying ritualists and cannibals regular fresh meat etc.

COMT 3: Why do the Igbos refuse to see that anything else will lack legitimacy and lead inexorably to war? Have the newly arrogant Igbos forgotten the lesson of 1966–1970? Why must Igbo candidates, Jonathan or Minimah rule us by force? Do the Igbos want a more brutal, blood-soaked civil war? The Igbo have started again.

Users employed various labels to express ethnic discrimination. In most of the comments, users, reacting to stories about alleged plans to scuttle the elections and keep President Goodluck Jonathan in office, insinuated that the Igbos are a "violent," "fetish," "money-loving," and "aggressive" tribe, labelling them as "hyenas" (COMT 1). Note also the labels "419, cocaine, human parts, fake drugs, career armed robbery, murder-for-hire, Okija necrophilia" (COMT 2). They also accused the Igbos of being forgetful, a clear reference to the bloody civil war of 1966 to 1970, in which Igbos were pitched against the rest of the country and were the apparent target of ethnic cleansing.[52] Insinuating that the Igbos were "unrepentant," the user in COMT 3 declared, "The Igbo have started again." This user, who labelled President Goodluck Jonathan an Igbo man because he was overwhelmingly supported by the Igbos during the elections, derided the Igbos as politically "insignificant" and "victims of the Nigerian civil war."

> COMT 4: You must be a bastard… If anything, Ndigbo have been more responsible for the existence and success of yeye Nigeria thus far. It took Prof. Humphrey Nwosu to get rid of IBB, Sen. Ken Nnamani to get rid of Baba Iyabo; it took late Prof. Dora Akunyili to rid you of Turai.
>
> COMT 5: Cabal … and all the while, the likes of Dr. Ngz. Iweala, Oby Ezekwesili, Ndy Onyiuke-Okerek, Prof. Onyekachi Chukwu, Prof. Bert Nnaji, Dr. Oti et al, to sustain your flustering Nigeria … while you lazy ewedu-lovers [the Yorubas] and Aboki [the Hausas] cohorts stole the country dry in fuel-subsidy scams, Pension funds scams, and so on.
>
> COMT 6: Stupid punk, how many Igbo Ministers have been charged for embezzlement in that useless country called Nigeria … compared to other ethnicities? Let's split it and see who runs a better ship.

Obviously reacting to users who attacked the Igbos, as shown in COMTS 1, 2, and 3, users in COMTS 4, 5, 6, 7, 8, and 16 expressed a lack of confidence in the Nigerian project, describing it as a *yeye* (worthless) entity (COMT 4), and attributed the country's very existence to some notable Igbos, who had helped to stabilize the "flustering Nigeria" (COMT 5) and contributed to the dislodgement of some "sit-tight politicians" from northern and southwestern Nigeria (COMT 4). In the comments, IBB refers to General Ibrahim Badamasi Babangida, the former military head of state (1985–93); Baba Iyabo refers to former President Olusegun Obasanjo (1976–79 and 1999–2007); while Turai is the wife of the late president Umaru Musa Yar'adua (2007–10).

> COMT 7: One Igbo is worth a million near-naked Aborigines like you stinking drunkards. Besides, we power One Nigeria economically, politically and socially ... while you lazy Ijaw drunks X thousands of bottles of Sapele Water. Homeless drifters stealing from every town they visit. Amnesty Days are numbered, better gather your fishing nets and get ready to return to your swampy and polluted reptile-infested enclaves.
> COMT 8: We the hardworking Igbos deserve to have money more than the lazy tribes but the lazy ones love pleasure and comfort more than any other working tribe. Why won't they sell themselves for anything?
> COMT 9: By this sagacious postulation, this brilliant egghead of Igbo extraction has proven that perhaps the Igbo man represents the true fabric of "One Nigeria."

Other users, presumed to be of Igbo origin, as exemplified in COMTS 5, 7, 8, and 9, extolled the virtues of the Igbos as "hardworking" (COMT 8) and labelled the Yorubas "racial," "lazy," "arrogant," "fetish," "coward," "greedy," and "untrustworthy" (COMTS 5 and 10). In COMT 10, the user described the Yoruba Obas (Monarchs) as "materialistic" and "selfish," accusing them of collecting dollars from President Goodluck Jonathan as inducements for political support. This user further insinuated that the Hausas, in particular, were "illiterates," a "savage race," "parasites," "beggars," a tribe in which men marry many wives, have many children, and abandon them on the street (CMTS 5, 14, and 15); in the same vein, the Niger Delta people, especially the Ijaws, were described as "alcoholic," with a natural thirst for Sapele water (a popular name for a brand of locally brewed alcohol in the Niger Delta parts of Nigeria), "parasitic," "predatory," "homeless," "half-naked," and "dirty" (COMT 7). "Parasites" as a label for the Hausas (COMT 15) is a reference to the belief among the southerners, especially those from the oil-producing states, that the North (dominated by the Hausa and Fulani ethnic groups) does not contribute significantly to the national treasury, given that Nigeria survives largely on revenue from southern crude oil. According to the Central Bank of Nigeria Economic Report, in the fourth quarter of 2017, Nigeria recorded gross oil receipts of 1.2 trillion nairas ($3.3 billion), or 60.1 per cent of total revenue, compared to 814.55 billion nairas ($2.2 billion) or 39.9 per cent of total non-oil revenue for the same period.[53] This trend persists, although the present government of General Muhammadu Buhari has claimed that it is focusing on non-oil sectors as a way to diversify the nation's economy.

> COMT 10: The Yoruba obas love money too much, they openly collected money from Jonathan without the feeling of their people.
> COMT 11: How many Yorubas can you be trusted? None, because they will be busy stabbing you for back.
> COMT 12: Igbos are just too cynical; they only care about today and don't give a damn about tomorrow.
> COMT 13: Mention your ethnicity if you're real human and not some cross-bred chimp from the creeks ... like I suspect. At least, I've told you I'm core Igbo and proud of every drop of Igbo blood in me.
> COMT 14: We Igbos cannot start having hundreds of wives and bringing bastards to the world ... Many of my Yoruba friends keep telling me how they envy Igbos and wish they were Igbos. I will never wish to be Yoruba or Hausa. That's the difference.
> COMT 15: These Hausa and Fulanis are animals of the highest order; they are cows ... What are these parasitic tribe talking about? All you (Hausa-Fulanis) do is to create violence everywhere you found yourself without adding any value to the community.
> COMT 16: Why are the Igbos too mischievous? Another Nzeribe's ABN, Kanu's YEAA or what?
> COMT 17: Jega and INEC do not need to re-print any ballot papers, they can hand-write the YDP on existing ones and say, "shikena." In the end, let it be known to you that Ndigbo couldn't care less either way dysfunctional One Nigeria goes ... kapisch? Stupid baastard!

As presented in COMTs 1 to 17 above, Nigerians engage in ethnic hatred in the virtual space provided by the news media. The findings are examples of intra-group bias and out-group prejudice as encountered in the tenets of SIT.[54] The ethnic distrust, rivalry, and intolerance that characterize Nigeria manifest themselves in the online community. As Blench,[55] and Ojie and Ewhrudjakpor,[56] among other scholars, have argued, Nigeria is a Western creation in which unique ethnic national-ities have been forced to live together. Besides expressing discrimination against other ethnic groups, users from some tribes – especially those who are presumed to be Igbos (as shown in COMTs 4, 5, 6, 7, 8, 9, and 17) – suggest skepticism about a united Nigeria. One could argue that the assertion made several years ago by Achebe,[57] that the Igbos were the "victims" of political discrimination and marginalization in Nigeria, is being reinforced in the users' comments. At the same time, users from other ethnic groups (e.g., the Yorubas) suggested in their comments that the Igbos are "mischievous" (COMT 16), "cynical," "profligate" (COMT 12), "greedy" (COMT 2), and "arrogant" (COMT 3).

POLITICAL DIFFERENTIATION

We conceptualize political differentiation as a phenomenon in which members of one political group believe that their political party or group has stronger ideological values while viewing other political groups as politically inferior or ideologically inept. Subsequently, members of one political group discriminate against the other political groups and their ideologies. In this study, two major political parties (the Peoples Democratic Party [PDP] and the All Progressive Congress [APC], which were the two leading political parties during the elections) featured prominently in the analyzed UGC, as shown in COMTs 18 to 32 below.

COMT 18: Kerosene is to be N50 not N180 but the PDP-led administration are stealing from the masses to overflow their pocket, their time is over.
COMT 19: PDP can remain in South East (SE) and compete with the All Progressives Grand Alliance (APGA), Both are now tribal parties ... PDP criminals – they are busy doing their thuggery in Rivers and Akwa Ibom.

COMT 20: Can any PDP in the house tell me who are the goats
and what is the yam in naija.
COMT 21: PDP – People Deceiving People. Their entire plan
is to discredit the Man (Buhari). Buhari has the West African
Examinations Council (WAEC) certificate for sure and the military
was used by PDP to discredit the Man. Doyin Okupe and co –
God see you ohhhhhhh.
COMT 22: PDPIG! Are full of heartless people who doesn't have
mercy on the masses. Gej it's surrounded by rouge people. Even
women in his cabinet are stealing at will.

In COMTS 18 to 25, users who demonstrated allegiance to the APC
labelled the ruling PDP as a party that oppresses the masses and "steals"
public funds (COMTS 18 and 20), a sectional and tribal party (COMT 19),
and a corrupt party of the "thieving elite." This is inferred in the coin-
age "PDPIG" to refer to the PDP (COMT 22). That coined acronym is
an apparent allusion to the pigs in George Orwell's *Animal Farm*, a
satire about totalitarianism, in which the pigs represent the ruling class
in the Animal Kingdom and end up deceiving and oppressing other
animals.[58] Users presumed to be APC loyalists also described the PDP
as the "monster" of Nigeria's politics (COMT 23) and as a corrupt and
failed party (COMTS 24 and 25). The phrase "chop and chop" in COMT 23
refers to the public perception that the PDP is a corrupt party that should
be displaced by the opposition party – the APC, whose presidential
flagbearer was General Muhammadu Buhari, a former military dictator
who was popular among the electorate for his discipline, integrity, and
anti-corruption track record.[59] Also in COM 24, "Breadth (breath) of
Fresh Air in federal governance is needed" is a reference to the popular
"Change Mantra" as the central campaign slogan of the opposition APC,
which capitalized on the ineptitude, recklessness, and sheer corruption
of the then ruling PDP.[60]

COMT 23: "Chop and quench" that is very rich coming from the
PDP, the very ugly monster of Nigeria present day politics.
COMT 24: PDP is a failure. Breadth of Fresh Air in federal
governance is needed.
COMT 25: Even if the Obas are billionaire; that does not stop them
from collecting more. It's over for PDP.

COMT 26: A vote for APC is a vote for Tinubu and One Man's rulership.

COMT 27: APC is bunch of sycophants, they see logs in other peoples' eyes but do not see it in their own eyes, only fools believe lies, rumors. APC cannot go far in this kind of politics. They rigged elections, used thugs bribed people.

For their part, the PDP's online supporters labelled the APC a one-man party (COMT 27), insinuating that it was in full control of Bola Hammed Tinubu, formal governor of Lagos State and a prominent APC financial backer. In COMT 31, the user coined the term "Thiefnubu" from Tinubu's name to suggest that he was a "thief" who enslaved his ethnic group (the Yorubas) by conspiring with the North to form the APC. In response to the APC's victory in the presidential election, most users described the party as a collection of sycophants who deceived and intimidated people, bribed the electorate, and rigged the elections (COMTS 27 and 28).

COMT 28: Liars will never bring Change. APC have nothing and have nothing to offer Nigerians than deceit.

COMT 29: The south west Obas should just rain causes on Tinubu, Fashola and the APC.

COMT 30: The Devil and the APC are one ... until recently, the Devil has lost the title of King of Lies to APC and has taken APC case to God for Judgement.

COMT 31: Let Failed Emperor Jagaban Thiefnubu continue to align to the Fulas for continued Slavery ...

COMT 32: APC's hypocrisy is transparent. It is an evil assemblage of the most hardened criminals and regions in Nigeria. That's why it is comfortable for the political wing of Boko Haram to field senile, illiterate certificate forger, perjurer and coup plotter, Buhari, as its presidential flag bearer.

Users also labelled the APC a "Devil" party (COMT 30), "a political wing of Boko Haram" (a terrorist group based in northeastern Nigeria) (COMT 32), and a party dominated by "criminals" and hypocrites. They accused the APC of fielding an incompetent presidential candidate (Buhari, now president and commander-in-chief of the Nigerian armed forces), whom they described as a dictator and an illiterate old man (COMT 32). Interestingly, the negative labels employed by users were linked to the core issues that dominated the pejorative campaign messages aimed at both the APC's presidential flagbearer, Buhari, and the PDP's presidential candidate, Jonathan, during the 2015 election.[61]

RELIGIOUS DIFFERENTIATION

People may see their religion as having acceptable values and other religions as lacking them. This study found that Nigerians' religious prejudices track political and ethnic contexts (see COMTS 33–45): the APC is labelled a Muslim and northern party, the PDP a Christian and south-south, southeastern political party. The PDP's presidential candidate was Jonathan, a Christian from predominantly Christian southeastern Nigeria; General Mohammadu Buhari, the APC candidate, was a Muslim from predominantly Islamic northern Nigeria.

> COMT 33: Are you corroborating the fact there is no forgiveness in Islam? If any Southern Nigerian did all Buhari did, he would not have been forgiven.
> COMT 34: Buhari is a radical Islamic zealot. All radical Islamic zealots are clerics.
> COMT 35: Useless people with their useless religion; this animals [?] are the problem of this country. Mother fuckers, go and educate your brainwashed maggots in the north. Useless nomads.
> COMT 36: All Xtians are believed to be mentally unstable ... how can the president drop money and you return it to him? The money should have been paid back to the treasury. I am quite convinced that you're a Devil worshipper.
> COMT 37: You are a very sick man to call all Christians mentally unstable. May God visit you with mental instability for calling His people mentally unstable. This goes to show that whoever you are, you are a fundamentalist in whatever you believe in.

As shown in COMTS 33 to 35, users – presumably Christians from southern Nigeria – attributed Islam to Buhari, describing him as an "unforgiving, radical Islamic zealot," and northerners as "nomads" and "brainwashed flowers of a useless religion" (a reference to Islam). Labelling Buhari as an "unforgiving Muslim" was an allusion to his actions during his first term as a military dictator, when he arrested and prosecuted politicians suspected of stealing public funds. For this, he had been accused of conducting a vendetta.[62] In response to users who made anti-Islam comments, other users – presumably Muslims – labelled the Christians "mischievous," "mentally unstable," and "devil worshiper(s)" (COMT 36).

> COMT 38: I dare you to openly profess your religion, I am a Christian and a true believer in Christ Jesus, the saviour of the humanity.
>
> COMT 39: I was born into a Catholic home. In fact, my late dad was a knight of the Catholic Church but I chose to worship like my ancestors did when I became a man. I do not believe in the white man's God.
>
> COMT 40: Jesus wept! God and religion my foot! Christians and Muslims my foot! My respect to Nigerians who are not Christians and not Muslims, for theirs is the kingdom of Nigeria.
>
> COMT 41: You Christians and Muslim will inherit Israel and Saudi Arabia while those of us who are no Christians and Muslims will inherit Nigeria and everything therein.
>
> COMT 42: You Christians and Muslims are strangers in Nigeria. A time comes when your time is up in Nigeria, so you could pack to Israel and Arabia leaving non-Christians and no Muslims to enjoy our forefathers' Nigeria.
>
> COMT 43: For a devout Muslim to collect dollar from GEJ, vote or no vote is haram, so who is fooling who here.
>
> COMT 44: For a devoted Christian, running from one church to another, kneeling before every pastor for deliverance, to loot the public treasury and share it with impunity; who is fooling who here?

Religion should not be a determining factor in Nigerian democracy. Some users, who appeared to be neither Christian nor Muslim, were critical of both religions, describing the two as "foreign faiths" (COMTS 39 to 44) whose adherents were equally "money worshippers" and "looters of public treasury" (COMTS 43 and 44). The users were referring to media reports that some traditional rulers and some Christian and Muslim leaders allegedly collected US dollars from President Goodluck in exchange for their political endorsement. The pattern of religious discrimination indicated here reflects that Nigeria's society is heterogeneous in matters of religion. Northerners are predominantly Muslim, and most of them belong to the Hausa/Fulani ethnic groups, whereas the South is predominantly Christian, with some adherents to traditional religions. In the Southwest, the people are Christian and Muslim in almost equal proportions, with a handful of traditionalists.[63]

SOCIAL ABUSE

Examples of social abuse are evident in COMTS 46 to 52, in which users employed derogatory names and terms when describing political figures belonging to out-groups. They also used images and symbols[64] when expressing social abuse.

> COMT 46: Rev. Fr. Mbaka, with fear of God and with respect for truth, please summon courage to ask the following question too.
> COMT 47: Bokohari can bribe Igbo man no whahala. But for the Niger Delta guy? Oil must be discovered in Sambisa forest. Bokohari get money?
> COMT 48: The Statement of Result bears Mohammed Buhari while the APC Presidential candidate is Muhammadu Buhari GMB and APC are Serial Liars like Liaing Mohammed ... Mindless Apostles of Change.

COMTs 47 and 48 deploy derogatory terms and names to express social abuse. In COMT 47, for instance, the name "Bokohari" (a blended word derived from Boko Haram and Buhari) has been coined to suggest that Buhari is a Boko Haram sympathizer. Also in COMT 48, APC supporters are described as "serial liars," and Lai Mohammed, the APC's press secretary, is described as "Liaing Mohammed," insinuating that he is a "liar" and suggesting a lack of confidence in the APC's "Change Mantra."

> COMT 49: Mama Peace has School Certificate, NCE and BSC, yet speaks the worst of English language and behaves worse than an illiterate.

COMT 50: The quality of education matters and military training both home and abroad provides great knowledge and leadership skills. Meanwhile, u need to proof that Buhari has no School Certificate.

The user in COMT 49 resorted to a satiric image to ridicule General Muhammadu Buhari regarding the allegation that he did not possess the minimum educational qualification of a school certificate to become the Nigerian president (Isika 2016). The image (which we removed from the comment because of its defamatory potential) shows a cartoon of Buhari, who looks guilty, confused, and depressed. It also demands "#Buhari Show Your Certificate." COMT 50 raises the same issue, but the user here is a supporter of Buhari who argues that the general possesses military training and experience that makes him socially and educationally more qualified than Patience Jonathan (former First Lady of Nigeria), who "speaks the worst of the English language and behaves worse than an illiterate," even though she "has School Certificate, NCE [National Certificate in Education], and BSC" (COMT 49). Patience Jonathan's husband was the main political opponent of General Muhamadu Buhari during the 2015 presidential election. Therefore, any abuse directed at her was also an indirect attack on her husband.

COMT 51: Why do you reason like a fool? The only thing going for Goodluck Ebele Jonathan is access to government money. He knows that he cannot win a free and fair election … and you are duller than the donkey in Aso Rock who has been there since 2009 unless you can prove that another donkey was in Aso Rock when Ya'ardua was sick.
COMT 52: And where are the Tompolos and Asaris threatening us we must return the Jonathan rogue to Aso Rock? Why has Ayo Kanye West Oritshejafor disappeared? Where is senile Edwin Clark? I hope Okupe has included bastard in his names on his official document.

COMTS 51 and 52 socially abuse former President Goodluck Ebele Jonathan (also called GEJ during the political campaigns). The user in COMT 51 has adopted a pseudonym (GEJisaDISASTER) that suggests that Goodluck Jonathan was a "disaster" as president. The user describes

Jonathan as a "donkey in the Aso Rock" who "could not win the election." COMT 52 contains further social abuse of Jonathan. The user indicts most of President Jonathan's aides and political supporters (with reference to Oritshejafor, former president of the Christian Association of Nigeria; Edwin Clark, an Ijaw man from Jonathan's ethnic group and his political godfather; and Doyin Okupe, his spokesperson).

Like the user in COMT 46, the user here in COMTS 51 and 52 resorts to satirical images (which we also removed from the comments) to suggest Jonathan's anticipated inglorious return to his village (Otueke) after losing the election on 28 March – which he did eventually lose. The salient element in the image[65] is a caricature representing Jonathan trekking along a waterlogged road toward a much-neglected, underdeveloped community: his home. This image further suggests that the former president neglected his community while he was in power.

This study's findings are rooted in the concepts of Otherness[66] and SIT.[67] As Al-Saidi explains, the concept of Otherness views the world as polarized into mutually excluding opposites, in which the Self is considered an insider who is rational, strong, standard, ideal, ordered, and good, whereas the Other is an outsider who is chaotic, irrational, weak, evil, substandard, lesser, disadvantaged, and unfortunate.[68] Similarly, a core tenet of SIT that is relevant to this current study is that group members are likely to express inter-group discrimination out of a belief that their own group is superior to others.[69] As established in this study, most users discriminate against other users along the divides of ethnicity (e.g., Hausa, Igbo, Yoruba, South-South minorities), politics (e.g., the PDP and the APC as the major political parties), religion (e.g., Islam, Christianity, and African traditional religions), and social class (e.g., level of civilization, education, or literacy) that together characterize the Nigerian nation. The online audience, as reflected in the UGC analyzed here, used negative, disparaging, and provocative tags to describe members of the other groups while displaying positive sentiments and support for their own groups. Our findings here corroborate the argument made by Daniels,[70] who submitted that the digital space has created serious consequences for race, ethnicity, and civil rights and that the myth that cyberspace is a peaceful enclave is rapidly disappearing.

The digital space represents Habermas's concept of the public sphere as a forum for citizens to share collective aspirations and concerns and to nurture deliberative democracy in ways that reduce the hegemonic control of the media by the political elite.[71] However, it has been argued that an ideal public sphere depends not only on access to critical information about state affairs but also on citizens' ability to engage in rational discourse that contributes positively to governance and social coherence (Haas 2004). Findings from our study confirm the concerns expressed by Haas and other scholars[72] that access to the digital public sphere has double-edged effects: citizens, as in Nigeria, can be active players in deliberative democracy even while engaging in negative rhetoric[73] that is counterproductive to the same democratic project.

Conclusion

Nigerians who use the comment sections of Nigerian online news media interact to discuss issues reported in the media; they also, even more aggressively, reflect the inter-group discrimination that characterizes the pluralistic fabric of Nigeria. The discrimination – in terms of ethnicity, political and religious affiliations, and social class – that is the result of Nigeria's colonial past[74] is being intensified in the digital space of the online community. Messages in the UGC sections of the Nigerian news media that attack members of other groups have implications for the social, religious, and political climate in the country. This could cause grave ethnic disaffection among Nigeria's various nationalities; it could also provoke social, political, and religious disorder. This study has established that when Otherness is promoted among Nigerians through the digital space, as when members of one ethnic group or religious sect view themselves as superior to the others and treat members of the outgroups as enemies, inferior, marginalized, or disadvantaged, the unity of Nigeria faces a serious threat. Unless this trend of cyber-harassment is addressed, it may intensify racial and ethnic segregation and social mistrust and encourage abuses of civil rights and freedom of expression among Nigerians.

This situation is all the more worrisome given that the Internet has provided a new gatekeeping order: the news media gate has become semi-porous.[75] In Nigeria there is no law restricting freedom of expression on the Internet, nor is there any effective regulatory framework for tracking and punishing cyber-culprits. Even in the United States, where online harassment and discriminatory comments are significant problems, the current legal landscape provides little help to victims. Section 230 of the Communications Decency Act, for example, largely does not require Internet service providers to take responsibility for UGC. The result is that online hosts (news media in particular) have no obligation to remove content, delete user accounts, or discipline users who post negative messages.[76]

This study contributes to the existing body of knowledge regarding the myriad consequences of social media. It also adds to studies on Internet participatory (citizen) journalism and UGC by employing the tenets of the SIT to explain Nigerians' participation in debates about public issues through the digital public sphere. This study has established that social media provide an open space for political engagement, deliberative democracy, social interaction and expression,[77] political activism, and social mobilization,[78] but also for negative discourse.

LIMITATIONS AND DIRECTION FOR FUTURE STUDIES

This study has relied on qualitative textual analysis of samples from readers' online comments to establish the presence of inter-group discrimination in the users' comments sections of Nigerian online news media. Although textual analysis of the selected UGC provides an in-depth qualitative picture of inter-group differentiation exhibited by users, the study is limited by a lack of quantitative analysis that would capture more expansive data, as qualitative data by itself may not be enough to adequately establish patterns. Nevertheless, this study offers direction and inspiration for future studies. We suggest, then, that future research focus on combining both qualitative and quantitative data that add depth and breadth to studies that seek patterns of hate speech and inter-group discrimination.

Notes

1 See Campbell and Kwak, "Political"; and Ojebuyi, "Negative."
2 Anorue et al., "Perceived"; and Jensen, "Social Media."
3 See Liu, "Communicating"; and Oladapo and Ojebuyi, "Nature."
4 See Attia et al., "Commentary"; Chatora, *Encouraging*; Al-Kandari & Hasan, "Impact"; Bosch, "Youth"; Hoffman et al., "Does My Comment

Count?"; Price, "Social Media"; Okon and Okogbule, "New Media"; and Van Rensburg, "Using."

5 Vesnic-Alujevic, "Political"; Edegoh and Anunike, "Assessment"; Chudnovskaya and Lipatova, "Impact."

6 Daniels, "Race," 129; Shifa and Pabón, "Interaction."

7 See, for example, Douglas et al., "Understanding"; Daniels, "Race"; Banks, "European"; Bernik et al., "To Fear"; Marwick and Miller, *Online*; Carney, "All Lives"; Gagliardone et al., "Mechachal"; Brown, "What Is Hate Speech"; Chudnovskaya and Lipatova, "Impact"; Ruzaite, "In Search."

8 See Edogor et al., "Influence."

9 See Chiluwa and Odebunmi, "Terrorist."

10 See Chiluwa, "Citizenship."

11 See Institute for Economics and Peace, "Global Terrorism."

12 See Chiluwa and Adegoke, "Twittering."

13 See Chiluwa and Ajiboye, "We Are After."

14 See Ndinojuo et al., "Descriptive."

15 See Isika, "Presidential."

16 Internet Live Stats, "World"; and Technext, "Nigeria."

17 See Miniwats, "Internet."

18 Internet World Stats, https://www.internetworldstats.com/stats1.htm

19 See Blench, "Position"; Ojie and Ewhrudjakpor, "Ethnic."

20 See Ojie and Ewhrudjakpor, "Ethnic."

21 Cited in Rafiu et al., "Nigerian State," 156.

22 See Osaghae and Suberu, *History*; Ojie and Ewhrudjakpor, "Ethnic"; Ahmadu and Yusuf, "Dynamics"; and Odaeyemi, "Political."

23 Achebe, *Image*, 66.

24 Chiluwa, "Media," 90.

25 See Omotola, "Nigerian."

26 See Al-Saidi, "Post-Colonialism."

27 Kane, "Franz," 353.

28 Al-Saidi, "Post-Colonialism," 95.

29 Ibid., 95.

30 See Meddaugh and Kay, "Hate Speech"; Al-Saidi, "Post-Colonialism"; Ibelema, "Tribal"; Kopytowska and Baider, "From Stereotypes."

31 Ibelema, "Tribal," 200.

32 See Blench, "Position"; Ojie and Ewhrudjakpor, "Ethnic"; and Chiluwa, "Media."

33 See Kopytowska and Baider, "From Stereotypes."

34 See Tajfel and Turner, "Integrative"; and Tajfel, *Social.*

35 See Ashforth and Mael, "Social"; Terry, "Social"; Douglas et al., "Understanding"; Hogg, "Social"; and Trepte, "Social."

36 Hogg, "Social," 111.
37 See Brown, "What Is Hate Speech."
38 See Hogg, "Social"; and Tajfel, *Social*.
39 Tajfel and Turner, "Integrative."
40 See Brown, "What Is Hate Speech."
41 See Douglas et al., "Understanding."
42 See Brown, "What Is Hate Speech."
43 See Omotola, "Nigerian."
44 See Techopedia, "User-Generated."
45 Catanzaro, "Using."
46 Cited in Elo and Kyngas, "Qualitative."
47 Bryman and Teevan, cited by Clarke, "Domestication."
48 See Tajfel and Turner, "Integrative"; Ashforth and Mael, "Social"; Terry, "Social"; Douglas et al., "Understanding"; Hogg, "Social"; Tajfel, *Social*; and Trepte, "Social."
49 See Brown, "What Is Hate Speech."
50 See Douglas et al., "Understanding"; Brown, "What Is Hate Speech."
51 See Hogg, "Social"; Trepte, "Social."
52 See Achebe, *Image*; Osaghae and Suberu, *History*.
53 Central Bank of Nigeria, *Economic Report*; and Abuja, "Nigeria."
54 See Brown, "What is Hate."
55 Blench, "Position."
56 Ojie and Ewhrudjakpor, "Ethnic."
57 Achebe, *Image*, 66.
58 "How George Orwell's Animal Farm," *New Nigeria*.
59 See Alemoh and Gambo, "Analysis"; Isika, "Presidential."
60 See Isika, "Presidential."
61 See Alemoh and Gambo, "Analysis"; Isika, "Presidential."
62 See Isika, "Presidential."
63 See Ojie and Ewhrudjakpor, "Ethnic"; Chiluwa, "Media"; Ahmadu and Yusuf, "Dynamics"; Odeyemi, "Political History."
64 See Marwick and Miller, *Online*.
65 See Van Leeuwen, *Introducing*; Kress and Van Leeuwen, *Reading*; Caple, "Playing"; Kress, *Multimodality*; and Bednarek and Caple, *News Discourse*.
66 See Meddaugh and Kay, "Hate Speech"; Al-Saidi, "Post-Colonialism"; and Ibelema, "Tribal."
67 See Tajfel and Turner, "Integrative"; Douglas et al., "Understanding"; Hogg, "Social"; Tajfel, *Social*; and Trepte, "Social."
68 Al-Saidi, "Post-Colonialism."
69 See Brown, "What Is Hate Speech."
70 Daniels, "Race."

71 See Molly, "Hegemony"; and Habermas, "Public Sphere."
72 See, for example, Banks, "European"; Bernik et al., "To Fear"; Marwick and Miller, *Online*; Carney, "All Lives"; Gagliardone et al., "Mechachal."
73 See Ojebuyi, "Negative."
74 See Rafiu et al., "Nigerian"; and Odeyemi, "Political."
75 Vesnic-Alujevic, "Political"; and Singer, "User-Generated."
76 See Marwick and Miller, *Online*.
77 See Conroy et al., "Facebook"; Halpern and Gibbs, "Social Media"; Yeku, "Akpos."
78 See Nam, "Dual."

Bibliography

Abuja, Benjamin Umuteme. "Nigeria Raked in N7.3trn Oil Revenue in 2017 – CBN." *Blueprint Newspaper*, 10 February 2018. https://www.blueprint.ng/nigeria-raked-in-n7-3trn-oil-revenue-in-2017-cbn.

Achebe, C. *An Image of Africa and the Trouble with Nigeria*. London: Penguin, 1983.

Ahmadu, H.J., and R.B. Yusof. "The Dynamics of Resource Conflict: Lessons from Nigeria and Malaysia." Universiti Utara Malaysian Institutional Repository, 2010. http://repo.uum.edu.my/2489/1/Hamman_JumbaThe_Dynamics_of_Resource_Conflicts.pdf.

Alemoh, T.A., and S. Gambo. "Analysis of Political Advertising Strategies Used by APC and PDP in the 2015 Presidential Election Campaigns." In *Mass Media and the Electoral Process in Nigeria*, edited by D. Wilson, 193–208. Uyo: ACCE, 2016.

Al-Kandari, A., and M. Hasan. "The Impact of the Internet on Political Attitudes in Kuwait and Egypt." *Telematics and Informatics* 29, no. 3 (2012): 245–53. https://doi.org/10.1016/j.tele.2012.02.005.

Al-Saidi, A.A.H. "Post-Colonialism Literature, the Concept of Self and the Other in Coetzee's *Waiting for the Barbarians*: An Analytical Approach." *Journal of Language Teaching and Research* 5, no. 1 (2014): 95–105. https://doi.org/10.4304/jltr.5.1.95-105.

Anorue, L.I., I.E. Onyike, O.C. Ekwenchi, and C.D. Chiaha. "Perceived Influence of Political Campaigns Carried Out on Social Media and Voters' Behaviour in the 2015 General Elections." In *Mass Media and the Electoral Process in Nigeria*, edited by D. Wilson, 239–52. Uyo: ACCE, 2016.

Ashforth, B.E., and F. Mael. "Social Identity Theory and the Organization." *Academy of Management Review* 49, no. 1 (1989): 20–39.

Attia, A.M., N. Aziz, B. Friedman, and M.F. Elhusseiny. "Commentary: The Impact of Social Networking Tools on Political Change in Egypt's 'Revolution 2.0.'" *Electronic Commerce Research and Applications* 10 (2011): 369–74. https://doi.org/10.1016/j.elerap.2011.05.003.

Banks, J. "European Regulation of Cross-Border Hate Speech in Cyberspace: The Limits of Legislation." *European Journal of Crime, Criminal Law, and Criminal Justice* 19, no. 1 (2011): 1–13.

Bednarek, M., and H. Caple. *News Discourse.* New York: Continuum International, 2012.

Bernik, I., B. Dobovšek, and B. Markelj, B. "To Fear or Not to Fear on Cybercrime." *Innovative Issues and Approaches in Social Sciences* 6, no. 3 (2013): 1–17.

Blench, R. "Position Paper: The Dimensions of Ethnicity, Language, and Culture in Nigeria." Prepared for DFID, Nigeria. Cambridge: Mallam Dendo, 2003. http://www.rogerblench.info/Development/Nigeria/Economic%20development/Ethnicity%20Position%20Paper%20Blench%20short.pdf.

Bosch, T. "Youth, Facebook, and Politics in South Africa." *Journal of African Media Studies* 5, no. 2 (2013): 119–30.

Brown, A. "What Is Hate Speech? Part 1: The Myth of Hate." *Law and Philosophy* 36 (2017): 419–68. https://doi.org/10.1007/s10982-017-9297-1.

Campbell, S.C., and N. Kwak. "Political Involvement in Mobilized Society: The Interactive Relationships among Mobile Communication, Network Characteristics, and Political Participation." *Journal of Communication* 61 (2012): 1005–24.

Caple, H. "Playing with Words and Pictures: Intersemiosis in a New Genre of News Reportage." PhD diss., University of Sydney, 2009.

Carney, N. "All Lives Matter, but So Does Race: Black Lives Matter and the Evolving Role of Social Media." *Humanity and Society* 40, no. 2 (2016): 180–99. https://doi.org/10.1177/0160597616643868.

Catanzaro, M. "Using Qualitative Analytical Techniques." In *Nursing Research: Theory and Practice,* edited by P. Woods and M. Catanzaro, 437–56. New York: C.V. Mosby, 1988.

Central Bank of Nigeria. *Economic Report: Fourth Quarter 2017.* https://www.cbn.gov.ng/out/2018/rsd/cbn%20economic%20report%20fourth%20quarter%20%20%20%202017%20published.pdf.

Chatora, A. *Encouraging Political Participation in Africa: The Potential of Social Media Platforms.* Pretoria: Institute for Security Studies, 2012. http://www.issafrica.org/publications/situation-reports/encouraging-political-participation-in-africa-the-potential-of-social-media-platforms.

Chiluwa, I. "Citizenship, Participation, and CMD: The Case of Nigeria." *Pragmatics and Society* 3, no. 1 (2012): 61–88. https://doi.org/10.1075/ps.3.1.03chi.

–. "Media Construction of Socio-Political Crises in Nigeria." *Journal of Language and Politics* 10, no. 1 (2011): 88–108. https://doi.org/10.1075/jlp.10.1.05chi.

Chiluwa, I., and A. Adegoke. "Twittering the Boko Haram Uprising in Nigeria: Investigating Pragmatic Acts in the Social Media." *Africa Today* 59, no. 3 (2013): 83–102.

Chiluwa, I., and E. Ajiboye. "'We Are After Ideals': A Critical Analysis of Ideology in the Tweets by Boko Haram." *Global Media Journal (African Edition)* 8, no. 2 (2014): 318–46.

Chiluwa, I., and A. Odebunmi. "On Terrorist Attacks in Nigeria: Stance and Engagement in Conversations on Nairaland." *Communication and the Public* 1, no. 1 (2016): 91–109. https://doi.org/10.1177/2057047315624926.

Chudnovskaya, I.N., and M.E. Lipatova. "Impact of Media on Shaping Ethno-Cultural Stereotypes in British and Russian Young People." *Media Watch* 9, no. 3 (2018): 426–36. https://doi.org/10.15655/mw/2018/v9i3/49487.

Clarke, J.N. "The Domestication of Health Care: Health Advice to Canadian Mothers 1993–2008 in *Today's Parent*." *Family Relations* 59, no. 2 (2010): 170–9. https://doi.org/10.1111/j.1741-3729.2010.00593.x.

Conroy, M., J.T. Feezell, and M. Guerrero. "Facebook and Political Engagement: A Study of Online Political Group Membership and Offline Political Engagement." *Computers in Human Behavior* 28 (2012): 1535–46.

Daniels, J. "Race, Civil Rights, and Hate Speech in the Digital Era." In *Learning Race and Ethnicity: Youth and Digital Media*, edited by A. Everett, 129–54. Cambridge, MA: MIT Press, 2008. https://doi.org/10.1162/dmal.9780262550673.129.

Douglas, K.M., C. McGarty, A.M. Bliuc, and G. Lala. "Understanding Cyberhate: Social Competition and Social Creativity in Online White Supremacist Groups." *Social Science Computer Review* 23, no. 1 (2005): 68–76. https://doi.org/10.1177/0894439304271538.

Edogor, I.O., A.A. Jonah, and L.I. Ojo. "Influence of Social Media on Youths' Usage of Traditional Mass Media in Nigeria." *New Media and Mass Communication* 31 (2014): 55–67. https://doi.org/10.7176/NMMC.VOL3155-67.

Edegoh, L.O.N., and O.W. Anunike. "Assessment of Social Media Use for Political Participation by Youth in Anambra State, Nigeria." In *Mass Media and the Electoral Process in Nigeria*, edited by D. Wilson, 125–40. Uyo: ACCE, 2016.

Elo, S., and H. Kyngas. "The Qualitative Content Analysis Process." *Journal of Advanced Nursing* 62, no. 1 (2008): 107–15. https://doi.org/10.1111/j.1365-2648.2007.04569.x.

Gagliardone, I., M. Pohjonen, A. Zerai, Z. Beyene, G. Aynekulu, J. Bright, Z.M. Teferra et al. "Mechachal: Online Debates and Elections in Ethiopia: From Hate Speech to Engagement in Social Media." *Report One: A Preliminary Assessment of Online Debates in Ethiopia*, 2 October 2015. http://ssrn.com/abstract=2782070.

Habermas, J. "The Public Sphere: An Encyclopaedia Article." In *Media and Cultural Studies, Key Works*, edited by G. Meenakshi and K. Douglas, 73–4. Oxford: Blackwell, 2006.

Halpern, D., and J. Gibbs, J. "Social Media as a Catalyst for Online Deliberation? Exploring the Affordances of Facebook and YouTube for Political Expression." *Computers in Human Behavior* 29 (2013): 1159–68.

Hodgkin, T. *Nigerian Perspectives: An Historical Anthology*. London: Oxford University Press, 1960.

Hoffman, L.H., P.E. Jones, and D.G. Young. "Does My Comment Count? Perceptions of Political Participation in an Online Environment." *Computers in Human Behaviour* 29 (2013): 2248–56.

Hogg, M.A. "Social Identity Theory." In *Contemporary Social Psychological Theories*, edited by P.J. Burke, 111–36. Stabford: Stanford University Press, 2006.

"How George Orwell's Animal Farm Suffered Rejection but Became a Classic." *News Nigeria*, 31 May 2016. https://www.thenewsnigeria.com.ng/2016/05/31/how-george-orwells-animal-farm-suffered-rejection-but-became-a-classic.

Ibelema, M. "Tribal Fixation and Africa's Otherness: Changes and Resilience in News Coverage." *Journalism and Communication Monographs* 16, no. 3 (2014): 162–217. https://doi.org/10.1177/1522637914534611.

Institute for Economics and Peace. "Global Terrorism Report – 2015." 2015. http://economicsandpeace.org/wp-content/uploads/2015/11/2015-Global-Terrorism-Index-Report.pdf.

Internet Live Stats. "World Internet Users." 2014. http://www.internetlivestats.com/internet-users.

Isika, G.U. "Presidential Election Campaign: Issues and Concerns of Multi-Party Democracy in Nigeria." In *Mass Media and the Electoral Process in Nigeria*, edited by D. Wilson, 47–58. Uyo: ACCE, 2016.

Jensen, M.J. "Social Media and Political Campaigning: Changing Terms of Engagement?" *International Journal of Press/Politics* 22, no. 1 (2017): 23–42. https://doi.org/10.1177/1940161216673196.

Kane, N. "Frantz Fanon's Theory of Racialization: Implications for Globalization." *Human Architecture: Journal of the Sociology of Self-Knowledge* 5 (2007): 353–62. http://www.okcir.com/Articles%20V%20Special/NazneenKane.pdf.

Kopytowska, M., and F. Baider. "From Stereotypes and Prejudice to Verbal and Physical Violence: Hate Speech in Context." *Lodz Papers in Pragmatics* 13, no. 2 (2017): 133–52.

Kress, G. *Multimodallity: A Social Semiotic Approach to Contemporary Communication*. London: Routledge, 2010.

Kress, G., and T. Van Leeuwen. *Reading Images: The Grammar of Visual Design*. London: Routledge, 2006.

Liu, J. "Communicating beyond Information? Mobile Phones and Mobilization to Offline Protests in China." *Television New Media* (2014): 1–8. https://doi.org/10.1177/1527476414544972.

Marwick, A.E., and R.W. Miller. *Online Harassment, Defamation, and Hateful Speech: A Primer of the Legal Landscape*. Fordham Center on Law and Information Policy Report. Fordham: Fordham Law School, 2014. http://ssrn.com/abstract=2447904.

Meddaugh, P.M., and J. Kay. "Hate Speech or Reasonable Racism? The Other in Storm-Front." *Journal of Mass Media Ethics* 24 (2009): 251–68. https://doi.org./10.1080/08900520903320936.

–. "Internet World Stats, Usage and Population Statistics: Internet Usage Statistics." https://www.internetworldstats.com/stats.htm.

Molly, P. "Hegemony and Heteronormativity: Revisiting the Political." *Journal of Women, Politics, and Policy* 35, no. 1 (2014): 87–9. https://doi.org./10.1080/1554477X.2014.863700.

Nam, T. "Dual Effects of the Internet on Political Activism: Reinforcing and Mobilizing." *Government Information Quarterly* 29 (2012): 590–7. https://doi.org/10.1016/j.giq.2011.08.010.

Ndinojuo, B.E., W.C. Ihejirika, A. Nikade, E.G. Godam, and S. Eludu. "A Descriptive Analysis of Twitter Followership of the Major Political Parties in Nigeria." *New Media and Mass Communication* 53 (2016): 1–10.

Odeyemi, J.O. "A Political History of Nigeria and the Crisis of Ethnicity in Nation-building." *International Journal of Developing Societies* 3, no. 1 (2014): 87–95. https://doi.org./10.11634/216817831403459.

Ojebuyi, B.R. "Negative Rhetoric in the User-Generated Content of Nigerian News Media." *Journal of Communication and Language Arts* 7, no. 1 (2016): 64–85.

Ojie, A.E., and C. Ewhrudjakpor. "Ethnic Diversity and Public Policies in Nigeria." *Anthropologist* 11, no. 1 (2009): 7–14.

Okon, G.B., and E.E. Okogbule. "New Media Application and Participation in the 2015 Presidential Election Campaign by Youths in Port Harcourt Metropolis." In *Mass Media and the Electoral Process in Nigeria*, edited by D. Wilson, 13–26. Uyo: ACCE, 2016.

Oladapo, O.A., and B.R. Ojebuyi. "Nature and Outcome of Nigeria's #NoToSocialMediaBill Twitter Protest against the Frivolous Petitions Bill 2015." In *Impacts of the Media on African Socio-Economic Development*, edited by O. Nelson, B. Ojebuyi, and A. Salawu, 106–24. Hershey: IGI Global, 2017. https://doi.org./10.4018/978-1-5225-1859-4.ch007.

Omotola, J.S. "Nigerian Parties and Political Ideology." *Journal of Alternative Perspectives in the Social Sciences* 1, no. 3 (2009): 612–34.

Osaghae, E.E., and R.T. Suberu. *A History of Identities, Violence, and Stability in Nigeria*. CRISE Working Paper no. 6, 2005. http://www3.qeh.ox.ac.uk/pdf/crisewps/workingpaper6.pdf.

Price, E. "Social Media and Democracy." *Australian Journal of Political Science* 48, no. 4 (2013): 519–27. https://doi.org./10.1080/10361146.2013.846296.

Rafiu, O.O., A. Owolabi, and S.N. Folasayo. "The Nigerian State, Political Assassination, and Democratic Consolidation: A Historical Exploration." *African Journal of Political Science and International Relations* 3, no. 2 (2009): 156–64.

Ruzaite, J. "In Search of Hate Speech in Lithuanian Public Discourse: A Corpus-Assisted Analysis of Online Comments." *Lodz Papers in Pragmatics* 14, no. 1 (2018): 93–116.

Shifa, M., and F.A.D. Pabón. 2022. "The Interaction of Mass Media and Social Media in Fuelling Ethnic Violence in Ethiopia." *CT4* 1 (2021): 139.

Singer, J.B. "User-Generated Visibility: Secondary Gatekeeping in a Shared Media Space." *New Media and Society* 16, no. 1 (2014): 55–73. https://doi.org/10.1177/1461444813477833.

Tajfel, H. *Social Identity and Intergroup Relations*. New York: Cambridge University Press, 2010.

Tajfel, H., and J.C. Turner. "An Integrative Theory of Intergroup Conflict: The Social Identity Theory of Intergroup Behaviour." In *The Social Psychology of Intergroup Relations*, edited by W.G. Austin and S. Worchel, 33–47. Monterey: Brooks/Cole, 1979.

Technext. "Nigeria Is Eighth in Global Ranking of Internet Users, Lagos Is First In Nigeria." *Technext* (blog), 28 August 2017. https://technext.ng/2017/08/28/nigeria-comes-eighth-global-ranking-of-internet-users-lagos-comes-first-in-local-ranking.

Techopedia. "User-Generated Content (UGC)." http://www.techopedia.com/definition/3138/user-generated-content-ugc.

Terry, D.J. "Social Identity and Diversity in Organizations." *Asia Pacific Journal of Human Resources* 41, no. 1 (2003): 25–35.

Trepte, S. "Social Identity Theory." In *Psychology of Entertainment*, edited by J. Bryant and P. Vorderer, 255–72. New York: Routledge, 2013.

Van Leeuwen, T. *Introducing Social Semiotics*. London: Routledge, 2005.

Van Resnburg, A.H.J. "Using the Internet for Democracy: A Study of South Africa, Kenya, and Zambia." *Global Media Journal African Edition* 6, no. 1 (2012): 93–117.

Vesnic-Alujevic, L. "Political Participation and Web 2.0 in Europe: A Case Study of Facebook." *Public Relations Review* 38, no. 3 (2012): 466–70. https://doi.org./10.1016/j.pubrev.2012.01.010.

Yeku, J. "Akpos Don Come Again: Nigerian Cyberpop Hero as Trickster." *Journal of African Cultural Studies* 28, no. 3 (2016): 245–61. http://dx.doi.org/10.1080/13696815.2015.1069735.

Contributors

SARAH AKROFI-QUARCOO is lecturer at the Department of Communication Studies, University of Ghana, Legon. She teaches broadcast journalism in addition to elective courses in gender and communication, media management, and international communications. She was one-time editor-in-chief of Radio Ghana newsroom. She holds a PhD in women's media history.

JORGE BARRERA, who was born in Caracas, has spent almost his whole career reporting on Indigenous issues from Yellowknife to northern Saskatchewan to northwestern Ontario. He is based in Ottawa for the CBC News Indigenous unit. Previously, Barrera worked for the Moncton Times & Transcript, Sun Media, and Canwest News Service.

EUGENE BROWN AGYEI is currently a PhD student at Michigan Technological University with research interests in new media technologies and social justice. Prior to starting his doctoral studies, Eugene worked as fact-checking journalist at the Media Foundation for West Africa (MFWA) and later at the Center for Journalism Innovation and Development (CJID).

DEREK BOWLER is a journalist specializing in digital verification and OSINT investigations. He is the hsead of Social Newsgathering at the European Broadcasting Union (EBU) in Geneva, Switzerland. Hailing from the village of Whitegate, County Cork, Ireland, he holds a BA (Hons.) degree in journalism and new media from the University of Limerick.

KENZIE BURCHELL is the co-director of the Specialist Program in Journalism and assistant professor of arts, culture and media at the University of Toronto. He is the principal investigator of the research project "Making Responsible Reporting Practices Visible," funded by the SSHRC Insight Development Grant and JHI-UTSC Digital Humanities Fellowship.

CAROLINA ESCUDERO is a professor and researcher. She has given seminars for the School of Journalism and the Women and Gender Studies, University of Missouri, since 2008, providing experience in global journalism and health, particularly with regard to trauma, gender, resilience, and human rights in the international context.

STEPHANIE FIELDING (she/her/elle) is a researcher, policy analyst, writer, and curator. As an analyst with Innovation, Science, and Economic Development Canada, she collaborates on national and international initiatives that focus on service innovation and digital policy. She holds degrees from McGill University and OCAD University.

TAMIKA FORRESTER is the senior producer for the CBC's Being Black in Canada initiative. She has worked in breaking news, social, and interview chase at the CBC. Tamika has also worked as an anchor/reporter in Jamaica.

INKYU KANG is associate professor of journalism at Penn State University. Before joining Penn State, he taught mass media and popular culture at the University of Wisconsin-Madison, where he holds a PhD in communication arts. Kang's major research interests are global media, cultural studies, and new media technology.

ANDREE LAU is a senior director at CBC, overseeing CBC News Network, the CBC News website and News App, and the CBC News Explore channel. She was editor-in-chief of HuffPost Canada from 2017 to 2020, after serving as its managing editor of news. Previously, she worked for the CBC as a TV reporter, videojournalist, and online writer in nine cities across Canada.

MICHAEL LITHGOW is associate professor of communication studies in the Faculty of Humanities and Social Sciences at Athabasca University. His research is broadly focused on public participation in cultural and political discourses. Current research includes critical technology practices, critical computational literacies, and pedagogical approachges to user-generated content in journalism training.

MICHÈLE MARTIN is professor emerita at Carleton University. Her research has focused on the politics of visual representations and the historical sociology of communication and media. Her book, *Images at War* (University of Toronto Press), won the Canadian Communication Association award.

NATALIE MILLER has worked as a journalist and editor for the BBC for over twenty years. In her career she has worked across a range of broadcast media including the BBC's Radio 5 Live, BBC News online, BBC News on social media, and most recently with BBC Newsgathering, where she led the BBC's User Generated Content Hub.

BABATUNDE RAPHAEL OJEBUYI teaches at the Department of Communication and Language Arts, University of Ibadan, Nigeria. His teaching and research interests include media studies and journalism, new media, health communication, media theories and ethics, development communication, and communication research methods.

TASHAUNA REID is a senior reporter with CBC News. She has worked behind the scenes and in front of the camera at CBC News since 2008, covering a range of topics across TV, radio, and digital platforms. Tashuana has worked in newsrooms across the country in Toronto, Edmonton, and Fredericton.

SHAUNA REMPEL has a master of journalism from Carleton University and is a social media strategist, educator, and consultant. She worked for ten years as an editor at the *Toronto Star*. She is a sessional lecturer at Ryerson University's School of Journalism, where she teaches multimedia journalism.

ABIODUN SALAWU is professor of journalism, communication, and media studies and director of the research entity, Indigenous Language Media in Africa (ILMA) at the North-West University, South Africa. He has taught and researched journalism for over two decades in Nigeria and South Africa.

MARCELO SANTOS is a researcher at the Center for Research in Communication and Social Observation (CICLOS) and an associate professor at Universidad Diego Portales in Santiago, Chile. He specializes in digital methods for social sciences with focus on the critical analysis of the crossroads between digital platforms and democratic processes.

JILLIAN TAYLOR has been with CBC Manitoba since 2012 and has been working as a journalist for nearly fifteen years. She was born and raised in Manitoba and is a member of the Fisher River Cree Nation. In 2014, she was awarded the Commonwealth Broadcasting Association's travel bursary, which took her to Australia to work with Indigenous journalists.

ASHA TOMLINSON is an award-winning investigative journalist with CBC News: Marketplace. She is also the co-creator, co-producer, and host of the CBC series *Being Black in Canada*. She previously worked for Global Television and Citytv.

Index

169–70, 172; produsers, xiii, xvi, xxii, 5; records as survival evidence, 164, 171; respect for victims and audience, 240; self-reflexivity, 163–4; squirm response to trauma, 169–70, 172; terminology, 134–5; types of, 163–4; Western assumptions, 130–1, 135. *See also* blogs; flesh witnessing
Witschge, Tamara, 134
Wochit, 58

Wolf, Herta, 163
Wolton, Dominique, 195
Wunsch-Vincent, Sacha, 184–5

Yemen, xvii, xvii(f), 136, 160
YouTube: citizen journalism, 214; monetization, 62; propaganda circulation, xiv–xv; statistics, 218; user channels, 186

Zimmer, Michael, 250